KING CHARLES THE SECOND

KING CHARLES II

BY
ARTHUR BRYANT

WITH ILLUSTRATIONS AND A MAP

LONGMANS, GREEN AND CO.
LONDON ◉ NEW YORK ◉ TORONTO
1931

LONGMANS, GREEN AND CO. LTD.

39 PATERNOSTER ROW, LONDON, E.C.4
6 OLD COURT HOUSE STREET, CALCUTTA
53 NICOL ROAD, BOMBAY
36A MOUNT ROAD, MADRAS

LONGMANS, GREEN AND CO.

55 FIFTH AVENUE, NEW YORK
221 EAST 20TH STREET, CHICAGO
88 TREMONT STREET, BOSTON
128-132 UNIVERSITY AVENUE, TORONTO

Made in Great Britain

TO MY FATHER

PREFACE

To all those who, by patient scholarship and research, have made some kind of highway through the forest of documents which encompass the reign of Charles II, the thanks of the author of this book are due. First and foremost to Dr. W. A. Shaw, whose titanic work on the Treasury Papers has revolutionized all knowledge of the later seventeenth century; to the editors of the Calendars of State Papers, the publications of the Historical Manuscripts Commission, Camden Society, and various other associations; to Thomas Carte and Leopold von Ranke among the dead, and Sir Charles Firth and Keith Feiling among the living. To the latter I owe not merely the inspiration and guidance of his brilliant study of English Foreign Policy from 1660-72, but the transcription of, perhaps, the most important Carolean document of modern times, Justice Warcup's Journal. There are many others who have made paths and vistas which have lightened my pilgrimage, to whom I pay no other tribute but a bare mention in the *List of Authorities Cited*; yet every student of the period will know how much I owe them.

These are for books: I have also to acknowledge more personal services. To Professor Wallace Notestein of Yale, who not only examined every word of my manuscript with the most critical care, but benefited the reader by eliminating some forty thousand of them; to Edmund Blunden, Hugh Sellon and Professor Andrew Browning who, despite heavy demands on their time, read my proofs and suggested much valuable emendation; to at least half a dozen other friends; to the Staff of the London Library, of the Bodleian, British Museum and Public Record Office; to the most forbearing of publishers; and, in overflowing measure, to my secretary and to my wife, I am in debt. To these, it would be ungrateful not to add the name of my father-in-law, Sir Walter Shakerley, who, seven years ago, placed at my disposal the vast collection of unedited seventeenth-century letters referred to in these pages as the Shakerley MSS.

But most of all an author should be grateful to his readers, for without the thought of them he would never write at all. If the view of the reign and character of Charles II which I have taken accords but ill with that with which they were presented at school, I must apologize. They will find no explanation in the text, for I have told my tale without arguments, believing that a simple narrative is the historical method best suited to our English genius. Those who justly demand reasons for my conclusions will find them in the reference notes at the end of the book : there is a key to these hieroglyphics on pages 373-84. The figures—renumbered in each chapter—which occur at the end of almost every paragraph refer to the group of authorities given for that paragraph in the Appendix.

I should add that throughout I have modernized the spelling of original letters, and employed the old (or English) calendar and the modern notation of years.

ARTHUR BRYANT.

THE WHITE HOUSE, EAST CLAYDON.
September, 1931.

TABLE OF CONTENTS

PRELUDE

PART I
CHARLES LACKLAND

INTERLUDE

PART II
THE KING OF ENGLAND

CURTAIN

LIST OF ILLUSTRATIONS

PRELUDE

THE CHILD OF VANDYKE'S PICTURES

PRELUDE

THE CHILD OF VANDYKE'S PICTURES

" Tell us, thou clear and heavenly tongue,
Where is the babe but lately sprung?
Lies he the lily banks among? "

In the month of May, 1630, the Queen of England lay at St. James's Palace, awaiting the birth of a child. The old manor-house of Henry VIII had been chosen in preference to Whitehall; it was quieter, with the fields and trees encircling its walls and courtyards. Northwards a green slope —in time to become St. James Street—stretched into a landscape that was bordered by the woods of Hampstead; southwards a deer park, watered by a stream. To the east the eye travelled across the tree-tops and gleam of the river to the vanes and towers of London.[1]

Here, on the morning of the 29th May, was born the heir of England. While the sound of the bells of London and Westminster, pealing together, was carried on the summer air, the King mounted his horse and rode citywards to give thanks to God for the Queen's delivery. As the royal cavalcade passed by the Maypole in the Strand, the City left its work and came out on holiday; coaches and drays ceased to rumble on the cobbles; pack-horses and porters crowded into the side streets; the vendors gave over their cries—Sweet Lavender, Hot Peascods, Cherry Ripe—and ten thousand heads looked down from the windows. At Paul's

3   A*

Cross, where the King dismounted before the Cathedral, a bright constellation was observed to be shining in the midday sky. Many, in that age of childlike faith, augured a great future. "To behold this babe Heaven seemed to open one more eye than usual . . . from which most men presaged that the Prince should be of high undertakings and of no common glory among kings." Yet it was only the planet Venus that shone so brightly, and shrewd observers with a talent for prophecy might have drawn a different conclusion.[2]

The christening took place at St. James's Palace on June 27th. The gilded officers of State and City, the white satin robes and crimson stockings of the guests filled the little chapel with colour. In the centre of all, in a cradle decked with precious stones, in white mantle and ermine train upheld by Earls, lay the babe, for whose reception into the bosom of the Church all this pomp was arrayed. The small, pudgy, and solemn countenance of this mighty Prince gazed up at the host of elder persons, and perhaps the ironical spirits were already flitting through that quick brain, suggesting laughter. As the Puritan Archbishop of Canterbury was unhappily prevented from officiating—his Grace having inadvertently shot a keeper instead of a buck a few days before—the High Anglican Bishop of London, Laud, presided over the long ceremony. Through the heavy-laden air arose the sound of his pious orations: "Double his father's graces upon him, O Lord, if it be possible." The polite doubt was received with befitting reverence, some holy water, specially secured from Jordan, was sprinkled, and the beautiful liturgy of the baptismal service chanted for the first time over a future King of England.[3]

The Prince, so heralded into the world, was no beauty. Unlike his parents he was swarthy and big—a reversion to some far Provençal or Medici ancestor. "He is so ugly,"

*wrote his mother, " that I am ashamed of him.   I wish you
could see the gentleman, for he has no ordinary mien; he is
so serious in all that he does that I cannot help feeling him
far wiser than myself."   From some forbear—perhaps his
grandfather, Henry of Navarre—he inherited grace of form,
a low, musical voice, and a fine constitution, that was in due
time to outlast many excesses and assure for him throughout
life an invincible good humour.*[4]

*Charles's childhood was spent in a world of pleasant places
—Windsor, Whitehall, Hampton Court, Theobalds, and that
river paradise at Greenwich before which the passing ships
struck their topsails.   We see him in the letters of the time,
welcoming his father home " with the prettiest, innocent
mirth that can be imagined," and in Vandyke's canvases,
standing in armour with his hand on the head of some great
dog, or playing with his brothers and sisters and the Villiers'
children in trim alleys of cypress and yew.   The children's
happy faces tell the story of their games.   And how glad
they must have been to exchange the silks and satins, the lace
collars, rosettes and cloaks, in which Vandyke painted them,
for holland smocks and overalls and romps in the garden, or
even good Master Fawcett's archery lessons.*[5]

*The boy's education proceeded apace.   He learnt to read
his criss-cross row on his horn-book—was taught French by
Gilbert le Moyne, and the art of clear and delicate writing by
Massonet—" the best writer for the fairness of his hand of any
age."   But mostly it was his mother's delight to train her
shy, dark child to " a wonderful civility "—by which he might
avoid his father's mistakes, and, by pleasing all men, find a
way to rule the hearts of this rude, stubborn, northern nation.*[6]

*At the age of eight, with many tedious ceremonies—borne
with a sweet and princely patience—Charles was made a
Knight of the Garter, and given a household of his own.   The
wooden billet he loved to sleep with was taken from him,*

and he was removed from the women and delivered over to the men. His new governors were the courtly Brian Duppa, Bishop of Chichester, and William Cavendish, Earl of Newcastle. This nobleman committed to paper the principles on which he desired his charge to frame his life. He was to study life, not books: "I would not have you too studious, for too much contemplation spoils action and virtue consists in that. What you would read I would have it history . . . that so you might compare the dead with the living; for the same humours is now as was then, there is no alteration but in names." Above all he was to be courteous and civil to everybody: "believe it, the putting off of your hat and making a leg pleases more than reward or preservation. To women you cannot be too civil, especially to great ones. . . . Certainly, sir, you cannot lose by courtesy."[7]

Newcastle did not always have an easy time with his charge, who early showed signs of possessing that obstinacy which was the spiritual heirloom of his race. The first letter from Queen Henrietta to her son was apparently written at his governor's entreaty, that nobleman having been nonplussed by his refusal to take physic. . . .

"Charles, I am sorry that I must begin my first letter with chiding you, because I hear that you will not take physic. I hope it was only for this day, and that to-morrow you will do it, for if you will not I must come to you and make you take it, for it is for your health. I have given order to my Lord Newcastle to send me word to-night whether you will or not."

A little while after Newcastle received from his charge a letter upon the same interesting subject:

"My Lord, I would not have you take too much physic, for it doth always make me worse, and I think it will do the like with you. I ride every day, and am ready to follow any other directions from you. Make haste to return to him that loves you."

The boy conceived a real affection for his stately governor.

*Like him he grew up with a love of music and of all courtly
and manly sports—an accomplished fencer, a graceful dancer,
above all a horseman. For Newcastle was the first master
of equitation of his age, and his power over horses was almost
miraculous. Charles spent many hours riding with him on
the commons round Richmond Palace.*[8]

*Before Charles's childhood passed, his tutor, the gentle
divine, Dr. Earle, painted its picture. " Nature and his
parents alike dandle him and tice him on with a bait of sugar
to a draught of wormwood. . . . He kisses and loves all, and,
when the smart of the rod is past, smiles on his beater. . . .
We laugh at his foolish sports, but his game is our earnest,
and his drums, rattles and hobby-horses but the emblems and
mockings of man's business." A year or so later—he was
nine now—Earle wrote: " He hastens apace out of his childhood, and is likely to be a man betimes, and an excellent man
if my presage deceives me not, and flattering and humouring,
the bane of princes, do not spoil him." Then the sky
darkened, and child and tutor passed alike into the limbo of
a breaking world.*[9]

PART I

CHARLES LACKLAND

CHAPTER I

THE MIRACULOUS PROVIDENCE[1]

" It being so rare, so excellent, that aged Time out of all the archives of antiquity can hardly produce a parallel."

As the last streaks of daylight, September 3rd, 1651, fell on the Worcestershire landscape, a tall dark fugitive drew in his horse on a lonely heath. About him clustered some sixty lords and officers, whose looks told a tale of peril and defeat.

At that moment the young King of England had touched a lower point than any to which his twenty-one chequered and poverty-stricken years had yet brought him. A few weeks before he had ridden at the head of a Scottish army along the moorland road by Shap Fell, watching, across the unclouded atmosphere of summer, the distant Derbyshire heights beckoning him on to London and a golden crown. Now his gallant gamble had ended in dust. All day he had fought at the head of outnumbered and despairing men as Cromwell's net closed in on Worcester. Only at evening, as the shattered Scots poured out through St. Martin's Gate, had King Charles, protesting that he would rather die than see the consequences of so fatal a day, been swept by the rout from the doomed city.[2]

At Barbourne Bridge, where the grass highway to the north was crowded with flying men, there had been a hasty consultation. The King himself had wished to ride alone to London, trusting to arrive before news of the battle and so

take ship to France.   But the day was already waning, and
his companions had dissuaded him from this desperate course.
Leaving the main line of fugitives to the west, they rode with
him across a land of wooded valleys and little hills, until at
nightfall they reached Kinver Heath.   Here the scout, who
was leading, admitted that he was lost.

In the confusion that followed, the Earl of Derby brought
forward a Catholic gentleman, Charles Giffard, owner of a
remote house in Shropshire, near which he had found
shelter a few days before.   To Giffard and his servant, Yates,
a poor rustic skilful in the ways of that country, the fugitives
entrusted themselves.   So guided they came down into the
hidden lands below.   As complete darkness fell, romance
spread her cloak over the King and hid him from the thousand
eyes that sought him.[3]

Nobody suspected the little party of Cavaliers, who walked
their horses through the streets of sleeping Stourbridge.   At
an inn near Wordsley, the King stopped for a hasty tankard
of ale: then rode on through the night, a crust of bread in
one hand and meat in the other.   Giffard rode at his side,
telling him of the secret hiding-places of Whiteladies and
Boscobel, while the broken lords and officers trotted behind.
For some hours they followed a maze of winding lanes, till
they came to the edge of Brewood Forest.   Here, fifty miles
from the battlefield, and a little before dawn, the tired King
saw the dark outlines of the ruined monastery of Whiteladies.[4]

The clatter of hooves and the whispered calls of Giffard
brought down the Penderels, the poor Catholic woodcutters
who tenanted the house.   To these humble folk the great
personages, crowding into the hall, turned for help and advice.
While a hasty message was sent to bring William, the eldest of
the five Penderel brothers, from Boscobel, the King, in an inner
chamber, broke his fast on sack and biscuits.   A few minutes
later Lord Derby brought in William and Richard Penderel

to him, telling them that they must have a care of him and preserve him.   To this they proudly and gladly assented. Richard went out to fetch some country clothes, while the King stripped and put on a rough noggen shirt.   The first lines of dawn were appearing when Richard returned with an old sweaty leather doublet, a green, threadbare coat and a greasy steeple hat without band or lining.   Lord Wilmot, the stoutest and merriest of the fugitives, began to cut the royal locks with a knife, but did the job so badly that Richard was commanded to finish it, which he did in great pride with a basin and a pair of shears.   Placing his hands up the chimney, Charles, who, despite peril and weariness, could not refrain from laughing, completed his make-up by blacking his face. Then, while his companions rode off to join the flying Scots, he went out into the dawn with Richard Penderel and a bill-hook.[5]

It was raining.   All day the King crouched in the damp undergrowth of a little wood, called Spring Coppice.   About midday Penderel's sister-in-law, Elizabeth Yates, brought him a blanket to sit on and a mess of milk, butter and eggs.   She told him news of the world outside the woods—of long streams of Scottish fugitives and pursuing Roundheads and of search-parties already at Whiteladies.   Afterwards he fell into a broken slumber.

Charles had changed much since Vandyke had painted him amid the silken dresses, the flowing hair, the lace, the pearls, the roses of his father's Court.   Before his twelfth year he had seen the lights of Whitehall darken into tragedy, while a blind mob, which cared for none of these things, bawled out for Reform and Liberty.   While still a child, he had become a wanderer on the face of the earth.   For three years he had followed his ill-fated father : seen the royal standard raised and blown down one tempestuous autumn evening at Nottingham, seen Rupert's men charge across the Warwickshire plain and played where gown and sword mingled in Christ Church meadow. Sent at fifteen to preside over the King's ruined fortunes in the west, he had spent a last year of boyhood on English soil, amid the squabbles and debaucheries of a broken army, driven back week by week towards the sunset until the royal banner floated in solitary loyalty above Pendennis Castle. Thence, on a March night in 1646, he had passed out of England.

He had become King at eighteen—of an estate of broken men and women, dangers, debts and beggary. Nor had he had anywhere to lay his head, for the rulers of Europe, over-awed by the " powerful devils at Westminster," had little wish to shelter him. Then the tempter had appeared in the homely guise of an elder of the Presbyterian Kirk and offered him the Scottish Crown in return for the renunciation of the Anglican cause for which his father had died. After many pitiful evasions, to find bread for himself and his followers, he had taken the Covenant and sailed for Scotland. In the year that followed, he had learnt many things. He had been humiliated and catechized; subjected to an infinity of dull, tedious sermons, made to do penance for the sins of his father and the idolatry of his mother, and threatened with betrayal to his iron foes. Yet by patience and a certain gentle persuasive-ness he had at last overthrown the supremacy of Argyll and the Kirk, and at the eleventh hour rallied a united Scotland behind him. But his triumph had come too late: half the country was in Cromwell's hands, and the sequel had been that bold, desperate march into England. Now an adventure, which had begun in shame, degradation and the sorrow of honest men, was ending in a little wet wood in a corner of the land he had come to conquer. But it was pleasanter to sleep under a hedge in England than in a palace in Scotland: even the rain and the weariness were better than that.[6]

In the intervals of sleep the King talked to Penderel. He had still hopes of reaching London and there taking ship for France, but his companion knew of no one on that road who could assist him. It was therefore decided that he should make for Wales, where he had many friends, and that Penderel should escort him that night to Madeley, ten miles to the west, where a Catholic gentleman of his acquaintance might secure them a passage across the Severn.

A little before dusk the two left the wood and made their way across a heath to Hobbal Grange, the cottage where Richard lived with his widowed mother. The old peasant came out to welcome her King, blessing God that she had raised up children to succour him in his time of need. She gave him bread, cheese and a fricassee of bacon and eggs, and wondered to see his appetite, half regal and wholly boyish. While she waited at the table, her son-in-law, Francis Yates— who not long after was hanged at Oxford for his share in the affair—came in with thirty pieces of silver, his all, which he offered to the King. The latter, who—though he perhaps did not realize the full grandeur of the sacrifice—was not unacquainted with poverty, accepted ten of them in his necessity.[7]

The night was pitch black, and Charles, after two days of continuous action and exposure, was tired out. He and Penderel made their way across country, avoiding the haunts of men and clambering the wet fences and pales of remote enclosures. After a few miles, the trackway they were follow-ing dipped down to bridge a stream, beside which stood a mill. The miller, hearing footsteps, appeared at the door, and called on them to stop. Instead of obeying, they ran blindly past him. The lane beyond the river was muddy and steep, and the darkness was such that Charles had nothing to guide him but the rustling of Penderel's breeches ahead and the miller's footsteps behind. When his breath and courage could carry him no longer, he flung himself into the hedge and waited for the end. Here Penderel joined him, and the two lay listening for their pursuer. But all was quiet, and after a time they resumed their journey through the briary, dripping night. Poor Charles was now in despair. His ill-made country shoes so racked his feet that he threw them away and walked in his slashed stockings. His nose began to bleed, his head throbbed and his limbs trembled with cold and weariness. " Many times he cast himself upon the ground with a desperate and obstinate resolution to rest there till the morning that he might shift with less torment, what hazard so ever he ran. But his stout guide still prevailed with him to make a new attempt, sometimes promising him that the way should be better, sometimes assuring him that he had but a little farther to go." Shortly after midnight they came to Madeley.[8]

At the edge of the village Penderel left the King in hiding and made his way to Francis Wolfe's house. The old gentleman—he was sixty-nine, and lived to see the Restoration—came to the door. Penderel asked him if he would help a Royalist fugitive of rank to cross the Severn. Wolfe replied that the town was full of troops, and all the passages across the river guarded, and that he would not undertake so perilous a task for anyone but the King himself. But when Penderel blurted out the truth, he expressed his readiness to venture his life and all that he had.

As the priest-holes in the house were known, the Wolfes and their daughter, Anne, sheltered the King all that day in a hayloft. In the evening they brought him food and money, and new shoes and stockings. Then, as the passage of the Severn was judged impossible, the two travellers started on the return journey for Boscobel. At Evelith Mill, fearing their challenger of the previous night, they left the roadway, intending to ford the river above the bridge. Here Penderel's courage, for the first and last time, failed him. The heavy rain had swollen the little stream, and, child of the Midlands that he was, he confided that he could not swim and that it was a scurvy river. Thirty years afterwards Charles dictated the story of that passage to Pepys. " So I told him that the river, being but a little one, I would undertake to help him over. Upon which we went over some closes to the river side, and I, entering the river first to see whether I could myself go over, who knew how to swim, found it was but a little above my middle, and, thereupon, taking Richard Penderel by the hand, I helped him over." At about three o'clock that morning, they passed the gateway of Whiteladies and came into the woods between that place and Boscobel.[9]

Leaving the King in the wood, Penderel went on to Boscobel to consult his brother as to the next step in their desperate enterprise. Here news awaited him. Lord Wilmot had found a refuge at the house of a neighbouring Catholic gentleman, Mr. Whitgreave of Moseley Hall, through the offices of Father Huddleston, a priest, who lived there. The other piece of news was that Colonel Careless, who two days before had led the last charge over the cobblestones of Worcester, was in hiding at Boscobel.

Careless accompanied Penderel back to the wood. He found the King, at the first stroke of dawn, sitting forlorn on a tree-stump, and could not refrain from weeping at the sight. The three then walked together across the high ground towards Boscobel, looking back, as the sun touched the Wrekin, on the far Welsh mountains beyond the Severn.

At Boscobel, a black and white hunting-lodge amid a jumble of barns and hayricks, the King breakfasted off bread, cheese and small beer. Joan Penderel, William's wife, washed and dressed his feet, cutting the blisters and inserting pads of paper between his toes. Then, as it was probable that the house would be searched by one of the numerous companies of soldiers in the neighbourhood, Charles and Careless went out again into the wood.

At the edge of the copse, overlooking the highway, was an old hollow oak. Into this, at Careless's suggestion, they climbed. The road below was soon busy with passers-by, and, through the veil of leaves that concealed them, they could see a party of soldiers searching the woods, where the Penderels, to allay suspicion, were " peaking up and down " with their nut-hooks. After a time Charles, worn out, fell asleep with his head in Careless's lap. As the hours passed and the King's fitful slumber continued, Careless's supporting arm became completely numbed. With infinite difficulty he awoke him, motioning him to silence lest the troopers below should hear.[10]

At nightfall, when the seekers had gone home to prepare for the Sabbath, the Penderels brought a ladder to the tree, and Charles and Careless, tired, cramped and hungry, returned to Boscobel. They passed through the big parlour of the house—it still stands—and up the stairs to a long attic gallery, used for storing cheeses. Here Mrs. Penderel, whom Charles christened Dame Joan, brought them a supper of chickens. Afterwards, as the night was fine, Charles sat for a while drinking wine in the garden, where Humphrey Penderel, the miller, came with news. While in the town that day, he had been questioned by a republican officer, who suspected that he knew of the King's whereabouts. Humphrey had stoutly denied all knowledge, whereupon the officer showed him a proclamation, threatening death to all who should aid " Charles Stuart, a long dark man, above two yards high," and offering a reward of £1,000 to anyone who should betray him. On hearing this Charles could not help reflecting on the temptation to which the poor men who sheltered him were exposed, but Careless, divining his thoughts, assured him that had the reward been a thousand times as great it could not have shaken their fidelity.

Before the King retired to rest, Careless asked him what he would like for breakfast. Charles suggested mutton—a reply which caused the Penderels to exchange glances, for suspicion might be aroused should they attempt to obtain so unusual a luxury from their neighbours. He then made his way upstairs to a hiding-hole beneath the attic floor, where he spent the night on a straw pallet in a space little bigger than his own body.

He awoke early on Sunday morning, and the first sounds he heard were the church bells of Tong. Careless had been up before him and brought home his breakfast from Farmer Staunton's sheepcote. Together they fried the mutton collops before the fire.

Charles spent the greater part of the day reading in a " pretty arbour " in the garden, where there was a stone seat and table. " He commended the place for its retiredness," and so rested. Here, as in other places, there is a touch of the *Pilgrim's Progress* in the narrative: one is reminded of the shepherd's boy in the Valley of Humiliation. The King's state was indeed very low. He was surrounded by his enemies, a price was set on his head, and his poor protectors were hard put to it to know where to turn for food for another day.[11]

While the King spent that Sabbath in the garden, John Penderel made his way to Moseley to consult Lord Wilmot and ask his help. He found Whitgreave and Father Huddleston, who informed him that Wilmot had left Moseley for Colonel Lane's house, Bentley, beyond Wolverhampton, intending thence to travel to the coast. As every hope of Charles's escape now depended on Wilmot, Penderel persuaded the others to take him to Bentley. Here Wilmot was found. In consultation with this cheerful, self-confident fugitive, who himself scorned any disguise but a hawk on

B*

his sleeve, it was decided that Charles should be brought that night from Boscobel to Moseley and that Wilmot should meet him there. On the way back, Penderel revealed the identity of their intending guest to Whitgreave and Huddleston. Having fixed a rendezvous at the foot of the garden, he returned with the news to Boscobel.[12]

From Boscobel to Moseley was eight miles: the night was dark and stormy. Charles was still too lame to walk, and Humphrey Penderel's aged mill-horse, with a " pitiful old saddle and rough bridle," was requisitioned for him. He bade farewell to Careless and set out, surrounded by the five Penderel brothers and Yates, who marched beside him armed with bill-hooks and pistols, ready to sell their lives in his defence. With this curious and devoted army, the King crossed Chillington Park and the dark Staffordshire woods. At Pendeford Old Mill, two miles from his destination, he dismounted, leaving the horse with William, Humphrey and George Penderel. He had gone a few paces on his way when he turned back and, begging their pardon that his troubles had made him forgetful of his friends, gave them his hand to kiss. The peasant brothers kneeling before the King in the storm are the epitome of this night. It was the supreme moment of their simple and pious lives.

In a little grove of trees in the corner of a field called the Moor, Father Huddleston was waiting for the King. He led him down a long walk of trees, through a gateway and across a garden. At the darkened door of the house Whitgreave did not know before which of the eight shadowy figures, all habited alike, he should kneel, until the light of the hall fell on the pale, kingly boy, with his cropped hair and shabby clothes, and Wilmot said: " This is my master, your master, and the master of us all."

While Whitgreave fed the Penderels, Wilmot led the King through the hall and up the broad staircase to a panelled chamber. Here Charles, sitting on the bed, asked questions about the fate of his companions. Presently Whitgreave and Huddleston joined them with sack and biscuits and a change of shirt.* Refreshed, Charles expressed himself fit for a new march and ready, should God bless him with an army of resolute men, to drive all the rogues out of his kingdom.[13]

Next morning, Monday, September 8th, the King awoke after the first night of comfort he had enjoyed since the battle. At breakfast he saluted old Mrs. Whitgreave, his host's mother, and made her sit with him at table while Huddleston and Whitgreave waited. The latter had sent all his servants to work in the fields, except a Catholic cook, who could be trusted with the half truth that the house sheltered a fugitive from Worcester. Charles spent most of this day sitting in a room over the porch, watching the high road that ran past the house. Three boys, who were living at Moseley as pupils of Huddleston's, were released from their lessons and told to keep guard, a task which they thoroughly enjoyed. That night at supper the eldest of them called to his companions, " Eat hard, boys, for we have been on the life-guard this day," an observation, as Whitgreave remarked, " more truly spoken than he was aware."

On Tuesday a message arrived that Colonel Lane would ride over that night to escort the King to Bentley, where he had arranged for him to start next day for the coast, disguised as a servant of his sister Jane, who had obtained a pass to visit a pregnant friend near Bristol. That morning Charles was in good spirits. He joined Huddleston and Whitgreave in the latter's study and amused them by stories of his usage by the Scots. Seeing a volume of Catholic devotions on the table, he picked it up and read for a time, commending

---

* Huddleston carefully secured Charles's old noggen shirt and blood-stained handkerchief, subsequently disposing of them to his friends, who found them most efficacious against the King's Evil and other maladies.

several passages to Huddleston's great joy and edification. In the afternoon there was an adventure. A servant arrived with news that a company of militia was on its way to search the house and arrest Whitgreave on a charge of having been present at Worcester. The latter at once hid Charles in the priest-hole, and, leaving all doors open to avert suspicion, went downstairs to meet the soldiers. A long and angry altercation took place in the doorway; in the end Whitgreave's neighbours were able to persuade the search-party that he had never left Moseley during the battle. When at last he was free to let Charles out of his narrow hiding-place, he found him in some fear that he had been abandoned for ever.

That evening the King asked Huddleston to show him his master's oratory, saying " he knew he was a priest, and he needed not fear to own it, for if it pleased God to restore him to his kingdom, they should never more need privacies." The priest led him to the little secret oratory. Charles looked with respect on this plain, decent room with its crucifix and candles, and with regard at the man who, without fear or cant, faced poverty and death in order to minister to his flock. Brought face to face with the same poverty and peril, Charles was perhaps nearer the inner truth of religion at that moment than at any other in his life. He stood there before the altar, no longer boy or king, but man in his simple dignity, humble in the presence of God.

At midnight Lane arrived from Bentley with two horses and waited in an orchard at the foot of the garden. At the top of the stairs old Mrs. Whitgreave was waiting to bid farewell to her King. Pressing sweetmeats into his hand, the old lady knelt down before him, and in this posture, she, her son, and Huddleston prayed God to preserve and bless him. Charles, deeply touched, gave them his hand to kiss, thanking them for their love and care, and telling them that, if ever it pleased God to restore him, he would not be unmindful.

After that he went into the garden.   In the orchard the horses were waiting.   The night was cold, and Huddleston lent the King his cloak; once more squire and priest knelt: then Charles and Lane rode off into the darkness.[14]

They made their way eastwards across a wilderness of heaths and wide fields.   On the high land between Willenhall and Walsall, where now the night sky is lit by blast furnaces, they came to Bentley Park.   Wilmot was waiting for them in the hall, and the three sat down to supper.   It was arranged that Charles was to start for Bristol at dawn, riding pillion with Jane Lane and disguised as William Jackson, a tenant's son in attendance, while the pair were to be escorted by Henry Lassels, a young cousin of the house.   Wilmot, who still refused to compromise his nobility by a disguise, was to travel with Colonel Lane at a short distance from the main party.   Charles retired to bed for the remainder of the night in the servants' quarters.

A little before dawn Lane called the King and gave him £20, a suit and cloak of country grey, and a high black hat. When Charles had dressed himself like a sober farmer's son on holiday and received the final instructions as to his part, he fetched the horses from the stables and waited, with his hat under his arm, before the house for his mistress.[15]

Jane mounted and took her seat behind the King.   Her mother stood at the door to see her go, ignorant of the honour done her daughter.   But the girl knew her prince and trembled as she touched his shoulder.   For the next week she carried the Crown of England in her hands, and never was trust more bravely or delicately performed.

For the greater part of the first day's journey the travellers were accompanied by a self-opinionated brother-in-law of the Lanes, John Petre, who was taking his wife to Buckingham-shire and knew nothing of the identity of Jane's servant.   All morning they rode through the broad, undulating country which now marks the western fringe of Birmingham, but which was then rural enough. At Bromsgrove, " a poor scattering village," Charles's mare cast a shoe. While he worked, the smith discoursed of current politics. No, he replied to the King's inquiry, he had heard no news since that of the victory of Worcester, nor had he heard that the chief rogue, Charles Stuart, had yet been captured. The King remarked that if that rascal were taken he deserved to be hanged for bringing in the Scots, on which the smith replied with an oath that he spoke like an honest man.[16]

In the afternoon they skirted the Forest of Arden. A little beyond Wootton-Waven an old woman, gleaning by the wayside, called out to them to have a care of soldiers on the main Stratford road. Charles was for riding on, but Petre, who had once been beaten by a band of drunken troopers, insisted on turning out of the way. Passing through Snitterfield, Shakespeare's paternal home, they came to Stratford by another route, only to meet the soldiers entering the town. Their foes, however, merely opened their ranks to let them pass, duly returning Charles's respectful salute. Here the Petres turned towards Banbury, while Charles, Jane and Lassels pursued their way southwards towards the Cotswolds. At Long Marston, having ridden fifty miles that day, they halted for the night at the house of John Tomes, a cousin of the Lanes. Charles supped in the kitchen, and, when the maid asked him to wind the jack, the well-nourished Cotswold servants gathered round, wondering what kind of a countryman he might be who could not perform so simple a task. But Charles knew his Staffordshire. " We seldom," he replied, " have meat, and when we do we rarely use a jack."[17]

Next day, September 11th, the travellers were abroad early, and the view from the Cotswold edge across western England was their recompense. As they crossed the hills by Chipping Campden, Charles could see a dark patch in the north,

" For the next week she carried the crown of England in her hands, and never was trust more bravely or delicately performed."

Worcester of fatal memory, westwards wooded Bredon and the Malverns, and far off the hills of Wales. For the next few hours, in all that busy, seeking kingdom, the pure winds and the tinkling sheep-bells were their only companions. They rode through Stow-in-the-Wold and Northleach, coming at dusk to Cirencester. Here Charles and Lassels slept together in the low upper room of an inn. After the chamberlain had taken away the candles, they changed beds, Lassels taking the little truckle mattress on the floor and resigning his bed to his King.

On Friday they reached Bristol. They entered the city at Lawford's Gate and crossed the Avon at Rownham Ferry. Charles remembered Bristol well : he insisted on riding about the town, inspecting the site of the former Royalist fortifications, and noting with surprise the many changes and improvements. Then skirting the left bank of the Avon, they climbed the upland to Abbots Leigh, the home of Jane's friend, Mrs. Norton, and her husband. As they reached the summit, the sun was sinking over the Bristol channel. Below them in the dusk was a gabled Elizabethan house, and from its trees and lawns arose the sound of rooks and of men playing bowls.

As they rode past the little group of players, Charles saw to his dismay a former chaplain of his, Dr. George—a most loquacious man—leaning against the railings watching the game. He took the horses round to the stable, and Jane Lane, on entering the house, told Pope, the butler—an old Royalist soldier—that her servant was sick of an ague and not fit to be below stairs. Accordingly Charles, who must have been feeling lonely on his separation from his charming fellow-traveller, found himself accorded a private room and a fire away from the other servants. At supper Miss Lane filled a little dish of broth and asked Pope to carry it to her retainer, telling him that he should have some more presently. Pope

took it with a napkin, spoon and bread, and spoke kindly to
the young man, whom he found very willing to eat. Meanwhile in the dining-hall, Dr. George, "being a man of a
cheerful conversation, asked Mistress Lane many questions
concerning William, of whom he saw she was so careful by
sending up meat to him, how long his ague had been gone
and whether he had purged since it left him and the like."
To these embarrassing questions poor Jane gave what answers
she could. After supper Dr. George, who much fancied
himself as a physician, paid a call on the invalid. He felt
his pulse, asked many questions, and wondered why he shrank
from him. His patient was not a little relieved when he heard
that he was leaving Abbots Leigh next day.[18]

In the morning the King rose early and, having an
excellent appetite, went downstairs to get his breakfast at
the buttery-hatch. Here he found Pope and two or three
other men. While they ate bread and butter, washed down
by the butler's ale, one of the men started to give a detailed
account of the battle of Worcester. Charles, asking him how
he came to know so much of the engagement, was not a little
alarmed to learn that he had actually been a trooper in his
own Guards. Hoping to allay suspicion, he asked him to
describe the King's clothes and appearance, which the other
did most accurately, looking hard at him and explaining that
the King was at least three inches taller than he. "Upon
which," Charles afterwards related, "I made what haste I
could out of the buttery, for fear he should indeed know me."

The surprises of that morning were not yet over. As
Charles stood by Pope's side, bare-headed at the hall door,
to let Mrs. Norton pass, he noticed that his companion was
staring at him very earnestly. Worried by this attention, he
went out into the fields for half an hour. On his return to
his chamber, Lassels came to him and told him that he thought
Pope had recognized him. Charles asked what kind of a

man he was, and, on being assured of his proven loyalty, decided to place his safety in his hands. He accordingly sent for Pope, who, looking upon him, fell upon his knees with tears in his eyes.

The good butler, hearing that Wilmot, who was lodging at a neighbouring house, was proposing to pay a visit to Abbots Leigh that afternoon, warned Charles that the servants were not to be trusted and that Wilmot would certainly be recognized. He contrived, therefore, to delay the latter and to bring him that night secretly to the royal chamber. Here a consultation was held, and it was agreed that Pope should try to find a ship at Bristol to carry the King to France.[19]

Charles spent that week-end resting quietly at Abbots Leigh, mostly sitting alone in the chimney corner and feigning illness. Miss Lane continued to express her anxiety for her servant in public, saying, " The boy will never recover— he'll ne'er be good again," while Margaret Rider, a maid of Mrs. Norton's, conceiving a romantic passion for the lonely young man, made him a carduus-posset and waited on him tenderly.

Pope's efforts to charter a vessel were fruitless. On Monday it was decided to remove Charles to Trent, near Sherborne, the home of an enthusiastic Royalist, Colonel Frank Wyndham, a brother-in-law of Charles's old nurse. Wilmot went on at once to warn Wyndham, while the others prepared to set out next morning. Just before announcing their intentions to the household, a disaster occurred. Their hostess miscarried, and poor Jane was at her wits' end to know what excuse to make to enable her to leave her friend at such a moment. The butler's resource saved them. He concocted a letter from Bentley, announcing the sudden illness of Jane's father, and handed it to her at supper : the girl's skilful acting did the rest.[20]

Early on Tuesday Charles, Jane and Lassels set out for

Trent.   They travelled eastwards for a few miles, as though
heading for Bentley, and then turned south.   Following the
old Roman trackway past Shepton Mallet, they reached Castle
Cary, where they were met by Lord Hertford's steward, who
found them accommodation for the night.   Next morning, a
fortnight after the battle, they came at about ten o'clock to
the retired and beautiful village of Trent, where Wyndham
and his young wife were awaiting them.   Charles, who was
in good spirits, called out, " Frank, Frank, how dost thou? "
He was escorted to the house, where a suite of black panelled
rooms had been set apart for him.   Here he was to make
his longest stay during the period of his flight, and here, in
a household of twenty persons, his presence remained unknown
to all but his host and hostess, their little cousin, Juliana
Coningsby, and two loyal maids.   Their names, Eleanor
Withers and Joan Halsenoth, are worthy of remembrance;
they waited upon him, passing the food, cooked in the kitchen
below, to his room by means of a rope in the chimney.

On the King's arrival a conference was held.   Wyndham
related a strange tale of his father, who, on his death-bed
fifteen years before, had called his sons about him, telling
them that they had seen serene and quiet times, but must
now prepare themselves for cloudy and troublesome ones.   " I
command you," he had said with his last breath, " to honour
and obey your sovereign, and, though the crown should hang
upon a bush, I charge you forsake it not."   In these dying
words, Wyndham perceived a prophecy, now nearing fulfilment.

The next day Jane and Lassels set out for Staffordshire,
and Wyndham paid a visit to his neighbour, Giles Strangways,
about finding a boat.   The latter sent him on to Lyme Regis,
where, after some delay, a Royalist merchant, called Ellesdon,
succeeded in chartering a coasting vessel, the master agreeing
for a substantial sum to convey two Royalist gentlemen to

France. It was arranged that on the night of the following
Monday, September 22nd, Limbry, the master, should bring
his ship to the little coastal village of Charmouth, where
Charles and Wilmot were to be in waiting. A room was
booked at the inn at Charmouth, and, to avert suspicion, the
landlady was informed " that there was a young man to
come thither the next Monday that had stolen a gentlewoman
to marry her." Having completed these romantic arrangements, Wyndham returned to Trent.[21]

On the Monday morning, Charles set out on his travels
once more, riding pillion, this time in front of pretty Juliana
Coningsby, with Wyndham as guide and chaperon. The
undisguised Wilmot and Wyndham's servant, Peters, followed
them at a safe distance. They went by Over Compton and
Berwick, crossing the high Dorset downlands at Pilsdon Pen.
At a house among the hills, a few miles above Charmouth,
they met Ellesdon, who was able to assure them that all
was ready. An hour later, as dusk fell, they rode down
the steep hill into Charmouth and put up at the Queen's
Arms. The wind was blowing for France and the auspices
were kindly.

It had been fair day at Lyme, and the little inn was
packed with horse-dealers. After supper Wyndham and
Peters went to the beach to await Limbry's long boat, leaving
Wilmot and Juliana, with Charles to wait on them, to
masquerade, before an extremely interested household, as
lovers. Hour followed hour, the disappointed company
retired to bed, and still the three waited. At dawn, after
what seemed an eternal night, Wyndham returned with news
that the tide had gone out and no boat come.

As the people of Charmouth were obviously intrigued by
their visitors, it was decided that Charles, Miss Coningsby and
Wyndham should set out for Bridport, where Wilmot and
Peters, after ascertaining the cause of Limbry's failure, should

join them later in the day.   Peters accordingly went to Lyme, while Wilmot sent his horse, which had cast a shoe, to be shod.   The blacksmith noticed that the remaining shoes were of Midland make, which tallied ill with the couple's tale that they came from Exeter, and confided his suspicions to the ostler, who confirmed them by recounting the strange behaviour of these supposed lovers.   Having finished his task, the smith therefore made his way to the house of the local minister to seek advice.   Finding the latter engaged in his morning devotions—a somewhat lengthy affair*—the honest craftsman, fearing to lose the hire of his labour, returned to the inn.   But when he had been paid and had seen the fat and jovial Wilmot ride away, his suspicions revived.   There was something, he reflected, very peculiar about that man.   Was not Charles Stuart at large in England, seeking to escape, and was there not a reward of £1,000 upon his head?   Once more he sought the house of the minister. He told his tale, confided his fears and hopes, and was rewarded when he saw the good man's eyes light with zeal. Together they hastened to the inn, where they wasted five minutes in upbraiding the indignant landlady.   Then they sought a Justice of the Peace.   But the latter was a true Englishman, with all an Englishman's love of deliberation and fear of rendering himself foolish in the eyes of his neighbours, and flatly refused to issue a warrant for a King's arrest upon such slender evidence.   In despair the two sleuth-hounds left him and made their way to Captain Massey, who commanded a troop of Roundhead militia.   He proved to be the man they were seeking, called out his soldiers, and at once set out in hot pursuit along the Bridport road.[22]

While these events were happening at Charmouth, the King's party had reached Bridport.   Here the town was full

---

* The minister, Mr. Benjamin Wesley, was a great-grandfather of John Wesley.

of red-coats on the point of embarking for the conquest of
Jersey.   While Wyndham and Juliana ordered a meal at
" The George," Charles, with the horses, pushed boldly
through the troopers in the yard.   At that moment an
ostler approached him and said he was sure he knew his face.
Charles, after discovering that this would-be friend had been
in service at a house in Exeter at which he had formerly
lodged, claimed to have been a fellow-servant with him there.
This satisfied the ostler, who asked him to drink, but the King
begged to be excused, explaining that he had to wait on his
master and mistress.   He found them in an upper room, with
a meal set before them, of which they made him eat before
he returned to the horses.   At this moment Juliana's sharp
eyes caught sight of Peters in the street below.   From him
she learned that Wilmot was in Bridport and was urging an
immediate departure: the imperturbable nobleman had at last
sensed peril.   Accordingly they set out at once along the
London road, joining Wilmot and Peters just outside the
town.   About a mile out of Bridport they decided to turn
up a lane northwards and work back across country in the
hope of tidings of the lost vessel.   It was well that they did
so.   A minute later Massey's pursuing troopers galloped past
the turning towards Dorchester.   Meanwhile the travellers
continued their rambling journey, unconscious that a whole
countryside was seeking them.   They lost their way and rode
all afternoon in a wilderness of downs and lonely valleys.
" Providence directed these strangers," leading them at nightfall to the little village of Broadwindsor, a few miles north
of Bridport.[23]

Here, in the heart of the bleak Dorset uplands, they
put up at a poor little inn, the best harbourage the place
could afford.   Happily the landlord was an old servant of
Wyndham's family, and he and his wife were both staunch
Royalists, having " according to their condition undergone

their share of troubles." Though they did not know the full
extent of the greatness they were entertaining, they bustled
about to make their guests comfortable. But the latter's perils
were not yet over. At midnight a company of soldiers
arrived, on march for the coast, and demanded quarters.
They swarmed all over the lower part of the house, completely cutting off the attic in which the King was trying
to sleep. One of their doxies who accompanied them was
unexpectedly brought to bed of a child on the kitchen
table: the clamour of this event and the furious dispute as to
the babe's future upkeep, which it occasioned between the
military and the parish overseers, made sleep impossible. For-
tunately the soldiers resumed their march at daybreak, and the
fugitives were able to breathe again. During the morning
Peters, who had been sent to Lyme to interview Ellesdon,
returned with the explanation of Monday night's fiasco.
Apparently Limbry had confided to his wife that he was about
to carry a dangerous cargo to France, and the latter, much
alarmed, had locked him up in his room and kept him there
till he gave his word that he would not sail. Further attempts
to embark from Lyme were plainly out of the question, and
the little party returned to Trent.[24]

Here the King remained for nearly another week. The
two maids and his pretty hostess waited on him, and he
passed his days cooking his own food and boring holes in
coins as keepsakes for them. On one occasion, hearing the
church bells pealing, he looked out of the window to see
a crowd of villagers dancing round a bonfire in celebration of
his own supposed capture and death. On another Mrs.
Wyndham was put to great fear for her guest—she had none
for herself—by the arrival of a mysterious troop of horse at
Sherborne, but Charles, who was growing used to dangers,
only laughed.

Meanwhile further attempts were being made to secure

a ship. Through the suggestion of a neighbour, Wyndham had got into touch with a little group of Royalists at Salisbury. One of these, Colonel Robin Phelipps, a younger son of the house of Montacute, undertook to find and charter a vessel from a Hampshire or Sussex port. His first attempt at Southampton was unsuccessful, but he transferred his efforts to Chichester. To be nearer the scene of action, it was decided to move the King from Trent to Heale, the residence of Mrs. Hyde, a widow.[25]

On the evening of Sunday, October 5th, Phelipps arrived at Trent to act as guide. Next morning the King took leave of his kind hosts. That day Phelipps and Charles rode fifty miles, the latter once more in front of Juliana, while Peters followed them in attendance. They passed, by Sandford Orcas and Wincanton, through a little frequented and lovely corner of England. At Mere, eighteen miles on their way, they stopped for a drink at the George Inn, where Phelipps knew the host, a good Royalist. They drank in the cellar, where the landlord turned to Charles with a " Thou lookest like an honest fellow. Here's a health to the King! " The subject of this loyal toast naturally hesitated, and mine host turned to Phelipps in disgust and asked him what kind of a Roundhead fellow he had brought.

In the afternoon the travellers, passing through Hindon, Chilmark and Teffont, skirted Salisbury Plain and came to Wilton. Here Juliana and Peters said good-bye, and Charles and Phelipps, leaving the main road, made their way across the plain towards the Avon valley. At nightfall they found the welcoming lights of Heale House.

Mrs. Hyde was waiting for them, and a cheerful little party of loyalists from Salisbury sat down together to supper, though the identity of the newcomer was not known to all. Mrs. Hyde recognized him at once and, though she tried to hide her feelings, could not refrain from showing her loyalty

c

by helping him to two larks instead of one. Among the guests was Dr. Henchman, a canon of Salisbury Cathedral, one of the chief agents in the search for a boat. After supper this wise and brave old churchman had a long talk with his King.*

It was not thought safe that Charles, who had been seen by all the servants at supper, should remain publicly at Heale, and it was decided that on the next day he should pretend to depart, returning secretly in the evening. Accordingly in the morning he rode off with Robin Phelipps. The pair spent the day pleasantly enough on Salisbury Plain, where there was no one to observe or disturb them. They galloped on the soft down turf, started hares and paid a visit to Stone-henge. Here Charles stood looking upon the stones for some time, and proved to his companion the fallacy of the popular belief that they could not be counted twice alike. At dusk Henchman met them in a meadow near Heale, where Phelipps took his leave. The King then re-entered the house by a back way and was escorted to a secret hiding-hole. Here he spent the next five days, waited upon by Mrs. Hyde and her sister, who alone knew of his presence. His quarters were cramped, but he was probably safer at this period of his wanderings than at any other. The Government had lost all trace of him.[26]

Meanwhile his faithful friends were seeking a boat. Wilmot and Phelipps, stopping at Hinton-Daubnay, near Hambledon, had recruited George Gounter of Racton, a Sussex Royalist. A much persecuted man, he had just returned from London, where he had been borrowing the wherewithal to pay the heavy fines laid on his estates. Without hesitation he undertook a new burden in the cause

* Fourteen years later, as Bishop of London, he was to prove that his courage was as great in the day of worldly success as in that of adversity, by remaining at his post during the plague, and at the end of his long and useful life his last blessings were to rest on the rising stones of Wren's St. Paul's.

for which he had already given so much. His poor wife, struggling to make both ends meet, wept when she heard of the new danger he had accepted, but encouraged him in his resolve. On Saturday, October 11th, this gallant gentleman found what he was seeking at Chichester, where, with the help of Francis Mansel, a loyal merchant, he negotiated a treaty with Nicholas Tattersall, the master of a Brighthelmstone coal-brig, who, for sixty pounds down, agreed to carry two fugitives from Shoreham to France.[27]

On Sunday, October 12th, Charles made ready for his departure from Heale. At three o'clock that night, Phelipps, with a lead-horse for the King, arrived at the appointed rendezvous. The lead-horse broke its bridle, and ran up the river; with great difficulty Phelipps recaptured it. The two horsemen then rode through the night, past Clarendon Park corner and Old Sarum. Dawn found them crossing the high and lonely hills to the east of Salisbury. All that morning they rode through Hampshire, by Tytherley and through the woods of the Test Valley, and so, by Mottisfont and Hursley, to Twyford. Here, leaving Winchester and the gleaming Itchen behind them, they trotted across the sweet, wind-swept open downs.[28]

On a hill called Old Winchester, the highest in those parts, above the little village of Warnford, Wilmot and his servant, Swan, Gounter and his brother-in-law were waiting for the King. They had left home early, calling at the house of Gounter's sister, Mrs. Symonds, at Hambledon, to borrow a brace of greyhounds on the pretence of coursing: they warned her that they might seek her hospitality that night. When the hour fixed for the rendezvous passed without any sign, Gounter rode down to Warnford. There, at the town's end, he encountered Charles and Phelipps. Pretending not to have recognized them, he continued his way into the village, drank a glass of ale and purchased some tobacco, and then rode back,

c*

catching up the travellers as they reached the summit of the hill.

On that high October afternoon with half England—rolling down and far woodland—spread around them, they held a council of war, deciding to spend the night in some quiet neighbouring house. " I know," said Gounter, " divers yeomanry men, where for a night we may be very welcome, and here is one who married my sister, and whose house stands privately and out of the way." " Let us go thither," replied the King.

As evening fell on the Hampshire landscape, they rode over Broadhalfpenny Down, where men already played a quaint game with stump and ball, towards the valley. Below them lay Hambledon, on the edge of the forest. At about candle lighting, they came to Mrs. Symonds' house; though all unconscious of her honour, she welcomed them and led them into a little fire-lit parlour, setting biscuits and wine before them.

That night was the pleasantest in all the King's travels. They sat down to supper at a round table, and, when the meal was almost over, the master of the house joined them. He, like an honest Cavalier, had been drinking in a tavern, and was filled with an hospitable desire to see all about him as merry as he. He settled down among his wife's guests, taking a stool by Charles, whose cropped hair and solemn aspect marked him out as a suitable object for conversion. Then, shaking his hand and mixing a bottle of strong waters in a tankard of beer, he called him Brother Roundhead and bade him drink deep. The scene is a delicious one—the wainscotted room, the firelight and the candles on the table, the faces of the hunted fugitives lit by the glow and the wine, and the hiccoughing host, half scared by the King's puritanical appearance, and wholly jovial. Whenever a bibulous oath escaped him, Charles was ready with the appropriate rebuke:

" Oh, dear brother, this is a scape : swear not, I beseech you."
But the other was incorrigible.   At ten o'clock, in order to let
Charles escape to bed, Gounter suggested to his host that the
Roundhead would be better away.   Symonds gladly assented.

It is not improbable that Charles awoke with a headache.
That day, the 14th of October, was the last of his pilgrimage.
Before he left Hambledon, a message arrived from Lord
Southampton, who had somehow learnt of his presence in
the neighbourhood, offering his services and hospitality.
Charles, having the promise of a ship, would not allow him
to run the risk, but ever afterwards gratefully acknowledged
his obligation to a nobleman, who, having great possessions,
was ready to sacrifice them all for his sake.[29]

Phelipps went to London to make arrangements for a
supply of money to await the fugitives in France, and the
King, Gounter, Wilmot and Swan set out alone.   For thirty
miles they rode eastwards through the forest.   On the fringe
of Arundel Park they saw the Governor of the Castle and his
men riding out to hunt : they did not like the look of his
" starched moustaches," so turned aside and led their horses
up the slope of the high woods.   Beyond the downs they
crossed the Arun at Houghton Bridge.   In the quiet village
street they halted before the ale-house door, and, while they
drank, Gounter pulled out a couple of Mrs. Symonds' neats'
tongues from his pocket.

East of the Arun they climbed, and for eleven miles rode
along the downs.   The thrill of the upland air caught their
hearts and, as the King gazed northwards from Chanctonbury
over the Weald, England seemed to him a country worth fighting for.   In Bramber, where they came down to cross the
Adur, the street was full of soldiers, and in the narrow lanes
beyond they heard horse hooves close behind them.   Boldly
they slackened pace, and the troopers, on some military errand,
pushed by unregarding.

Near Beeding they parted company, preferring to approach Brighthelmstone by different routes. Charles and Wilmot climbed Edburton Hill and cantered over the nine miles of down which divided them from the sea. At Brighthelmstone, then only a cluster of fishermen's cottages, they pulled up at " The George." When Gounter and Swan arrived, they could hear the King's voice in the parlour, toasting Wilmot: " Here, Mr. Barlow, I drink to you! "

At the inn, Mansel and Tattersall, who as yet only knew of Charles as a Royalist fugitive, met them. They all sat down together to supper. Though there was some anxiety about the wind, the King was in excellent spirits.

That evening witnessed two last touching pieces of loyalty. After supper Tattersall, who had looked much at Charles during the meal, drew Mansel aside and told him that he had not dealt fairly with him, " for, though he had given him a very good price for the carrying over of that gentleman, yet he had not been clear with him; for he was the King, and he very well knew him to be so. But, said he, be not troubled at it, for I think I do God and my country good service in preserving the King, and, by the grace of God, I will venture my life and all for him, and set him safely on shore if I can in France." To such simple men it was given to see further than the politicians in their wisdom.

There was a further incident. As the King was standing alone by the fireside after supper, with his hand leaning on his chair, the innkeeper, an old guardsman, came in and started to talk. Suddenly he raised the King's hand and kissed it, saying, " God bless you wheresoever you go; I do not doubt before I die to be a lord and my wife a lady." Charles laughed and hastily left the room, but he had no cause to fear the old soldier's loyalty.

For a long time they sat up drinking and smoking, Charles desiring to keep Tattersall with him, lest he should decline the venture at the last moment, as Limbry had done. When it became known that the wind had changed and set fair for France, Charles and Wilmot lay down for a brief rest. At two o'clock Gounter called them, showing them the time on his watch. They rose and made their way on horseback through the night to a creek at the mouth of the Adur, where Tattersall's brig, *The Surprise*, was lying. They climbed aboard and lay down in the little cabin, waiting for the tide. Here Gounter bade them farewell.[30]

At about seven o'clock of the morning, being high water, they went out of the port, steering a westward course as though for Poole, the boat's normal destination. At that very hour another fugitive from Worcester, less fortunate than Charles, was waiting for the axe to fall in Bolton market square. A few days before his death, Lord Derby had written to his wife : " Though I be never so close, my heart is my own—free as the best." It was such a spirit that made the Restoration a certainty.

All that day Gounter followed on the beach with the horses, watching those vanishing sails. On board *The Surprise*, the King, who had learnt to love ships during his first exile in Jersey many years before, suffered a sea change; he walked the deck, happy and at home, talking to Tattersall and winning that loyal sailor's admiration by directing the course. The crew, four men and a boy, stood watching and smoking.

One further subterfuge was necessary. Tattersall had not broken the news of the vessel's unwonted destination to his men. He now approached the King and begged his help. The latter accordingly confided to the crew that he and Wilmot were merchants, who had suffered losses and were in debt, and offered them twenty-five shillings to drink if they would second his endeavours to persuade the Master to set them in France. This speech made a strong appeal to the thirsty throats and romantic hearts of the English seamen. They at once agreed, and the Master was quickly persuaded. About five in the afternoon, while still in sight of the Isle of Wight, the brig stood off with a northerly wind for France.

At dawn on Thursday, October 16th, Charles landed at Fécamp. When his mother's Court rode out to welcome him back to the Louvre, his friends could scarcely recognize him. The gentle boy, who had left Paris two years before, was now shorn and bearded, his build was manly and powerful, his features had coarsened, his expression grown reckless. Yet to shrewd observers, the long mouth and level eyes told their tale. Young though he was, he had met as intimates hunger, weariness and peril; he had shared the companionship of the very poor; he had known courage and fidelity. And, if the Commonwealth's spies noted, beneath his outward cheerfulness, a certain sadness, it was because his heart was still in England with the loyal men and women who had shared his perils and from whom he was now divided.[31]

CHAPTER II

" For loyalty is still the same,
    Whether it win or lose the game,
    True as the dial to the sun,
    Although it be not shined upon."
                    —SAMUEL BUTLER.

IT was a forlorn prospect upon which Charles gazed from his mother's windows in the Louvre that winter. On land and sea his enemies were invincible. All imaginable ways for the recovery of the royal interest had been tried and failed. With the last surrender in Ireland and the fall of Jersey, nothing remained. In England, returning exiles were making their peace with the usurpers by compounding for their estates.[1]

A faithful few, hastening from lodging-houses and garrets in Antwerp or Caen, now joined their King in Paris. Of what stuff these companions in adversity were, let the letters of Edward Hyde tell. Before the war a rising lawyer and Parliamentarian, he had thrown in his lot with Charles I rather than see the two things he cared for most—English liberty and the Church of his youth—trampled down by a Faction more despotic than any king. Appointed to his Council, he had followed the Prince of Wales out of England in 1646. Since then he had passed through most of the vicissitudes which human life can offer—poverty, exile and humiliation; had seen his advice rejected and scorned, his home beside a Wiltshire chalk stream made the spoil of

41

strangers, his wife and babes hungry for bread.* Through all this, though like others he could have made his peace with the usurpers and returned to England, he never faltered.†
" I know of no other council to give you," he told the old Cavalier Secretary of State, Nicholas, " than by the grace of God I mean to follow myself, which is to submit to God's pleasure and judgment upon me, and to starve really and literally, with the comfort of having endeavoured to avoid it by all honest means. . . . Indeed, all discourse of submitting to those rogues in England hath so little sense or excuse in it, that there needs no reply to it. You and I must die in the streets first of hunger."[2]

When this honest man and good hater rejoined the King that Christmas, he found a great change. Gone was all reliance on Scots and Presbyterians; Charles was the best of Anglicans now. To Hyde and his friend, Lord Ormonde— the exiled Viceroy of Ireland—he henceforward gave his entire confidence. It was Hyde's policy to restore the England of his youth—with its balance between Church and State, Throne and Parliament, Liberty and Prerogative, and its subordination of all to the " known laws of the land." That ideal he had long ago laid before Charles I, who had sometimes forgotten it but in the end had died for it:‡ he now held it before his son. To achieve it, he refused all com-

* " Be of good cheer," he conjures her, " and keep up the spirits of thy company . . . and be as merry as poor, honest, undone people can be." (Sir Edward Hyde to his wife, 20 Feb., '50, *H.M.C. Bath,* II, 88.)

† " My prayers are for my friends," he wrote to Lady Isabella Thynne, " that God will preserve their innocence whoever enjoys, or rather possesses, their estates. . . . While I have bread and books I shall think myself very rich, and when I want both, I shall do no ill thing to get either." (*Clarendon MSS.* xxviii, f. 297.)

‡ " It is not my case alone," Charles I had said at his trial; " it is the freedom and liberty of the people of England. And—do you pretend what you will—I stand more for their liberties. For if power without law may make laws, may alter the fundamental laws of the kingdom, I know not what subject he is in England that can be sure of his life or anything that he calls his own." (*State Trials,* IV, 1082.)

promise with other ideals which were at heart contradictory:
whether those of the ruling militarists—who had set aside
even the pretence of established law; of the Presbyterian
oligarchs—" so inconsiderable in England, so false in Scotland, and both so adverse to monarchy that the very conditions
they offer upon which to assist the King evidently destroy
him "; or of the Catholics, with their fatal dependence on
foreign arms.   The last, championed by the Queen-Mother
and her fat, opportunist major-domo, Lord Jermyn—" full
of soup and gold " and the one prosperous figure in that Court
of hungry exiles—were his chief bugbear.   " I do more fear,"
he had written many years before, " a French army than
the Presbyterians and Independents; it must be the resurrection
of English courage and loyalty must recover England to the
King."[3]

Good councils the King certainly needed.   He was as
poor as the mice behind the wainscotting of his little chapel.
He was surrounded by men and women, who had sacrificed
all for his cause, and who looked on him as their sole means
of subsistence.   In penniless days he was forced to support
them, who now, forgetful of his own necessities, clamoured
ceaselessly that he might relieve theirs.   Having nothing else
to do, these unhappy exiles quarrelled perpetually.   " It is
a very hard thing," wrote Hyde, who, as Chancellor of a
more or less non-existent Exchequer, had to bear the brunt
of their importunities, " for people who have nothing to do,
to forbear doing something which they ought not to do."
Him they all attacked.*   " You have great reason," he told
a correspondent, " to lament the animosities which govern
too much this little Court, and which, no doubt, give great
scandal to all our friends.   I wish it were as easy to cure as
to lament it."[4]

* " I have an excellent time and have the good fortune to be equally dis-
liked by those who agree in nothing else." (Hyde to Nicholas, 13 June, '53,
Cl.S.P., III, 171.)

To repair his fortunes, Charles sent embassies, proud and out-of-heel, to every Court in Europe. Those who have known wealth seldom make good beggars, and the ambassadors, where their creditors permitted them to do so at all, generally returned more penniless than they went. During his first year in France—when the Wars of the Fronde drove the Court of his cousin, the little French King, from Paris—Charles was left to subsist on whatever small contributions threadbare loyalists in England and Scotland could smuggle to him: by September, 1652, his servants were no longer able to provide his diet, and he was reduced to taking his meals in taverns. The plight of his followers was far worse: the once prosperous Hyde—so cold that he could scarce hold a pen—had not three sous to buy a faggot, and some were almost starving.* Even when the French Court returned and a small pension was granted to Charles, things were not much better. " We are all here in the same beggarly condition you left us," wrote Hyde at the New Year of 1653, " which I think long custom will grow second nature to us."[5]

Chiefly, it may be said, the exiles lived on hopes. These rose and fell as regularly as the tides of the Channel. They were high in the autumn of 1652 with the outbreak of war between the Dutch and English Republics, when Charles impetuously offered his services to a cold and unresponsive States General. In the following spring came Cromwell's bold ejection of the Rump—the corrupt and hated remnant of politicians who had usurped the name of the Long Parliament. But exiled hopes fell to zero when Cromwell set himself up in its place. Installed as Protector, before the end

---

* " I do not know that any man is yet dead for want of bread, which really I wonder at," wrote Hyde in June, 1653. . . . " I am sure the King himself owes for all he hath eaten since April, and I am not acquainted with one servant of his who hath a pistole in his pocket. Five or six of us eat together one meal a day for a pistole a week, but all of us owe for God knows how many weeks to the poor woman that feeds us." (Cl.S.P., III, 174.)

of the year, his enemies were repenting in dungeons and the princes of the earth crowding to do him homage, while beneath his window, at Roberts' Ordinary in Whitehall, Anna Trapnell, the prophetess, fasting on toast and small beer, celebrated his eminence by singing extempore hymns for a continuous fortnight. The only comfort left the exiles was at the farthest corner of Scotland where the Royalist, Middleton, had been dispatched, with a thousand men, a few barrels of powder and a large number of letters from the King to the Highland chiefs.[6]

Yet the men who shared the King's lot never quite gave up hope. Plotting, intriguing, begging, quarrelling, they made the lives of the proud Commonwealth's agents and ambassadors perpetually uneasy. " They are in all places beyond the sea," reported one of these, " and have an influence where they are." Their intense conviction of the iniquity of their enemies—" those bloody reigning villains " who had defiled in their eyes the very foundations of the earth—sustained them. " If I did not assuredly believe," wrote Hyde, " that . . . they will at last determine the confusion and be each other's executioners, I should be very melancholic."[7]

The centre of these exiled hearts was the young King. His adventures had improved him: the shy, reticent boy of a few years before had now, as one fine lady testified, " *la meilleur mine du monde, douce, civil, galant.*" Moreover, the old dependence on his imperious mother had gone: he was possessed of a will and character of his own, far from palatable to the Palais Royal, whither after 1652 the Queen moved her Court. His judgment of men was far beyond his years: even in boyhood his counsellors had noticed his quickness to see through a humbug or recognize an honest man. But this astuteness was impaired by a temper far too gentle for the troubled rôle which he was forced to play. His softness in Council and dislike of rebuking anyone, however unruly, wrung from Hyde a despairing: " Until the King be more a king in his own house, all will not be well." Yet this very gentleness sometimes proved an asset, for, though unable to enforce quiet in his Court, he could act the peacemaker where others failed, whether the quarrel lay between jealous Ministers or two ladies blackening one another's reputations. It was in his own nature to forgive so easily that he was the more able to make others forgive. And occasionally, when a big issue was at stake, he could show a surprising firmness. Throughout the nine years of his second exile, the attacks on his chief adviser were ceaseless, yet Hyde's position in his Councils was never shaken.*   When at the beginning of 1654, the latter's enemies concocted two simultaneous petitions, one from the Catholics about the Queen, the other from the Presbyterians, requesting his removal, Charles obtained advance copies of both and made great sport at their curious similarity; when they went further and accused Hyde of a secret correspondence with the English republicans, he dismissed the charge as a foul and wicked lie. Even the all too truthful tale—raised suddenly at the Council table—that Hyde had once spoken of him as idle and given to pleasure, could only elicit a laughing: " Why, that is no news, for he has told me so twenty times to my face."[8]

Indeed to those who had won his love, he was most loyal: witness the constancy with which he upheld during long absence his boon companion, Henry Bennet, against the attacks of his mother and brother, or the rollicking Ned Griffin against the more serious enmity of Hyde. When Jane Lane, driven by suspicion from England, arrived at Paris, he rode

---

* Hyde's omniscience did not help to make him popular. " He is wiser than all men in all things," wrote a colleague, " and it seems because he can speak well, he thinks he may do anything, and never considers how great envy attends him, and how few friends he has in this Court." (Nicholas to Jane, 8 Dec., '54, C.S.P.D. 1654, 408.)

out to meet her, and before all the Court embraced her, calling her " his life," found her a home as a lady-in-waiting
to his sister in Holland, and throughout his exile carried on
an affectionate correspondence with her, constantly deploring
his inability to serve her more until the Restoration brought
an end to his penury.*⁹

Yet this very tenderness of heart proved his undoing. His
extreme susceptibility where women were concerned was the
Achilles heel of his armour : through that gap every arrow
could pierce. Even as a boy in England, Hyde had observed
with sorrow how ready he was to lend an ear to the jests and
licentious conversation of the debauched soldiers of his army.
During his adolescence in Paris, his mother's firm rule had
given him small opportunity for illicit pleasure;† indeed he

* A charming letter of Charles's to her, dated the last of June, is printed
in *H.M.C. Rep. 6 (Raffles)*, 473 : " I did not think I should have ever begun
a letter to you in chiding, but you give so just cause by telling me you fear
you are wearing out my memory, that I cannot choose but tell you that I take
it very unkindly that, after the obligations I have to you, 'tis possible for you
to suspect that I can ever be so wanting to myself as not to remember them
on all occasions to your advantage." . . . Another will be found in *Seward's
Anecdotes* and Lyon's *Personal History of Charles II*, while there are some
delightful references to the friendship in Charles's correspondence with his sister
Mary, published in *Cal. Clar. MSS.*, II, No. 2061, and *Thurloe*, I, 665.

† Burnet, who was then only a child in distant Scotland, is responsible for
the statement that at this time the young Duke of Buckingham introduced Charles
into all the vices of the age, but as this is nowhere corroborated by contemporary
evidence and is contradicted by Madame de Motteville, who was in Paris at the
same time as the Prince, it may—like most of Burnet's statements where he is
not speaking from his own personal experience—be disregarded.
    I have ignored altogether the story that Charles became father of a child
before he was seventeen, as the result of a liaison during his first stay in Jersey.
The tale rests on certain letters—in possession of the Jesuits College at Rome
—alleged to have been written by Charles in 1665 and 1668, to, and on behalf
of, a hypothetical Jesuit son. These were printed in English in the *Gentleman's
Magazine*, 1866, I, 531, and II, 65, and were made the subject of a famous
essay by Lord Acton. In two of them Charles is made to refer to the presence
in England of his mother, who—as all the world knew—was then, and had
long been, in France, while another letter purports to have been written from
Whitehall at a date when the King was at Oxford. Apart from these suspicious
circumstances, it is almost inconceivable to anyone acquainted with Charles's
very marked epistolary style, that he could have written these long, dull,
verbose letters.

had been made to woo, most shyly and reluctantly, his cousin, Mademoiselle de Montpensier, the richest heiress in France and, in her own estimation at least, the despair of an adoring Court. On Charles's heart she had made no impression, and when she rejected him for higher game, he had turned with a sigh of relief to her lovely maid of honour, the young Duchess of Châtillon. This also had proved an incomplete affection, for though Charles long loved her and twenty years later was still doing Bablon—as he called her—little acts of kindness, the affair remained platonic. But when, at the outbreak of the second Civil War, Charles, then eighteen, had hurried to the Dutch coast to lead a mutinous English fleet to his father's aid, he had fallen within a week to the blue eyes of a ruined Royalist's daughter—"a brown, beautiful, bold but insipid creature," named Lucy Walter. Nine months later there was born, beside the Zeeland water-meadows, that eldest and beloved son, whose story ended thirty-five years after with Kneller's painting of Monmouth's severed head.[10]

Now that he was a man and his own master, Charles did not long deny himself the pleasures to which his vigorous body and all too tender heart prompted him. "The greatest heroes and sages of antiquity," wrote his mother's friend, Madame de Motteville, "did not guide their lives by grander principles than this young Prince at the opening of his career, but when he found that his struggles were doomed to failure, he sank into indifference and bore the ills of poverty with reckless nonchalance, snatching at whatever pleasures came in his way, even those of the most degraded kind." To this fall his enforced idleness at Paris* and the comradeship of his old playmate, the Duke of Buckingham†—the worst rake of his age—contributed. For those who loved him best, this

---

* "That cursed place and company makes all people mad," Hyde had written in 1650. (*Cal. Clar. MSS.*, II, No. 471.)

† "The Duke of Buckingham is here at the old rate, and is good for nothing." (Hyde, 25 July, '53, *Cal. Clar. MSS.*, II, No. 1284.)

frailty was most tragic. " It is too true," wrote Hyde, " and cannot be denied that the King is exceedingly fallen in reputation, which cannot be recovered but by some bold attempt. . . . He is so much given to pleasure that if he stay here he will be undone."[11]

Yet his friends never doubted that he would outlive the scandals about him and give the world evidence of another temper of mind. Though he refused to read through all the long dispatches and memoranda, with which Hyde's " eternal pen " filled his exiled Cabinet, and could only be " brought very unwillingly to the work of writing letters," he could, when need arose, show an energy which amazed everyone. It had been so in Scotland, during his brief period as head of an army; it was so again in the early summer of 1654, when at last a chance occurred of escaping from the debts which imprisoned him at Paris and finding a new refuge for himself and his Court in Germany.* And when, that November in Cologne, he received sudden news that his mother, whose hobby was conversion, had been practising against the Protestantism of her youngest son, the fourteen-year-old Henry, Duke of Gloucester, Charles acted with a speed and vigour that completely shattered the ill-judged attempt.†[12]

---

* " Every three or four days some new difficulties break out, which put the King to his own best activity, and may in the end do him more good than a greater calm and less distresses would do." (Hyde to Rochester, 27 March, '54, *Cal. Clar. MSS.,* II, No. 1802.)

† " If you hearken to her, or anyone else in that matter," Charles wrote that day to his brother, " you must never think to see England or me again. Therefore consider what it is not only to be the cause of the ruin of a brother that loves you so well, but also of your King and country, and do not let them persuade you by force or fair promises. The first they neither dare nor will use, and for the second, as soon as they have you . . . they will care no more for you. . . . If you do not consider what I say to you, remember the last words of your dead father, which were to be constant in your religion and never to be shaken in it." To the Queen he wrote with no less eloquence but more fire, that he could only suppose that she never wished him to regain his crown. As for Jermyn, whom he regarded as the villain of the piece, he told him roundly that if he did not use all means to prevent his brother from being seduced, " and not only say but give testimonies of it," he would never

D

Indeed there was something about him that won all hearts.* " May I never drink wine," wrote the rough Irishman, Lord Taaffe, " if I had not rather live at six sous a day with him than have all the pleasures of this world without him." Often dissolute and quarrelsome, and always haunted by debts and poverty, his exiled Court was rendered tolerable by the perpetual gaiety and charm of its master. Though idleness and perpetual disappointments at times dejected him, Charles never lost hope or allowed others to do so. To every situation he brought an unfailing sense of humour—chuckling at the kindly reception by a too soft-hearted German lady of an impostor who had taken his name, telling his mother that the fat Hyde, disguised at a masquerade, was the naughty man who had done all the mischief and set him against her, or writing ironically of a much-canvassed Scotch rising: " Who would have thought, after so much discourse of an army in the Highlands that had taken Inverness and would quickly drive all the English out of the kingdom, that there should indeed be no men there but such as lodge in their own beds and only project what they will do when they are able? "[13]

Perhaps the secret of his personality lay in his perennial delight in the little, ordinary things of life. Even in the twenties he was a master of the art of living. The purchase of a sword or suit of clothes, a day's hunting through the Duke of Neuburg's woods—even though he killed but one hare at the end of all—a good bottle of wine or a new song from the Paris ballet, could give him the liveliest pleasure. In the dullest moments, he could betake himself, as Hyde testified, " with great cheerfulness to compose his mind to his fortune in studying French and Italian." And when some

speak to him again, " being so full of passion," he added, " that I cannot express myself." (*Clarendon MSS.* xlix, 10 Nov., '54.)

    * See the amazing tribute of the Puritan, Walter Gostelowe, in 1656 (*Thurloe*, V, 673), or the presbyter Baillie's praise of seven years before (*Baillie*, III, 86-90).

all-too-rare treat or gala day offered itself—such as the holiday visit to the Spa with his beloved sister Mary, the young Princess of Orange—Charles knew how to seize the fleeting happiness with the zest of a child. " I am just now," he had written to his aunt, Elizabeth of Bohemia, in July, 1654,

" beginning this letter in my sister's chamber, where there is such a noise that I never hope to end it, and much less write sense. . . . I shall only tell your Majesty that we are now thinking how to pass our time, and in the first place of dancing, in which we find two difficulties, the one for want of fiddlers, and the other for want of somebody both to teach and assist dancing at dancing the new dances. I have got my sister to send for Silvius as one that is able to perform both. For the fiddledidies my Lord Taaffe does promise to be their convoy, and in the meantime we must content ourselves with those that make no difference between a hymn and a coranto."

A year later, on a further visit, he was writing to his friend, Bennet: " You must not expect to hear from me very often as long as my sister is here . . . for, from having very little company, and some of those worse than none, we have now as good as can be, and pass our time as well as people can that have no more money, for we dance and play as if we had taken the Plate Fleet."[14]

Of the King's courage, since the day when, a boy of eighteen, he had taken his stand by Prince Rupert's side on the quarterdeck as his mutinous ships bore down on the Parliamentary fleet, there had never been any doubt. Early in 1655, it seemed likely to be put once more to the test. An angry England, oppressed by ever-growing taxation, was stirring. That winter John Corbin of Kidderminster, travelling through Bewdley Forest, heard about sunset three strangers talking of war. Deal boxes of mysterious weight were consigned to protesting country carriers; questioned, that indignant loyalist, Sir John Pakenham, assured the authorities that they contained nothing but a rundlet of wine and two

D*

firkins of soap: picture his surprise when they were found to be full of guns. In Dorset there were strange faces at the Wimborne cock matches, and a mysterious barque, ballasted with ammunition, slipped by night into Lulworth Cove.

While Cavaliers whispered to their neighbours, "if the Pretender were in, the crown settled on's head, how sweetly he would govern, give a just and due conscientious liberty and take off taxes," men of very different political views were everywhere plotting to overthrow Cromwell. " Because he hath oppressed and forsaken the poor, because he hath violently taken away a house he builded not, surely he shall not feel quietness in his belly," thundered Rogers, the preacher. " The flying roll of God's curses shall overtake the family of that great thief." In every corner of England men were spoiling for a rising.[15]

As the news of these events filtered across the Channel, impetuous swords flew everywhere from exiled scabbards. Ormonde, starving at Antwerp, clamoured to be gone, " ready," he said, " to try for a hanging." Charles did his best to check him: " You do not wish," he wrote, " to be more in England than I do that you should be there, but I must tell you I will not venture you there unless something be first done, and in such case I will be ready to venture myself." Events proved the King wise. On January 22nd Cromwell dissolved his first Parliament with bitter reproaches. Then the iron hand fell on Royalist and Anabaptist alike. The spies had done their work.[16]

The Sealed Knot, the little group of high-born conspirators who directed the English Cavaliers, had planned a rising for February 14th. At the beginning of that month, an emissary from the bolder Royalists arrived at Cologne to obtain Charles's consent to proceed with the rising despite the discoveries. Charles agreed. A few days later came a letter from the Sealed Knot, urging a postponement until more

favourable times.   In this dilemma the King, with the cautious
Hyde at his shoulder, followed the " fatal custom of his
family " and replied in an indecisive letter, which was a
masterpiece of vacillation.   Such flickering lanterns do not
lead revolutions.[17]

Yet, if Charles could not mould circumstances, he could
at least wait on them.   On February 14th, accompanied by
Ormonde and a single groom, he vanished from Cologne.
For several weeks the wildest rumours of his whereabouts
circulated in England.   When he reappeared at the beginning
of March, it was in his old disguise of " Mr. Jackson " at the
house of a friendly Dutchman in Middleburg, waiting, amid
sands and sea mists, for a call.[18]

It never came.   March was the strangest of months in
England.   Royalist agents poured into the country; the
dungeons of Dover Castle were perpetually full of them, yet
they never failed to escape.   At Gravesend the authorities
reported a horde of strangers, voluble with explanations; they
had come, they said, to see the country, to learn to speak
English, to " see fashions," to " spend money."   In London
there arrived, after two arrests on the way, the stout and
jovial Wilmot (now Earl of Rochester), with the King's commission as Commander-in-Chief in his pocket and no disguise
but a yellow periwig.   Here, as Hyde related, " in the hours
of good fellowship, which was a great part of the day and
night, he communicated his purpose to anybody he did believe
would keep him company and run the same hazards."   For
such conspirators, Cromwell was more than ready.   On
March 8th the long expected rising broke out, and as quickly
went out.   Kent was packed with troops; in the far west,
the arrest of all the Royalist squires left the populace leader-
less.   On Hexham Moor, the Cavaliers dispersed almost
before they assembled, " strangely frightened with their own
shadows."   Only in Wiltshire, where gallant Penruddock

raised the King's standard at Salisbury, was there any serious fighting. Fortune never smiled on the little rising. Two days later a forlorn remnant, hungry, weary and outnumbered, laid down their arms at South Molton.[19]

All this was unknown to Charles, who was still waiting at Middleburg for news. Here, at the end of the month, came Manning the spy, having tracked him from Cologne, proclaiming that the blood of his father (a true Cavalier) " boiled within him and kept him from sleep lest there should be any sword in England drawn before his." And here also, to Charles's intense embarrassment, arrived unexpectedly an English relative of his hostess, with her husband, daughter and two servants. " They were in the house before we knew of it," Ormonde reported, " so there was no avoiding the necessity of trusting them. What effect their coming may have upon us in other respects I know not, but the daughter, though little more than a girl, makes Mr. Jackson's confinement more supportable."[20]

Before the end of March, buoyant rumours from across the Channel sank into truth. Sadly the King knighted his host and, with scarcely a penny in his pocket, returned to Cologne. There was nothing left for the exiles but to reproach one another. In these recriminations Charles did not join. " Those who will not believe anything to be reasonably designed unless it be successfully executed," he wrote to a friend in England, " had need of a more difficult game to play than mine. I hope we shall shortly see a turn and, though deferred longer than I expected, that I shall live to see you at Whitehall." A great planner of revolution he was not, but his perpetual cheerfulness was no small asset in dark days.[21]

That year in England was the saddest men had known. " Of all mine acquaintance," wrote an old Parliamentarian, " there is scarce one who is not in a borrowing condition."

The country was now parcelled into military districts, and over each a Major-General wielding almost absolute power. From Northampton General Butler reported that he had decimated the Cavaliers' " very home and without trifling." In Manchester, Worsley, declaring that he saw " the finger of God going along with it," was busy pulling down alehouses, bribing witnesses and multiplying spies.   In that time many a humble Englishman shared Thomas Stafford's daily prayer that it would please God to " grant us a speedy deliverance out of the power of the Major-Generals and restore us to the protection of the Common Law."*   But those in whose hands the power of these things lay, remembering that it ever pleased God to save by few and not by many, could little understand the discontents of their people.   " How happy may these nations be," wrote that Christian soldier, Colonel Coplestone, to the Protector: " and what hath that bloody and restless generation to complain of? "²²

Though Charles was now poorer than ever,† the imperial ambitions of the dynast who sat on his throne brought him new hope.   That year Evelyn had seen Cromwell launch a great warship, bearing on its prow his own effigy trampling six nations beneath his feet.   It was a portent.   The empire

* Little over a year before, Cromwell—a man of a magnanimity far greater than that of his associates—criticizing the Rump's arbitrary rule, had spoken with indignation of the victimization of Royalist squires: " Poor men, under this arbitrary power, were driven like flocks of sheep by forty in a morning to the confiscation of goods and estates without any man being able to give a reason why two of them had deserved to forfeit a shilling." (Carlyle, *Cromwell, Speech*, III.) Now, when there was no Rump, an old Devonshire squire of seventy-six could be transported to the West Indies without trial, for no other offence but an expression of sympathy for a party of Royalist fugitives. (*Thurloe*, I, 746.) Those who believe that the experiment of the Commonwealth was a pleasant one for the ordinary Englishmen who lived under it, should study the seven volumes of contemporary letters contained in the *Thurloe Papers* (they repay reading), and supplement it by any collection of family papers that cover this period: a good example is the *Verney Memoirs*.

† One of his followers, the aged Earl of Norwich, complained that he must needs retire into some cave or bush to mend his " ould breeches." (*Nicholas*, III, 15.)

upon which this tornado burst was the giant, dying carcass of Spain—a fit prey for Puritan crusaders and the heirs of Drake's buccaneers. " The Lord himself hath a controversy with your enemies, even with that Roman Babylon of which Spain is the great underpropper," wrote the Protector to his admirals in the West Indies. " In that respect you fight the Lord's battles, and the Scriptures are most plain." In all this Charles saw a chance of retrieving his fortunes. The Spanish Netherlands, with their ports opening across the narrow seas on England, offered a hopeful haven. Yet, before the longed-for invitation came from Spain, there were many delays and disappointments for him who lay, as one of Secretary Thurloe's spies described him, " lurking behind the hangings, with no part to act upon the theatre of the world."[23]

Though England and Spain were now at war, New Year 1656 found the King still waiting for a call to Flanders. But delay was the genius of the Spanish system, and week followed week without a word, until he could wait no longer. At dawn on February 26th, with two servants and a dozen horsemen, he slipped away from Cologne. Three days later, to the horror of the slowest and most ceremonious people in the world, he arrived unannounced at Brussels.[24]

The cup of humiliation from which Charles now drank was a deep one. Courteously but coldly ignored by the Viceroy of Flanders and his Ministers and frustrated at every turn by the " unnecessary Spanish gravity," it was many weeks before he could obtain even a bare recognition of the alliance which he was seeking, and many months before he could procure enough money to redeem his followers from the debts which imprisoned them at Cologne. The pension which he had hitherto received from France—Spain's perpetual enemy—was now stopped, and, though the Spaniards declared themselves anxious to compensate him, their manners were so exquisite that they felt they could offer him no allowance that was not worthy of their King's dignity, and their coffers so empty that such was altogether beyond their power. To angry entreaties they were unfailingly polite, and as unfailingly dilatory. " God send me to deal with men of passion," exclaimed Ormonde, " who will be angry when they are contradicted and be moved by reason that they cannot answer."[25]

But hope was an undying plant in the hearts of the exiles. Bruges, where Charles now set up his beggared Court, was many leagues nearer England than Cologne, and even Hyde, never prone to be over sanguine, spoke of living to eat cherries at Deptford again. There was the usual talk that summer of a rising. The English Levellers—formerly the greatest republicans of all—were now displaying surprisingly monarchial sentiments. In a Declaration to Charles they referred to his father as " a gentleman of the most strong and perfect intellectuals, and one of the best and purest morals of any prince that ever swayed the English sceptre," admitted their former errors, and announced their intention to overthrow " that ugly tyrant who calls himself Protector." Charles replied that he had read few things in his life that had touched him more, but the difficulty with these allies was that they wanted money and he had none. Therefore, though there was much talk, no rising occurred.[26]

Meanwhile an ever-growing number of necessitous and discontented men, driven from England by Cromwell's rule, flocked to Charles's Court. These formed the nucleus of an army, which, not for the last time in his life, was to prove too much for his purse. They ranged from runaway London apprentices—representatives of a new generation to whom the royal cause was beginning to appeal—to Scotch Highlanders, whose " right native apparel " much amazed the good people of Bruges. When Charles recalled to his side his brother, the Duke of York—who as Turenne's industrious apprentice had at one moment commanded the French Army*—these were joined by the Irish regiments under his command.[27]

This army was at once the pride and curse of Charles's life. To find money to pay it, and obtain from the ever-delaying Spanish authorities quarters to house it, became the first task of his Ministers. In this they were helped for a time by that volatile genius, George Digby, Earl of Bristol— a nobleman who passed with boundless spirits from one misfortune to another, his lack of character as invariably making the end of his undertakings disastrous as his personality made their beginnings favourable. After a service in the French Army, made notorious by his violence against the Spaniards, he now had the audacity to offer to act as Charles's agent at Spanish headquarters. Discovering that the new Viceroy, the royal bastard Don Juan, had a passion for astrology and an eye for the throne, he so played upon these frailties, casting horoscopes and talking perpetually of crowns and sceptres, that he completely won him. Thereafter, till his erratic genius discredited him, he did his master much useful service. His task was anything but easy, for, confronted by the utter poverty of the Spaniards, he was bombarded with long, angry letters from Hyde, stressing the desperate needs of the exiles and upbraiding his delay.[28]

There was little to be done that year of grace, 1657, but wait for something to turn up and news from England. There was no hope now of a rising, so long as Cromwell lived. The Levellers had taken to trying to assassinate him: a fire-work left in a hand-basket at Whitehall was their New Year's gift, but as usual it did not go off. As tit-for-tat, two attempts were made to lure Charles and his brothers to an English port and there shoot them. As for the Spanish Ministers, with

---

* James was thus the only man who ever commanded both the French Army and the English Navy. He also achieved for a short time the command of the Spanish Army in Flanders and the Admiralty of Spain. (Clarke, *James II*, I, 264, 365, 381.)

their promises, their poverty, and their unfailing delays, Hyde could only exclaim, " All the divels in Hell take them! "[29]

One small gleam of hope came with the spring. Bristol had an unexpected success, and induced the Irish troops in the French garrison at St. Ghislain to betray the town to the Spaniards. Don Juan was delighted, and Bristol quite lost his head in his triumph. " I wish the stars would permit him to stay till I come," wrote Charles to Ormonde, " or at least that we might see him before he suffers a second disapparition. Pray God that Taurus be as successful to him as Aries has been, and then I hope he will think a little more of terrestrial things." In the meantime Stuart shares rose, and Charles was invited to Brussels, where he was handsomely fêted by the authorities, and, as usual on such occasions, behaved to admiration at all the State balls. While he did so, Blake with his stately ships passed under the cliffs of Teneriffe to an exploit so daring that even the exiles' hearts thrilled at it.[30]

They had little else to rouse them that summer. Hopes that Cromwell would overreach himself by accepting the Crown proved to be dupes, and the wants of the Court grew worse than ever. Hyde told Langdale that they owed for every loaf since their coming, and Ormonde spoke with a bitterness, rare in his sunny nature, of " the want of money that makes us mad." But the worst embarrassment of all was the Army. Unpaid, ill-disciplined, despairing, it became the bane of northern Flanders. Charles begged to be allowed to take the field and lead it against the French, but the Spanish were as evasive as ever.[31]

Charles would not have been himself if he had not sought relief in pleasures that were not always wise or creditable. There was indeed no hiding his master failing.* Ormonde,

---

* A little while before, the appearance of Lucy Walter in England had led to the publication of a royal pension warrant, found on her person, in a

who never breathed a word against him except to his face, wrote to expostulate. " God's blessing on your heart for your letter to the King," Hyde answered. " An honester, and a wiser, I never read, and truly I think it has made a deep impression. I am sure it has given me occasion of preaching at large." Charles bore it all in good part, but showed no sign of leaving Brussels for the country. But what distressed his advisers most was his unkingly taste for every sort of company: in his love of society, he made no distinction of persons.* " You speak ignorantly," Ormonde told Hyde, " when you talk of the pleasures of any place that has not visitable company in it to take up every afternoon of the year."[32]

In September, after Hyde had found every bit of meat, every drop of drink, all the fire and all the candles entirely owed for, the longed-for permission was at last given for Charles to visit his army, then serving with the Spanish forces at Dunkirk. Opposed to them in the French lines were six thousand of Cromwell's janissaries, " stout men and fit for action, each with a new red coat and a new pair of shoes." To win over their commander, Reynolds, the King and his brother walked daily on the sand-dunes; once Reynolds came out and assured the Duke that he wished the King well: subsequently he sent him a present of wine and forbade the

Commonwealth journal. Though the lady's association with Charles had ceased, her behaviour had been causing his friends considerable embarrassment: in 1656 she had narrowly escaped being drummed out of the Hague as an infamous woman. Yet, though every idle action of hers brought him on the stage, Charles continued, regardless of his reputation, to send her money and kindly messages. (See *Thurloe*, I, 683-4; III, 100; V, 178; *Evelyn*, IV, 222; *Cal. Clar. MSS.*, III, Nos. 1024, 1029, 1061, 1071, 1200, 1206, 1214, 1230; *Ellis, Orig. Letters*, 2nd S., III, 352. And see also *Camden Misc.*, XI (*Burnet Letters*, 31).)

* " But till the King shall himself take more majesty on him he will always, and from all these peoples, find every day more and more neglect and disesteem, for they abhor the ridiculous freedom of the French, which makes no distinction of persons. I wish the King would set a better value on himself and not use familiarity with persons of so much inferior quality." (Nicholas to Hyde, 5 Sept., '57, *Nicholas*, IV, 13.)

English ships to fire at those solitary walkers. But soon afterwards Reynolds was drowned, and the attempts came to nothing. As usual on such occasions, Charles exposed his life recklessly, much to the disgust of poor Hyde,* who found it depressed the exiles' credit with the Bruges shopkeepers.[33]

That winter was a bitterly cold one, and in England the crows' feet were frozen to their prey. At Bruges the exiles shivered and tightened their belts, and at far Madrid Harry Bennet wrote of his longing for old England, where one turf was worth all Spain. " Pray, sir," he begged Hyde, " be pleased to use a little diligence to get us thither." It was a forlorn land for Cavaliers. " The High Court of Justice is erected to put some of those unquiet spirits out of the world that nothing will quiet but death," wrote one republican grimly. The Anglican Church was at its last gasp, its services forbidden, its cathedrals desecrated and offered for sale, and its ministers in dens and caves of the earth.[34]

New Year 1658 came and passed. There was much talk in Flanders of an invasion of England, and Bristol and Don Juan pored together over maps. But the Spanish refused to move without some assurance that the invasion would be supported, and it was finally agreed that Ormonde should cross the Channel to report. On January 20th he landed at West March, where he sat up all night at an inn, playing at shuffle-board with four Suffolk brewers. Thence he made his way to London. Here with his hair dyed—unhappily it turned a variety of colours—he interviewed many Royalist sympathizers and received as many views. Betrayed, he was driven from house to house, and barely escaped. A fortnight later all hope of a rising ended in a tornado of arrests. Executions —the sledge, the gallows, the reeking quarters—followed.

---

* " I am none of those who think that you are like to recover your three kingdoms without being in danger of your life, but let it be when the adventure is of use and there is a recompense in view. Truly, sir, you ought to take some compassion on our fears." (Hyde to the King, *Cl.S.P.*, III, 374.)

Even the most sanguine of the exiles now despaired. " If we are to tide out another year, the Lord have mercy on us," prayed one, and Norwich thought that the only hope of a return must be " such a hope as St. Paul mentions, that we must be saved by—a hope that is not soon and with patience waited for."[35]

Once more Charles spent the summer at Brussels—the shadow of a king—so thin and attenuated now that his enemies could almost forget him. Some feared that, in that enforced idleness, his immoderate delight in empty, effeminate and vulgar conversation might become part of his nature. " I received last night," Hyde wrote to him that July, " a very discreet and sad letter from my Lady Abbess, and in it a letter from London concerning you. I confess I heartily wish you out of the town and, if it were possible, out of the reach of the scandalous tongues there. . . . I pray you burn this letter, and God of Heaven preserve you and rouse up your spirit to do what you ought yourself, and then you will make us all do as we ought." It was with some relief that his servants saw him leave Brussels in August to take the country air at Hoogstraeten on the Dutch-Flemish border and hunt and hawk. The sport was poor, and Charles consoled himself by wooing Henrietta, the younger daughter of the Dowager Princess of Orange. The young lady smiled on her lover, but the Dowager, who had no use for penniless kings, did not. Charles therefore crossed the border incognito to visit some Dutch friends. Here, though he knew it not, he was in deadly peril. There came by night to his inn an old, reverend-looking gentleman with a long beard, who sought an interview. When the door was closed the stranger locked it, threw off his disguise and revealed himself as Downing, English ambassador at the Hague. Kneeling at Charles's feet, he entreated his pardon, and, this granted, warned him that he was bound to apply for his seizure under a treaty between the Dutch and the Commonwealth, and begged him at once to return to Flanders. It was the first sign that very wise and far-scented rats were leaving a sinking ship.[36]

Back at Hoogstraeten, Charles's world suddenly went mad. A trumpeter from Dunkirk brought delirious news, and Stephen Fox hurried post-haste to tell his sovereign, then in the midst of a game of tennis, that it had " pleased God out of His infinite goodness to do that which He would not allow any man the honour of doing." Cromwell was dead. " As for this town," wrote Culpeper from Amsterdam, " they are mad with joy. No man is at leisure to buy or sell; the young fry dance in the streets at noonday ! " The King acted at once, and proposed in writing to the Princess Henrietta. The young lady swooned, the Dowager wilted, and he, to whom the situation appeared mainly in the light of his love-affair, spent a pleasant week-end at the Oranges' palace at Turnhout, under the impression that his hand had been accepted. There his rejoicings ended. On his return on September 13th to Brussels, the familiar tale of debts and beggary closed round him once more. His house was let, his goods sold or pawned, and he ate, so we are told, " such things as he could get to eat." In England nothing very startling appeared to happen, after all. The prudent Dowager announced that no engagement had taken place.[37]

Yet for all the debts and the closing in of another starving winter, things *were* happening in England. They buried the great Protector, and Evelyn saw the superb equipage, the effigy, the royal robes, the crown in life he dared not wear. " But," he added, " it was the joyfullest funeral I ever saw, for there were none that cried but dogs, which the soldiers hooted away with a barbarous noise, drinking, and taking tobacco in the streets as they went." The Army was now supreme—but it was an army without a head. At Gresham

College, young Christopher Wren could lecture no more on the stars, for a soldier stood at the gate with a gun.[38]

In that time, a weary winter in Flanders, a sowing time in England, one man saw the future. The old exile Culpeper, fixing his eyes on the Commander of the Commonwealth Army in Scotland, wrote:

" The person that my eye is chiefly on as able alone to restore the King is Monk, who commands, absolutely at his devotion, a better army, as I am informed, than that in England. He is a sullen man, that values himself enough, and much believes that his knowledge and reputation in arms fit him for the office of Protector better than Mr. Richard Cromwell's skill in horse-races and husbandry. . . . The way to deal with him is . . . to show him plainly . . . that he shall better find all his ends with the King than with any other way he can take. Neither are we to boggle at any way he shall propose in the declaring himself . . . so it oppose the present power, it will, at last, do the King's business. When he is engaged past a retreat, he will want you as much as you want him, and you may mould him into what form you please."

In December Royalist agents were given instructions to open secret negotiations with Monk.[39]

All through the spring of 1659 a great reaction was setting in for Charles. In the Parliament that February he had almost more friends than the Protector, and in the lobbies men whispered the terrible conundrum, " If a single person, why not the King? " The extremer republicans fell much on the arbitrary acts of the Government, and Sir Henry Vane declared that he had not thought to have seen the day when free-born Englishmen should be sold as slaves by their own countrymen. In May the " men of buff " dissolved Parliament and restored the Rump. By an angry nation the latter was sardonically nicknamed the " Representative," for, out of five hundred members of the original Long Parliament, scarcely more than fifty were allowed to sit. By the end of May the Protectorate had vanished, the new Council of State was busy demolishing Cromwell's monument in the Abbey, and its members were privately engaged in stocking their larders with the remaining deer from the royal parks.[40]

At such a moment the wisest counsel for Royalists was to leave their enemies to fight each other.　Yet to have followed it, they must have been more than human.　In England many feared a massacre by the fanatic soldiery.　In Flanders hungry men were clamouring to draw their swords and be home again.　Even Hyde, with his prayer not to gratify Thurloe with a plot, was carried away by the tide.　By mid-summer, plans for a joint Presbyterian-Cavalier rising had been laid in every county in England.[41]

The rising was to have taken place on August 1st.　Before it began, a secret communication arrived from Samuel Morland, Thurloe's under-secretary, that Sir Richard Willis, one of the Sealed Knot, had been for long betraying the inner councils of the Royalists to the Government.　It was a terrific blow for Charles and Hyde, and at first, so deeply grounded was their faith in Willis's loyalty, they could not believe it. But proofs from Morland convinced them.　At that moment the King was on the point of embarking for Deal, where he was to have been seized and murdered.[42]

It was too late to prevent a rising.　Many were warned, but others were too far distant to be reached or refused to believe in Willis's treachery.　The plans went forward there-fore in the usual spasmodic, uncertain manner.　To be near at hand, should the call come, the King slipped away to a little house at Tervueren, ostensibly to hunt and hawk.　Thence at 4 a.m. on August 3rd he left for Calais with only Ormonde, Titus and O'Neill.　Learning that the rising in Kent had miscarried, he went on to Rouen to find a boat for the western countries.　Here, full of hope, he wrote to Hyde:

" To-morrow we set forth, and do not doubt but by the help of God to get to our friends . . . for upon the whole matter I am

E

very cheerful, and, though I am not altogether so plump, I begin
to grow as sanguine as Mr. Skinner.   Sure never people went so
cheerfully to venture their necks as we do."

Like all his race, Charles was at his best in the heather.[43]

Again the call did not come.   In England, their plans
everywhere betrayed, the Royalists never rose.   Only in
Cheshire did four thousand men under Booth, a great
Presbyterian magnate, take the field.   These, after much
squabbling among their leaders, were routed by Lambert at
Winnington.   It was a miserable battle.   " In short, sir,"
reported the Cavalier Mordaunt, " 'twas never fought.   The
foot saved themselves in the enclosures, the horse trotted away
—which is the civilest term."   Booth himself, appropriately
disguised as an old woman, was found a few days later at
Newport Pagnell.[44]

When the news reached him, the King, with his usual
philosophy, abandoned the idea of an English rising and fell
back on the old one of a restoration by foreign aid.   At that
moment the representatives of Spain and France were about
to meet at Fuentarrabia to conclude a peace, and it was hoped
that they might combine to do something for the exiles.   For
the Pyrenees Charles, still incognito, accordingly set out, and
with O'Neill to attend to the commissariat, Bristol to amuse
him and Ormonde—" in an old threadbare French suit "—
to add respectability, travelled lazily southwards.   While
Hyde at Brussels fumed and swore that he would be undone
by such delay, Charles wrote cheerfully:

" You will wonder to find me no farther advanced than this
place, where I arrived last night, for the truth is our greediness for
getting into Spain with all haste has made us lose time . . . I hope
God hath decreed all for the best.   Our journey hath hitherto been
very lucky, having met with many pleasant accidents "—(if some
had worn petticoats beneath dark southern eyes, one can feel
certain that they were none the less welcome)—" and not one ill
to any of our company, hardly so much as the fall of a horse.

But I am very much deceived in the travelling in Spain, for by all reports I did expect ill cheer and worse lying, and hitherto we have found the beds, and especially the meat, very good. The only thing I feel troublesome is the dust. . . . God keep you, and send you to eat as good mutton as we have every meal."

As Charles predicted, all turned out for the best. At Fuentarrabia he charmed every heart and obtained all the courtesy from Spain and France that the most sanguine of his supporters could reasonably have hoped. And at that moment of great opportunities, when even Hyde itched to be up and doing, the King's easy, pleasure-seeking philosophy provided the necessary antidote and secured that element of time in England which in reality was the exiles' trump card.[45]

The royal party left Fuentarrabia highly satisfied—indeed, as O'Neill told Hyde, so much so that they believed themselves already at Dover. In the hopes of clinching matters Charles offered to marry Hortense Mancini, niece of Mazarin, France's virtual ruler, a proposal politely declined by the cautious Cardinal. On November 13th he set out for the north, intending to visit his mother and his fifteen-year-old sister, Henrietta —" Minette " as he called her. The child, who made a hero of the poor wandering King, wrote to thank him for the honour he was doing her, blissful that he should take " so much trouble for a little sister that does not deserve it." With only his valet, Toby Rustat, to accompany him, Charles travelled swiftly and happily across France.[46]

At Colombes Minette was waiting for him with her mother. She was so grown that after six years' absence he did not recognize her and kissed the wrong young lady by mistake. In the presence of this sweet Princess, the quarrels of the past were forgotten. Even Jermyn, now all smiles and compromise—with a fat weather-eye cocked on England— was awarded an earldom. " The spirit of peace," O'Neill reported, " reigns here as well as at the frontiers."[47]

E*

On December 7th Charles resumed his journey to Flanders. The roads were heavy with thaw after frost, and he made slow going.   At Amiens he held a military conference with the great Turenne; thence passed, shadowing future history, by Peronne, Cambrai and Mons.   On December 16th, a little before it was dark, in very good health and humour, he reached Brussels.   He found his followers cold, hungry and depressed, in the gloom of a Flemish winter.   They were almost without hope.[48]

CHAPTER III

" I pray God send we may live to see peace in our time and that friends may live to joy in each other."—PENELOPE DENTON.

YET in London all the boys were singing. They sang old ballads, printed on broadsides; of justice and the gallows, and the Rump and " England's murthering monsters," under the very noses of the soldiers. And, added those cheerful prints:

> " 'tis hoped before the month of June
> The birds will sing another tune! "

And, though no one dared say it openly, everyone knew what they meant.[1]

That October the Rump had cashiered Lambert, and Lambert, aping his former master, had turned out the Rump. These events had determined the Commander-in-Chief in Scotland to act. Monk—" Old George," as his soldiers called him—had been bred a Cavalier, and had only taken service under the Parliament when the royal cause was lost. Shrewd and Devonshire to the bone, he was the first professional English soldier of that unique school which believes that the military arm should be subordinate to the civil. With a rapidity strange in so slow a man, he now secured the strong places throughout Scotland and disarmed his Anabaptist officers. Then he assembled his troops and told them what he proposed to do—to march into England to assert " the freedom and rights of three kingdoms from arbitrary and

69

tyrannical usurpations." On December 5th, with seven thousand men, he was at Berwick, and Lambert was marching north to oppose him. " They say the nation will be involved in a new and bloody war," Hyde had written, " I pray tell me what will be the end of that war? "[2]

The rough youth of London, the City apprentices, had never a doubt. When on December 5th they rose and clamoured for " a Free Parliament," and the wicked old one-eyed cobbler, Colonel Hewson of Drogheda fame, was sent to subdue them, they pelted his soldiers with old shoes and slippers, turnip-tops, stones and tiles. In the country the Army fared no better; Puritan Bristol rose against the troopers, and at Southampton, when the garrison went out to drill, the townsmen locked the gates. Men dreamed of massacres and ruin; it was " a crazy time everywhere." By the end of December, the Army, hopelessly divided among itself, was being tossed on the surge of an angry countryside. Its rank and file, unpaid, had broken into mutiny, while its commander, the " weeping Anabaptist," Fleetwood, sat " peaking in his chamber, as if it were moulting time with him and birds of his feather." On Boxing Day, escorted by a vast crowd of soldiers and apprentices, Speaker Lenthall processed, with mace before and Rump behind, to take possession of Westminster.[3]

Far away on the bleak border at Coldstream, Monk prepared to march. On a December night, between two and three, his chaplain, Price, roused him from the wooden form on which he was resting, and spoke to him of his duty—to restore the known laws of the land. " Mr. Price," he replied, " I know your meaning and I have known it. By the grace of God I will do it." On January 1st he crossed the Rubicon. " It was the Lord's day too, and it was His doing," wrote Price. " The frost was great and the snow greater, and I do not remember that we ever trod upon plain earth from

Edinburgh to London.   The air this day was very clear too,
so that we could distinguish the very colours of the pebbles
in the Tweed."[4]

As Monk marched, resistance crumbled away.   All Yorkshire came out in arms to aid him.   Fairfax, forgetting his
gout, left his heavy country life and raised his tenants:
"became another man, his motions so quick, his eyes so
sparkling, giving the word of command like a general."
There was a great work to be done, though still none dared
call it by its name.

In London rumour ran riot.   Wild excitement and
depression followed in succession.   Men were resolved to
"shake off the soldiers," and the young clerks, over their
evening bowl at the Dog Tavern, spoke privately of—no one
would say who.   Merry doggerels—not very kindly, exceedingly lewd—about the Grandees of the Rump went the
round of the town.   And on January 30th Pepys, as he
woke in the morning, fell a-singing of his song, "Great, good
and just," and "thereby put himself in mind that this was
the fatal day, now ten years since, his Majesty died."   What
did these things portend?[5]

The exiles in Flanders, warming chilled fingers before
starved fires, could scarcely imagine, and they dared not hope.
Hyde pleaded patience: "to sit still till they are in blood."
In his bones he could feel something stirring.   But the debts
and poverty were worse than ever, and it was bitterly
cold.   "In this terrible weather," he wrote to Langdale
on February 2nd, "we have all some envy towards you that
are in a place, where you can want no fire, which we all do;
if, and when it will change, we yet know not."[6]

In the midst of the cold and the distractions, the King
remained unmoved.   He had someone now to love.   So,
though he sent a hundred letters to England on public affairs,
he wrote to his little sister in Paris of other things:

" I begin this French letter by assuring you that I am very glad to be scolded by you. I withdraw what I said with great joy, since you scold me so pleasantly, but I will never take back the love I have for you, and you show me so much affection that the only quarrel that we are ever likely to have will be as to which of us two loves the other best. In that respect I will never yield to you. I send you this letter by the hands of Janton, who is the best girl in the world. We talk of you every day, and wish we were with you a thousand times a day. . . .

" When you send me the scapular, I promise to wear it always, for love of you. Tell me, I beg of you, how you spend your time, for if you stayed long at Chaillot in this miserable weather, you must have been not a little bored."[7]

All the while Monk marched. At York he was deluged with petitions for a Free Parliament. He said nothing, " was dark," and, when incautious men spoke of a king, frowned. But though he came ostensibly to protect the Rump, the members of that body were dubious and made secret efforts to undermine his authority. On February 3rd his troops entered London—likely men, with the officers wearing red and white favours in their hats and trumpeters going before in liveries of scarlet and silver. Next day the Rump offered him the Oath of Abjuration of the House of Stuart, and he refused to take it.[8]

A decision of the City fathers to pay no taxes until a Free Parliament should be called gave the Rump its chance. On February 8th it ordered Monk to march into the city and pull down the gates and portcullises, thereby offering him the alternatives of disobeying the Civil power or incurring the hatred of London. Still obedient, he marched into a puzzled and angry city. Royalist hopes fell to zero. But on the night of the 9th, Monk called a council of his leading officers. With their aid he penned a letter to the Rump, demanding the issue of writs for filling up the House with excluded members and an early dissolution to make way for a Free

Parliament. The letter was at once printed. Monk had done his work.[9]

Again—it was Saturday, February 11th—Monk marched into the city, the people silent and watching. At the Guildhall he told the Mayor and Aldermen what he had done. Within half an hour all men's faces had changed. That night was such a one as no man could remember. One observer counted thirty-one bonfires in a single street, and at every one a rump roasting; the butchers in the Strand rang a peal on their knives, " and all the bells in all the churches as we went home were a-ringing. . . . The common joy was everywhere to be seen; . . . indeed it was past imagination, both the greatness and the suddenness of it."

By Monday all England knew, and from Hampshire John Stewkeley, jumping to conclusions, wrote that Monk had declared for " a single person (you may imagine whom) and for a Free Parliament. . . . We may all soon meet if the wind blows from Flanders, which I pray for as a subject, as a member, as an Englishman." That week it was quite surprising how many times young Mr. Pepys, secretly in taverns and wine-vaults, drank the health of his exiled sovereign. And as the news of these doings filtered across to the Continent, there was a wild flutter of hope in the breasts of the exiles and their landladies.[10]

Yet still Monk showed no signs of recognizing that there was a king across the water, and angrily reproved any who spoke to him of Charles Stuart. In this he was wise, for the Royalist tide was running so strongly that there was some danger of a reaction. Dispossessed Cavaliers in their cups spoke wildly of revenge and restoration of property, and Monk was heard to observe that, if there was a fanatic party on one side, there was a frantic one on the other. Yet beneath the surface, he was going with the tide as fast as any man. " I cannot omit," wrote a Royalist agent, " that his little son being asked who he was for, whether a King, a Protector or a Free State, he answered that he was for the King, and so was his mother." The good lady represented the feeling of almost every woman in England. " My head is so testicated with the times," wrote one of them, " between hope and fear, that I know not what to do; if things be not as I hope, my heart will break, I cannot outlive it; but I do not despair, for I am confident it will be."[11]

On the afternoon of March 15th, just before the Exchange closed, there appeared a humble workman " with a ladder upon his shoulder and a pot of paint in his hand, and set the ladder in the place where the last King's statue had stood, and then went up and wiped out that inscription, *Exit Tyrannus,** and as soon as he had done it threw up his cap and cried, *God bless King Charles the Second*, in which the whole Exchange joined with the greatest shout." Next day, by the votes of the excluded members, the Long Parliament brought its existence to an end, and Monk, judging the time ripe, gave a secret interview to the royal emissary, Sir John Grenville.[12]

On March 30th Grenville reached the King at Brussels, where he delivered Monk's message, advising him to leave the territory of a state with whom England was still at war. Next morning, before it was light, or the Spaniards had time to stop him, Charles galloped across the frontier to Breda. Here, with Hyde at his shoulder, he signed the famous Declaration, which secured at once a bloodless revolution and a restoration without conditions. The unquiet wraiths of twenty years, confiscated property, religious settlement, vengeance for bloodshed, were exorcized by Hyde's magic formula—the King would leave all to the will of a " Free

---

* After Charles I's execution, the royal statue outside the Exchange was thrown down by order of the Government, and over the empty niche the words inscribed : " *Exit Tyrannus, Regum Ultimus* "—The tyrant is gone, the last of the kings.

Parliament." To the Declaration, Charles added letters to Monk, to the speakers of both Houses, the Council of State and the City of London. For Monk he enclosed a commission as Captain-General of his forces and a blank warrant to appoint a Secretary of State. Grenville himself refused all honours, but before he left for England Charles slipped into his pocket a grant for the Earldom of Bath—promised to his father, the great Sir Bevil—and the posts of Groom of the Stole and First Gentleman of the Bedchamber.[13]

When Grenville reached England in the middle of April, the elections for the new Parliament were still uncertain, and Lambert, escaped from the Tower, was in arms in the Midlands. Monk therefore put the King's letter into his pocket and bade Grenville wait with the others till summoned by the Council of State. Then Lambert was defeated at Daventry, the successes of the Cavaliers at the elections became known, and " every man began to be merry and full of hopes." On the 25th the new Parliament met, the great Presbyterian, Dr. Reynolds, preaching to the assembled members at St. Margaret's from the text: " Behold, unto you that fear my name shall the son of righteousness arise with healing in his wings." Meanwhile " plain, homely, dowdy " Mrs. Monk was busy preparing Whitehall.[14]

On Saturday, April 28th, Grenville officially handed the King's letter to the Council, who decided to pass it unopened to the House of Commons. The following Tuesday was the pleasantest of May Day mornings, and Pepys, with the Fleet off Deal, wished himself in Hyde Park. As soon as the House assembled, Arthur Annesley, President of the Council, announced that Sir John Grenville was at the door with a letter. He was ordered to be brought in, and the Speaker took the letter and read it aloud, while the members stood bare-headed. Afterwards Monk's cousin, William Morrice, moved that the constitution of England lay in King, Lords and Commons. Without a dissentient voice the vote was carried. After that, all restraint went. They voted thanks to Grenville, and £50,000 to the King and that he should be invited to return at once and rule them. And Luke Robinson, the fanatic, " all bathed in tears," stood up and spoke for an hour and a half, recanting all his former opinions and promising to be a good subject in future. But nobody paid much attention to him, for a thing had happened " never read of in history, when monarchy, laid aside at the expense of so much blood, returned without the shedding of one drop." " This government was as natural to them as their food or raiment, and naked Indians dressing themselves in French fashion were no more absurd than Englishmen without a Parliament and a King."[15]

In the afternoon the whole nation went mad, with " ringing of bells and drinking of the King's health upon their knees in the streets "—which Pepys thought a little too much —and loyal Mr. Dobeson, a great sufferer for the cause, actually burnt the windmill at Charlton in his joy. There were, of course, a few dissentients: the Minister of Gawthorpe, Lincs, kicked the local bonfire out, and a certain Captain Southwold remarked that if the King came in he would cut him up as small as herbs in a pot. But for the vast majority of the nation it was " the happiest May Day that had been many a year to England." And down at Deal lay a fleet in her pride with pennants loose, guns roaring, caps flying and the loud *Vive le Roys* echoing from one ship's company to another.[16]

All the while the wonder grew. " The change is so great," wrote Lady Derby, " that I can hardly believe it. . . . This passes human wisdom and, in all humility, we ought to recognize in it the hand of the Eternal; it is beyond our understanding." " Good God! " cried another astonished Cavalier, " do the same people inhabit England that were in it ten or twenty years ago? Believe me, I know not whether I am in England or no, or whether I dream." On May 8th the King was proclaimed in Westminster and London, the Lords and Commons going in procession with the Heralds through the packed streets. " At the word *Charles* in the Proclamation, the King-at-Arms, lifting himself up with more than ordinary cheerfulness, the people took it up and on a sudden carried it to the Old Exchange," with such a shout that though all the bells of the city rang, they could not be heard. And down at Claydon in Bucks, Parson Butterfield wrote: " Such universal acclamations of wild and sober joy I never yet saw; we had our bonfire too and bells ringing even at Claydon. . . . Heaven and earth seem to conspire to make a fair and fruitful spring of plenty and joy to this poor kingdom. . . . The fields and pastures begin to put on their best dress as if it were to entertain his Majesty in triumph and make him in love with his native soil."[17]

The subject of all this joy was at Breda, writing tenderly to Minette about the purchase of clothes and ribbons, and waiting to learn the terms upon which a Restoration would be admitted. When Bernard Grenville arrived with a letter from Monk, preceding by a few hours the official invitation from the House, Charles was at supper. After he had read the letter, he embraced Grenville, telling him that no man had ever been more welcome, for now he could say he was a king and not a Doge.[18]

Thereafter life became an unbelievable dream. On the following day came eighteen deputies from the States General to invite him to the Hague and offer £30,000 for his expenses. On May 14th, accompanied by the Dukes of York and Gloucester, his sister Mary, and her child, William of Orange, Charles set out from Breda. At the Hague, where he dined off covers of gold, he was waited upon by the Committee of the Lords and Commons, with a promise of £50,000 and an

invitation from Parliament that he " would return and take
the government of the kingdom into his hands." There
followed fourteen London citizens with a trunk containing
£10,000, round which the exiled family gathered to gaze with
wonder at so much gold.[19]

It was a busy and crowded time. All day long the King
interviewed delegations and supplicants, and all night, since
there was no other period available, wrote letters. To one
delegation only he returned a short answer—a bevy of
ministers who begged a pledge that he would forbid surplices
and the Book of Common Prayer in his Chapel Royal—replying that in giving liberty to others, he did not intend to
surrender his own.[20]

The only business that now remained was to bring the
King to England. On May 15th the fleet under Admiral
Montagu sighted the Dutch coast, all hands making ready
painting royal coats of arms where formerly the Commonwealth Harp had been, getting out silk flags and cutting up
yellow cloth to initial C.R. upon them. Next morning Pepys,
made Secretary to the Admiral by the Muse of History for
the purpose of recording these events, visited the Hague
and was much impressed by the neat, clean town with its
maypole at every door and the burghers with their muskets
as bright as silver. Indeed, after the drabness of Commonwealth London, he was unable to find words to express a full
sense of its gallantry and, in the emotion of that morning,
lost his new Copenhagen knife. In the afternoon, on the
Naseby, the Admiral, resplendent in gold and silver, sent
for him, and the two had a most significant talk about
religion, in which Montagu declared himself wholly sceptical,
an enemy to enthusiasm and intolerance and a believer in
uniformity of worship and prayer. When Pepys, being unable to stand, retired that night to his bunk, a new age had
dawned for England.

On the 17th, a day of reception, the King wrote to Monk, fixing the place of his landing.

" I need say little to you since I have informed Dr. Clarges of my purpose, and he will tell you with what difficulty I get one-quarter of an hour to myself. I have thought the best I can of the place where I should disembark . . . and have resolved, God willing, to land at Dover. . . . But you can hardly imagine the impatience I have to see you, for, till then, I shall take no resolution of moment. I pray bring Mrs. Monk with you, and believe me to be very heartily your affectionate friend."

The touch about Mrs. Monk was typical, and showed a proper appreciation of a real power in the land.[21]

On the night of May 22nd fifty thousand people waited for dawn on the sand-dunes. At 2 a.m. the drums beat, and the crowds stirred with excitement. Then the King, with his brothers, his sister and his aunt, the Queen of Bohemia, escorted by a great cortège came down to the waterside, where the Admiral awaited them. It was a lovely day, and Pepys had put on his linen stockings and white canons. As the royalties came aboard the crowded flagship, all the guns in the Fleet broke into thunder.

At eleven o'clock the royal party dined together, " which," thought Pepys, " was a blessed sight to see." Afterwards the *Naseby* was rechristened the *Royal Charles*, and the memory of many old sorrows and glories buried. The time came for the shore boats to leave, and the witty Queen of Bohemia, with shining eyes—" The Tempest " had been written for her wedding day fifty years before—took her leave of the King, while Mary clung to him weeping. Then the anchor was weighed.

All the afternoon the King walked up and down the deck, examining everything on the ship. Later he told to the wondering courtiers the tale of his escape from Worcester, and Pepys, clinging to the fringe of the listening crowd, wept to hear it. In the evening he supped alone in his cabin, glad

to be away from the crowd and the stir for a little. Afterwards he stood on the moonlit poop, looking back at the
vanishing coast-line. Such days are memorable and deeply
stamped on the mind.[22]

At dawn on the 25th, the Fleet anchored off Dover, close
inshore. Monk, summoned by horse, was hurrying from
Canterbury, and a vast concourse was waiting in the little
sea town. From the decks the exiles watched the scene.
The King, active as ever, called his brothers to try the sailor's
victuals, and the three breakfasted like true Englishmen off
peas, boiled beef and pork.

About three o'clock Charles was rowed ashore in the
Admiral's barge. Pepys followed in a smaller boat with the
footman and "a dog the King loved." The beach was
dense with spectators, and, as the barge ran across the shingle,
the guns on all the forts and ships burst into flame. Other
guns down the coast took up the echo, till four hours later
the Tower artillery proclaimed to the listening citizens that
the King had come into his own. As he stepped ashore, he
knelt down and thanked God for this strange and wonderful
deliverance. Then he rose and, drawing Monk to him, kissed
him and called him father. As every eye in the multitude
fixed its gaze on that little group by the water's edge, the
soldier placed his sword in his master's hand and cried *God
save the King*. All took up the mighty sound, but in the
midst of it the young Duke of Gloucester was heard crying
God save General Monk.

The Mayor of Dover approached and presented his
insignia of office (which was returned) and a fine Bible which
the King declared he loved above all things in the world.
Then while the people shouted continuously, Charles, under
a canopy of state, passed through them to his coach. So,
with all Kent running and riding after him, he drove towards
Canterbury.[23]

Two miles out, the King left the coach and mounted his horse to sniff the air. It was fifteen years since he had seen England in May. Then he rode across Barham Downs to Canterbury. The bells of the Cathedral were ringing as he passed through the narrow streets. That night, before he slept, he scribbled a line to Minette: " My head is so dreadfully stunned with the acclamations of the people, and the vast amount of business that I know not whether I am writing sense or nonsense."[24]

At Canterbury he spent the week-end; saw a multitude of suitors, invested Monk, Montagu and two great English Cavaliers, Southampton and Hertford, with the Garter, and attended Anglican service in the Cathedral. On Monday, through roads lined all the way, he went on towards Rochester.

On Tuesday, May 29th, the sun rose early to welcome the King's thirtieth birthday. Many thousands of his subjects rose earlier. On Blackheath, before the serried regiments of the fallen Army, with a rural triumph of morris dancers, with tabor and pipe, the Lord Mayor and a hundred and twenty thousand citizens were waiting. All the way to the capital the concourse grew. Then, amid an indescribable colour and din, " with a triumph of above twenty thousand horse and foot, brandishing their swords and shouting with inexpressible joy; the ways strewed with flowers, the bells ringing, the streets hung with tapestry, fountains running with wine," the long procession passed over London Bridge into the crowded streets. A hundred thousand heads looked down as Colonel Browne's regiment, in silver doublets and black scarves, trotted by, but the roar drowned even the bells when the King rode into view. Here he was at last, " the Black Boy," whom so many had secretly toasted and mentioned in bated breath and dreamt of. Tall, slim, and dark, he rode bare-headed between that dazzling crowd, bowing now to left, now to right, to the

F

ladies in the balconies and windows.   The smiling eyes looked
with approval at the companies of " proper maids all alike in
white garments," and the long hands drew in his fine horse
and took the Bible which the London ministers proffered him.
And Evelyn, remembering the long years of oppression, " stood
in the Strand and beheld it and blessed God . . . for it was
the Lord's doing, and such a restoration was never mentioned
in any history, ancient or modern, since the return of the
Jews from the Babylonish captivity."

Towards evening the King came to his Palace of Whitehall.   The Houses of Parliament with their Speakers were
awaiting him.   After a brief rest he received the Address of
the Lords,* and made his answer—" disordered by my journey
and with the noise still sounding in my ears (which I confess
was pleasing to me because it expressed the affections of my
people ")—promising them that he would endeavour by all
means to restore the nation to its freedom and happiness, and
ever defend its faith and laws.   Then he went up to the
Banqueting Hall to hear the long oration of the Speaker of
his faithful Commons.   " I am so weary," he answered, " that
I am scarce able to speak, but I desire you may know . . .
that whatsoever may concern the good of this people I shall
be as ready to grant as you shall be to ask."

It had been the King's intention to attend a service of
thanksgiving at the Abbey that evening, but the strain of the
long day had proved too much for even his strength.†   Instead
he offered his oblation in the Presence Chamber of the

---

* " . . . Dread Sovereign! I offer no flattering titles, but speak the words
of truth. You are the desire of three kingdoms, the strength and the stay
of the tribes of the people, for the moderating of extremities, the reconciling of
differences, the satisfying of all interests, and for restoring the collapsed
honour of these nations." (*Parl. Hist.*, IV, 56.)

† There is a story that Charles spent the first night of his return in the arms
of Barbara Palmer. It rests on the testimony of a footnote of Lord Dartmouth's,
made in *Burnet's History* half a century later, and on the statement of the historian
Oldmixon, who, writing in the reign of George I, is no more a first-hand authority
on the Restoration than I should be on the Crimean War.

Palace. Yet, at that supreme moment, there was a glint of irony behind the tired, smiling eyes; he was foolish, he remarked, not to have come home before, since every man in England was protesting that he had always longed for his return. Down in Buckinghamshire, the rector of Maid's Moreton wrote with joy in the church register: " This day, by the wonderful goodness of God, his Sacred Majesty King Charles II was peacefully restored to his martyred father's throne, the powerful armies of his enemies being amazed spectators and in some sort unwilling assistants to his return. . . . And from this day ancient orders began to be observed. *Laus Deo!* "[25]

INTERLUDE

ENGLAND OF THE RESTORATION

INTERLUDE

ENGLAND OF THE RESTORATION

"For all that I have yet seen, give me old England."
—EDWARD HYDE.

IT was a rough England to which the King returned, nor had twenty years of suspicion and despotism done anything to soften it. Fighting was the darling pastime of its boisterous people. In Moorfields on holidays the butchers out of hereditary hatred fell upon the weavers, till they were glad to pull off their aprons and hide them in their breeches; or sometimes it would be the weavers who won, wounding and bruising all their rivals and calling out round the town: *A hundred pounds for a butcher!* Since there were no police, the warlike tastes of the people were quite untrammelled. The very Inns of Court were riotous, and when the Lord Mayor elected to go to dinner in the Temple with his sword borne before him, the students pulled it down and besieged him all day in a councillor's room. Even in Oxford, a learned antiquary belaboured one of his fellow dons whenever he met him, giving him many a bloody nose and black eye.[1]

Among the gentry of a people so turbulent, duels were almost incessant. Two strangers at night, jostling for the wall about the New Exchange, whipped out their swords and killed each other on the spot. Honest John Reresby, lord of many hundred acres, related with pride how, dining at a neigh-

bour's house, he quarrelled with a young gentleman engaged
to his host's daughter and all but spoilt the match: " we
should have fought the next day, but considering better of it
he submitted—though it was he who received the affront, for
I threw a glass of wine in his face." The King was always
trying in vain to moderate this passion in his people.[2]

This pugnacity the English carried into the concerns of
State, which after twenty years of wont, they regarded as
peculiarly their own. In this they astonished foreigners; a
Frenchman reported that the very boatmen wanted the milords
to talk to them about State affairs while they rowed them to
Parliament. With those who disagreed with their views, they
had a short and ready way. When the French ambassador
omitted to light a bonfire at his door to celebrate an English
victory over the Dutch, the mob smashed his windows and
all but grilled him on his own furniture. Their pet political
aversion was Popery, and any demagogue, who was unscrupulous enough to play on their feelings in this particular,
could loose a murderous wild beast. Once a year the London
mob processed through the city with effigies of Pope,
Cardinals and Devils, which they stuffed with live cats to
make them squall realistically and burnt amidst shouts of
delight at Smithfield.[3]

Their sports matched their politics. Pepys has left us a
picture of one of their cockfights:

" After dinner . . . directed by sight of bills upon the walls,
I did go to Shoe Lane to see a cock-fighting at a new pit there . . .
but, Lord, to see the strange variety of people, from Parliament-
men to the poorest prentices, bakers, butchers, brewers, draymen
and what not; and all these fellows one with another in swearing,
cursing and betting. I soon had enough of it, and yet I would not
but have seen it once, it being strange to observe the nature of
these poor creatures, how they will fight till they drop down dead
upon the table, and strike after they are ready to give up the ghost,
not offering to run away when they are weary or wounded past

doing further, whereas a dunghill brood . . . will, after a sharp stroke that pricks him, run off the stage, and then they wring his neck without more ado, whereas the other they preserve, though both eyes be out, for breed only of a true cock of the game."

The more squeamish Evelyn, at the Bear Garden, saw a bull toss a dog into a lady's lap many feet above the arena; saw also two dogs killed and the show end, amid applause, with an ape on horseback.[4]

Living thus, they drank deep. Roger North, entertaining the Mayor and Aldermen of Banbury at his brother's house, Wroxton, so plied them—sitting, standing and walking— that they spent the night in ditches homeward bound, while he himself retired "like a wounded deer to a shady, moist place," and there lay down and "evaporated four or five hours." The Puritan Monk, who could speak of God's "providences" and "melting bowels" with the best of them, was a toper worthy of the people he saved. In May, 1663, after a notable dinner at the Earl of Oxford's, he took some of his fellow-guests home, where each resolved to see his companion aground. But the General struck a master stroke and "presented to each a goblet of the deepest. Some swallowed the contents and some not, but all peaceably remained where they were till the following morning." Only Monk went to Parliament as usual, his mind nothing impaired. When the great Van Tromp, as deadly with a bottle as a cannon ball, visited England, he met his match—and it was our senior University that had the honour. For Dr. Speed, with five or six more as able as himself at wine or brandy, got him to the Crown Tavern, and there so filled him with both that at twelve at night he was carried unconscious to his bed.[5]

A people used so to live could scarcely fail to possess a marked character of its own. Their very phrases suggest individuality; they were coarse, but vulgarity, the bane of modern civilization, was almost unknown. Squire Oldfield, in Cheshire, stayed at home on a January day because " it was slabbie weather "; Pepys was " vexed to the guts " by a quarrel with his long-suffering wife; and John Verney asked that his prospective bride might be paraded up and down Drapers' Garden for an hour or two to assure himself that there was " nothing disgustful " about her. At Claydon, an elderly rustic, at an Easter Communion, " drank up all the wine in the silver chalice and swore he would have his penny-worth out of it, being he paid for it." Mrs. Dobson wrote to her hectoring lawyer husband that " 'twas not the fashion in Cheshire for wives to be beaten or throttled into kind-nesses," and when the amorous Pepys sidled up his pew in church to take a pretty, modest maid by the hand and body, the girl, to his dismay, took pins out of her pocket and made as to prick him should he touch her again.

For a fine delineation of seventeenth-century character, take Roger North's portrait of Lord Chief Justice Saunders. Bred a parish foundling, his observance and diligence had made him an exquisite entering clerk; thence by the same course of self-improvement he became a special pleader, was called to the Bar and won a leading practice at the King's Bench. With all this he continued to live with a poor tailor's family in Butchers' Row, never went into society, played jigs on his landlady's harpsichord, and was seldom without a pot of ale or brandy by his nose. Since he never took exercise, his body became so fat and beastly that his neighbours at the Bar could scarcely bear it; " those whose ill-fortune it was to stand near him were confessors, and in summertime almost martyrs. As for his parts, none had them more lively than he. Wit and repartee in an affected rusticity were natural to him. He was ever ready and never at a loss. . . . With all this, he had a goodness of nature and disposition in so great a degree that he may be deservedly styled a philanthrope. He was a very

Silenus to the boys, to make them merry whenever they had a mind to it.   He had nothing rigid or austere in him. If any near him at the Bar grumbled at his stench, he ever converted the complaint into content and laughing with the abundance of his wit.   As to his ordinary dealing, he was as honest as the driven snow was white; and why not, having no regard for money and no desire to be rich?   And, for good nature and condescension there was not his fellow.   I have seen him for hours and half-hours together, before the Court sat, stand at the Bar with an audience of students over against him putting of cases, and debating so as suited their capacities and encouraged their industry.   And so in the Temple he seldom moved without a parcel of youths hanging about him, and he merry and jesting with them."[6]

Cleanliness the English did not affect.   In all Pepys's nine years of recording his minutest movements, there is only one mention of his having had a bath—and that (it was at Bath) curiously shocked his sense of hygiene, for, said he, " methinks it cannot be clean to go so many bodies in the same water." On January 23rd, 1669, this rising official entertained no less than three lords at one meal, the best of its kind and the fullest of honour and content that ever he had.   After his guests had left, he called his wife to cut his hair, " and when she comes to all, she finds that I am lousy, having found in my head and body about twenty lice, little and great . . . being more than I have had, I believe, these twenty years.   And so with much content to bed."   As for the sanitation of the day, it was oriental in its simple grandeur.   There was a standing feud between Pepys and his neighbours because their houses of office perpetually overflowed into each other's cellars.*[7]

Of the soil that nursed this rough, humorous people,

* So Mrs. Pepys, taken ill at the theatre, unconcernedly went out into Lincoln's Inn Walks and " there in a corner did her business." (*Pepys*, 5 Sept., '67.)

London was the core. Till the fire of 1666 it was still the huddled, wooden city of the Plantagenets and Tudors. For six miles it crowded along the northern bank of the river, which was its glory. There was no quay, but the houses came down to the water-side. And below them and the narrow steps that divided them, lay the ships of all the world. This winding blue canal was the Londoner's highway and the ceaseless background of his life. It was ruled by a corporation of jolly, swearing, Wapping watermen, who brooked no competition and whose ribaldry was proverbial; though what it was they shouted to the western bargemen about the women of Woolwich which made them so mad, we shall never know, and perhaps it is as well. For fear of them—though at any hour of the day coaches, drays and cattle were mingled in profane confusion on London's single bridge—no other bridge could be built, and the King, who called them his nursery of seamen, supported them. Their rivals were the hackney coachmen, who congregated for their fares beneath the Maypole in the Strand and were ever ready with whip and fist to vindicate their exorbitant charges. Whenever political feeling ran high these two trades could be relied upon to come out on opposite sides and pay off old scores.[8]

In some respects that London has its counterpart to-day. It had, for instance, its traffic problem, and on two successive days angry Mr. Pepys in his fine new coach was held up for half an hour by the block in Exchange Street. And it was certainly noisy, for the wheels never ceased to rumble on cobbled stone, or the apprentices and hawkers to bawl their wares, in an age when the art of advertising was more vocal than visual.[9]

But where the London of 1660 differed from ours was in its dirt and its beauty. Of the former we have already spoken; and the latter pervaded every corner. Partly it was because the green fields were never far away; the trees invaded the streets and squares; there were gardens lurking behind the houses, and nightingales in Lincoln's Inn. It was still an agricultural town, and the rich earthy smell of the fruits and beasts of the home counties lay about it. So, on a July day in 1671, a cow went merrily mad in King's Street, tossed half a dozen people, and, trotting into Palace Yard, caused a panic in Westminster Hall, where frightened judges and lawyers supposed the Fifth Monarchy men to be up in arms; Serjeant Scroggs, who had long been crippled by gout, flung aside gown and coif, and miraculously vaulted over the bar. This dreadful beast was driven back up Whitehall, hocked and escorted by two anxious butchers; the sentinel at the Cockpit burst out laughing, asking how anyone could be afraid of a poor lame cow, whereupon he and it vanish hastily from history through an archway.[10]

Since the fields were so near, the recreations of the citizens were still rural. On May Day the milk-maids, with garlands upon their pails, danced down the Strand with a fiddler playing before, and Nell Gwynn, in smock-sleeves and bodice, stood at the door of her lodgings and watched them go by. One might sit in one's coach and drink ale at a tavern door, or take a morning mess of cream and sillabub at " The World's End " in Knightsbridge, or visit the Mulberry Garden—a pretty place by moonlight, and a vast contrast, with its " rascally, whoring, roguing sort of people," to the trim Victorian palace which, in due season, rose in its place. Farther afield lay Kensington's grotto, the cherries of Rother-hithe, and the cakes of Islington; the Jamaica House at Bermondsey—where Pepys's maids ran races on the bowling-green; or, best of all, wooded Vauxhall, with its spring blossoms, where one could listen to the nightingale and other birds, and " here fiddles, and there a harp, and here a Jew's trump, and here laughing, and there fine people walking."

And as the day began before dawn, and most folk left their business at midday, there was plenty of time in the long summer afternoons for such recreations.[11]

If the London of Charles II seems rural to us, it was metropolitan enough to our forefathers. Such a one would visit it in an Easter term to sample its towny joys—to the destruction of tarts and cheese-cakes—to see a new play, buy a new gown, take a turn in the park. There were naked lunatics to gape at for treats at Bedlam, and lions in the Tower. One might sup at the Hercules Pillars in Fleet Street or at the sign of Old Simon the King—or, if one chose to be very fashionable, at the new French house in Covent Garden, Chatelin's, with its fricassee, ragouts and salads, its music and gay company, and its unforgettable bills. And everywhere were sociable little taverns in blind corners, " The Trumpet," " The Sugar Loaf " or " The Green Lettuce "; " The Old House " at Lambeth Marsh where Pepys on his unlawful occasions wheedled the wives of his naval subordinates; the little bawdy-house behind the House of Lords where he went to drink wormwood; and the fair, frail ladies whom Mother Temple and Madam Bennet in Drury Lane or Moorfields vended to all and sundry.[12]

This was London, but England was the country. The French ambassador, travelling westwards, was surprised to see how empty it was, passing, in a distance of thirty leagues of fine land, but very few villages and scarcely a soul on the road. Yet how lovely this open, lonely land was, and how rich its people in everything that made life worth living! " I wish I were with you a little in the sweet country," wrote town-tied Mrs. Shakerley to her Cheshire neighbours. In Devon the folk clotted their cream with sugar to crown their apple-pies, and, in the fields beside the Ouse in Huntingdonshire, the milk-maids bore home their pails with music going before them. In that county, so rich was it in corn, it was the custom, whenever a King of England came, to meet him with a hundred ploughs.[13]

Here in the country quiet, the old ways of life persisted. Pepys, walking on Epsom Downs, far from any house or sight of people, found an old shepherd reading the Bible to his little boy. Parson Moore of Horsted Keynes did his shop-keeping by barter, receiving a box of pills and sermons in return for a ribspare and hog's pudding, and in remote parts of Lancashire boon services were still unsuperseded by rents. The colliers of the Tyne rowed merrily by verdant flats and woods, with a trumpeter and bagpipes making music in the stern, and west of the Pennines the country people went bare-footed, leaping as if they had hoofs. Rich and poor alike talked and spelt in the dialect of their own county, Cheshire Mrs. Dobson writing to tell her husband:

" I leve heare tow and twentey milke coues and a boll, three big hefers and a boleke and seven which are yer old bes; and one boll calfe which runs upon one of the coues and seven other calves which ar this yeare rered, and on fat tegg."

It was a world of country squires and parsons, of yeomen and cottagers and ragged, cheerful squatters, making their own wares and their own pleasures after the manner of their ancestors. For " that great hive, the city," its vices and graces, country folk had nothing but pity. To cousins there imprisoned they sent vast cheeses and pies of game; " there was two very fat geese, eight wild ducks, and eight wood-cocks, and in the box a pair of stockings " in one such that Lady Shakerley sent her sons in London. " When I came home," wrote Robert Paston, " which is the sweetest place in the world, I found my children and Mrs. Cooper pretty well, and she and the gentleman are taking their pleasure to see an otter hunted in the pond." It was so all over England.[14]

In a people so bred, beauty moved and had its being.

Poetry strayed even into their official memoranda: a diplomat in a dispatch described how the Lisbon mob chased its victims to the seashore, where " it pleased him who bridles the sea with a rope of sand to put bounds to the fury of the people." Colour and the pomp of life, moving in gilded majesty, came back with the King; these things, in which all shared, were the visible signs of an inward and spiritual grace. Pepys clothed his boy in green lined with red, and went abroad himself in a summer suit of coloured camelot, with a flowered tabby vest, very rich, and gold lace sleeves. And on May Day, 1669, when he drove in Hyde Park in his new coach, the horses' tails were tied with red ribbon, the standards gilt with varnish, and all the reins were green. No wonder the people looked mightily upon him.[15]

Of this beauty, music was queen. The Cambridge trumpeters came before dawn to the Bear Inn to give the travellers a levet; Pepys, going down the river, shared a boat with a stranger who, proving a man of music, sang catches with him all the way; on a moonlight night he, with his wife and maids, sang in the garden, with mighty pleasure to themselves and neighbours, " by their casements opening." Every substantial family in town and country made its own music as it made its own jam; the men and the boys on viol, harpsichord and double bass, the girls with lute, spinet and guitar. In their rough, amateur, but very competent way, they excelled in the old English music—" like sitting," as Roger North remembered it, " in a pleasant cool air in a temperate summer evening, when one may think or look or not, and still be pleased."[16]

Across this land and its people, darkened by a generation of war and anarchy, broke the rays of a new dawn. It had been long due. Ten years before the King returned, a little group of men, sickened by fanatic extravagances, had begun to meet in Wadham College to discover something of the real world they lived in.   Discussion of theology and State affairs was forbidden; for these they substituted the circulation of the blood, the valves in the *venæ lactae*, the Copernican hypothesis, the improvement of telescopes, the possibility or impossibility of vacuities.   Their purpose, wrote one of their number, " was . . . the satisfaction of breathing a freer air and conversing in quiet, without being engaged in the passions and madness of that dismal age. . . . By this means there was a race of young men provided against the next age, whose minds, receiving from them their first impressions of sober and generous knowledge, were invincibly armed against all the enchantments of enthusiasm. . . . Nor indeed could it be otherwise, for such spiritual frenzies, which did then bear rule, can never stand long before a clear and deep skill in nature."   It was an appeal from lunacy to truth.[17]

With the return of the King, who had little use himself for abstract religious formulas, and preferred to test everything by his own keen common sense, the new generation came into its own.   Shortly after the Restoration, the Royal Society was founded in Christopher Wren's room in Gresham College, and the King became its first patron.   When its members placed a spider in the midst of a circle of unicorn's horn, and the insect, disregarding the hallowed beliefs of centuries, " walked out "—as the Society's minutes briefly record—something momentous had happened.   At their weekly meetings, the conversation was philosophical and cheerful, and the experiments ranged all nature.   They employed an itinerant, who each year made a report of his discoveries in England, bringing not tales of new Messiahs or godly judgments on the wicked, but dried fowls and fish, plants and minerals.   When Prince Rupert was about to lead a fleet against the Dutch on the Guinea coast, the virtuosos requested him to employ his leisure in sounding the depths without a line and fetching up water from the bottom of the sea.   In their boundless curiosity they were laying the foundations of the modern world. Even in death's dark vale, when the plague was at its height, Evelyn, calling at Durdans, discovered Dr. Wilkins, Sir William Petty and Mr. Hooke contriving chariots, new rigging for ships, a wheel to run races in, and other mechanical inventions.[18]

Pneumatic engines, æolipiles for weighing air, calculating machines, quench-fires, even a "new fashion gun to shoot off often, one after another, without trouble or danger, very pretty," all came alike to this remarkable generation. In our own age of marvels but dimly understood, we are standing, as Newton said of himself, on the shoulders of giants. And with all this achievement, these men were not specialists, but versatile beyond our imagination. Wren, at twenty-four, was a Professor of Astronomy and the wonder of Europe for mechanical invention, and was over thirty before he ever thought of architecture. The learned Lord Keeper Guilford, besides attaining to an exquisite skill in music, devoted much time to the Torricellian experiments; his younger brother, Roger North, barrister, musician, author, architect and yachtsman, mastered the theory of light; "the very remembrance of these things," he wrote in after years, "is delight, and while I write methinks I play. All other employments that filled my time go on account of work and business: these were all pleasure."[19]

Under such a lead, a boundless curiosity filled every mind. Captain Baker went out to find the north-west passage, and came back with prodigious tales of ice, blue as sapphire, and as transparent. Pepys delighted to hear a traveller tell of the high hills in Asia, "how clear the heaven is above them, how thick like a mist the way is through the clouds that wets like a sponge one's clothes, the ground above all dry and parched, nothing in the world growing, the stars at night most delicate, bright and a fine clear blue sky." Men loved to think they lived on such an earth. Where science and beauty blended to reveal the wonderful works of God, the mists of religious mystification parted for a moment in a clap of laughter. When four months after the Restoration, godly Mr. Rowe preached his farewell sermon at the Abbey, and the Reader desired the Almighty to imprint his words on the thumbs of men's hands and the great toes of their right feet, the congregation could not restrain its merriment.[20]

G*

PART II

THE KING OF ENGLAND

AN EARLY 17TH CENTURY VIEW OF WHITEHALL.

"It lay for nearly half a mile beside the river, a warren of galleries, apartments and gardens, the home not only of the King,

CHAPTER I

THE FIRST FINE CARELESS RAPTURE

" Though for a time we see Whitehall
  With cobwebs hanging on the wall,
  Instead of silk and silver brave
  Which formerly it used to have,
  With rich perfumes in every room,
    Delightful to that princely train,
  Which again you shall see when the time it shall be
  When the King enjoys his own again."
                                  —MARTIN PARKER, 1643.

FOR a generation the old Palace of Whitehall had been stripped
of its glories. It lay for nearly half a mile beside the river,
a warren of galleries, apartments and gardens, the home not
only of the King but of the Ministers of State, servants high
and low, courtiers, chaplains, ladies and all the gilded army
which encompassed the English throne. One entered it
either from the river or the lane—spanned by the two gate-
ways which linked Charing Cross with Westminster. Its
buildings were of all sizes and ages, from the classic
Banqueting Hall to the little octagonal Cockpit.[1]

The centre of this courtly city was the long Stone Gallery,
the very hub of the Stuart Government of Britain. On its
walls hung the pictures which Charles I had collected and
his enemies dispersed, and which his son partly reassembled.
Here they made a kind of National Picture Gallery, for the
place was open to all comers: Pepys spent a happy and
instructive hour looking at them with the painter Hales on

103

Good Friday, 1666. Yet most of the crowd that walked continuously up and down the Galleries did not come there for the pictures; places, preferment, sight-seeing, above all news, was the ceaseless business of that place of rumours. "It runs through the Galleries," was the prefix which sped the national gossip.[2]

Well it might, for those who waited here saw the outward stir of all that was moving the wheels of State. The velvet curtains across the doors would part and the King himself pass through the crowd, followed by a group of Ministers and suitors from Bedchamber or Council Room, still contending for that royal ear, whose retention was at once the hardest and most precious achievement of a careerist's life. Here in the Gallery, for a moment, opportunity flitted by.*[3]

From the Stone Gallery, guarded doors opened into the royal apartments. In the Withdrawing Room, the waiting lords warmed hands before the fire in winter; and here the King would sup, talking wittily and without restraint to those about him. Beyond was the holy of holies, the Bedchamber. In this great room, with its windows looking on to the tides and shipping of the river, the most secret affairs of State were transacted at all hours of the day between the bed and the wall. Yet even here, though the entrée of those who might enter was strictly limited by Court etiquette, there was no privacy for a badgered monarch.[4]

Up a tiny flight of steps was the King's Closet. Of this inner shrine he kept a private key, of which only his trusted servant, Chiffinch, had a duplicate. Here dwelt his treasures, the "brave pictures" of Raphael, Titian and Holbein which so enchanted Pepys, the jewels and crystal vases, the rare

---

* So Chaplain Teonge, brought by his Captain, waited in the Gallery until the King appeared; then dropped on to his knee, while his sovereign paused to say, "God bless you, God bless you"—a genial and inexpensive greeting to which he was much addicted—and, before he could be stopped, walked away at "his usual large pace." (*Teonge Diary*, 203.)

cabinets, the book of maps four yards wide, and the models of ships. Here also ticked and chimed in exquisite disunion an army of enamelled clocks and watches which it was the delight of this mechanical monarch to collect. He loved to display these rareties to appreciative connoisseurs; one day in the autumn of 1660 he showed them all to Evelyn with his own hands.[5]

Like his father, this King had a taste for the arts. He made his Court a home for artists : Streater, of " landskip " fame, whom he created his Serjeant Painter and loved; Cooper, " the rare limner "; Danckerts from the Hague to paint his ships and palaces; Verelst, " king of flowers," by whose leafy dewdrops Pepys was so impressed, and the fashionable Lely. He liked to look on pleasant things, and so his library was filled with old illuminated breviaries and finely bound volumes that a busy man might finger and turn over, not caring to read too deeply.[6]

It was not here that the world saw him, nor even in the Ante-Room where the Foreign Ministers daily awaited his return from the park, but in perfumed Banqueting Hall and Chapel. He dined in state, a little after midday, before a background of tapestry, while the massed lords of the household served him on bended knee, and all England came and went in the galleries above to share the pageantry. Yet to one who had learned to live otherwise and loved to talk at ease to companions as he ate, it was a little lonely to sit there at the great table in solitude; sometimes afterwards he was seen to slip softly away to his Bedchamber without allowing anyone the leisure to speak with him.[7]

Every Sunday morning, a stream of citizens flowed westwards by boat or coach to see the King pray. It was a fine sight for a people accustomed to the drab worship of Puritanism. Pepys, who was a regular spectator during the months following the Restoration, noted the rapidity with which the old rites were restored at the Chapel Royal. The very first Sunday the King was in London, Bishop Wren—newly released from a twenty years' sojourn in the Tower—was preaching before him in lawn sleeves; and a fortnight later the organs played after the silence of a generation. Before long there were crimson cushions to kneel on and cloth of gold on the communion table. Then there were the joys of watching the King come down to take the sacrament upon his bended knees—" a sight very well worth seeing "—the new music he introduced, and the long sermons to which it was his constant privilege to listen. These, in that age, were serious matters, and were of every variety: Dr. Creighton preached on the promising text, " Roll yourself in dust "— " very learned," comments Pepys, " but his application most comical "; a Greek professor, " though a great scholar, made a most dead flat sermon . . . and very long beyond his hour which made it worse," and an Oxford canon, throughout his, insisted on the sin of adultery. Even a king might count on hearing home-truths on Sundays. It was not surprising that Charles once wrote to his sister: " We have the same disease of sermons that you complain of, but I hope you have the same convenience that the rest of the family has of sleeping out most of the time, which is a great ease to those who are bound to hear them." " My lord, my lord," cried a preacher to the sleeping Lauderdale, " you snore so loud you will wake the King! "[8]

Within the Palace walls were the Privy Gardens where Charles would set his watch of a morning by the sun-dial, the bowling green where he walked in windy weather, the little Physic Garden, where he culled herbs for his laboratory. The latter, which he had made beneath his Closet, was a constant delight to him. Here his chemist, Le Febvre, presided over the chemical glasses which so puzzled Pepys, and his successor, Williams, made the famous King's Drops, which not only cured the sick but, surreptitiously dropped by the invaluable Chiffinch into the wine of guests, made cunning tongues babble secrets.   The King loved to work here, making researches into the heart of things more exact and curious than the nebulous nature of political life afforded, dissecting, composing cordials or endeavouring to fix mercury.[9]

Beyond the Cockpit lay the park of St. James.   It had fallen into neglect during the interregnum, but by September, 1660, disbanded soldiers were employed making a canal through it, to the delight of the Londoners who loved to watch the engines drawing up water.   A year later all the world came to see the King's brave improvements and the birds with which he was stocking his lake.   These ranged from the little ducks he used to feed to that "melancholy water-fowl, between a stork and a swan," brought by a Russian ambassador from the wastes of Astrakhan.*   The Whitehall typists, who to-day take the sun beside the lake, still view their progeny.[10]

The King, who loved all animals, made his park a home for them.   Evelyn thought it a strange and wonderful thing to see the wildfowl breeding so near a great city.   Beyond the lake were deer of all kinds: antelopes, an elk, guinea goats and Arabian sheep.   And everywhere Charles planted flowers and walks of trees, making a green paradise for old age and coming generations.[11]

In this park, the resort of all the world, he was wont to take that "bewitching kind of pleasure called sauntering and talking without any constraint."   "He loved," says Aurelian Cook, "a smart walk, a mouthful of fresh air and a little ingenious raillery."   Here he might be seen of a morning before lunch, as Pepys saw him one autumn morning in

---

* They included a Balearian crane, with a jointed wooden leg made by an old soldier: this unfortunately has not been transmitted to posterity. (*Evelyn*, 9 Feb., '65.)

1667, with a great crowd of his idle people about him, and here he would listen to all comers. Yet, it should be added, he walked " by his watch, and, when he pulled it out, skilful men would make haste with what they had to say to him."[12]

He loved talking and, since " his apprehension was quick and his memory good," conversed during his walks incessantly and on every subject. Evelyn records four successive conversations with him in 1661 : at the first he talked of astronomy, at the second of smoke abatement, architecture and gardening, at the third of his collection of curiosities and at the fourth of bees. Best of all he liked to tell stories, of which he had an endless repertoire. It is needless to say that, though nearly always witty, they were not always refined.[13]

In his park the King took the exercise with which he preserved his superb health and good humour. On its edge was the old tennis court of Henry VIII where, eschewing the long, crowded levée of Sundays and more formal occasions, he would be at play before six, and, farther afield, the Pall Mall court he built for that swift pastime. Waller has left a picture of his game :

> " No sooner has he touched the flying ball
> But 'tis already more than half the Mall,
> And such a fury from his arm has got
> As from a smoking culverin 'twere shot."[14]

One thing park and palace offered in abundance—beauty. One must picture it in crimson and gold. The trumpeters and kettle-drummers marched in scarlet cloaks with facings of silver lace, and from their trumpets hung taffety ribbons and banners of gold. Fringed hangings of crimson brocade, glorious gilt mirrors from France, a world of shining and gleaming fabric, formed the background of the public show which Whitehall offered to all comers. And everywhere was music—the King's fiddlers, glorious to behold, sweet to hear in concert-room or boarded gallery, with their airs of Byrd and Lawes and the young Purcell; and in the private apartments of the Palace, when the candles were lit and Charles supped with Castlemaine, little groups of friends and lovers touched the strings of chamber music and raised their voices in harmony.

Music the King could never be long without; among the imports from Flanders at the Restoration was the royal guitar. His taste was for violins and light instrumental music of the French school. He gathered round him a remnant of the great English musicians, who had loved his father and shared his misfortunes, and a host of foreign masters collected in the days of exile.[15]

In this, for good or bad, the King was educating his people. He had brought back from France and Flanders the germs of a new culture, and England, after a long winter, was ripe for change. It came from Paris, where young Louis —" the sun King "—was inaugurating that wonderful era in every form of art which bears his name. Into England flowed after 1660 an ever-increasing stream of French ideas, and modes of life. Fine Gallic gentlemen surprised simple Englishmen with their quaint airs and graces;* French modistes appeared with fans and petticoats and " the fashones " to tempt the purse and adorn the persons of our English ladies. Everything new came from Paris, the Mecca of the civilized world, from sedan chairs, and dainty silver brushes for cleaning the teeth, to Chatelin's famous fricassees and ragouts. In 1666 Charles wrote in despair to his sister in France to beg for some gold sealing-wax, for there was none to be had in London, and three years later the English ambassador at Paris reported that no less than four thousand gilt mirrors had been sent into England in one summer.[16]

* Pepys observed with wonder the new way of drinking healths, after the French manner : " Bow to him that drank to you, and then apply yourself to him whose lady's health is drunk, and then to the person that you drink to." (*Pepys*, 19 June, '63.)

To many plain Englishmen, this love of things French was an unpleasing feature of Charles's Court. Even Evelyn complained that France had now the ascendant and we were become quite another nation, and much of the later bitterness against the Stuarts is attributable to this cause. For the common folk loathed the French and all their elegancies; a foreigner recorded how a London mob, mistaking an Italian for a Frenchman, proceeded as a matter of course to throw him into the river. Yet, for all this, Charles did achieve a change in English taste far greater than any transient turn of fashion. For it affected everything: our architecture, our dress, food and manners, our books, our whole attitude of life. Through France, England drew at this moment a deep draught from those eternal waters which have their spring in ancient Greece and Rome, and from which she has drunk at every great era of development in her existence. The calm, the balance and beauty of the eighteenth century is Charles's legacy to his people.[17]

In this respect the King was a creator. In a quarter of a century he went far to transform his rough realm into a gentler and more urbane mould. His conception of a gentleman was the model by which the chivalry of England dressed itself for many succeeding generations; it was, in a nutshell, "to be easy himself and to make everybody else so." It was a conception not unneeded, for in neither of these respects did the English excel in the years before the Restoration. "But, Lord!" observed Pepys, when the Russian envoys drove through the streets of London, "to see the absurd nature of Englishmen that cannot forbear laughing and jeering at everything that looks strange." "I can say nothing for him," Charles wrote to his sister after one flagrant act of rudeness on the part of his envoy at Paris, "but that it was a fault for want of good breeding, which is a disease very much spread over this country."[18]

In the first fine, careless rapture of the Restoration the summer of 1660 glided swiftly by like a coloured dream. " Now is comed in a blessed time," wrote one happy exile. All England flocked to Whitehall : ruined Cavaliers begging grants and places, mayors with addresses and gifts, politicians on their unchanging quest, ministers of pleasure jostling divines seeking loaves and fishes, and an entire countryside of ecstatic starers. For this happy host the King kept open house. " Whitehall is like a fair all day," wrote one entranced squire, and a witness of that crowded time recorded how Charles tried to do his duty. " The eagerness of men, women and children to see his Majesty and kiss his hands was so great that he had scarce leisure to eat for some days, coming as they did from all parts of the nation; and the King being as willing to give them that satisfaction would have none kept out, but gave free access to all sorts of people." One could scarcely move. Seven weeks after the Restoration, a royal official tried to get into the inner park, but could not succeed, and even saw a man basted by the Keeper for carrying people over on his back through the water. Even the King's dogs got spirited away in the crush as an advertisement in *Mercurius Publicus* reveals :

" We must call upon you again for a black dog between a greyhound and a spaniel, no white about him, only a streak on his breast, and his tail a little bobbed. It is his Majesty's own dog and doubtless was stolen, for the dog was not born nor bred in England and would never forsake his master. . . . Will they never leave robbing his Majesty? Must not he keep a dog? The dog's place (though better than some imagine) is the only place which nobody offers to beg."

From this merry start the Court of Charles II never quite recovered. History offers a thousand evidences of its charming informality, but none better perhaps than this vignette from a letter of 1670 :

" There were lately several bullets, to the number of forty, shot into the King's gallery and garden; the Politicks judged there was treason intended . . . but at last it is found to be an ordinary fellow that keeps tame pigeons, which it seems his neighbour's cats are very lickorish of; he, to be revenged, watches to kill all cats with his stone-bag, and some of his shots have reached into Whitehall."[19]

Yet in all this the King, well accustomed to make shift, somehow contrived to live a life of his own. If there was a conference with his Commons in the afternoon, to be followed by a Council meeting, he rose at five and rode to Hampton Court in the cool of a June morning before the crowd was up, getting back by midday to dinner and business. And if there were too many functions—a grand dinner at the Countess of Devonshire's, from which the gallants returned in a thunder shower looking like drowned rats, or a magnificent entertainment of the whole Court and Parliament by the City—there were many ways in which a wise prince might enjoy himself. Of these the river that flowed beneath his windows offered plenty. " The King and Duke of York come every evening as far as Battersea, Putney or Barn Elms to swim or bathe themselves, and take a great delight in it and swim excellently well," recorded one Londoner. That summer Charles was on the water almost every day; his barges and dinghy lay always off the piers which jutted out from the Palace wall. One morning he was down the river before five to view a Dutch yacht, and it was rumoured that he was tiring all his Court with early rising.* Yet, though he got through an enormous amount of business in the day, he was equally indefatigable at night. When Cromwell's Admiral, Montagu—now Lord Sandwich

---

* " His Majesty," reported another of his subjects, " is very active, and oft abroad between four and five in the morning, sometimes upon the river in his pleasure boat, and sometimes in hunting, in both which recreations he takes great delight." (*H.M.C. Hastings*, II, 140.)

—joined the royal supper-party, he lay long next day in bed. Only the King was up as usual at dawn for his "morning physick at tennis."[20]

One of those evenings—it was July 13th—Pepys, at Lord Sandwich's house in Whitehall, heard great doings of music next door, and was told that the King and the Duke of York were supping with " a pretty woman they had a fancy to." She was Barbara Palmer, one of the loyal and noble house of Villiers and " the finest woman of her age." She was then just twenty, and, having already passed through one notorious affair, was now married to the kind of husband who figures so frequently in the plays of that time as one born to be a cuckold. He was soon made one, for no man was less able to resist this kind of temptation than that " known enemy to Virginity and Chastity, the Monarch of Great Britain."[21]

So, in a world of business and pleasure, summer passed into autumn. " His Majesty," wrote one, " is in continual action and merciful expression, in so much as he rejoiceth all men's hearts who behold the cheerfulness of his countenance." In the exuberance of such a year, a burst of confidence swept the nation, and by October a merchant could write the cheering words, unfamiliar after many years of disuse, " Trade begins to flourish."[22]

H

CHAPTER II

THE AUGEAN STABLE

" 'Tis true, that when the nation has been so long mad, after so many changes and revolutions, and our progress from bad to worse, we might with reason have expected God should have sent us the worst of tyrants, some infidel or usurper, to scourge us with whips, as we well deserved. But He was so gracious as to send us our own King to redeem the nation from all the infamy it had undergone and to restore it to all it had lost and to make the people as happy as they ought to be."—BULSTRODE, *Memoirs*.

IT is not in the nature of honeymoons to endure, and King and people had yet to know each other. The difficulties facing the new Government were gigantic. For beneath the surface the country was still bleeding from the wounds, religious and political, which for twenty years Englishmen had inflicted on one another; a vast national debt had to be liquidated; the Army and the Navy were several years in arrears of pay, and there was war with a foreign power. Such realities could only be forgotten in the first wild joy of release from captivity.

The new Government, formed to represent both Royalists and moderate Presbyterians, fell to the control of an unofficial inner cabinet, consisting of Lord Chancellor Hyde and Secretary Nicholas, old Lord Southampton, the Treasurer, Monk (now made Duke of Albemarle) and his nominee, Morrice, as the other Secretary of State. It says much for these men, and for the King who presided at their meetings, that, at this moment of delirious reaction, they made not the slightest attempt to impose limitations on the old, inefficient and—from a governmental point of view—highly inconvenient parliamentary system. They might easily have done so, for not only was the tide of monarchy running more strongly than ever before, but both abroad—where medieval parliaments were everywhere crumbling—and at home—where the authority of central government had been absolute for the last ten years— there were powerful precedents for increasing the authority of Whitehall. There were some who urged the King to adopt the usurped prerogatives of the Commonwealth, treble his income by resuming possession of the old Crown domains, and so make himself independent of Parliament, and govern by a standing army. But such ideals were incompatible with his easy, tolerant nature, and they were utterly alien to the great counseller who held his ear. For Hyde had never moved from the position he had taken up in 1641, when he had begged Charles I to throw himself on the hearts and affections of those who had been the severest assertors of the public liberties, so that he might rule—a great and glorious King— over a free and happy people. This ideal of kingship, reaching back to the great days of Elizabeth, he held before his sovereign, and Charles never lost it, though he sometimes wandered in delectable fields by the way. Long afterwards he told Reresby that he would ever govern " according to the known laws."[1]

It is this which explains the lofty levels of magnanimity and forgiveness reached in the opening months of the Restoration. The first business of the Government was to procure the passage of an Act of Indemnity and Oblivion, and in this the Royalist Hyde, who had suffered so much at the hands of the late rulers of England, proved more forgiving than the Presbyterian magnates who had shared their prosperity. The measure at once came before the Commons,

H*

who instead of giving it the immediate passage, which the peace of the nation required, wasted all June adding names to those who were to be exempted from pardon.

Charles had to make repeated entreaties before they could be persuaded to send up the Bill to the Lords. Meanwhile that assembly, growing impatient, was inquiring into the deaths and trials of its own murdered members. It was the volatile Bristol who, in a brilliant speech, persuaded it to give effect to the King's wishes by exempting from death all but the Regicides, and at the same time gave expression to the injured feelings and memories of many thousands of Englishmen: "I find myself set on fire when I think that the blood of so many virtuous and meritorious peers and persons of all ranks, so cruelly and impiously shed, should cry so loud for vengeance and not find it from us!"[2]

Yet the debates still continued, and on July 27th the King found it necessary to go down to the Lords and urge them once more to expedition. "My Lords," he told them in the course of an extraordinarily frank speech, "if you do not join with me in extinguishing this fear, which keeps the hearts of men awake . . . you keep me from performing my promise, which, if I had not made, I am persuaded neither you nor I had been now here. I knew well there were some men who could neither forgive themselves, or be forgiven by us, and I thank you for your justice towards those—the immediate murderers of my father—but I will deal truly with you, I never thought of excepting any others. . . . This mercy and indulgence is the best way to bring men to a true repentance, and to make them more severe to themselves, when they find we are not so to them. It will make them good subjects to me and good friends and neighbours to you."[3]

On August 21st the Lords, finding the King set on unconditional pardon for all but the Regicides, sent back the measure to the Commons, who had to content themselves with only three other exemptions.   To everyone else save the Regicides, free pardon and forgetfulness of the past was offered.   On August 29th Charles came to the Lords to pass the Bill.   A fortnight later, when the Convention Parliament adjourned for the vacation, Hyde set the seal to his work of conciliation in the words with which he dismissed the members to their homes:

" The King is a suitor to you . . . that you will join with him in restoring the whole nation to its primitive temper and integrity, its old good manners, its old good humour, and its old good nature; good nature, a virtue so peculiar to you . . . that it can be translated into no other language, hardly practised by any other people, and that you will, by your example, by your precepts and by your practice . . . teach your neighbours how to pay a full obedience to this clause of the statute, how to learn this excellent art of forgetfulness.

" Whilst we conspire together to execute faithfully this part of the Bill, to put all old names and terms of distinction into utter oblivion, let us not find new names and terms to keep up the same. . . . If the old reproaches of Cavalier and Roundhead and Malignant be committed to the grave, let us not find more significant and better words to signify worse things.   Let not piety and godliness grow into terms of reproach and distinguish between the Court and the City and the Country, and let not piety and godliness be measured by a morosity in manners, an affectation of gesture, a new mode of speaking. . . . Very merry men have been very godly men, and, if a good conscience be a continual feast, there is no reason but men may be very merry at it."

Many things that belonged to that consecrated England of his dreams, from the far times before the wars, this good man could not restore; the old Elizabethan balance between Crown and Parliament, Church and State, were, though he knew it not, gone for ever.   But one thing he could and did achieve—the restoration of the English character.[4]

Public affairs cannot for long admit of such lofty levels, and the path of the Restoration Government ran also along the dusty roads of finance.   Here lay from the first its overwhelming problem, more acute even than that of divided religion. The annual income of Charles I had been in the neighbourhood of £900,000, the actual expenditure some £200,000 more. Under the Commonwealth, the national expenditure had doubled, rising to over £2,200,000, of which by far the greatest part went to the Army and Navy. For a time this was met by the sale of Crown and Cavalier estates, but, when these sources were exhausted, the burden proved altogether beyond the capacity of the country. In the year before the Restoration the annual deficit was nearly a million, and the accumulated debt over two million pounds. Against this, the cash resources of the Exchequer at the time of the King's return amounted to £11 2s. 10d.*[5]

In addition to this load of debt, the new Government found itself saddled with three tremendous burdens: an army costing £55,000 a month, which was both feared and loathed by the nation, a navy which, so long as the Spanish War continued, swallowed £6,000 a day, and that highly expensive trophy of Cromwellian imperialism, Dunkirk, whose garrison alone cost another £100,000 per annum. To effect a reduction of armaments and taxation, immediate overtures were made to Spain, resulting by September in a formal peace. At the same time steps were taken to disband the Army. By an Act of Parliament, continuing the monthly assessments of £70,000 —under which the nation had groaned for a generation—for a further few months, and a Poll Tax, estimated to produce £210,000, the Government was enabled to satisfy most of the arrears, without payment of which the Army would never have consented to its dissolution. On September 13th Hyde—somewhat to his master's sorrow—was able to sing the requiem of the finest military machine since the days of imperial Rome. " No other Prince in Europe," he told

---

* In thinking of these figures, it must be remembered that the purchasing power of money was far greater and the national population far less than it is to-day.

Parliament, " would be willing to disband such an army, an army to which victory is entailed, and which, humanly speaking, could hardly fail of conquest . . . an army whose order and discipline, whose sobriety and manners, whose courage and success, hath made it famous and terrible over the world." On the same night the Army officers, dining together in King Street, expressed their willingness to do the people's pleasure, and within three months forty thousand matchless troops had passed into civil life. To their arrears, the King added from his own private purse a week's extra pay.[6]

Yet the financial troubles of the Restoration had only begun. During the past generation few Englishmen had escaped loss, while many had been completely ruined. Before Parliament had made the slightest provision for the royal revenue, or before even the confiscated Crown lands could be restored, half England was presenting, in complete confidence that they would be immediately honoured, a myriad obligations incurred by the King's predecessors. Chief among these were those of the original Cavaliers. To them it seemed obvious that, since the King enjoyed his own again, they also should enjoy theirs. On the very day he entered London, twenty Sherborne officers petitioned that they might be made partakers in the universal joy, referring to a promise of Charles I, made when they took up arms in 1642, that their pay should continue for ever. Sir Jonathan Wiseman, eleven times tried for life, placed on·a ladder to be hanged till his wife brought his judges the leases of his lands, carried five miles strapped beneath a horse's belly and escaping without a penny in the world, " tost and tumbled up and down and hated of all men," petitioned for compensation. The dispossessed Clerk of the Court of Wards and Liveries, now a hundred and ten years old, begged a mark of favour before going to the grave. Ann Dartiguenave, whose relations were

all ruined and she " left to inherit nothing but sadness,"
Bridget Cawley driven naked out of doors with her children,
George Duke imprisoned for years on pump water and
pottage, with many thousands of others, looked with confidence
for relief.   Even the widow Carey, whose son Peter had
followed Charles I to Oxford and there been bitten by his
dog, Cupid, demanded her share of the bounty.[7]

The petitioners for cash mingled with an army of place-
hunters.   For every Government post, from the highest to the
lowest, there were at least two or three claimants, who all, at
one time or another, had had some right or promise to it.
Pepys, newly appointed Clerk of the Acts, was so disturbed
on hearing that his predecessor was coming up to town to
petition for his place that he missed the treat of seeing a bride
to bed.   Bridget Rumney begged for her old office of providing sweet herbs for the Court, Richard Rosser for the Exeter
Post—not on account of his own sufferings, but for the sake
of his wife and children, " those patient partakers of all his
troubles "—and Adrian Bolte, who had concealed the royal
staff for twenty years, for the making of the King's cabinets.
When it became obvious to even their blinded eyes that there
were not enough posts to go round, these anxious seekers
petitioned for odds and ends, such as the right of selling
baronetcies or, like old Colonel Duncan—who had lost
£10,000 and several limbs in the royal cause—for the roots
and underwoods in the King's forests and chases.

The Government did its best, but all the wealth of the
Indies could not have met the needs of this long impoverished
and defrauded generation.   The King himself, by his reluct-
ance to deny these poor importunists, added to the general
confusion.   To his personal adherents in exile and those who
had befriended him after Worcester, he showed, for all his
own embarrassments, a never-failing generosity; even at the
darkest moment of his career they were provided for.

The humble Penderels all received pensions fitting to their services and condition, and to the end of the reign gifts were being made to their grandchildren. Jane Lane, in addition to a handsome pension, received an endless shower of presents —miniatures, jewelled watches, snuff-boxes; her brother a large grant; Wyndham a baronetcy and £600 per annum, with pensions for his wife and maids; Robin Phelipps £400 per annum and two Household offices; Tattersall a ship in the Navy; old Wolfe, who declined a pension, an augmentation of arms, and the convivial Symonds a superb silver punch service. Gounter was dead, but Charles adopted his son, educating him at Winchester and Oxford.[8]

But for those who had lost their estates in the royal cause, little could be done. Crown and Church lands, and such properties as had actually been confiscated, returned to their rightful owners, but for the unfortunate squires, who had been forced to sell their birthrights on a drugged market to pay fines and decimations for their loyalty, there was no redress. For the King had been restored, not by their victorious arms, but by the rest of the nation, many of whom had benefited by their ruin; their lands had in some cases passed through a dozen hands since their first purchase and could only have been returned at the expense of grave injustice to third parties. There would have been a revolution had not the Government reassured the fears of existing holders by passing an Act to confirm all sales and leases of property since the Civil Wars. Even the restoration of the Crown lands— without which the administration of the country could not have been supported at all—involved hardship: witness the petition of John Tracey, merchant, who had bought Crown lands in Hyde Park worth £7,000 in 1652, and now begged a grant of two houses, which he had built beside the Knightsbridge road, to save him from ruin.[9]

But the embarrassments of the Government were naturally unperceived by the Cavaliers in the urgency of their own need. To them it seemed as though the King had passed an Act of Indemnity for his enemies and Oblivion for his friends. The feeling of this party was well summarized by the honest Essex squire, who held that Monk and the crafty old Parliament men had persuaded the King and Hyde that they owed their restoration to them, and so got all the employments, whereas it was the Cavalier party, the loyal gentry, who had in truth brought him home. There was much in what he said, for the worst feature of all wars and revolutions is that they inevitably leave the profiteers in possession. Long afterwards Ailesbury saw in this disillusionment of the loyalists the beginnings of Whiggery, the poor wasted gentry, whose children were forced to take service in rich men's families, losing all affection to the Crown. One certain result was the hatred of all that party for its greatest member, Hyde, in whose moderation they saw only a sword drawn between them and the promised land.[10]

Even without these embittering difficulties the ordinary financial problems of the Government were enough to daunt any man. Apart from the debts of Fleet and Army, which even after the disbandment amounted to nearly a million, there was a burden of long matured debt to be liquidated— a Commonwealth civil debt of about £400,000, £320,000 incurred by Parliament before 1648, £530,000 by Charles I, and the debts of the King's own exile. For certain of these the Convention at first assumed responsibility, but no parliamentary provision was ever made for their payment. It says much for Charles that, crippled as he was from the very start, he continued throughout his life to pay off, as best he could, the debts of his predecessors.[11]

From the first, the main anxiety of the King and his Ministers was to obtain an adequate revenue. In this they showed great moderation, and many afterwards blamed them

that in doing so they left the Crown too dependent on the
whims of factious Parliaments. When Charles passed the
Act of Indemnity in August, no revenue had yet been settled.
In his Speech, therefore, he referred to this omission :

" I am so confident of your affections that I will not move
you in anything that immediately relates to myself, and yet I must
tell you that . . . I have not so much money in my purse as when
I came to you. The truth is I have lived principally ever since
upon what I brought with me, which was indeed your money,
for you sent it to me, and I thank you for it. Nor have I been
able to give my brothers one shilling since I came into England,
nor to keep any table in my house but what I eat at myself. And
that which troubles me most is to see so many of you come to
me at Whitehall, and to think you must go somewhere else to
seek your dinner."

So appealed to, the House informed its hospitable sovereign
that it proposed to make up his standing revenue to £1,200,000,
a sum which it thought adequate to meet the ordinary charges
of State. But in actual fact £70,000 was all the King ever
received from the Convention for the ordinary expenses of his
first year of government.[12]

In the meantime the straits of the Administration were
serious. The bakers refused to supply any more biscuit to
the Fleet till the debts of the Commonwealth had been paid,
and when the Queen-Mother came over, the captains reported
that there was not enough powder for a royal salute. In
Flanders the King's old Guards were starving; at home the
Household was without pay. To meet these needs Charles
tried to borrow from the United Provinces and Spain, but in
both cases failed on account of his refusal to make concessions
which would have damaged English trading interests.[13]

It was not till Christmas that the Convention—before
its dissolution to make way for a legal Parliament—granted,
in return for the King's surrender of the ancient Crown
emoluments from Wards and Liveries, an excise on wine,

beer and spirits, which, it was assumed, with the customs, would bring the annual revenue up to the requisite £1,200,000. Charles returned thanks in a graceful little speech, saying that he had always held an extraordinary affection and esteem for Parliaments, but that this was now much increased by their behaviour, and that though other Parliaments had been styled learned and unlearned, and sometimes had worse epithets, this would be known as *the Healing and Blessed Parliament*. It was left to an obscure Buckinghamshire squire to add the chorus: " Mercy so generally rules the land that traitors themselves are preferred to their desires! "[14]

But not quite all traitors. On Tuesday, October 9th, the Regicides were formally indicted at Hicks Hall, and next day twenty-eight of them—all, that is, that the Government could gather together—were brought to the Bar of the Old Bailey. The trial was conducted with scrupulous fairness by the Court, though the triumphant shouts of the spectators could not always be suppressed. One who knew him well believed that Charles's compassion was such that, if the law had permitted, he would have had the prisoners acquitted. But the nation demanded a sacrifice; it was not only the King's blood which called for vengeance but the ten years' suffering and humiliation of a whole people. No time was wasted. On Saturday, October 13th, the enthusiast Harrison was drawn on a hurdle to the gibbet at Charing Cross and there hanged with his face towards the window from which his own victim had stepped out twelve years before. The rest of the horrible sentence was then executed, the people shouting all the while. Pepys, who had also seen Charles I executed, was one of the spectators, and afterwards went home unconcernedly to arrange his new book-shelves. Evelyn missed the sight, but saw the reeking quarters, mangled and cut, as they were brought in baskets to the hurdle, and attributed all to God's miraculous providence. The others followed in quick succession, dying, all but the miscreant Minister, Peters, like brave men. But they got no sympathy from the nation. " The hand of God is powerfully against those cruel murderers," reported one, " and no man pities them." Even the Quaker, Fox, rejoiced.[15]

But Charles had had enough and scribbled across the Council table to Hyde, " I confess I am weary of hanging —let it sleep." When ten* had suffered, the rest were reprieved and taken back to prison. The Convention accordingly turned its attention to the dead. On December 8th, Lords and Commons concurred in an Act for digging up the carcasses of Cromwell, Ireton and Pride and reburying them, after hanging and execution, beneath the gallows at Tyburn. On the anniversary of the King's execution the order was carried out, and there, where the Maida Vale buses now roll, they rest for ever. " This day (O the stupendous and inscrutable judgments of God!)," recorded Evelyn, " were the carcasses of those arch rebels . . . dragged out of their superb tombs in Westminster among the Kings to Tyburn and hanged on the gallows there from nine in the morning till six at night, and then buried under that fatal and ignominious monument in a deep pit, thousands of people who had seen them in all their pride being spectators." Pepys, whose washing day it was, saw their green and grinning heads winking at him from the spikes of Westminster Hall, and Nicholas wrote to an old friend to describe how Cromwell and his choicest instruments had finished the tragedy of their lives in a comic scene at Tyburn.[16]

One other stall there still remained to be cleansed in England's Augean stable—religious discord. The King liked to be easy and to see others so too, and would not split hairs, but his subjects were theologians to a man.

---

* Three more only, captured from Holland, were executed in the following year.

Four great parties struggled for supremacy: the Anglicans, with twenty years of suffering and persecution to avenge; the Presbyterians; the sects who had shared the Army's domination, and the Papists. The first three were at one in hating the last, whose only friend, outside their own ranks, was the King. The sects were for the time discredited and unpopular. The struggle for supremacy therefore lay between Anglican and Presbyterian. And supremacy of some sort or another there must be, since the English people were still unable to conceive the possibility of peace under a divided Church. To them toleration, the most hated word in the language, meant freedom for the blasphemies of fanatics and the idolatry of Papists.

It was certain that episcopacy, in some form or another, would be re-established. But the King harboured a hope that it would prove possible to unite old opponents in a single creed and ritual, and to this end he worked hard to reconcile Anglican divines—still elate with the consciousness of martyrdom and eager for loaves and fishes so long withheld—with Presbyterian doctors, to whom the chief attraction of religion lay in its infinite possibilities for splitting hairs. On the afternoon of Sunday, June 17th, while all England was making holiday and Pepys was walking in Lincoln's Inn Fields to spy out the beauties, Charles presided at the first of a long series of disputations between the leaders of the two parties.* By the patience with which he bore with their tedious speeches and angry faces and his unwearying insistence that both sides must yield something of their high demands and meet midway, he won golden opinions, old Mr. Ashe bursting into tears of joy at the gladness he had put into his

* " There were unhappily two men of that number who were much better fitted to widen old differences and create new ones: these were Dr. Gunning on one side and Mr. Baxter on the other; men so very disputatious that they were the best to spoil so good a design of any I ever knew. They spent often whole days in their disputes, as if the whole business in hand had been to try their skill at that fencing work." (*Burnet Supplement*, 68.)

heart.   But for all his patience he did not succeed.   If, after
his failure to make either side yield—and of the two the
Presbyterians were slightly the more intractable—he threw in
his lot with the party which had stood by him in his sufferings,
he is scarcely to be blamed.[17]

There dawned a golden age for the Anglican Church.
The old bishops were restored, first to their former sees or
better, and then to the House of Lords.   Morley, from grub-
bing around the Antwerp bookstalls, was enthroned as Bishop
of Worcester, half starved Dr. Cosin became Prince Bishop
of Durham, and Juxon, the good old Bishop of London, who
had stood beside his former master on the scaffold, was made
Archbishop of Canterbury.   Charles's episcopal appointments
were nearly always admirable, and in no other age have men,
more distinguished and saintly, filled the English bishoprics.
Places were even kept for the Presbyterians; Reynolds accepted
Norwich, though Baxter and Calamy ultimately refused the
honour Charles and Hyde pressed on them.   Yet as a whole,
and particularly in Presbyterian London, the new regime was
not popular.   The hatred felt a generation before towards
Laud's bishops had not yet died away; the high episcopal
rites—altar, surplice and bowed knee—were unfamiliar and
to many savoured of Popery; and the English, theologians as
they were, had little respect for priests.   " Lord! " observed
a Londoner, after watching a batch of bishops at the Abbey
in their new robes, " how people did most of them look upon
them as strange creatures and few with any kind of love or
respect! "   And a Scot, observing the family propensities of
this new hierarchy, wrote of having seen the bishop and
bishopess, the little bishops and the little bishopesses.   Though
Dr. Basire might claim with justice that, for purity of doctrine,
substance, decency and beauty, the Anglican Church was the
most perfect under heaven, and England a very land of Goshen,
there was a widespread feeling, which even good churchmen

like Evelyn shared, that far too much was restored to the high ecclesiastics, and that the golden shower that descended on them had been better deflected towards the innumerable gallant gentlemen who had ruined themselves in the Civil Wars. For this the Anglican Church was indebted to Hyde, from first to last the staunchest supporter it had.[18]

To the squabbling divines who met at Sion College to find peace, the King offered on September 4th a compromise contained in a Royal Declaration. When it was debated a month later in his presence, he proposed a clause for a universal toleration for tender consciences. It was received in iron silence, for both sides were determined to oppose any liberty of worship which might be extended to include the Papists. The Declaration was subsequently published without this clause, but the King's interest in it was now gone, and when on November 28th the Commons rejected a Bill to make it legal, the matter was tacitly allowed to drop. The bishops had triumphed, though more from the obstinate blindness of their opponents than from any other cause.[19]

Charles had other trials that autumn. On September 13th, while Hyde was making his great conciliation speech in the House of Lords, the young Duke of Gloucester lay dying of small-pox. A week later the King saw his body buried according to the rite of that Church to which in his brief life he had proved so staunch a son. After death, an indiscreet marriage is held the worst disaster which can befall a British family. This also was vouchsafed the Stuarts. On September 3rd the Duke of York secretly married Hyde's daughter Anne.[20]

At this juncture the precipitate heir presumptive appeared before the King, fell on his knees, and, in floods of tears, informed him of what he had done. Charles was naturally taken back, but after a little thought summoned Ormonde and Southampton and asked them to break the matter as tactfully as they could to Hyde. When they told him, he declared that he would rather see his daughter the Duke's whore than his wife, and that he hoped the King would send her to a dungeon in the Tower until Parliament had had time to pass an Act for cutting off her head. At this moment the King entered the room, and, sitting down at the table, asked if they had resolved on anything, to which Southampton replied that he had better consult with more sober men, for Hyde was assuredly mad. Charles, who had had some experience in such matters, turned to his Chancellor, who was standing with swollen and tear-stained eyes, and with a look of wonderful kindness told him that, since the business was done, they must needs make the best of it. But shortly afterwards the Duke allowed himself to be deluded by lying tales into a belief that Anne had misconducted herself with other men, and tried to disown her. The King, who alone throughout the affair behaved like a gentleman, refused to listen to the scandal, spoke of the defamed lady and her father with the greatest tenderness, and visited her at the time of her lying-in—an event which almost immediately followed the marriage. Furthermore, he showed a gossiping world that he meant to support Hyde, by insisting on his immediate acceptance of a peerage and a grant of £20,000.[21]

In the midst of these distractions, first Mary of Orange and then the Queen-Mother arrived in England, bent on preventing the *mésalliance*. The latter, now " a very little, plain old woman," reached Dover on October 30th, bringing with her Minette, whose hand was being sought in marriage by the French King's brother, the Duke of Orléans. Charles met them and escorted them to London, being much entertained on the way by the Kentish gentlewomen, who flocked to see him, and persisted in holding up their faces, country-wise, for him to kiss.[22]

The King delighted to have Minette near him. He

I

arranged balls for her pleasure, and, when she was at Tunbridge, scribbled across the Council table to Hyde:

" *I would willingly make a visit to my sister. . . . When do
you think I can best spare time?* "
" I suppose you will go with a light train? "
" *I intend to take nothing but my night bag.*"
" You will not go without forty or fifty horse? "
" *I count that part of my night bag.*"

During her brief stay she won all hearts, lovely as an angel,
as one beholder saw her, in a little mob-cap and coloured
gown.[23]

The ill-fortune of the Stuarts did not desert them in this
moment of reunion. Before Christmas Mary was stricken
down by the same disease that had killed her brother, and all
one week the King watched by her bedside. She died on
Christmas Eve, leaving behind a darkened Court, and only
two of that little group of brothers and sisters who had dined
together on the *Naseby* seven months before. But that old
saint, Colonel Francis Basset of Taunton, accustomed as he was
to sudden death, saw in the event the hand of God, testifying
to the faithful that all the children of Belial should shortly be
destroyed.[24]

CHAPTER III

SETTLING IN

" In all affairs of Church and State,
　　He very zealous is and able,
　Devout at prayers, and sits up late
　　At the Cabal and Council table;
　His very dog at Council board
　Sits grave and wise as any Lord."
　　　　　　　　　　　　　—ROCHESTER.

EARLY in January, 1661, Charles set out for Portsmouth to see
his mother and sister off to France. He had scarcely turned
his back on London when trouble began. The very mildness
of the Restoration settlement made the position dangerous.
The chief channels by which news and rumours circulated
were still in the hands of men who, a little before, had
exercised absolute power: the Post Office, where the Independents, Wildman and Thompson, reigned; the tippling
houses whose keepers had been licensed by the old Commonwealth justices, as had been also the wandering pedlars and
petty chapmen, on whom the remoter villages depended for
contact with the outer world. But the most dangerous of all
the weapons of insurrection were the pulpit and the press.
While the Government struggled with its policy of inclusion
and toleration, it received every day reports of inflammatory
sermons by Presbyterian divines or Anabaptist preachers, and
of printed libels, packed with imaginative and scriptural
accounts of divine judgments on the King's supporters—

malignants stricken dead in the streets, sheets of fire and earth-quakes, companies of toads (many bowlfuls of them) invading the houses of godless magistrates! In days of easy credulity and slow communications such falsehoods were hard to dis-prove. Before the year's end the Government had been apprised of plans for a widespread rising of Anabaptists and disbanded soldiers. Arrests were made, and it was hoped all would now be well.[1]

On Sunday, January 6th, while the King was at Portsmouth saying good-bye to Minette, an inspired wine-cooper called Venner, recently returned from the invigorating air of New England, urged a congregation of Fifth Monarchy Saints in Swan Alley to arm and seize the kingdom. That night— it was the children's feast of the Epiphany—a handful of enthusiasts broke into St. Paul's and challenged the wayfarers in the starlit streets, shouting for King Jesus, and slaying all who resisted. Within an hour the capital was in crashing terror, the streets filled with running multitudes, and every tower and steeple rocking with bells. Then in the darkness the Saints vanished. The next evening a regiment of foot —almost the entire military force at the Government's disposal—found them in Ken Wood, and drove them from an entrenched position in a gravel pit, while a sleepless City awaited fire and massacre. Before dawn on Wednesday they were in the streets again, still shouting for *King Jesus*, and slaying all they met, running here and there in little isolated parties till they were cut down or captured. That morning the shops were shut, and peaceable men stood at their doors with sword and pistol.

The rising thoroughly alarmed the Government. Reports from other parts confirmed its fears: at Newcastle a band of horse had tried to surprise the town; old Commonwealth men had been seen distributing powder among disbanded troops; "pulpits blew sparks," and rumour said the monarchy would not last a year. Farther south, through the towns of the West Riding, naked Quakers passed and repassed on market days crying *Woe to Yorkshire!*, and at Deptford the seamen turned out with handspikes on a night alarm that horsemen were galloping through the streets shooting at the watch. Charles, returning in haste to London, took the opportunity to lay the foundations of our regular army, reincorporating Monk's *Coldstreamers*, the last of the old regiments to be disbanded, and raising a loyal Guard of Horse —to-day the Blues—from the Cavaliers who had served him in Flanders.[2]

One inevitable result of the rising was to intensify religious bitterness. On January 10th the Government issued a Proclamation against Conventicles, meetings for public worship held elsewhere than in licensed churches or private houses. The Quakers were particular sufferers; in London they were attacked by the mob, and several would have been killed but for the timely intervention of the Duke of York. They were universally suspected of blasphemy, a belief which the singular behaviour of some of their members did much to encourage.* Before the Restoration every prison had been packed with Quakers. The gentle King had released large numbers of them, promising peace if they lived quietly. Now once more he had to intervene and empty the prisons.[3]

Despite the alarm, the Government still remained in most matters pacific and conciliatory—a milder one in England there had never been. Presbyterians continued to receive encouragement; and the King did his best to persuade the Anglican incumbent at Kidderminster to accept preferment so that

---

* One, for instance, had for some years made a practice of visiting market-places and rich men's houses, stark naked and smeared with that which is rightly forbidden puppy-dogs to eat, informing all and sundry that the Lord God would besmear their religion as he was besmeared. Rather naturally the poor man was subjected to " many grievous whippings with long coach whips, stonings and diverse imprisonments." (*Kennet Register,* 296.)

Baxter might be gratified with a living on which he had set his heart. As this saintly man, melting for once, observed—could anything be more serious, cordial and obliging? About the same time he was given a licence to preach—he had hitherto done so without one—by the Bishop of London, with every mark of friendliness. But in the country Anglican Justices of the Peace were beginning to prosecute ministers for not using the Prayer Book according to the old pre-war law of the land. The wind was coming from a new quarter.[4]

That January, a season so mild that the ways were dusty and haunted by flies and the rose bushes full of leaves, Charles rode almost daily to Hampton Court to supervise his workmen, returning in time for Council meetings at noon. He was nest-making, and, now that his only remaining brother and sister were married, it seemed fitting that he should find a mate. And, since the financial needs of his Government were so great, she must needs be a rich one. So there was talk of dowries, and several eligible ladies flitted across ministerial minds, their incomes and religions being carefully considered by the Councillors, and their persons a little pensively by the King. The Spanish were particularly anxious that the English Crown should be tied to their policy by matrimony, and presented, in Charles's own words, a whole " litany of marriages "—Saxon, Danish, and even Dutch princesses—offering to endow them all impartially. Charles, who had some memory both of Spanish promises and German ladies, waved them aside: " Odd's fish, they are all foggy! " He turned instead to the princess of a little nation, then engaged in a life or death struggle for independence against Spain. A few months before, Lord Winchelsea had reported a most interesting interview with the aged Queen Regent of Portugal, in a room filled with ancient matrons standing still as statues, while from behind a screen the royal sage, like Moses in the Mount, spoke oracular words. She now offered a dowry for her daughter such as no other woman ever before brought to England—over half a million in cash, Tangier, the island of Bombay, and, most munificent of all, free trade with Brazil and the East Indies, a key for English merchants to the treasure trove of the world.　The impecunious Charles jumped at such an offer.[5]

In vain did the Spanish ask indignantly if there was no other woman for the English King to marry but the daughter of Braganza, proffer other and better brides, and threaten war. A secret intimation from Louis that France in such an event would stand by England strengthened the King's resolve.　In early March, when the Portuguese ambassador arrived, he was cordially received, and to his great satisfaction given a private key to the royal garden.[6]

But before the marriage negotiations could be concluded there was another business to be done.　For the King was now settled and loved of all, and it was time for his subjects to crown him.　All February the scaffoldings and triumphal arches were going up.　A few Puritans thought them the greatest vanity ever beheld, but everyone else was determined, after a quarter of a century's cessation of the ancient pageantry of England, to do the thing in style.　While the King made the best of the pleasant spring weather by driving a chariot and two horses in Hyde Park, learned antiquaries pored over books to discover forgotten ceremonies and rites.[7]

On April 20th Charles created sixty-eight Knights of the Bath and next day conferred a number of peerages, including the Earldom of Clarendon for the faithful Hyde.　Being England and April, there were showers, and the gilded arches and vast gaping crowds in the streets were frequently wetted. On Monday, 22nd, according to the ancient custom of the realm, the King, leaving Whitehall at dawn by barge, rode in state from the Tower to the Palace.　Bells pealed, fountains ran wine, the windows were filled with carpets and ladies, and

eyes were blinded with gold and silver. Even Pepys who
had a magnificent view from Mr. Young's, the flagmaker
in Cornhill, found himself unable to express the glory of the
day and the grandeur of the men and horses.

On St. George's Day they crowned the King. The sun
rose fair and serene, and Pepys before it, taking his place on
the scaffolding at the north end of the Abbey at four o'clock
and watching for many hours, with a great deal of pleasure,
that busy kaleidoscope—the raised and carpeted throne, the
clergy in cloth of gold, the very fiddlers in scarlet vests. And
when at last the King, robed and bare-headed, with sword and
wand borne before him, was met at the west door by the
singing choir, when the crown was placed on his head and
the aged Archbishop cried out " Lift up your hearts," there
was such a shout as the grim ghosts of the Regicides beneath
the Tyburn gallows must have stirred to hear. Three times
Garter strode to the open places on the scaffold and proclaimed that if any could show reason why Charles Stuart
should not be King of England he was to come now and
speak. But no one came.

Then, amid anthems and rare music, lutes, viols and
trumpets and the thunder of organs, the King passed out
through the watching multitudes to the hall in which his
father had stood his trial. There he sat down to eat. In
that tapestried, feasting splendour, Dymoke, the King's
champion, rode in armour among the tables and, with spear
and target, flung down the gauntlet to all challengers. And
when it was over, and Pepys had scrambled four rabbits
and a pullet from one of the tables and listened to the music
and looked upon the ladies, the King passed out again beneath
the canopy of state with its silver pillars and tinkling bells.
So he went down to his gilded barge, and vanished into the
quiet of Whitehall.

That night the city had a " light like a glory round it

with bonfires." Pepys, swaying down packed streets, stumbled
on many gallants, men and women, who laid hold of him
and made him drink the King's health on his knees, wondering much, did that good secretary, to see the ladies tipple.
A little later—he did not quite know how—he was in the
royal wine cellar, and there, with the yeoman Keeper and
some young sparks, drank the King's health over and over
again.   And in Mr. Shepley's bed—while Evelyn, sober as
ever, was presenting his sovereign with a panegyric poem—
this honest citizen concluded a great day with a burning head
and a vomiting stomach; "and if ever I was foxed," he
added, " it was now! "[8]

A fortnight after the Coronation, the King met his
new Parliament. The first election returns in London had
favoured the Presbyterians, but, though the forces which had
made the Great Rebellion were well represented in the
Boroughs, the country as a whole chose a House of Commons of Cavalier squires, more Royalist, some said, than the
King himself. The latter welcomed them genially—" I
know most of your faces and names and can never hope
to find better men in your places "—and then turned to an
important and welcome piece of news:

" I have often been put in mind by my friends that it was
high time to marry, and I have thought so myself ever since I
came into England.   If I should never marry till I could make
such a choice against which there could be no foresight of any
inconvenience, you would live to see me an old bachelor, which
I think you do not desire to do.   I can now tell you, not only that
I am resolved to marry, but whom I resolve to marry, if God
please. . . . And trust me, with a full consideration of the good
of my subjects as of myself, it is with the daughter of Portugal."[9]

In that country the news was received with enthusiasm,
in England with more tempered joy and a burst of petitions
for salaried posts about the Queen.   Opinions were canvassed

as to her person and nature; one, who had seen her portrait at Whitehall, reported that she was a lovely little woman, another that she was short, but pretty, dark and black-eyed. Old Nicholas, always inclined to anticipate events, implored heaven to bless the royal pair with a numerous progeny. Others were a little scornful of England's new ally. Captain Cocke, "a man of great observation and repute," said that Lisbon was a poor, dirty place, its palace windows unglassed, the King a rude, simple fellow, and the royal family accustomed to dine off nothing but fruit, with an occasional hen; and a Member of Parliament declared that if the Spaniards took their country from the Portuguese, we must needs marry the whole nation. The King, better mannered and more far-sighted than his subjects, wrote his future wife charming letters, and sent his ambassador at Lisbon instructions for increasing commerce with India and South America and, for engrossing, if practicable, the entire sugar trade of the West Indies.[10]

The chief business of the new Parliament was to confirm the Act of Indemnity. A House of Commons with a majority of unforgetting Cavaliers proved even more reluctant to forgive than its predecessor, and it again needed the intervention of the King to get them to pass a Bill for affirming the Acts of the Convention.* "Let us look forward and not backward," he told them, "and never think of what is past. . . . God hath wrought a wonderful miracle in settling us as He hath done; I pray let us do all we can to get the reputation at home and abroad of being well settled." In the affairs of Scotland, Charles showed the same generous temper, insisting, despite the racial prejudices of both Houses, on withdrawing the English garrisons from that country. "The

---

* " . . . His Majesty is most fixedly honourable and true to that business as in all things else." (Andrew Marvell to the Mayor and Aldermen of Hull, 15 June, '61, *Marvell*, II, 30.)

King," wrote a country parson, " is honest in spite of the Parliament. They could not have done more to make him loved and themselves hated."[11]

If his subjects required indemnity, Charles needed money. In his speech to Parliament, he pointed out that the revenue granted had fallen far short of what had been promised, and that the pay of the seamen—whom he specially commended as people on whom the very happiness and security of the nation must depend—was still several years in arrear. The general poverty of the country after its long revolution and the extravagance of Cromwell's warlike government had brought about a general shrinkage of revenue; neither Customs, Excise nor Hearth Money produced anything like the sum which had been estimated, and the Government was left to struggle with a heavy deficit.* The new Parliament at first did its best to assist the King in this dilemma, voted a collection of free gifts, which, as wise men predicted, did not come to much, and tried various ways to bring the revenue up to the promised £1,200,000. But, since it represented very accurately the tax-paying classes in the community, it did not try very hard, and during the next twelve years the revenue remained about £400,000 less than the necessary expenditure of Government. Charles, who bore these financial difficulties with commendable humour, was forced to borrow money from city bankers at exorbitant rates in order to carry on the administration at all.[12]

This loyal Parliament which denied an adequate revenue to the King, denied also religious toleration to his subjects. On April 15th a further Conference of Divines had met at the Savoy to find some agreement between Episcopalians and Presbyterians. It failed even more signally than its pre-

---

* Thus the Customs, estimated by Parliament to bring in approximately £400,000 per annum, only produced an average revenue of £285,000 during the first seven years of the reign. (*C.T.B.*, VII, Part I, xv-xvi.)

decessor, partly on account of Baxter's furious eagerness for
theological argument, but mainly because the Anglican squires
in the Commons were in no mood to offer toleration on their
own terms to those who had oppressed them and their
creed for so many years: ministers, they held, must either
conform to the observances and liturgy of the Church as it
was or leave its communion. When the Conference broke up
at the end of July, the bishops still maintained that there was
not the least justification for the changes which their opponents
demanded.[13]

The Cavaliers in Parliament in no way shared their
sovereign's capacity for forgetting the past. Already they saw
signs that the Presbyterian pulpits were at their old task of
inciting the people against established order. As early as
March little Zachary Crofton was telling his fashionable city
auditory that episcopacy was a human institution and led to
Papacy. It was not long before he went further and published a book, urging the carrying on of the work of the
Covenant by force and claiming that the people had lawful
power to bind their kings. It was this kind of thing, the
Commons reflected, that had begun the troubles in '40 and '41.
Overseas were more dangerous enemies. In Holland and
Switzerland little groups of Regicides were meeting for prayer
and talk of revenge, while at Sedan John Desborough, whose
house was furnished with gold and purple hangings from
Whitehall, was making military plans. Parliament showed
its feeling by passing Acts to restore the bishops to the House
of Lords and strengthen the Militia.[14]

Amidst all this, the King preserved the even tenor of his
way, and contrived to make the best of a lovely summer. He
was scarcely crowned but he gave orders to put ten tons of
ballast into his new pleasure boat, and thereafter at least once
a week sailed down the river to visit his ships at Woolwich
or the Nore. Evelyn spent a long and memorable day aboard

this yacht, with its neat, panelled cabins, velvet hangings, and damask furniture, while the King at the tiller raced another boat from Greenwich to Gravesend and back for a wager, and talked the while of gardens and buildings, the improvements he was making at Greenwich, and the smoke nuisance in London.[15]

Another royal recreation that summer was the theatre. In July Charles took his aunt of Bohemia—who had once seen Shakespeare's plays acted in his own lifetime for her girlish delight—to witness Davenant's *Siege of Rhodes*, at the new Opera House in Lincoln's Inn Fields. The theatre was packed, and the long wait before the royal party arrived was enlivened by the breaking of a board overhead, which precipitated a great deal of dust down the ladies' necks, making, as one present records, good sport. The show itself was magnificent and well acted, all but the eunuch—a naturally unpopular part—who was hissed off the stage. On at least six other occasions that autumn the King was present at one or other of the two public theatres.

In all this Charles was helping to create a new English stage. The old, rough suburban playhouses of former days gave way to two elegant little theatres, whose audiences were drawn chiefly from the Court and the smart young folk of the western faubourgs. For such, the old plays would not do; they demanded something less wild and imaginative, better mannered and more intimate. This theatre was the microcosm of the new age. From its little picture stages, with their tall wax candles and velvet curtains, dainty actresses, with impudent, alluring ways, looked down on bewigged, approving gentlemen.[16]

His people saw their bachelor King in many aspects that year: now supervising his workmen in St. James's Park, now on Banstead Downs at a horse-race, now joining the hands of an old courtier and Ormonde's little daughter to point a smiling contrast between age and youth, or delighting good Mrs. Evelyn by offering to enshrine a Madonna she had copied among the treasures in his Closet.   In early May he sat up all night to watch the eclipse of Saturn through his great telescope with a party of mathematicians from the Philosophical Society; later in the summer he granted a Royal Charter to that body.   Henceforward he took the keenest interest in their proceedings, attending occasional meetings, making them gifts, sending to them to know why sensitive plants contract on being touched, or urging the admission of a learned London haberdasher, whose social status, he argued, was so far from being a prejudice that they ought to elect him without ado.   He talked that autumn of a progress in the west to visit the scenes of his escape, but somehow never went, and remained in London, making occasional expeditions to hunt the stag in the great forests round the capital, where he tired all the horses and came home with scarcely an attendant to keep up with him.   To the faithful Clarendon, holiday-making in the great forest pleasance he had given him, he wrote:

" He must be a harder-hearted man than I that can refuse you a few days in a place you are so well pleased with as I perceive you are with Cornbury.   'Tis good reason I should give you now a little time to play, after the passing of so many ill hours in my service. . . . Have a care of the game, that I may have good sport next year when I come thither."[17]

When the Houses reassembled in November the country was again full of reports of unrest, blown far and wide from pulpits, where fanatic saints or learned Presbyterians spoke contemptuously of the new order and praised the good old times.   Parliament now determined to act.   In December it passed the Corporation Act, compelling every municipal office-holder to receive the Anglican sacrament and repudiate the doctrine that lawful war could be waged against the King. The first step in the exclusion of the Nonconformists had been taken. The two great religious parties whose union had brought about the Restoration were once more at logger-heads.[18]

CHAPTER IV

BENEDICT—THE MARRIED MAN

" Then Israel's monarch, after Heaven's own heart,
His vigorous warmth did variously impart."
—DRYDEN.

THE New Year of 1662, which opened with the King's playing
a part in ancient rites that had lain rusty for a quarter of a
century—the old solemn fooleries of the Lincoln's Inn Revels,
the traditional Twelfth Night gaming in the Privy Chamber
—brought also the familiar tale of deaths. Charles knelt by
the bedside of his old tutor, Brian Duppa, to crave his dying
blessing; a little later Elizabeth of Bohemia, after all her
sorrows and afflictions, breathed her last in his arms. They
buried her—Wotton's Queen of Hearts, Shakespeare's Miranda
—in the Abbey, on a night of hail, thunder and lightning.
The loss bound Charles's heart the more tightly to Minette
across the water; she was all he had to love now, for his
mother with her hard, decisive nature had never been a
companion, and James, for all his fine looks and honest
energy, was somewhat of an ass.[1]

She, the frail, penniless Cinderella of a year before, was
wife now of the Duke of Orléans—the centre of a thousand
fêtes, and *Madame* of France. But her gentle heart, husband,
lover, wit, never once touched; it had been given in childhood
to her tall, dark brother, and long years of absence did not
alter it. Nearly every Sunday, before the French mail left,

144

. . . " The centre of a thousand fêtes and *Madame* of France."

Charles sat late, penning her long, tender letters. " I do intend to write to you very often in English that you may not quite forget it," he told her. " For God's sake, my dearest sister, have a care of yourself and believe me that I am more concerned in your health than I am in my own, which I hope you do me the justice to be confident of, since you know how much I love you. . . . I am sure," he added, " I shall be very impatient till I have the happiness to see *ma chère Minette* again."[2]

She sent him that January a little protégée, Frances Stewart—" the prettiest girl in the world "—to be Maid of Honour to his Queen. He made much of her, with her lovely motions and childlike grace and mind; at a Court ball a few weeks later she was the only blazing star. For Charles it was the commencement of a long and, though he often wished it otherwise, virtuous friendship.[3]

But the Queen was coming at last, and a British fleet waiting at Lisbon to bring her over. On March 1st Charles, appealing once more for an adequate settlement of his revenue, begged Parliament to expedite business, so that he might be free to welcome her when she landed, and to pass an Act to repair the highways near Whitehall lest she should find it surrounded by water. But as usual the Commons were dilatory. Since January they had been hot on the trail of their old enemies, and had introduced a Bill for Uniformity in public prayer, with a proviso that any minister who refused it should be deprived of his living. The needy King, after a fruitless attempt to persuade them to make provision for ejected ministers, let them go their own way, telling them a little wistfully that his was the worst luck in the world if, after all the reproaches of his being a Papist while abroad, he should now be accused of being a Presbyterian. He was still trying to bring their debates to a conclusion on May 14th, when the Portsmouth guns thundered out a welcome to his

K

little bride, as the Fleet carried her into harbour—very shy, very solemn and very sick.[4]

It was not Parliament alone that gave Charles anxiety. There was Barbara. All the previous year peering eyes— half scandalized and wholly delighted—had watched her progress. In December a patent had passed the Privy Seal for the poor cuckold, her husband, to be Earl of Castlemaine, the honour to be tied up in the heirs of her body : everybody knew why. And now that the Queen was come, what was to happen to the pretty, termagant thing that shared the King's pleasures. She was expecting a baby, and spoke of lying in at Whitehall; there were tears, expostulations, and Charles, who could not bear to see a woman cry, was at his wits' end to know how to make her happy without offending his bride. When he supped with her the night the news of the Queen's landing reached London, observers noted that there were bonfires at every door but hers.[5]

On the evening of Monday, May 19th, when the Bills were at last ready for his approval, he prorogued Parliament and at once posted away, reaching Guildford by midnight. Next day soon after noon he arrived at Portsmouth. He found his bride indisposed in bed, a little solemn, dark creature with lovely hands and feet. At eight next morning he was writing, not very delicately, to Clarendon describing it all :

" It was happy for the honour of the nation I was not put to the consummation of the marriage last night, for I was so sleepy, by having slept but two hours in my journey, that I was afraid that matters would have gone very sleepily. I can only now give you an account of what I have seen a-bed; which, in short, is, her face is not so exact as to be called a beauty, though her eyes are excellent good, and not anything in her face that in the least can shock one. On the contrary, she has much agreeableness in her looks altogether as ever I saw; and, if I have any skill in physiognomy, which I think I have, she must be as good a woman as ever was born. . . . You would much wonder to see how well we are acquainted already."[6]

On Wednesday, May 21st, a lovely day of early summer, they were married, at first secretly to please her according to the rites of Rome, and in the afternoon publicly by the Bishop of London. After the ceremony Catherine laid aside her rose-coloured English dress, and rested, while Charles supped beside the bed, talking merrily to her and all the company. She was already in love with him, for his shining eyes made him the most charming prince in the world.[7]

"I think myself very happy," he wrote to Minette. "I was married the day before yesterday, but the fortune that follows our family is fallen upon me, *Car Monseigneur le Cardinal m'a fermé la porte au nez!* But I flatter myself I was not so furious as Monsieur was and shall let this pass." To the bride's mother he wrote more decorously to say how charmed he was: "Being now freed from the dread of the sea and enjoying in this springtime the company of my dearest wife, I am the happiest man in the world. . . . I cannot sufficiently either look at her or talk to her." The rest of the week the young pair lingered at Portsmouth, waiting for carts to carry Catherine's train of young ladies and their vast Guarda Infantas, without which, as Charles told Clarendon, there was no stirring.[8]

These ladies were somewhat of a trial. Of apparently the highest virtue, their modesty was such that they would not so far wrong their virginity as even to sleep in sheets once touched by man. They were accompanied by a chorus of very pious, very dirty Portuguese monks, each of whom had with true family feeling brought a little following of relations. On the 27th they all set out together through a world of pleasant hills and woods and staring rustics.[9]

At Hampton Court Charles and Catherine spent their honeymoon. He had made the place very pleasant, filling it with incomparable furniture and tapestries, and crowning all with a bridal bed of crimson and silver velvet. Outside were gardens with parterres, and fountains and copper statues, and the park—of which he was so proud—planted with rows of lime trees. With picnics on land and water, music and dancing, in a world of green lawns and June roses, the idle weeks passed.[10]

When England came to do homage to its Queen, it was not disappointed. A fine handsome lady she seemed to be—though her teeth did stick out a little—and very discreet, and would, it was hoped, put Lady Castlemaine's nose out of joint.* Even her ladies were found to be more tolerable than they appeared, and had soon learnt to kiss and look freely up and down after the English fashion; by mid-June scandal said that one of them had presented her new country with a child.[11]

But what really enchanted England was the satisfaction which the royal couple seemed to take in each other. Country-bred Doll Leeke hoped such connubial virtue would work on some of the Court ladies and make them more grave. For if Charles's Restoration had a thorn in its side for his best subjects, it was the scandal of his easy, pleasure-loving Court; now that there was a Queen doubtless all would be respectable and charming.[12]

Alas! That June Lady Castlemaine gave birth to her first son; he was christened Charles after his father, who obligingly stood sponsor. A week later the lady left her indignant husband and, with her genius for precipitating delicious public scandals, moved to Richmond. Her tears, her prayers, her beauty, were such that the King could not keep away. It was not that he intended to fall again—he meant to be the best

---

* The Queen is a very beautiful, handsome princess, but low and slender, and of a solid, grave countenance, quick wit and a great housewife. The King is very much taken with her and very fond of her. (Henry Bodvel to Maurice Wynn, 3 June, '62, *Wynn Papers*, 370.)

of husbands—but Barbara loved him, needed him, and it was not in his nature to abandon her when all the world thought her lost. She begged that he would show his friendship for her by making her Lady of the Queen's Bedchamber—a fine and fashionable pinnacle of refuge for an injured lady. Weakly he promised.[13]

The Queen had heard of Barbara and, when she was presented with the lists of the ladies of her household, angrily struck her name out. In the strained days that followed there were not wanting companions in the jolly supper company—which always offered relief from an unquiet wife—to tell Charles that a King's love was above rebuke, and that, like his famous grandfather, Henri IV, he should cause all the world to pay the same respect to Barbara as he did himself. It was not the part of a man, still less of a generous prince, they told him, to abandon her, now that her husband had left her and her name was tarnished. The advice, given merrily across the lighted candles and wine cups, met the whisperings of his own heart: he had given her his word, he was a king, and he would keep it. So the little wife, in her lonely, angry room, who could scarcely speak a sentence in his language, who had never known the world, who was helpless because she adored him and could not control her jealous passion, was made to suffer. He did not mean to be unkind, but he would not be argued out of justice to an old friend.[14]

When Clarendon, foreshadowing very accurately the feelings of his subjects, protested—as usual a little too loudly —Charles wrote him one of those rare letters which reveal the hidden strength of will beneath that calm surface:

" I forgot to desire you to give Broderick good counsel not to meddle any more with what concerns my Lady Castlemaine, and to let him have a care how he is the author of any scandalous reports; for, if I find him guilty of any such thing, I will make him repent it to the very last moment of his life. And now I am entered on this matter, I think it very necessary to give you a little good counsel in it, lest you may think that, by making a further stir in the business, you may divert me from my resolution, which all the world shall never do; and I wish I may be unhappy in this world and the world to come, if I fail in the least degree what I have resolved. . . . And whosoever I find use any endeavour to hinder this resolution of mine (except it be only to myself) I will be his enemy to the last moment of my life. You know how true a friend I have been to you. If you will oblige me eternally, make this business as easy as you can, of what opinion soever you are of; for I am resolved to go through with this matter, let what will come of it."

Faced by such a letter Clarendon protested no more. In the course of several tearful interviews, he tried to persuade the Queen that the only way to keep her husband's affection was to give way. He reminded her of the universal practice of seventeenth-century sovereigns, and asked, with a significant hint at the morals of her own brothers, whether she believed a Queen of Portugal would find that Court so full of virtuous affection. He might have added the story of Louis XIV's bride, whom the Spanish ambassador had recently found weeping because her husband had taken La Vallière into his coach. " For this does your Majesty cry? " asked the astounded diplomat. " Before God Almighty, I have seen the King your father with four mistresses at a time in his coach! "[15]

But Catherine would not yield. For a time her husband tried to win her by caresses; then, as the poor child's jealous fury turned to morosity, avoided her company, put on an air of affected gaiety and threw himself into the merry life of his young Court. Yet every night he returned to his solitary Queen, and once—but once only—those in that quarter of the Palace heard the sound of angry voices. Such a scandal soon spread; Pepys knew all about it before July was out.

Yet, while Charles was injuring one woman, he was

showering kindnesses on another and inviting his lonely
mother to make a home in England with such tenderness
that even old St. Albans was touched.   On July 16th
Pepys saw him going down the river in pelting rain towards
the Downs to meet her, and it somewhat lessened his esteem
of him to see him get so wet.   Mother and son met in mid-
Channel in a raging storm—" Mam's ill luck at sea," Charles
called it—but the yachts, to their great honour, rode out the
gale, and all came safe to Greenwich.[16]

The coming of the older woman, who could remember the
difficulties of her own youth, made life easier for the Queen.
The two, diverse as were their characters, had much in
common—most of all their religion.   A few weeks later—it
was August 23rd—Charles brought his bride to London.   The
river was packed with boats, and a hundred gilded pageants
played upon the water.   It was a fit entry for a Sea King's
bride to her husband's capital.   They came together in an
antique-shaped open vessel, covered with a cupola of gold, its
Corinthian pillars wreathed with garlands.   Pepys, standing
on a roof top of the Palace, observed Lady Castlemaine watching this wonderful spectacle.   He saw her curtsy coldly to
her husband when he bowed to her, saw her run down, alone
of all the great ladies, among the rabble when a child was
hurt by the fall of a scaffold; saw her put on a Cavalier's
plumed hat to keep the wind off her hair: it became her
mightily, he thought, as did everything else.[17]

When it was too late, and Charles, with an easy shrug of
his shoulders, had resumed his old relations with the lady,
Catherine surrendered.   Nor was she content with this, for,
in her anxiety to win back her husband's love, she showered
on her proud, lovely rival every mark of attention, and thereby
made Charles think that all her anger before was but womanly
contrariness.   The honeymoon was now over.   In early
September, at a party at Somerset House, his subjects were

privileged to obtain a glimpse of that strange admixture which
was Charles's idea of matrimony. He came with his wife,
Castlemaine and a pretty boy, James Crofts—his son by Lucy
Walter—whom Henrietta had brought from France. Charles
and Catherine were very merry, he pretending she was with
child, and she denying the soft impeachment with a lisping
" You lie ! " whereupon he was merrier still, and tried to make
her say in English, " Confess and be hanged ! " Afterwards
husband and wife, mistress and former mistress's son, went
affectionately home together in the same coach.[18]

It was not surprising that the nation was shocked; the
English people were unaccustomed to such behaviour in their
rulers. After this, almost any scandal, however improbable,
about the King passed for truth. It was unfortunate that this
fall in reputation should have coincided with the collection
of the highly unpopular Hearth Tax and the tightening of
the laws against the Nonconformists. On August 24th
the new Act of Uniformity came into force, and some two
thousand ministers resigned their livings. The moderate
Presbyterians were thus thrown into the arms of the real
republicans. From every part of the country came reports of
seditious sermons, armed meetings and secret conclaves. Men
in taverns whispered that the King minded only his mistresses,
that the Queen-Mother and her cabal carried on the government from Somerset House, and that Popery was coming in;
and in their cups republicans hinted darkly that Charles
was often alone on the Thames in a single pair of sculls, where
a good man might easily do his business. As for the traitor
Monk, he should starve in an iron cage above St. Paul's.[19]

Money difficulties added to the general uncertainty; these
were more acute than ever. With its annual deficit of over a
third of the total revenue and its burden of unpaid debts, the
Government was forced to borrow from the City bankers on an
ever-falling credit. To make matters worse, though the higher

officials were mainly honest, and did their best under over-whelming difficulties, the lower grades of the administration were hopelessly corrupt.   Everybody cheated the Government. The ranunculi planted in St. James's Park, worth about £14, were charged for at the rate of £118; Jonas Shish, the aged shipwright at Deptford, whom Evelyn described as a most respectable man, regularly swindled the Navy to the tune of twelve shillings for every twenty-eight feet of timber cut; the Woolwich dockyard officials stole the old cordage off the ships and resold it to the Service as new.   " I see it is impossible," commented the Clerk of the Acts, " for the King to have things done as cheap as other men."   That August, rowing down the Creek, he discovered two warships lying without a soul on board and everything stolen.   And since nearly every salary was several years in arrears, Charles could not rid himself of his servants, however dishonest, inefficient or superfluous they might be.[20]

To relieve its pressing necessities, the Government, that October, sold Dunkirk to the French for five million livres. Though the place was quite useless, and was costing £130,000 a year to maintain, the country affected to be much humiliated by the transaction;* Clarendon in particular became most unpopular.   The great suburban palace he was building him-self in the fields to the north of Piccadilly was christened Dunkirk House by the mob, and the purchase price, which was most religiously employed to meet the deficiences in the national exchequer, popularly supposed to have found its way into his pockets.[21]

In these circumstances it is not surprising that the King

* " The only news here (which drowns all other) is the sale of Dunkirk to the French; most say 'tis gone already, but I hope, if the Londoners will but contribute anything like towards the charge of keeping it, 'tis yet retrievable.   Howbeit the merchants are all of a flame, and the discontented parties interpret everything in the worst sense, and to the dishonour of the King and his Council."   (G. Wharton to W. Legge, *H.M.C. Dartmouth*, I, 10.)

determined on a change in the Government. That October he abruptly told Clarendon that he had resolved to replace old Secretary Nicholas by Sir Henry Bennet, and then walked away so briskly that there was no time for protest. Nicholas, who was close on seventy, was offered a peerage and a grant of money for his long and faithful service, and, after commuting the honour for a little additional cash, the old man came to the conclusion that he had made no bad bargain. But to Clarendon it was a severe blow, for Bennet had strong and uncongenial views of his own, and his promotion from the Privy Purse offered that strategic post to the King's friend, Charles Berkeley, whom he loathed.[22]

It was a bitterly cold November, and as though to emphasize the wintry chill, a delegation of Muscovite ambassadors from the barbarous north-east came, bringing with them furs so welcome that for once Charles refrained from his disconcerting habit of giving away all his presents in advance. Such weather proved too much for the Chancellor, who was stricken down with severe gout. For the next four months Bennet reigned in his stead.[23]

While snow lay thick in the streets and the skaters were cutting rings on the lake in St. James's Park, Charles and his new advisers were inaugurating a policy that was to make Clarendon start in his bed. A little before Bennet had placed before his master a memorandum, urging him to strengthen his authority before the general dissatisfaction culminated in revolution. The Militia was now called out, and the discovery of a conspiracy to surprise Whitehall, followed by such a tornado of arrests that Pepys dreamt that he had been taken up as a plotter.[24]

But while the Government was acting with such vigour, it was preparing measures of a different kind. On December 26th the King published a Christmas greeting which electrified the nation. In it he stated that he still, despite the Act of

Uniformity, intended the Indulgence to Tender Consciences promised at Breda, and that, until a Bill could be laid before Parliament, he would, out of his mercy, dispense with the execution of the penal laws against all religious dissentients who should live peaceably. Nor—and here lay the greatest shock of all—were good Catholic subjects to be excluded from this toleration. A few weeks later the prisons were opened, and a mixed assortment of Anabaptists, Quakers and Recusants stepped out into a slightly puzzled world.[25]

In all this the King was merely expressing his natural distaste for religious coercion and the bloody laws which disgraced the statute books. But the opponents of the measure did not err when they suspected that he was actuated by far gentler feelings towards the persecuted Catholics than was then held compatible with Protestant zeal. His experiences after Worcester were still fresh in his memory; he had made promises, then and subsequently, to Catholic loyalists which he was determined to honour, and many of his dearest friends, including his mother and sister, were devout adherents of the old Faith. In its order and the beauty of its outward observances,* above all in its insistence on authority, it offered much which appealed to him. Therefore, though he had no great respect for any form of religious dogma—he once observed that Harrow Church was the only *visible* church he knew— and regarded many Romish practices, such as the Confessional, with considerable amusement, he had every intention of making things easier for the Catholics. Nor did he regard a reunion between the Roman and Anglican Churches as impossible. A paper of this date addressed to the Romish

---

* From the time when as a friendless young King he had insisted, despite the protests of his Presbyterian masters, on receiving the sacrament kneeling, Charles had always shown respect for the outward decencies of religion. After the Restoration, when a Puritan prebend of Windsor refused to bow to the altar, Charles remarked: " If he will not bow to God, let him not bow to me," which, noted the narrator, " made him the more supple next day." (*Livingstone, Life,* 177-8, and *Woodcock Papers,* 63.)

see suggests that he was ready to accept the tenets of the ancient Church, provided that the Papacy would agree to the maintenance of the independent hierarchical system of England, the existing settlement of former Church lands, and toleration for Protestants of all denominations. By such he would have established in Great Britain a compromise similar to that of his grandfather in France, with the joint advantages of a union with the continental Catholic powers and a cessation of the religious discords which for ever divided his subjects— English, Scotch and Irish. It would also have freed him from the ceaseless and maddening interference of Parliament in matters of ritual and dogma. But in supposing such a solution to his difficulties to be possible, he entirely under-estimated the insensate hatred felt by his people, Anglican and Presbyterian alike, towards Catholicism. He had been so long absent from them that he did not as yet quite understand them.[26]

CHAPTER V

THE COURT OF CUCKOLDS

" The King was inferior to none, either in shape or air; his wit was pleasant; his disposition easy and affable; his soul, susceptible of opposite impressions, was compassionate to the unhappy, inflexible to the wicked and tender even to excess; . . . his heart was often the dupe, but oftener the slave, of his attachments."—Anthony Hamilton.

" He sat down out of form with the Queen, but he supped below stairs."—Halifax.

On the last night of 1662 there was a great ball at Court. Watchers in the gallery saw the King, when all were seated, take out the Duchess of York to dance a Bransle. Afterwards he led a single maiden in a Coranto, and, while he danced, the Queen and all the ladies stood. But the fun of the evening set in fast and furious, when the time came for country dances, and Charles called out for the first, which he said was " Cuckolds all awry! The old dance of England."[1]

In that immortal phrase, uttered amid the laughter and fiddles beneath the tall wax candles, the King epitomized his Court. Love was its main pursuit—" the effect of idleness and having nothing else to employ their great spirits upon," as Pepys observed. The latter heard much that winter: how Lord Chesterfield, himself no mean cuckold-maker, hurried his lady off to lonely Bretby to be out of York's clutches; how little Jermyn, the most absurd of conquerors, was banished the Court for ogling Barbara; how the King supped three or four nights a week with that scandalous lady, walking back to his lodgings across the still garden in the early morning, so that the very sentries spoke of it.   Much of this was idle gossip, but not all.[2]

In other respects, however little seemly in this one, this Court, so rich in lovely women and brilliant men, was elegant enough.   Grammont, accustomed to the grandeur of that of France, was surprised at its graceful manners. Drunkenness was almost unknown, and gambling—though its master was too much of a gentleman to spoil the ladies' pleasure at cards—tacitly discouraged.   After all, Charles reflected, it was he in the long run that paid for their losses. So he sent an agent to the Foire de Saint Germain to buy little things to play for, in the hope that it might keep the charming creatures out of debt, and gave them plenty of balls and masquerades, though the latter presented difficulties, as he told Minette:

" We had a design to have a masquerade here, but we were not able to go through with it, not having one man here that could make a tolerable entry.   I have been persuading the Queen to follow the Queen-Mother of France's example and go in masquerade before the carnival be done : I believe it were worth seeing my Lord St. Albans in such an occasion.   My wife hath given a good introduction to such a business, for the other day she made my Lord Aubigny and two other of her chaplains dance country dances in her bedchamber !   I am just now called for to go to the Play."

In all such activities Charles was irrepressible.   " The King doth me the honour to dine here," wrote the French ambassador.   " Not that I have asked his Majesty, but he *would* come and be one of a party which will include the most illustrious libertines of the kingdom."[3]

Though the King made the best—or, as some supposed, the worst—of his soft hours, the ever-growing lines of that dark face spoke of sterner interests.   In February, 1663, Parliament was to meet again, and great was the speculation as to how it would take the Declaration of Liberty for Tender Consciences. Doubts were soon resolved. The Commons made short work of it, and immediately presented the King with an uncompromising request for stern dealing with all who differed from the Act of Uniformity. Deeply in debt, he had no alternative but to yield, which he did with his usual grace, telling them that he was sure no prince had ever been happier in his Parliament than he. A month later he accorded their request for a proclamation banishing Papist priests and Jesuits; he could take good care, he reflected, not to enforce it. Yet, though he hid his ill-humour from all but a few, he was angry and humiliated.

When the promised Bill for indulging tender consciences was introduced in the Lords, Clarendon himself was among those who spoke against it and ensured its rejection. Desperately jealous of the rising power of Bennet and Berkeley, he welcomed the defeat of his master's policy as a check to their influence. Charles, still grateful to his old servant, showed little signs of resenting this extraordinary behaviour, which many imagined would ensure his dismissal. Clarendon, on the other hand, supposed that the humiliating failure of his Declaration had sickened the King of his new advisers, and that he would rid himself of them. Yet the truth was Charles had no intention of abandoning any of his Ministers, however much they might hate one another.[4]

Though Clarendon might pour out his soul to Ormonde about his rival, and declare that he was weak and unskilful, Bennet—raised that year to the peerage as Arlington—was by far the better administrator of the two. The dispatches of the English ambassadors of the time ring with delight at the accession of a Minister who understood foreign languages and thought it worth while to answer letters. His diplomatic experience was far wider than the older man's, and, if he never understood the English people as well, he was less obstinate in a mistaken course.   And his personal devotion to his master's interests—marked by the famous black plaster, worn so proudly over the wound he had won in the royal cause twenty years before—was as devoted as Clarendon's. He had been in his youth a close personal friend of Charles, who never forgot an intimate affection of this kind, and this was gall and bitterness to the other, who never had been.[5]

As for Berkeley, the King really loved him.   Simple, unaffected and without ambition, he gained the respect of everyone save Clarendon.   Even Burnet records, across the mists of party passion, how generous he was, and believed that, had he outlived " the lewdness of that time," he would have initiated great and noble designs.   The stoic, William Coventry, remembered his goodness of nature, his desire of public good, and his low thoughts of his own wisdom; the gay Grammont his unfailing generosity to those in need. " Never," recorded the latter, " did disinterestedness so perfectly characterize the greatness of his soul; he had no views but what tended to the glory of his master; his credit was never employed but in advising him to reward services or confer favours on merit; so polished in his intercourse that the greater his power, the greater was his humility; and so sincere in all his proceedings that he would never have been taken for a courtier."*[6]

With spring, the King opened the season on the first Saturday in April by driving round the fashionable coaching-ring in Hyde Park, saluting at every turn the fair Castlemaine,

---

* See also the Duke of York's glowing description of his generosity and utter neglect of his own interests to serve his master's.   " He was of so generous a nature that when any project of advantage to himself had been brought to him, and he had obtained the King's promise of a grant of them, if some old suffering Cavalier happened at the same time to put in for them, he released the King of his promise to himself and got them given to the others, saying that for him, sooner or later, the King would provide." (Clarke, *James II*, I, 397.)

and enchanting the staring crowd. A fortnight later he was at the wedding of his boy James, now Duke of Monmouth, and betrothed to the child heiress of the great house of Buccleuch. He wrote to Minette to tell her how he was about to sup and dance with the young people, and see them to bed, where, however, he added, the ceremony should stop. So great was his love of this son, that some supposed he would settle his brother's future crown on him.[7]

To the Queen, the sight of that handsome, active boy, though she could not help liking him, was not a little bitter. Seeing how passionately her husband loved children, she longed to bind him to her by giving him an heir. As far back as the previous November she had had fainting fits, which had caused the ladies about her to become very significant and Charles very kind. With spring hopes were again rising; she spoke of visiting Tunbridge Wells to help forward the work. Her spirits improved, she became another woman, grew brisk and played as other ladies; and Charles told Minette how often she called him away to dance.[8]

She still had her trials. Castlemaine had lodgings in the Palace and the King continued to sup there nightly. Yet it was not altogether for the sake of Barbara that he did so, for, if the French ambassador is to be believed, he told his hostess that unless her rival, pretty little Frances Stewart, was his fellow-guest, he would prefer to stay away. One of the most beautiful girls in the world and one of the most modest, he thought her; the King's heart was plainly touched. Yet, though others knew it not, the best of it still rested with his sister. " I hope you believe I love you as much as 'tis possible," he wrote her. " I am sure I would venture all I have in the world to serve you, for I have nothing so near my heart . . . as that tender passion I have for my dearest Minette."[9]

It was a busy summer for Charles. Public business poured in from every side. The French ambassador was trying to conclude an alliance between the two countries, much hampered by the Chancellor's gout and refusal to speak any language but his own. " We must have patience," wrote the former. " Men here scarcely know themselves; they have almost no form of government; the evils that they have suffered are yet so recent that all their efforts aim at preventing the return of the same. They are cold, slow, phlegmatic, motionless, frozen." The main business between the two nations was the defence of Portugal against the invading armies of Spain. Here a small English expeditionary force was struggling against overwhelming difficulties, not the least of which was the utter inability of the home Government to support it when the Portuguese Ministers left it to starve. " Alas," wrote Clarendon to the ambassador at Lisbon, " we have no money to send fleets or troops upon adventures, nor can anybody suppose that the burden of a war of Portugal can be sustained upon the weak shoulders of the Crown of England." It was commonly supposed that summer that the ruin of our little ally was certain. Yet the miracle, sometimes vouchsafed to a hungry English army, occurred. Before the end of June the boys were crying in the streets news of a great victory in Portugal, won with glorious resolution by a handful of Monk's old Redcoats.[10]

More urgent than any foreign affairs to the King, was the state of his own exchequer. He had hoped that by giving way to his faithful Commons on the question of religion, they might be prevailed upon to redeem their promise to settle an adequate revenue, or at least make provision for some of the debts. Unfortunately, they were in that angry, pettish mood often incident to public assemblies, and were more inclined to institute searching inquiries into maladministration of public funds than supply the money which alone could bring such maladministration to an end. Above all, they were filled with a sense of the extravagance of the Court.

One of their members endeavoured to prove that Charles had spent four millions since he came in, though where he had obtained it was not explained. It was not till the third week of June that they could be persuaded by the royal oratory* to vote four not very generous subsidies.[11]

So situated, Charles's only course was drastic economy. He gave orders that the cost of the Navy should be halved, his household reduced, and his family put to board wages. There was much murmuring at this, but it was hoped that when the Court returned from the autumn vacation, the new frugality would be regarded as a *fait accompli*.[12]

The troubled state of affairs in Scotland and Ireland claimed much of the King's time that summer. From the former, where Lauderdale was bringing to an end a bad and unpopular military system, came ceaseless and lengthy dispatches. The King read them all, leaving, as Robert Moray recorded, everything to do so, except it were his dinner; he remarked, as he eyed one of them, that if Lauderdale would not write with better pens, he would have Scotland billeted again. From Ireland, where Ormonde was grappling with the overwhelming task of settling a country of which every acre of ground was being fought for by at least three different claimants, came reports as ceaseless. It is only when the miscellany of the King's business is added together—the Council meetings, the dispatches from every quarter with his marginal notes upon them, the perpetual interviews granted to ambassadors, Ministers and suitors of every kind—that the full magnitude of his share in turning the wheels of that over-centralized administration becomes

---

* " Let me and you think never so well of ourselves, if all the world knows or believes that we are poor . . . if our friends think we can do them no good, or our enemies believe we can do them no harm, our condition is far from being prosperous. . . . If you do not give me some present supply of money to enable me to struggle with those difficulties I am pressed with, I shall have a very melancholy summer." (King's Speech, 12 June, '63, *Parl. Hist.*, IV, 267.)

L*

apparent. When the ingenious Samuel Morland had perfected a secret method of opening and resealing letters, it was the King himself who, slipping away from a sleeping palace in a private gentleman's coach, spent three midnight hours at the General Post Office testing the process. A clerk of his Council recorded that, though Charles suffered from his father's fault of being diffident of his own judgment, nobody understood business better than he; and a Minister of State declared that, only when the King was present at every Committee, could anything ever be done.[13]

Many men would have allowed themselves to sink under such a burden. Not so Charles. His very interviews he turned to pastime. Pepys saw him, obviously enjoying himself, in argument with a pretty Quakeress, telling her that if her desires were as long as the petition she carried, she might not obtain them. He would rise at five and be found later eating cherries at Woolwich, or read dispatches booted and spurred, and then vanish for a whole June day to hunt the deer in Epping Forest.[14]

Parliamentary session and London season closed that July with a glorious farrago. For some time men had spoken of Clarendon as lost, and his old rival, Bristol, determined to test the matter. Despite a warning from Charles, he suddenly impeached him in a meteoric speech in the Lords on a wildly libellous charge of treason, as damaging to the King as to his Minister. In a subsequent and highly theatrical interview with his sovereign, Bristol all but committed violence in his presence. When the judges had declared that the articles did not constitute treason and he persisted in his disturbing behaviour, a warrant was issued for his arrest. But as there was no police force and, as Clarendon was highly unpopular, Bristol remained at large. The whole episode amazed the French ambassador, accustomed to more seemly ways of government. " Here we have a regular suit," he wrote to his master, " between a private person and the Chancellor, this last having his high rank, his past services, the goodwill of the King and of all the Court; but the other walks about the town as if nothing were the matter. . . . I confess that I am at my wits' end and that it seems to me as if I were transported beyond the spheres of the moon. . . . May God spare your Majesty such subjects and such a lack of power! " he added.[15]

The Queen was now in a state of high elation, for the promised visit to the Wells was drawing near. On July 13th Pepys saw her riding hand in hand with the King in the park, in a white-laced waistcoat, crimson short petticoat and hair *à la negligence*; Castlemaine, following with the Maids of Honour, looked out of humour. Afterwards he watched them in the Presence Chamber, talking and laughing, and fiddling with one another's hats, and little Frances Stewart merriest of all, " with her cocked hat and a red plume, with her sweet eye, little Roman nose and excellent *taille*." A day or two later poor Barbara called for her coach and drove off at a quarter of an hour's warning to her uncle's house at Richmond. But the kindly King followed her there, under pretence of going hunting, and dried her tears.[16]

On July 23rd Charles escorted Catherine to Tunbridge, leaving her in tears three days later to return to pass the usual batch of Bills and prorogue the House. The same night he posted back to her, again returning to London on the 29th to settle some urgent Irish business and thence back to the Wells by August 1st. " One of the greatest towns in the world is now turned into a solitude," wrote one left behind; " neither ladies nor courtiers are to be seen there; the gentlemen, without any compassion for those who stay, have taken their wives with them." The silly season had begun. At Harwich a strange, dreadful fish appeared off the hoy, with long grey whiskers, looking " exceeding gasfully."

At Tunbridge Charles found his wife grown very debonaire—" now hugs and meets him galloping up the road, and all the actions of a fond and pleasant lady that can be! " —the Court of England was better fun than a convent, after all. For the rest the waters—*les eaux de scandale*—ruined what was left of the fair fame of the maids and ladies, nor did the Queen show any certain signs of producing the promised heir. At first hopes had been high, but it proved to be no more than the effects of the waters, which were *si vitriolées.*[17]

On August 11th Charles was called back to London for further business, fetching his wife a few days later, preparatory to a visit to Bath. Nothing, a foreign ambassador reported, would be left unattempted to give an heir to the English Crown. Before the end of the month, in depressingly cold weather, the royal party set off down the western road, spending a night at a country squire's on the way and receiving a variety of feasts, presentation purses and mayoral addresses. At Bath the weather was so bad that it was ten days before the Queen could take the waters, entering them in stately privacy with her husband and " sweating vastly." They solaced themselves by paying visits to neighbouring country houses and once to Bristol, where the King, by a generous burst of knighting, aroused terrific struggles for precedence among the merchant princes. Even here Charles was pursued by business. Robert Moray, bearing a sheaf of Scotch dispatches, found him one morning waiting in his wife's bedchamber till her mass was done and she could start for Longleat, where they were to dine; he had scarcely read one when the Queen appeared and carried him off. No sooner was he back from the day's expedition—so rough a one, with the frights of the coach overturning in the country lanes, that Catherine declared she would never more venture out in such a mountainous country—than Moray was at him again with his dispatches, and so he settled down to read them, while he changed his clothes and had his hair combed.[18]

At the end of September King and Queen were due at Oxford. Charles wrote to Clarendon, who was pressing the decorous hospitality of his country home: " My wife and I intend to dine with you at Cornbury the day we come to Oxford, which I think sufficient trouble for you; it would have been impossible for us to have lain there with half the women we have, for you know the baggage and baggages of an army are the troublesomest part of it." Travelling by Badminton, Cirencester and Cornbury, they reached the University town on September 25th. Here they spent an edifying week of orations, Latin plays and sermons, returning on October 1st to town. Castlemaine was so delighted to see Charles again that she declared—when the cook announced that the Thames had got into her kitchen—that she should burn the house down if needs be to roast his supper.[19]

Scarcely was the King home, but his Government was vouchsafed its annual alarm. This time it was Yorkshire that provided armed Quakers riding through the night and preachers " blowing the bellows of rebellion among the ignorant." The insurrection, which broke out at Farnley Wood near Leeds, was quickly suppressed by the local gentry, and the King refused to press home the trials of the conspirators too vigorously.* But the country as a whole was still highly inflammable; the French ambassador reported that it was so gnawed by false religions that nothing but a miracle could save it. " We are in the land of prophets," he wrote, " we have here a new Jeremiah who speaks only of fires and flames; another asserts that he has had a vision in which God

* Yet Charles was fully aware of the reviving strength of the opposition to monarchy, speaking in the Privy Chamber a few weeks later of a political libel " so pernicious as it were almost fit to be dispersed to let the people see the desperate spirits of the contrivers, who not only seek to overthrow him but all Government whatsoever." (R. Southwell to Sir G. Lane, 23 Feb., '64, *Carte MSS.* 33, f. 324.)

has declared to him the day and place of judgment. This one has accepted six Jacobuses to go and disclose his revelations outside London." The art of prophecy, he concluded, was both paying and simple, and consisted in running about the streets, making grimaces, raising the eyes to heaven, and being very dirty.[20]

But Charles had more urgent worries of his own. Early in October the Queen fell dangerously ill. The King, who had been intending a visit to Newmarket, remained by her bed in a deep melancholy. After her Portuguese priests had kept her from sleep for two nights, he put his foot down. His firmness saved her life. By the 21st there was a marked improvement, and Charles, thinking the worst was over, took a few hours' rest and supped with Barbara. But next day Catherine's fever was worse and her life again despaired of; he knelt beside her, and begged her to live for his sake, and she, weeping to see him cry, did so. When her almoner told her she owed her life to a cap of precious relics, she whispered no—to her husband's prayers.[21]

She mended slowly: a week later she was still delirious, babbling that she had been brought to bed at last but lamenting that it was but an ugly boy. Charles assured her that it was a very pretty one, and she was comforted, and when she woke next morning she believed that she had three fine boys and a girl. At the end of the month she was out of danger, and the King in such good humour that when he met three of his Admiralty officials in the Matted Gallery, he called out: *Here is the Navy Office!* and made them walk up and down it twenty times, talking merrily. But his hair, one of them noticed, had gone mightily grey. "My wife is now out of all danger though very weak," he told his sister; "it was a very strange fever, for she talked idly four or five days after the fever had left her." Three weeks later Catherine was still too weak to stand, but her recovery was past all doubt, and Charles, in the chapel at Whitehall, while his choir sang the anthem, contentedly beat time with his hand.[22]

By the beginning of December Charles could tell Minette that Catherine had watched a ball the night before in the Privy Chamber, where there were enough pretty faces to have done credit to Paris itself, and begged her to buy some images to put in her Prayer Book. Her illness had made her still more religious than before. It did not seem greatly to have changed her husband, for when, that Christmas, Castlemaine announced her conversion to Rome and her agitated relations begged him to intervene, he replied that, as for the *souls* of the ladies, he never meddled *there*.[23]

Whitehall was now itself again. Charles's attempt to reduce his household had proved a failure, for the family, knowing how easy it was to touch its master's heart, had set up such a howl that there was no doing anything. Pretty Catherine Boynton bewailed about the stay of her pension and the loyal debts of her dead father; George Kirk clamoured for the continuance of the grant given him by the late King; and before long Charles was flooding a tearful Treasurer with orders to forbear this or that cut, since it would inflict hardship on some servant. He was not of the stuff of which economists are made.[24]

Even the scandals began again. This time it was Frances Stewart—and in this event, at any rate, better and direct evidence proves the gossips liars, for the lady's virtue was king-proof. Yet there was no doubt that Charles's heart was stirred, deeply; his doctors thought he was falling into a consumption. He even wrote a song to express his passion:

" I pass all my hours in a shady old grove,
　But I live not the day when I see not my love;
　I survey every walk now my Phillis is gone,
　And sigh when I think we were there all alone;
　　O then, 'tis O then, that I think there's no hell
　　Like loving, like loving too well.

While alone to myself I repeat all her charms,
She I love may be locked in another man's arms,
She may laugh at my cares and so false she may be
To say all the kind things she before said to me:
    O then, 'tis O then, that I think there's no hell
    Like loving too well.

But when I consider the truth of her heart,
Such an innocent passion, so kind without art;
I fear I have wronged her, and hope she may be
So full of true love to be jealous of me;
    And then 'tis, I think, that no joys be above
    The pleasures of love."

He made his engraver stamp her, with trident and helmet, a
little inviolate Britannia to watch over his coinage, and went
abroad with his wife. " I have been all this afternoon playing the good husband," he told Minette, " and 'tis now past
twelve o'clock. And so good night, for I am fast asleep."[25]

CHAPTER VI

SWORD, PESTILENCE AND FIRE

" Shipping and sea affairs . . . seemed to be so much his talent,
both for knowledge as well as inclination, that a war of that kind
was rather an entertainment than any disturbance to his thoughts.
. . .'Tis certain no prince was ever more fitted by nature for his
country's interest than he was in all his maritime inclinations."

—BUCKINGHAM.

IF Charles was master of soft pleasures, he was also King of
England and therefore sovereign of the sea.   Ever since he
had first felt the throb of the tiller as a boy, he had loved her,
and now his Ministers noted that twenty leagues by water
were pleasanter to him than two by land.   His pride was in
the gilded ships that swung with the tides at Spithead and
the Nore; the symbol of his power their brass guns.   By the
ancient law of Admiralty, all ships that saw his flag in the
narrow seas must dip their pennants in homage, and never did
English King insist more steadfastly on this scarce-won right.
" I extremely wonder," he wrote, when a proud French
monarch dared challenge it, " at that which you write me of,
for certainly never any ships refused to strike their pavilions
when they met any ship belonging to the Crown of England.
. . . Therefore all I say to you is that my ships must do their
duties, let what will come of it."[1]

These punctilios were the outward signs of a never-
ceasing warfare which his subjects waged for the commerce
of the world.   On every sea—by fog-bound, frozen Lab-

rador, coasting the Gambia mud-flats, battling the monsoons of Malabar—sailed the English merchant adventurers. The sugars and spices they passed through the Customs were the means by which the State was supported.

Wherever Englishmen were free to sail, sailed also their Dutch rivals. Arrogant and capable, the hated *butterboxes* took toll of all the world. To the merchant princes of the republic in their palaces at Amsterdam, sea commerce was life itself—the spirit that moved alike the brush of Rembrandt and the vast arm of the Dutch sailor as he raised his dram of brandy. They could not but hate the English who dared wrest it from them. Though peace might keep the seamen of the two nations from each other's throats in home waters, beyond the line they waged ceaseless war.

Daily fights between Yarmouth and Enkhuizen fishermen over herring-shoals, English encroachments and Dutch cruelties amid the Moluccas, scrambles for slaves and gold on the burning marshes of West Africa, were the mile-stones that led to war. Angry lawyers and pamphleteers struggling for compensation for long-captured, never-forgotten ships, English revolutionaries lurking in Dutch republican towns, lecherous cartoons of Charles sniggered over in the print-shops of the Hague, did nothing to calm the air. By the spring of 1664 every Englishman who earned his living by the sea was clamouring for war.[2]

In April a Parliamentary Committee of Trade reported, *nemine contradicente*, that the wrongs suffered by English merchants at the hands of the Dutch were the ruin of trade. The Commons thereupon petitioned the King to demand redress from the United Provinces, and offered to stand by him with their lives and fortunes. Three days later the Clerk of the Acts was instructed to buy naval stores.[3]

Thus in the same month as they widened still further the divisions across English life by passing an Act against

Nonconformist Conventicles, the Commons, by raising the banner of a popular war, offered what seemed the surest means of uniting the nation.   Charles sent Downing to the Hague with the English demands, but checked the passion for immediate hostilities, telling Minette:

" The States keep a great bragging and noise, but I believe when it comes to it, they will look twice before they leap.   I never saw so great an appetite to a war as is in both this town and country. . . . But all this shall not govern me, for I will look merely to what is just and best for the honour and good of England, and will be very steady in what I resolve, and, if I be forced to a war, I shall be ready with as good ships and men as ever was seen and leave the success to God."

Meanwhile he was on the Thames almost daily to visit his fleet.   The weather was hot and dusty, so he flung aside his periwig at Tilbury and wrote to his sister when he got home that the wind had made his head ache.   But it was not the wind that was to blame, but fever; and it was a fortnight before he could tell her again that he was just come from seeing a play, and that it was almost midnight—" a fair hour for a sick man to think of going to bed, and so good night."[4]

All Autumn, while Charles was testing how much could be wrung from the United Provinces without war, minimizing differences in interesting conversations with Dutch diplomats, and telling Minette that she was an Exeter woman and must therefore use her good graces to keep France neutral, guns in far seas were going off of themselves.   Late in September came news that our ships in Guinea, carefully sent there by Charles, had beat the Dutch " out of their castles almost," " which," thought Pepys, " will make them quite mad."   The King thought so too, but wondered what on earth he should say to the Dutch ambassador.   " And pray what is Cape Verde? a stinking place ! " he asked that

indignant diplomat; " is this of such importance to make
so much fuss about? "   Before long it was worse.   " You
will have heard of our taking of New Amsterdam, which
lies just by New England," he wrote to his sister.   " 'Tis a
place of great importance to trade.   It did belong to England
heretofore, but the Dutch by degrees drove our people out
and built a very good town, but we have got the better of
it, and 'tis now called New York."[5]

That October, at the Lord Mayor's Banquet, the French
ambassador saw the King surrounded by his Ministers and
richest subjects, the plate of gold, the infinite cheer, the
shouting spectators, the trumpets and guns sounding at every
health.   At that moment a mighty and puissant nation, at
the height of its newly recovered wealth and splendour, was
moving confidently to war.   A few days before the wondering diplomat had heard Charles chaffing his old Cromwellian
sea-dogs at the Nore and seen the glory of his fleet.   He
had been deeply impressed and, thanks to a sudden squall
after a heavy dinner, very sick; at which the King, with a
twinkle in his eye, had invited him to return to London
by water.[6]

With the Duke of York hoisting his pennant aboard the
Royal Charles, and Admiral Teddiman jealously eyeing the
flags of Dutch merchantmen in the Channel, Parliament
listened hopefully to the King's opening speech in November.   " I have been able to let our neighbours see," he told
them, " that I can defend myself and my subjects against
their insolence. . . . By borrowing very liberally from myself
out of my own stores, and by the kind and cheerful assistance
the City of London hath given me, I have a fleet now at sea
worthy of the English nation and not inferior to any that
hath been set out in any age."   In gratitude, they voted him
two and a half millions—a sum such as he had never known
before.   But though he had no love for the " stinking

Dutch," and was full of pride in his fleet, he still held his people on the leash, hoping to bring the merchant princes of Amsterdam to terms. He was the only man in all his dominions, he told his sister, that did not desire war.[7]

Yet there was no avoiding it. The United Provinces were resolved not to yield a jot of their hard-won commercial sovereignty, cost what it might, and from every quarter came reports of angry British ships grappled in battle with blazing Dutchmen, and homecoming merchantmen brought captive into the English harbours, which lay so conveniently across the trade routes. " The truth is," Charles confessed, " hardly any escapes us that pass through the Channel : I believe that we have already taken above four score, and every day there comes in more. They brag very much that they will eat us up in the spring, and so they did some two months ago, but as yet we are all alive."[8]

A little tensely the nation awaited the coming of that spring and the breaking of the coldest winter in the memory of man. It was not quite certain of its strength now the Rubicon was crossed. But when three ambassadors from France, anxious for peace lest either of the sea rivals should, by destroying the other, obtain absolute mastery of the seas, landed at Dover, the country people on the road told them they might as well go home. And the tension broke into laughter when a ballad, written by one of Charles's courtiers with the Fleet, appeared :

" To all you ladies now at land
    We men at sea indite;
But first would have you understand
    How hard it is to write. . . .
Our paper, pen and ink and we
Roll up and down our ships at sea—
With a fal, la, la, la, la.

Should foggy Opdam chance to know
    Our sad and dismal story,
The Dutch should scorn so weak a foe
    And quit their fort at Goree :
For what resistance can they find
From men who've left their hearts behind? "

There was no reasoning such a nation out of its desires.
When little Courtin, the brain of the French delegation,
informed Charles that unless the war ceased, France would
be bound by her treaties to support the Dutch, he replied
that, though he had a fair respect for the French King, his
people had none. When Courtin continued to argue, the
King called to old St. Albans, who was listening behind
the door : " Do come; here is a little man I cannot convince
or silence," and slipped away to supper. A few days later
he was at Portsmouth inspecting his fleet.[9]

That spring, while Dutch capers and British colliers
chased each other and shots played among the white houses
of Whitby, the North Sea was cleared for as fierce a duel as
any in our history. For the Dutch were rivals worthy of
England : in wealth and ships they were unsurpassed, and
Albemarle, who knew them of old, predicted that they would
certainly fight. And fight they did. For while York and
the British Fleet, after a month off the Texel, lay refitting
in Solebay, and Charles at Whitehall obligingly promised to
help the lovesick Courtin to a lady's heart, Opdam put to
sea. On Friday, June 2nd, Commissioner Pepys, all fat and
lusty and ruddy from being in the sun, and rather out of
breath, broke into Castlemaine's lodgings, where King and
Court were supping, with the news that the Fleets were in
sight of each other.[10]

All next day Londoners could hear the guns. Then the
sound died away to the eastwards and for three days rumour
ran riot. But on Tuesday evening, just as a cool breeze
sprang up from the river, a messenger arrived with news of

an overwhelming victory. That night furniture hurled from windows lit scorching bonfires, the bells challenged sleep, and Albemarle was like a man out of himself with joy. Bab May, with dispatches from York, confirmed all next day: twenty Dutch line of battle sent to the bottom, Opdam blown to the darkened skies on his own flagship, ten thousand Dutch seamen drowned and slain. But in the gilded room beside the river, tears were running down Charles's face, for first among the names of the English dead was Berkeley's.*[11]

The victory amazed England: nothing quite like it had been known before. Few knew how ill equipped the country was for a war. The millions which had been voted by Parliament were, in reality, scarcely sufficient to support the peace establishment, and were as yet far from being in the Treasury coffers, and Charles had had to bear the cost of equipping the Fleet on his own shoulders. The credit of the administration was so weak that the City bankers refused to advance it money even at 10 per cent., and when Pepys— though the kind King stroked him on the head for his care —complained to the Council of the want of money for the Navy, the old Treasurer could only hold up his hands in despair and ask what could be done. The very postilions who rode before the King's coach were over three years in arrears of pay. At Portsmouth the ropemakers discharged themselves and tramped off into the fields to make hay.[12]

Yet a fiercer agony than this wasting consumption was in store for England. While the captured Dutch standards waved above the Tower, passers-by in Drury Lane saw red crosses on the doors. The plague had come to town. That burning June, while Charles visited the dying Puritan Admiral Lawson, or listened to Evelyn's account of the crowded naval hospitals, panic set in. By the 21st the roads were full of coaches and wagons for the country.[13]

* Before his death in action, Berkeley had been created Earl of Falmouth.

M

Though the plague was already at the Palace gates in King Street, Charles made no great hurry to be gone. He had already determined on a western progress, and accordingly dispatched the seraglio to Hampton Court, remaining behind himself to escort his mother, who was returning to France, to the Nore. Thence he proceeded on a visit to the Fleet at Portsmouth, returning in sweltering weather to Hampton Court for Council meetings at Sion, and a world of public business—the war, the French negotiations, treaties for a Spanish alliance, and the eternal problem of Ireland. On July 26th he went by river to pay a last visit to Greenwich, viewed his new buildings, inspected a ship, and made his company sit down with him to dinner. Pepys was given a lift home on the royal barge, and was much struck with young Monmouth, who was with his father—" a most skittish gallant, always in action, vaulting, leaping, or clambering." As they passed through the doomed city, the bells were everywhere tolling. But nobody took much account of the poor, for the plague was their almost exclusive prerogative. Next day Pepys, at Hampton Court, watched the royal party setting out for the west: it was pleasant, he thought, to see the young, pretty ladies, in their velvet coats and caps.[14]

After a detour to inspect the fortifications in the Isle of Wight, Charles rejoined his wife at Salisbury. Here he remained for a month, wearily pursuing business, coursing hares on the downs, or teasing the young ladies at their bowls on their love affairs and dreams.* When the plague came to Salisbury, and a house was shut up, he called up to the windows as he rode by to ask if all was well and promise help. By the end of the month he was ill himself; could not sleep, was out of humour, and weary of everything. He attributed

---

* Frances Stewart dreamt that she was unaccountably in bed with all three French ambassadors; on her confiding this to the King, he called the gallant Courtin to come and listen, upon which she blushingly added that she was on the side of M. de Verneuil, who happily was a bishop and nearly seventy. (*Jusserand*, 248.)

it to the damp of the Avon valley, and in September took a turn in South Dorset, visiting the home of his Minister, Lord Ashley, and the remote villages through which he had ridden a hunted fugitive fourteen years before.[15]

While King and cuirassiers trotted by sun-mellowed cottage and wooded combe, elsewhere men and women awaited the " great sweep of mortality " their God had sent them. In the alleys of London death reigned putrescent on his rat-haunted throne of baking brick and rubble; pale ghosts, muffled and crippled with sores, shunned one another in the streets; and night was a delirium of terror. In the country round the capital, corpses rotted in the fields, and armed men besieged the starving survivors in plague-haunted farms. Stout Albemarle and Craven, the Cavalier, remained in London, keeping their master's peace, and duly distributing such pittances as the charity of the rich could afford an unhappy people.[16]

Yet while a thousand died daily in London, and the plague crept into the Fleet, England fought on. Sandwich missed snapping a rich homecoming armada at Bergen; De Ruyter took the seas; a battered English fleet was back in Solebay to refit, and then—" God be praised "—out to sea again, bearing fire and sword to the Dutch coast towns. Thirty-five enemy ships were sunk and taken off the Wellbank, and the Admiralty officials at supper at Greenwich, forgetting plague and horrors, almost died with laughing as Evelyn, in the gaiety of the occasion, improvised comic verses.[17]

But though the honours of that year remained with the stricken English, and only a few sheep, raped from Margate meadows, with the Dutch, the victors were half broken. The Navy Office groaned under the horrible pressure and lamentable moan of poor starved seamen; fighting ships lay in the river unmanned and unequipped. When Parliament met the King at Oxford in October, the Commons, undaunted, and

M*

with an angry eye cocked at France, voted further supplies for war, with the whole world if need be. It availed the Government but little, for the plague had broken the back of the nation's trade, the Customs were wasting away, and the London chimney money brought in next to nothing. The French ambassadors, getting only silent answers to their suggestions for peace, packed up their trunks and made homewards, leaving the Commons debating a Cattle Act against the Irish and a Five Mile Act against Nonconformist ministers. Charles fought their mad mood as best he could, but was forced to yield.[18]

For him the year 1665 flickered out amid Oxford mists and meadows. The pestilence was creeping through village hovels westwards, but in Christ Church, where Mistress Stewart sang sweet French songs one after another for her sovereign's delight, the jovial crew danced continuously, and all the world was merry *à la mode*.

With the coming of 1666, the King returned to Hampton Court, and thence in a few days to Whitehall. " I have left my wife at Oxford," he told Minette, " but hope in a fortnight or three weeks to send for her to London, where already the plague is in effect nothing. But our women are afraid of the name of plague, so that they must have a little time to fancy all clear." Yet, though he made light of the pestilence, he was quick to express his sense of the courage and devotion of those who had faced its dangers. " Mr. Pepys," he said, " I do give you thanks for your good service all this year, and I assure you I am very sensible of it." When Evelyn waited on him with a report of his charge of the wounded, he ran towards him impulsively with outstretched hands.[19]

France, bound by an old treaty to the Dutch, declared war that January, the English taking up the gauntlet with the greatest cheerfulness. It was the worst mistake Louis ever made—" the good example of being a martyr to his word," commented Charles—for it roused racial hatreds in English hearts that nothing could appease.   Charles himself— though sorry to fall out with a people he admired, and possessing, like his Admiralty officials, misgivings as to the ability of his exchequer to sustain the war—took the double odds with calm.   As usual with him, what weighed most was the purely personal consideration that it must bring to an end his correspondence with his sister.   A little before he had written her after his easy fashion:

" I am very glad to hear that your indisposition is turned into a great belly.   I hope you will have better luck with it than the Duchess had here, who was brought to bed Monday last of a girl. One part I shall wish you . . . that you may have as easy a labour, for she dispatched her business in little more than an hour.   I am afraid your shape is not so advantageously made for that convenience as hers is; however, a boy will recompense two grunts more, and so good night, for fear I fall into natural philosophy before I think of it."

Now he had perforce to bid her good-bye.   " Nothing," he assured her, " can alter that passion and tenderness I have for you, which is so rooted in my heart as it will continue to the last moment of my life."   Careless, ever turning away from pain, unthinking, he was none the less speaking the truth.[20]

With the coming of spring England found herself faced by the combined navies of Holland and France.   In this emergency, her admirals made the fatal mistake of dividing the Fleet, Rupert being detached with thirty sail to watch the French in the Channel, while Albemarle remained with the rest in the North Sea.   On June 1st, a famous day in the naval annals of England, Albemarle encountered the Dutch Fleet under De Ruyter, and with stoic courage gave battle, despite the advice of his captains.   Though this Homeric encounter was begun off the Dutch coast, the thunder of the guns could be heard in the Thames.   All next morning Charles paced up and down the park, torn between hope and fear; in the afternoon he rowed down to Greenwich to be nearer that never-ceasing sound.   It was not till the afternoon of June 4th, a Monday, that two officers, their faces blackened with tar and powder, arrived at the Navy Office, with news that Rupert had joined the fight.   Pepys hurried them to Whitehall, where the King, in the Vane Room, heard their story, afterwards emptying the gold from his pockets into their hands.   But at sea, for four blackened days and nights, the carnage continued.   On Wednesday, the 6th, the sound of the guns at last ceased, and then suddenly delirium came to London.   For a courier brought news that the Dutch Fleet was flying broken to its ports; the King, told in chapel, rose to stop the service, and in half an hour all the bells in the town were ringing.   Next day truth came with the official report; Albemarle, bent against wind and tide to give the Dutch their bellyful, had all but shattered England's Fleet in one of the hardest fought struggles of her history.   At that moment, ruin staring her in the face, her ships tattered and charred, and plague stalking her towns, England never wavered.   There came to the windows of the coach, in which Pepys and William Coventry were returning from the burial of Admiral Mings, a knot of rough seamen, with tears in their eyes, to beg a favour.   " We are here," they said, " a dozen of us that have long known and loved and served our dead commander, and have now done the last office of laying him in the ground. We should be glad we had another to offer after him and in revenge of him.   All we have is our lives; if you will please to get his Royal Highness to give us a fireship, here is a dozen of us, out of all which choose you one to be commander, and the rest of us, whoever he is, will serve him and, if possible, do that which shall show our memory of our dead commander and our revenge."   The request was granted.   While the King was working feverishly at Sheerness to refit the Fleet, England sprang to arms on the threat of a French invasion—" 30,000 mounsieurs, yet we fear them not!" Everywhere country gentry and yeomen turned out, confident in their ability to drive the regiment of Picardy into the sea; "we must rely," wrote the future Marquis of Halifax, "on the oak and courage of England to do our business!" Before the end of July the Fleet was once more at sea in search of the enemy, and the Court full of smiling faces. Then, on July 25th, while Charles and his brother stood tense on the leads of Whitehall, listening to that far sound, the seamen beat the Dutch into the Weelings. Three weeks later rough Robin Holmes, anticipating Zeebrugge by two and a half centuries, landed a thousand men at Schelling, burnt two towns, a hundred and fifty ships, and a million pounds of Dutch property.[21]

But the Dynasts had not yet finished their sport with England. On August 27th the Commissioners for repairing old St. Paul's listened to Christopher Wren's plans for a new form of church building not yet known in England, to be crowned with a noble cupola. Their conservative hearts, staunch for restoration according to the old pattern, revolted, and they adjourned to consider the matter.[22]

On the morning of September 2nd Pepys arrived at White-hall with the news that a fire, broken out the previous night in Pudding Lane, was being driven at great speed by a hot, easterly gale into the city. The King, much troubled, ordered him to return and command the Lord Mayor to pull down all houses in its path. But the citizens were too busy removing their goods, and the Mayor could do nothing but wring his hands. In the evening Charles himself came down the crowded river, passing Worcester House where Clarendon's endless belongings were being rocketed into the lighters below, to inspect the situation. As it grew dark, the fire took on "a most horrid, malicious and bloody aspect," stretching in a mile long arch across the sky.

Tuesday saw it more terrible than ever, when its flames

flashed up the mighty height of St. Paul's and the great roof poured a molten torrent into the aisle below. Charles, realizing that nothing could be hoped from the City fathers, took control himself, called out the trained bands, and gave battle in defence of his people. All that day he was King of England, riding up and down the line of his workmen with a bag of guineas at his side, commanding, threatening, rewarding, sometimes dismounting at the fiercest points to pass the buckets with his own hands, or standing, ankle deep in water, amid sparks and falling masonry, to see his orders for blowing up houses carried out. It was not till early on Thursday morning that the fire, defeated at last, fell back. " All that is left of city and suburbs," wrote a subject, " is acknowledged to be wholly due to the King and the Duke of York."[23]

But the best part of the proud city, that had housed a tenth of the kingdom and more than half its wealth, lay a mass of blackened stones, so that a northerner, looking towards the Thames from the spot where Cheapside had once stood, was reminded of his own fells; at Kensington, four miles out, the gardens were covered with the ashes of paper and plaster blown there by the wind. The King himself rode up and down Moorfields, quieting the fears of the poor fugitives who huddled there and giving orders that they should be fed by his officers.[24]

Almost before the flames were out, Charles was considering plans for rebuilding. The first ideal, formed by his surveyor, Wren, of a completely new city proved impracticable, partly because the citizens were too eager to build at once, but still more because the masses of masonry left standing necessitated a close following of the lines of the old town. Yet in one respect the new London that arose at the King's bidding was immeasurably the superior of its predecessor. The regulations, which he supervised with such attention at the Council table, were strictly enforced; the new houses were of neat brick or stone, grouped in uniform and well proportioned types; they were fewer, better spaced and consequently healthier. That they were adorned by the crowning glory of Wren's churches was good fortune, but that eighteenth-century London arose in the form it did was largely the work of Charles. In our homelier northern medium, like Augustus, he found his capital built of earth and left it of marble.[25]

The country put a bold face on this new disaster, spoke of revenging it upon the Dutch, who, with French Papists, were suspected of having caused the disaster, and resolved never to submit to a base peace. At Whitehall defiance was even flung at French fashions—a gesture also directed towards giving work to London clothiers. In October the whole Court turned out at Charles's bidding in long black vests with white underskirts of a Persian design. Evelyn thought them a comely and manly habit, too good to hold, but Charles himself admitted, a little ruefully—on seeing the result—that he and his courtiers looked rather like magpies. A month later came news that Louis had retaliated by putting his servants into the same quaint garb—such an affront, thought Pepys, as never before had been put by one Christian monarch on another.[26]

Yet for all its brave show, the nation's nerve was shattered. The whole country dissolved in panic at the thought of fire-balls, massacres and Papist armies under furse bushes; frightened Members of Parliament produced mysterious daggers, and at Berwick the very sentries saw " the likeness of abundance of ships in the air." Indeed the fire had much the same effect on the popular mind and politics of the last half of the seventeenth century as the Gunpowder Plot on those of the first. All the old rumours against the Catholics and their friend, the King, revived; even his efforts at the fire were

turned to slander: he had come there, it was said, to exult
over the doom of the city which had slain his father.
Prophets, predicting further divine judgments, appeared;
shrill voices were heard speaking out of the clouds that
worse was to come; everywhere sinister republican figures
began to stir.   In Scotland there was open insurrection.   As
for the war, with ruin universal, prices rising—coals were selling at £30 a chaldron that December—and crowds fighting the
press gang, all heart was out of it.   " The true English valour
we talk of," wrote Pepys, " is almost worn out."[27]

Faced with such a situation, the Government opened
negotiations for peace.   The chief hope was a secret agreement with France, and Charles was writing to Minette again
in October, telling her: " As I do not think this to be an
eternal war, I should be very glad that you should have part
in . . . the ending of it."   Old St. Albans was employed
as mediator, and by April, 1667, Charles and Louis were in
secret agreement as to the terms on which the peace conference, which assembled in May at Breda, was to be concluded.
" I look upon the peace as made," St. Albans reported.*[28]

Meanwhile the financial plight of the Government made
that peace imperative.   When the alarmed Commons had
met after the fire, the King had once more pointed out the
urgent need for money; how much and how it was to be
raised, he left to them.   They voted £1,800,000, a great sum,
as an Admiralty official said, were it not for the existing
debts which swallowed more than all of it, nor, in the ruined
state of the country, did there seem much chance of being
able to collect it.   Creditors of every kind, from hungry seamen to contractors, besieged the Admiralty; no one would
lend the Government a penny, and bankruptcy, long threat-

---

* " I wish," commented one shrewd observer, " my Lord St. Albans has not
been too sanguine and taken promises for performances." (Orrery to Ormonde,
21 June, '67, *Orrery*, II, 170.)

ened, stared it in the face.   During the previous summer,
Sir George Carteret, Treasurer of the Navy, had kept the
Fleet at sea mainly by pledging his own private credit—just
as a generation earlier he had saved the King from starvation
in Jersey.   Now he could go on no longer; on November 25th
he told Pepys there would be no money to equip a fleet next
year.   The Navy was over a million in debt, and the seamen
in open mutiny; in January the King had personally to
suppress a riot in the Strand, riding into the midst of
the shouting sailors to tell them that every care would be
taken for their payment but that, if they assembled in such
a manner again, it should be with the gallows; whereupon
the honest matelots, who knew how to respect pluck, gave
three cheers and dispersed.   In early February the inevitable
decision was made, and the Council—Charles, York, Rupert,
Albemarle, and the Archbishop alone weakly protesting—
determined not to equip the battle fleet but to rely on an
early peace and the harbour guns in case of accident.   The
alternative was bankruptcy.*[29]

The Dutch, uncrippled by such financial constipation, did
not lay up their fleet.   Peace they needed as much as the
English, but they believed that it could be obtained by a deed
more effective than all the talk at Breda.   While Charles and
York busied themselves in strengthening the fortifications of
the Medway and a slow paralysis crept over a weary and
dispirited nation, the Dutch put to sea.[30]

On June 7th they were off the Gunfleet, seventy strong,
and next day listeners at Bethnal Green could hear their
artillery.   The Militia turned out in thousands; Albemarle with
pistols breathed defiance from the Kentish shore, and all the
gay young Hectors from the Court posted Essexwards—Pepys

---

* The King's poverty was such that the unpaid Council clerks had perforce
to give up supplying paper for the table, and his stock of neckwear was reduced
to three linen bands. (*Pepys*, 22 April, 2 Sept., '67.)

thought to little purpose but to debauch the countrywomen thereabouts. Then was seen with what majesty England can fight without a navy. Silently and with a vast concourse on either shore, the Dutch passed up the Thames. On the night of June 10th, though their great admiral, De Ruyter, declared the attempt to be desperate, they stormed Sheerness. Next day, while the drums beat to arms in London, and the King called out the entire military force of the country, twenty Dutch ships glided up the Medway past the ammunitionless guardships, broke through the chain set to stop them as though it were string, and there, as Commissioner Pett with his models scuttled ashore, made fast to the English flagship. Then, with five of her companions blazing, and an impudent trumpeter on her quarterdeck sounding " Joan's Placket is torn," they withdrew with the *Royal Charles* towed behind them.[31]

In vain did Charles summon the Militia on Tower Hill to tell them that they should venture no farther than he would himself : in vain hasten from his silent Court to block the river by Barking creek with sunk merchantmen. With that shame in their hearts and the Dutch Fleet riding in triumph from the North Foreland to the buoy of the Nore—" as dreadful a spectacle as ever Englishmen saw, and a dishonour never to be wiped out "—the faith of his people was shaken to the core. While the King hurried to and fro, travelling by night for coolness, raising men and arming forts, a nation of moralists beheld in his misfortune the judgments of God on the follies and vices of his Court. The Quaker—naked but for a cloth " civilly tied about the privities to avoid scandal "—who ran through Westminster Hall with a dish of burning coals on his head crying *Repent*, seemed to their hurt and angry hearts to indict the cause of England's troubles. Yet in this case, had they but known it, a chartered accountant would have proved the better prophet.[32]

CHAPTER VII

" Never was such a Faith's Defender,
    He like a politick prince and pious,
    Gives liberty to conscience tender
    And doth to no religion tie us.
    Jews, Turks, Christians, Papists, he'll please us
    With Moses, Mahomet or Jesus."
                                    —ROCHESTER.

REVOLUTION was in the air.   On the north downs the
Presbyterian oligarchs, as of old, met in conclave at Lord
Northumberland's house, and in London the mob pulled up
the trees and smashed the windows of Clarendon's Piccadilly
palace.   Men feared a sack of the city, there was a run on
the Exchequer, and Pepys had his savings buried in the garden
at Brampton; there were rumours that the Government had
dispersed and the King secretly fled.[1]

   Amid this panic, Charles kept his head.   His people were
clamouring ominously for an immediate assembly of Parliament; and, deeming that while they were in such a mood it
would be madness to resist them, he overruled the protesting
Clarendon and called a meeting of the Houses for July.   It
was as though a great pressure of steam had been suddenly
loosed; angry and frightened men felt there was no longer
any need to act for themselves, for the magic word would set
all right.   " Great matters," wrote one, " is expected when
the Parliament sits; much wrong has been done; God Almighty
find out the authors and bring them to condign punishment! "[2]

   Though Charles knew when to give way, he did not mean

189

to yield an inch more than he need. When rumours were spread that he was about to use the new troops which he had raised for the defence of the kingdom to overthrow its liberties,* and he learnt that their instant dismissal would be demanded, he resolved, though he had every intention of disbanding, to prove that he was still master. Accordingly, when the Houses, after a preliminary adjournment, assembled on July 29th, he informed them that he had just concluded peace at Breda, and that, having given them one mark of his affection by summoning them in his need, he would now give them another by sending them home till October. As for the insinuation that he meant to rule by an army, he added, it was a lie, for he was too much an Englishman to wish to govern by anything but the law.[3]

But the national anger was far from allayed, as Charles knew, and in the three months remaining to him before Parliament met again, he had need to set his house in order. The people demanded a scapegoat; it was natural that they should turn to the head of the administration—the old, proud, pompous vizier, whose vast palace, still rising daily, contrasted so ill with their poverty and humiliation. To them he seemed an upstart, whose family had crept into every vantage post in the State—even into a royal bridal bed. " Here lies," they wrote when one of his sons died,

> " Tom Hyde :
> It's a pity that he died;
> We had rather
> It had been his father;
> Had it been his sister,
> We had not missed her;
> If the whole generation,
> It had been better for the nation."

* Pepys heard on July 7th that the Parliament were afraid that the King would " try for a general excise, raise a land army and keep them all down like slaves," and that Bab May had been heard to say that £300 per annum was enough for any country gentleman, " which makes them mad."

The Cavalier Parliament men, who would never forgive Clarendon for having stood between them and their lost estates; the Presbyterian lords who hated the Tudor administrative prerogative which he upheld; the younger and keener brains in the Council, like William Coventry and Arlington, who saw in him the barrier to all progress, were at one in loathing him; to say nothing of the "buffoons and ladies of pleasure," who hated him quite as cordially as he did them. He belonged to another age, which he tried to preserve too long, and the new age was resolved to shake him off. A great blow had already been given his prestige that summer by the death of the old Treasurer, Southampton; to Clarendon's anger the King had placed the vacant Treasury in commission with some younger administrators of the new school. His health had long been failing: Council meetings were held at his house, where he lay bedridden on a couch, and the King compelled to attend him there; and with age he had grown increasingly domineering, and too apt to suppose that none but he could ever be right. In his two latest tasks—the management of Parliament and the war—he had failed. For the last, though he shared the responsibility of laying up the Fleet with others, he was much to blame; he was never made to direct a war. As for Parliament, instead of being able to coax it to do whatever he liked—as he had promised the King —he had so alienated it, that not only was the administration kept perpetually short of money, but the members believed him to be plotting for the government of England by military force.[4]

For five years one thing alone had sustained him—his master's protection. The King, though many thought that he was weary of the old man—his heavy avuncular behaviour and his constant rebukes*—had visited him with every mark

* As a sample of Clarendon's frank tutorial style: "This debate is worth three dinners, and I beseech you be not weary of it, but attend with all patience," or, "Indeed you are to blame that you have not yet given your warrant; I pray do not defer it." (*Lister*, III, 491-2.)

of affection on his wife's death that summer, and even now, when the clamour for his removal was deafening, seemed as though prepared to maintain him for ever. Yet it was plain that Clarendon's continued tenure of office would render the Cavalier Parliament as unanimous against the Crown as its predecessor had been in 1640; nor could the Government, in its financial embarrassment, continue any longer without parliamentary aid. Short of establishing military rule, the only alternative to his dismissal was to dissolve the House of Commons and try a new one; and that, in the existing state of the country, would bring in the old republicans and open the floodgates of revolution. Pressed by William Coventry and Arlington, Charles yielded. Indeed, no other way remained open to him, either to save himself or Clarendon. He sent a kindly message to the old man by his son-in-law, York, to say that, as he had certain intelligence that he would be impeached in the next session, it would be better for his own safety and honour, as well as the Crown's, that he should resign the seals—adding that, in view of his ill-health and domestic loss, a retirement into private life might well be a relief. But Clarendon was not a statesman of the school who can find peace in retirement and a country life. In an angry interview with the King, he told him that he would never willingly surrender the seal, and that to throw over an old and faithful servant after thirty years could only discredit the Crown, and from thence passed on to refer to the royal association with Castlemaine, whom he supposed to be at the bottom of the trouble. After two hours Charles rose and left the room in silence. To those watching outside, the King's anger was apparent; and, as the old man passed sorrowfully through the garden, the lady ran out into her aviary in her smock and blessed herself at his going away.[5]

Even now the King, remembering Clarendon's long years of service, delayed. It was not till August 30th that he accepted the inevitable, and sent Secretary Morrice to take the seals from him. " I cannot but be of the opinion that . . . public affairs will be bettered by this change," Arlington told Ormonde. To the latter the King himself wrote a few weeks later to justify his action: " The truth is his behaviour and humour was grown so insupportable to myself and to all the world else, that I could not longer endure it; and it was impossible for me to live with it and do those things with the Parliament that must be done or the Government will be lost." It was a hard but, on the whole, just summary of the situation.[6]

Yet still the old man, whose weakness it was, as he himself confessed, that he was too proud of a good conscience, remained disconsolately in London. He was still there when Parliament met in October, proudly awaiting his accusers with the proofs of his innocence. Such a display of righteousness maddened them, and, within a fortnight, feeling, as one country squire put it, that it was " rash to show the teeth to so big a beast unless prepared to bite to the bone," the Commons impeached him of a long array of crimes.* A few weeks later, while the Houses were still disputing the impeachment, Evelyn found his old friend sitting in the garden of his new-built palace, sadly watching the gates setting up towards the fields to the north. Next day he heard that he had fled from England.[7]

The dismissal of the old pilot gave universal satisfaction. By this—combined with the disbanding of the troops, a proclamation for suppressing Popery, and the peace—Charles, with considerable tactical skill, had broken the back of a

* These, enumerated in *Lister*, III, 530, included peculation, alienating Crown lands, " snipping in public employments," raising " monuments of his greatness, while the kingdom groaned under his oppressions," insolence to the King, declaring the latter to be popishly affected, mismanaging the war, disparaging Parliament, advising government by an army, hindering the operation of the Act of Uniformity, and " that upon all occasions he discouraged the poor and suffering Royalists."

N

serious movement against the Crown.   In a brief speech at the
opening of Parliament he increased the new goodwill—
promising the Commons leave to call to account whom and
whatever they pleased.   They were so delighted that they
voted him thanks.[8]

One new right however, which a year before he had
skilfully evaded, Charles had to yield—a parliamentary commission to examine his accounts and officers.   It was
universally supposed that the latter had been guilty of grave
irregularities, and that the money, granted for the war, had
been misappropriated.   In this, however, Commons and
country were wrong.   Though little over four millions had
been voted by Parliament for a war, on which the Dutch had
spent three times as much,* Charles—by transferring to the
needs of the Navy money required for the ordinary peace
administration—had actually spent nearly six millions on it.
Yet the Commissioners—whether from misunderstanding of
the complicated accounts submitted by the departments, or
from mere factiousness—continued to convey to the country
an impression that vast sums had found their way into the
royal pocket, and that Charles was richer for the war, instead
of being, as was actually the case, another million or so nearer
bankruptcy than before.[9]

The King had hopes that, when he had thrown to his
Commons the things they hungered for, he would then be
able, as he put it, to take his measures with them and obtain
such a grant as could alone solve his difficulties.   But they
gave him nothing, occupying themselves with the more con-
genial tasks of passing an Act to banish Clarendon and baiting
the Admiralty officials.   Accordingly, in December, Charles
adjourned them till February, 1668, trusting that the intricate

* A fact of considerably more importance in fixing the responsibility for the
Medway disaster than Pepys's famous third-hand story of the royal moth-hunt. (See
Cal. Treas. Books, II, Intr.)

diplomatic somersault he was about to turn would put them into a more giving mood.[10]

The peace which England had concluded at Breda, though it had consolidated her colonial empire in the west by the cession of New Jersey, New York and Delaware, had brought little credit to the Government. It was now forgotten in the startling advance of the French armies across the Spanish Netherlands. The old balance of power between France and Spain broke suddenly, as the legions of the great captains drove towards Scheldt and Rhine. In sudden panic all Europe strove feverishly to find some stop to this flood-tide towards what seemed like to be " a universal monarchy."

Even the Grand Monarch was perturbed by the ease with which a rotting empire crumbled before his young power— or rather by the effect it had on the European mind. He therefore put forward peace terms which he felt might prove acceptable, but hinted therein at the possibility of withdrawing his Queen's former renunciation of her claim to the Spanish Crown. From a suggestion so momentous, sprang in one or two prophetic minds—the Austrian Lisola's, the English Temple's—the ideal of a great European league to crush the encroaching power of France—an ideal in due course to transform a slim young country page, then serving the Duke of York, into the greatest soldier of his time.[11]

It was natural in such a moment, when the rulers of Europe were regrouping themselves for a new age, that the support of England should become a matter of consequence. France, Spain and Holland were all anxious to secure her, though the price they were prepared to pay proved incommensurate with that which her King required. For Charles had learnt that wars were expensive, and henceforward he regarded continental commitments solely in the light of whether they could be made to pay. Europe to him was a

N*

meadow-land of milch cows. His urgent need for money at home made it needful for him from time to time to visit such pastures.

The abstract ideal of the balance of power, so dear to the grandiloquent Whig statesmen of the next century, made no appeal whatever to Charles's concrete and unjealous mind. Nor did he think it of any benefit to tie England indefinitely to any particular alliance; expediency, not principle, was the basis of his policy. Yet he was keenly alive to her commercial and maritime interests, and any threat of a rival power to dominate the Netherland ports alarmed him quickly. One nightmare in particular haunted him—that of an alliance between France and the Dutch to partition between them, without any compensation to England, the Spanish Netherlands and American Empire. That, at all costs, he was determined to prevent.*

Yet Charles was too much of a realist to suppose that anything worldly could not be made a subject of barter, and he was quite ready to allow France liberty to overrun the Netherlands, Spain, or any other country, provided that she yielded him certain safeguards in the shape of Flemish ports and compensating commercial advantages elsewhere, and, above all, that her encroachments were at the expense, not to the advantage, of Holland. His personal predilections were, for family and dynastic reasons, French, and accordingly he intimated that he was ready to accept Louis's overtures for English neutrality—or, better still, offer an active alliance against the hated Dutch—in return for a cash payment, a commercial treaty, a cession of ports in the Netherlands, and the lion's share of Spanish America. Not unnaturally, Louis felt that such a price was too high to pay for a bare neutrality,

---

* Some years later Charles summed up this view with the words: " France will have us or Holland always with them, and if we take them not, Holland will have them." (*Foreign Entry Book*, 177, 16 Sept., '72. See also *Thurloe*, VII, 915.)

and the proposal came to nothing. About the same time Spain also discovered that the price for which an English alliance could be bought—it included the coveted right of trade with South America—was too high.[12]

Unable to come to terms with either of the warring powers, Charles and Arlington—still faced by the nightmare of a Franco-Dutch partition of the Spanish Empire that would establish France without a rival on land and, far worse, Holland without one on sea—acted with startling decision. In the last weeks of 1667, the enthusiastic William Temple was dispatched to the Hague to sound De Witt as to the possibility of either an Anglo-Dutch alliance for the protection of Belgium or, alternatively, a league to enforce a Franco-Spanish peace. To render the Dutch republican rulers the more amenable, he was to hint at the possibility of England securing the Belgian ports through an alliance with France or Spain. Thus threatened, and alarmed as she was by the French victories, Holland accepted the second alternative. By January 13th a treaty was signed, binding England and Holland to secure peace between France and Spain, and if necessary to enforce it. It was typical of Charles that the agreement to compel Spain to accept an unpalatable treaty was made as gentle as possible. "For the indecency of the word" (force), he wrote, "I would willingly have it left out."

If the pacification of Europe at the peace of Aix-la-Chapelle that April—the desired fruit of this famous league, shortly afterwards, by the addition of Sweden, extended into the Triple Alliance—was in reality due to other causes, Charles had none the less secured a real diplomatic triumph. Apart from the minor achievement of fulfilling his nuptial obligation of securing a Spanish recognition of Portuguese independence, he had proved to Louis and the rest of Europe that English friendship was worth paying for, and had rehabilitated his

honour in the eye of his own subjects. " God be thanked,
it is done," wrote Arlington, " and that both the world abroad
and at home understand it to be both honourable and safe for
his Majesty and foretell we shall find the Parliament much
better complexioned for it."[13]

With the majority of the English people, the new alliance
could not but be popular, for not only did it help to appease
their growing hatred and fear of France, but it suggested,
in the spectacle of their King heading a league of Protestant
states to intimidate two great Catholic powers, a most agree-
able reformation in his heart. In this they were wrong, but
a belief in a royal leaning towards advanced Protestantism
was enhanced that winter by a marked slackening of the laws
against Nonconformists, and even by overtures made to their
leaders for comprehension within the Church. In reality
Charles, freed from Clarendon's monotonous Anglicanism,
was merely displaying his grandfather's propensity for achiev-
ing national unity on a secular basis. In this he was much
encouraged by the Duke of Buckingham, who now with
Arlington shared his inner councils, and who, so far as he
had any religion at all, leant towards the Puritan sects,
possibly—for there appeared no other reason—because they
might require a new Protector, and his furious vanity made
him desire such a post.[14]

But Charles's moderation, much as it delighted the saints,
was far from pleasing to his faithful Commons. When they
met on February 10th, before the King even arrived, they
carried a vote for enforcing the Act of Uniformity.* Therefore, though they welcomed the announcement of his
diplomatic achievement, his plea for steps to bring about a

---

* " The comprehensive Bill hath made almost a great uproar among us; and
the honest old gentry of England are so much the Church's sons still that,
hitherto, notwithstanding all the vigorous and powerful prosecution thereof, they
have been able to suppress it." (Letter to Duchess of Ormonde, 21 April, '68,
Orrery, II, 350.)

better understanding among his Protestant subjects fell upon deaf ears. So also did his familiar entreaty for an adequate grant of money. It is true that in the face of his obvious necessities, they voted him £300,000, but so small a grant was of little avail to stave off his ever-nearing bankruptcy. Meanwhile they returned to their attack on the Admiralty officials, though here on March 5th they met their match, for Commissioner Pepys, having received the royal permission to plead lack of money in his defence, and being well fortified by a dram of brandy and mulled sack, made at their Bar such a two hours' speech as completely confounded all their elaborate and ill-informed accusations. After this intellectual treat, they proceeded in a body to Whitehall to request the King, who was writing at the time to Minette, to enforce the laws against Nonconformists. As usual, he promised to oblige them. He derived, however, some consolation from the thought of their discomfiture by his admirable official, for, when someone in Council expressed a fear that the Commons would vote the recruitment of sailors a miscarriage, he replied cheerfully: " Why, 'tis then but Mr. Pepys making of another speech to them! " And how he laughed, leaning out of his window over the river, when Pepys, taking boat, called out that he was going " to wait on our masters at Westminster! " The latter, after much boggling about raising the money they had voted, concluded a factious session by an apparently endless and unseemly quarrel with the Lords over their privileges concerning an unfortunate litigant called Skinner. After that there was nothing for it but to adjourn them till August, which Charles did, to everyone's relief, on May 8th. He was just too late to save one of their victims, Admiral Teddiman, who died three days later—" very ill of a fever and a double thrush by the fright they had put him into." The last observation of this poor old tar was that he had a very good King, God bless

him, but that the Parliament had very ill rewarded him
for all the service he had endeavoured to do them and his
country.[15]

From the contemplation of an imbroglio of squabbling
politicians, it was a relief to Charles to turn to the more
intimate pleasures of his palace.   Early that year he had made
an addition to his seraglio.   A revival of Fletcher's *Two
Noble Kinsmen* had introduced to his indulgent eye the
person of a charming little actress, Moll Davis, who had
enchanted the audience with her melting rendering of a song
that began:

> " My lodging it is on the cold ground,
>   And very hard is my fare,
>   But that which troubles me most is
>   The unkindness of my dear."

Thereafter her lodging was in a far better place.   As she was
a sweet singer and the loveliest dancer in the world—" all
air or else all flame and spright "—she proved a great source
of pleasure to Charles, though at times rather less so to the
Queen.*   But the latter's love for her husband was now too
deep for jealousy; once visiting him in the morning and
talking with him, she noticed a tiny slipper beside the bed,
and laughingly withdrew lest " the pretty little fool " in
hiding behind the curtains should catch cold.   About this
time also the royal supper-parties began to be graced by the
irresistible figure and gaiety of a little Cockney comedienne,
whom all London called affectionately Nelly.   To Charles
her wild humour and mocking wit proved a constant diver-

---

* Yet, though an unfaithful husband, Charles was not an inconsiderate one.
" The other night," wrote a courtier in January, 1667, " the Queen fell sick when
the King was in bed with her.   He did rise in his shirt to fetch her a basin, but
before he came with it she laid up all in the sheets, and then he put on his gown
and slippers and fetched a towel and dried the sheets clean about her and laid her
on his clean side and then called her women and went to his own chamber, but
came three times, before he would go to sleep, to see her."   (*House of Lyme*, 240-1.)

sion.   Yet two years passed before she first bore him a son
or withdrew from the stage which her genius lighted.[16]

Of older loves, Frances Stewart had been absent from the
Court for a year, leaving it after a runaway money match
with the Duke of Richmond—a heavy, drunken, stupid
cousin who was Charles's pet aversion.   The circumstances
of her departure had been so distressing and insulting to him
that for a time he refused to see her again.   But in the spring
of 1668 she fell ill of small-pox, that fatal foe to woman's
beauty, and one whom he described as " a little fantastical
gentleman called Cupid," drew him back to visit her.   " I
must confess," he told Minette, " this last affliction made me
pardon all that is past; I cannot hinder myself from wishing
her very well."   That May his subjects were whispering that
their sovereign had been seen one evening sculling himself
alone down the Thames to Richmond House, where his
charmer lay, and thence, finding the door locked, dis-
appearing over the garden wall—a " horrid shame," thought
Pepys.[17]

As for Castlemaine, her day was over.   She consoled herself with little Jermyn, though the King recommended her
to bestow her favours upon Jacob Hall, the rope-dancer, as
one better able to return them.   Yet, though Charles might
weary of his lights o' love, he never abandoned them; indeed,
they grew more expensive with the years.   At this time, when
his old association with Barbara finally ceased, he borrowed
a large sum of money from a City banker to buy her Berkshire
House.[18]

Dearer than these kaleidoscopic ladies, there remained his
sister.   It was more than seven years since he had seen her,
yet still he wrote constantly to assure her of " that which
I can never tell you too often, how truly and passionately I
love my dearest Minette," or to inquire anxiously of her
health : " For God's sake have a care of your diet, and believe

the plainer it is the better health you will have; above all have
a care of strong broths and gravy in the morning." Ill-treated
by a half impotent, jealous and vicious husband, Minette's life
had resolved itself into one great hope—her brother's ultimate
welfare.*   At this moment when his own embarrassments
were so great, it seemed as though a vista opened before her
for its achievement.[19]

It was the summer of 1668, when the Jansenists acknowledged the supremacy of Rome, when the eloquent Bossuet
brought back Turenne to the ancient fold, and when, throughout Europe, the flood-tide of Roman culture was at its height.
She—whom her mother had made, alone among her children,
a Catholic—longed to see her brother safe in that harbour, in
which her own frail soul rode out the gales of existence.
Might it not be that God had set her apart—she, the careless, the lover of laughter and dancing—to win back the souls
of the lost, heretic people of whose royal house she came?
All her life she had passed far from them in a land where
the King but spoke and subjects obeyed: might not the
union of these two, her royal brother, and more royal brother-
in-law, bring to each incalculable benefits—sovereignty and
peace to Charles, conquests to Louis, Europe to the Lilies and
the New World to England?   Might not the true faith—
the ancient beacon from which God gave forth his light to
men—be the means by which this vision should be achieved?[20]

With all a woman's cunning and patience, and with
infinite love, she wove her web.   Once more she persuaded
Louis of the importance of winning England's friendship,
lest the growing jealousy of France should leave him without
an ally in Europe.   Charles, who had never quite given up
hope of a French alliance, and was finding that any league
with the anti-French forces in Europe must prove a drain,

* " She is truly and passionately concerned for the King, her brother."
(Montagu to Arlington, 6 Sept., '69, *H.M.C. Buccleuch (M.H.)*, I, 437.)

not an aid, to his strained financial resources, gladly received her overtures. In May he told Ambassador Ruvigny that he would willingly make a treaty with his master as " between gentleman and gentleman." But he added, since all his subjects, on whose goodwill he depended for money, were of a very different way of thinking, he must be assisted. Already he saw the possibility of outside relief from that hopeless financial and religious siege in which the parsimony and intolerance of his Commons imprisoned him.[21]

All through the year 1668, Charles was negotiating with Minette and Louis for a " stricter friendship " with France. In this he was alone. Suggestions that he might be swayed, either by his Ministers or his mistresses, he particularly resented. " One thing," he told Minette, " I desire you to take as much as you can out of the King of France's head that my Ministers are anything but what I will have them, and that they have no partiality but to my interest and the good of England. If they take any other measures than that," he added a little later, " they will see themselves mistaken in the end." Only to one of his Ministers, the faithful Arlington, did he at first venture to reveal anything of the *grand design*, which was being formed in his mind.[22]

It was indeed not the divergent interests and personalities of his Ministers that proved the difficulty: Charles knew how to fool them, to the top of their bent. The first obstacle was France's new commercial and maritime policy: a matter so important that he refused to proceed unless given security on this point, writing: " The thing, which is nearest the heart of this nation, is trade and all that belongs to it." The other were his commitments under the Triple Alliance, " which I am sure," he told Minette, " the King, my brother, would not have me violate upon any terms. . . . But," he added, " when I have said this, I do believe we are not so tied, that, if we received satisfaction on the principal matter of the sea, there is scope sufficient for a very near alliance."[23]

To square all these difficulties was Minette's task. Events in England were all conspiring to bring about the fulfilment of her wishes. Parliament remained prorogued, while Charles's advisers, both in England and Scotland, attempted to carry out the one policy on which they were in agreement, and one (however much Commons and Anglican Bishops might loathe it) which the state of public feeling made advisable—an extension of religious liberty to the dissenting Protestants. To Charles such a policy was, as always, the threshold to a wider one, a broad scheme of toleration which should include all his divided subjects—Anglican, Presbyterian, Independent and Catholic—and enable him to fulfil the vow made in Whitgreave's little oratory at Moseley.* Once more the mighty figure of his grandfather, Navarre, passed across his vision. It was as though in answer to his sister's prayer.[24]

Yet here, as ever, was that overwhelming problem of money, which held up everything; unless he could master that, all was in vain. The Anglican Commons would certainly give him nothing so long as he showed the least tolerance to any creed but their own—it was doubtful if they would give it then—and some of his Council, notably Buckingham, who loved to walk, in his less rakish moments, with Anabaptists, urged him to summon a new Parliament. But though Charles trifled with the idea, he could never quite bring himself to take the plunge: in those dark waters what icy chills of republicanism might not lurk? Albemarle, now in the last chamber of life, announced that he would

---

* When in August, 1669, three Devonshire men were sentenced under an old Elizabethan statute to forfeit a large sum of money to the Crown for having forborne to attend church, Charles not only pardoned the fine, but declared that he would not have this remunerative statute enforced hereafter, " it being his judgment that no man ought to suffer merely for conscience sake." (*H.M.C. Rep. 6, Ingilby,* 367.)

leave the country rather than face the anger of his former allies in a Parliament with a Presbyterian-Independent majority.[25]

Thus for the two things which Charles most urgently needed—money and loyalty—Minette's policy seemed to point a way. There was only one man likely to offer the former —his cousin, Louis. And of all his subjects, the loyalest were the persecuted Catholics, as he had once learnt—did he but care to recall it—in the secret places of Whiteladies and Boscobel. His sister's pleading was becoming very clear now: for all the odds against him, might not hers be the one way out? He resolved to follow his grandfather's example.

In the greatest secrecy the *grand design* took shape. "I must again conjure you," he told Minette in January, 1669, "that the whole matter be an absolute secret, otherwise we shall never compass the end we aim at." On the 25th of that month York—by now secretly converted to Rome—the Catholic Arundell of Wardour, and a young Royalist Minister, Thomas Clifford, who was bold enough for anything, were admitted to the secret. In the same month Minette sent an Italian astrologer, Pregnani, to England to press forward her plan. The choice was an unfortunate one, for the profession of prophet did not commend itself to Charles. "I give little credit to such kind of cattle," he told Minette, "and the less you do it the better, for if they could tell anything 'tis inconvenient to know one's fortune beforehand, whether good or bad, and so, my dearest sister, good night." At Newmarket, whither the seer accompanied him to the March races, he had an opportunity of testing his powers. "I believe he will give you some account of it," he reported afterwards, "but not that he lost his money upon confidence the stars could tell which horse would win, for he had the ill luck to foretell three times wrong together." After this,

Pregnani never stood a chance. More successful was the mission of Lord Arundell, who was sent to Louis in March, 1669, to settle the outlines of the design.[26]

The path which Charles was now taking was one of extreme peril: should Protestant London get wind of the true object, before his plans were ready, revolution would be almost certain. Already disquieting rumours of an understanding with France and an abandonment of the Triple Alliance were current. The danger of betrayal from within was small, for the King's Catholic servants were the staunchest of all his friends, and of the loyalty of Arlington—the only Protestant in the secret—even Minette, previously doubtful of his Spanish sympathies, was now convinced. He had obtained for her that summer a small sum of which she stood in great need— " You never saw anybody perkt up as she is since this money," reported the English ambassador. But across the water, an ever-increasing circle of French Ministers and diplomats were entrusted by Louis with the secret: and a fear sometimes haunted Charles and Arlington that France might be planning a trap, a fear which explains the slowness of the negotiations and their frequent vacillations.[27]

To allay his suspicions, Buckingham, to his own intense gratification, was entrusted with the secret of the negotiations and made by Minette, whom he adored, to believe that he was their chief mover. But with their innermost purpose— the King's design to declare himself a Catholic—he could not be, and was not, entrusted. One or two of the other Protestant Ministers, who could not indefinitely be denied knowledge of an Anglo-French understanding, were also admitted into the outer courts of the secret.[28]

Meanwhile Charles took what steps he could to safeguard his position. He placed the forts and arsenals—wherever he could do so without arousing suspicion—in the hands of officers upon whom he could rely, and busied himself with improving the morale of his little army. Remembering the beginning of his father's troubles, he took care to secure the outposts of his other two kingdoms. In Ireland, the Anglican Ormonde was recalled, to be replaced by the Presbyterian Lord Robartes. In Scotland, the red-faced vizier, Lauderdale, moderated the high proceedings of the bishops and, widening the basis of religious toleration, tried to procure an Act of Union with England, and coaxed through the Scottish Parliament a Militia Act by which twenty-two thousand troops were placed at the King's disposal for use in any part of his dominions.[29]

For all Charles's schemes money was the necessary preliminary. At first he asked for £800,000 to sustain the alliance and £200,000 to precede his conversion; in return for these he would connive at Louis's accession to the Spanish throne when its present holder should die, receiving as his own share the South American colonies, Minorca and Ostend. But other considerations were moving Charles—his passionate desire for revenge for the Medway, and the never-ceasing warfare which Dutch and English merchants waged beyond the line for the trade of Africa and the East. For England peace with Holland and world commerce were hardly compatible.

In the summer of 1669 the idea of an Anglo-French war to humble the detested Republic was first formed. Whatever scruples Charles had on the point of the Triple Alliance were put to rest when Louis revealed to him De Witt's secret overtures for a Franco-Dutch partition of the Spanish Empire. " There is all the reason in the world," he now assured Minette, " to join profit with honour . . . and the King will find me as forward to do Holland a good turn as he can desire; we shall, I doubt not, agree very well in the point, for that country has used us both very scurvily."[30]

By the autumn Charles's need for money was so pressing

that a meeting of Parliament, prorogued since the early summer of the previous year, could no longer be averted. No sooner were they met in October but the Commons, instead of voting the supplies needed, fell to their old game of persecuting dissenters, baiting officials, and seeking for defalcations in the royal accounts. Secretly instigated by the impossible Buckingham, whom the King, for old friendship's sake, continued to gratify with the appearance of power, they fell upon Arlington's friend, Sir George Carteret, the Navy Treasurer, hounding that unfortunate official in their usual manner.* "But, Lord!" wrote Pepys, who saw them at their work, "what a tumultuous thing this committee is, for all the reputation they have of a great council . . . there being as impertinent questions, and disorderly proposed, as any man could make."[31]

Accordingly the King prorogued them in December till the middle of February, in the meantime taking the trouble himself to examine both the Commissioners and the war accounts, about which they were making so much fuss. He satisfied himself that, far from there being a default of a million pounds, his officers had devoted to the war at least a million and a half more than had been voted for it. Therefore, when he met Parliament at the beginning of the new session, he spoke out his mind:

"When we last met I asked you for a supply and I ask it now again with greater instance. The uneasiness and straightness of my affairs cannot continue without very great ill effects to the whole kingdom. Consider this seriously and speedily. It is yours and the kingdom's interest as well as mine, and the ill consequence of a want of an effectual supply must not lie at my door. And that no misapprehensions or mistakes touching the expenses of the last war may remain with you, I think fit to let you know that I have fully informed myself in that matter, and do

---

* "Behaving themselves like most insolent and ill-mannered men," was Pepys's description (27 May, '68).

affirm to you that no part of those moneys that you gave to me for that war have been diverted to other uses, but on the contrary, besides all those supplies, a very great sum hath been raised out of my standing revenue and credit, and a very great debt contracted, and all for the war."

After that the wind was out of the Commission's sails. The Commons, the more amenable for a disgusted surrender on the part of Charles to their desire for religious persecution,* and somewhat touched by the just and tactful way in which he had ended the old quarrel between them and the Lords, voted him a wine tax for seven years, which was calculated to increase his annual income by £300,000 and so redeem the promises of 1660. But it was ten years too late, and Charles was all that distance nearer bankruptcy.[32]

To counteract the influence of his brother, who—fearful lest a peer's Divorce Bill then under discussion should serve as a precedent in royal circles—was opposing it with might and main, Charles, for the remainder of the session, took to attending the debates in the House of Lords. At first his unexpected presence caused some embarrassment, but after a few days, finding that their sovereign kept himself silently and discreetly in the background, the peers expressed great appreciation of the honour paid them. He, for his part, thoroughly enjoyed his new recreation and declared it was better than going to a play. When the Bill passed, Buckingham, who loathed the heir presumptive, flattered himself that the King would take the opportunity to rid himself of the childless Catherine who, poor lady, had by now suffered her last miscarriage—a pet fox of her husband's having one night followed him to her room and there changed the fate of England by leaping unexpectedly on to the bed. But

---

* Charles's friend, Sir Robert Moray, had written to Lauderdale on December, 1669: " He is now beginning to declare himself more vigorously against persecution of people for their religion, and says upon that subject things most pungent and unanswerable." (*Lauderdale*, II, 170.)

Charles pooh-poohed the suggestion; if his conscience, he said, would permit him to divorce Catherine, it would also allow him to dispatch her out of the world. Yet he fully appreciated the passionate desire of his subjects for a Protestant heir. When one evening a country squire assured him that, would he but beget a Prince of Wales that night, he would make his people the happiest on earth, he answered: "I'll promise you I'll do my best."[33]

Meanwhile the *grand design* was hanging fire, partly, perhaps, through Arlington's timidity and secret regrets for his dying child, the Triple Alliance, still more on account of Charles's unexpected success with Parliament and his natural inclination—now that the need for it was a little less urgent —to delay taking so irrevocable a step. For three weeks that April he was at Newmarket, recovering from a slight indisposition and diverting himself with horse-racing. Nor was his passion for chemistry easily compatible with any great zeal for a martyr's crown; the French ambassador noted that, however inconstant Charles might be in some things, he invariably spent several hours a day making experiments in his laboratory. It was left to Minette to initiate a last great effort. With the Dutch pressing for a completion of the terms of the Triple Alliance, her own health failing and a jealous husband growing every day more reluctant to allow her any life of her own, it was her one chance to realize her dream. Making the utmost of a temporary reconciliation with Monsieur, she obtained the longed-for authority to visit England and conclude the treaty.[34]

To Charles, who had not seen her for over nine years, it was a joyous moment; all the Court, the music, the players and the bravery, hastened after him to Dover, where he went out on the water to meet her. But to Minette, who moved through the warm days of feasts and ballets with bright eyes and a flush on her gentle face, it was the testing time of all

her hopes for this world and the next. Only a week had
been originally allowed her by her grudging husband, but of
those unforgiving hours she wasted not one minute. Within
six days of her landing her brother, who could deny her
nothing, least of all this on which her whole being was set,
had consented. On May 22nd, 1670, the Treaty of Dover
was signed and the die cast beyond recall. On that unforgetting scrap of paper, signed in the utmost secrecy by four
English statesmen—Arlington, Arundell, Thomas Clifford,
and the faithful Richard Bellings—Charles promised to
declare himself a Catholic and to join the French in war
against Holland, Louis providing the subsidies that alone
could enable him to do either.* On June 2nd, brother and
sister, after their brief romance, parted in mid-Channel; then
Minette, laden with presents, passed beyond his keeping,
bearing with her that strange paper to the French King.
Just three weeks later a courier from the English ambassador
at Paris brought the " saddest story in the world." Minette,
stricken down in a single night of agony, was dead.†[35]

* Louis was to pay Charles two million livres (roughly £150,000) within six months
to enable him, whenever he thought fit, to declare himself a Catholic; Charles was
to declare war on Holland when Louis was ready, and receive from the latter
three million livres (£225,000) a year while the war lasted. Of the fruits of
that war Charles was to receive the Zeeland islands. He was to assist Louis
in making good any new claims that might accrue to him for the Spanish
throne, but was not to be called upon to do anything that infringed the Triple
Alliance. (*Lingard*, XI, 364.)

† Throughout the torture of her last hours, she spoke of her brother again
and again: " I have loved him better than life itself," she whispered to
Montagu, " and now my only regret in dying is to be leaving him." (*Ady*, 352.)

CHAPTER VIII

THE RETURN OF ODYSSEUS

" Thy sword within the scabbard keep
  And let mankind agree :
Better the world were fast asleep
  Than kept awake by thee.
The fools are only thinner
  With all our cost and care,
But neither side a winner
  For things are as they were."
                                    —DRYDEN.

THE news found the King in London, remaking his world to fit that strange and romantic dream which his sister's pleading had turned to reality. The young Englishman who brought it was disturbed by the tears which troubled his dark, sphinx-like face and the volcanic fury of his resentment against Monsieur. In his first anguish Charles half believed the angry rumours of poison, to which his subjects attributed Madame's sudden death. The bitterness of his comments to Colbert were such that the ambassador feared that it would break the alliance.

Yet it was never in Charles's nature to struggle against the inevitable. " My grief for her is so great," he told a friend, " that I dare not allow myself to dwell upon it, and try so far as possible to think of other things." When an embassy from Louis had satisfied him Minette's death was due to natural causes,* he spoke no more against France, but set

---

* The doctors pronounced that she had died of cholera. More probably the cause was an acute attack of peritonitis. (*Ady,* 360, 371.)

himself to carry out her great desire. Nor indeed could he easily have turned from it, for somewhere in Louis's keeping was that unrecallable piece of paper.[1]

Lonely and desperate as was the game Charles had chosen, his every move now showed how well fitted he was to play it. Even the hated intolerance of his Commons he turned to advantage. By enforcing the Conventicle Act, with which they had just saddled him, against all places of dissenting worship, he counted on arousing such a spirit of opposition among the Protestant Nonconformists as would make his plan of universal toleration almost popular in comparison. Yet, while Surveyor Wren was kept busy removing the seats and pulpits from meeting-houses, and delighted Anglican Justices employed " smart actings against Conventiclers," Charles was taking steps to commit the Protestant members of his Council still further to his most un-Protestant design. The chief of these was Buckingham. In three things, though in nothing else, this man could be relied on—in his vanity, his adoration for Madame, and his hatred of Arlington. These Charles employed to enchain him. Early in August he dispatched him with a magnificent equipage on an embassy of condolence to Paris, where he was to be flattered into initiating a secret Anglo-French treaty. To render him the more ready, Buckingham was to be given the impression that the idea was his alone, while his rival, Arlington, was to fan his eagerness by a maddening display of Dutch sympathies. The deception was to be crowned by obtaining his signature, and that of his colleague, Ashley—a freethinker in close touch with the Dissenters—to what Charles christened a *Traité Simulé*, establishing a secret alliance with France in every respect similar to that of Dover, save that the £150,000 promised for the royal conversion was to be disguised as part of the war subsidy. To these Charles also proposed to add the Scotch Presbyterian Lauderdale, counting, as he divined he could, on his absolute

loyalty to his commands. Once they had signed, fear of
exposure must compel them to follow wherever he chose to
lead.[2]

Yet, though the crown, and perhaps life itself, were staked
on that gambler's throw, nothing disturbed the even tenor of
Charles's way. That August, after obliging Barbara, who
was just off to Scarborough, by creating her Duchess of Cleveland, he took a quiet holiday at Windsor. Here he passed his
time in hunting the stag, walking in the park, which he was
planting with rows of trees, and planning the restoration of
the castle. The picture of that brief sojourn still lives in
Robert Moray's letters: of the King sleeping a little in his
chair after a morning's hunting, or rising at five to ride to
Hampton Court to watch his wife fishing. Moray once asked
him when he expected the dilatory Buckingham back from
France, and received the surprising reply, " At the day of
judgment in the valley of Jehoshaphat! "[3]

In October Charles stole a second holiday. Every spring
and autumn now—setting out from London before it was
light—he took his Court to Newmarket. Here he was at his
happiest. " The King is highly pleased," wrote one of his
attendants, " with all his Newmarket recreations; by candle-
light yesterday morning and this morning hunting the hare;
this afternoon he hawks and courses with greyhounds. . . .
As thou prizest earthly felicity, bring a Maid of Honour behind
thee." Such felicity was seldom wanting. Under the genial
patronage of such a prince, himself no mean horseman or
judge of horseflesh, the first of English sports found a fitting
home. Charles loved the informality of the place, the fleet
running of the delicate shaped creatures he imported from
the East, the evenings among the jockeys where he " put off
the King." On the great wind-ridden heath, the very centre
and epitome of England, he was free.[4]

He was back in London before October 24th, for the

opening of Parliament. He met the Houses with the usual fruitless request for some consideration of the State's debts and a demand for subsidies for the Fleet, giving as reason the growing navies of France and Holland, though he only meant the latter. But it was essential to deceive a Parliament, who regarded the Triple Alliance as the principal support of its anti-French, anti-Catholic policy. At the same time it was necessary to prevent the Dutch, who were already suspicious, from strengthening that alliance—a task committed to the invaluable Arlington.[5]

While Arlington was engaged in deceiving the Dutch ambassador—" a prying, talking, pressing man "—Charles was busy entertaining his nephew, the Prince of Orange. Both for the sake of his father's kindness to him twenty years before, and the love he had borne his mother, he was anxious to restore the young man, if possible, to the authority of his ancestors. He had therefore proposed to reveal the secret of the treaty to him, and offer him the sovereignty of Holland as soon as its republican rulers were overthrown. Louis demurred, and Charles soon discovered that he was right, for the boy was far too good a Dutchman to connive at such a plan. As this " hopeful and personable prince " was also somewhat cold and heavy, Charles had him well plied one night to see if there was anything in him, and found there was, for William smashed the windows of the Maids of Honour, and was only prevented with difficulty from following up his missiles in person.[6]

Charles had another visitor that November—Louise de Queroalle, a lovely little Breton who had waited on his sister at Dover, and whom the Queen had offered to make a Maid of Honour. Dark, refined, with a soft childish face, she made an irresistible appeal to him—perhaps the more so because she was his only link with Minette. She was soon in high favour, though the French ambassador, who hoped

she would tie Charles with silken fetters to France, noted
with sorrow that she was distressingly coy.[7]

Just before Christmas, while the Commons were discussing
ways of raising money for equipping the Fleet, and arguing
the pros and cons of an Entertainment Tax,* Charles was
setting the last seal to the *Traité Simulé*. On December 21st
the treaty was secretly signed by the leading members of the
Committee of Foreign Affairs—Clifford, Arlington, Buckingham, Ashley and Lauderdale. These—the famous Cabal—
were now committed beyond recall to their master's policy.[8]

Very reluctantly, Charles had been compelled to add to the
Traité Simulé a note in his own hand, admitting that the fatal
£150,000 added to the war subsidy was in reality the aid
promised for his conversion. Louis had no intention of
allowing him to escape from the trap into which Minette had
so uncomprehendingly led him. For a trap Charles was
beginning to see it might well be. The more Colbert—wishing to tie him still further—urged that he should take the
preliminary step of conversion, the more did Charles, freed
from his sister's influence, struggle to postpone that spiritual
event. First it was because the Pope was dying—he could
not confide, he urged, his secret to *un Pape moribond*; then
he must receive inspiration from an Englishman, and no
one suitable was available; then the theologian who was to
perform the great work must also be a chemist, since he had
still some lingering doubts, grounded in natural philosophy,
which such a one alone could resolve. The difficulty was
to find so peculiar a divine, for the Roman Church was hardly
as Catholic as that. Indeed, it was becoming painfully obvious
that Charles's professions of zeal for the true faith coincided
only with the more severe crises of his eternal need for money.[9]

---

* " That towards his Majesty's supply, everyone that resorts to any of the
Playhouses, who sits in the Boxes shall pay 1s., and any who sits in the Pit shall
pay 6d., and any other person 3d." (*Parl. Hist.*, IV, 460.)

That zeal diminished almost to zero in the spring of 1671, when Arlington—no crusader by nature—was able to show him the extent of anti-Catholic feeling in the country. Both within and without Parliament arose bitter complaints of the growth of Popery, while alarming rumours began to circulate about French subsidies and troops for overthrowing English liberties and religion. And the keenest resentment was shown at the King's repeated demand for money to pay his ever-pressing debts; it was significant that this opposition was most marked among the loyal country gentry, who, blind to the real cause of such liabilities, saw in them the fruits of Court extravagance and the seeds of future taxes on their beloved land. By April the position had become so critical that Charles prorogued the Houses—once more at loggerheads with each other—without waiting for the passage of two of the bills of supply which they had reluctantly voted him.[10]

Libellous pamphlets, scandalizing Charles and his Ministers; Boanerges* in the House of Commons asking, apropos of the Government opposition to the Entertainment Tax, whether the King's interest in the drama lay most among the actors or the actresses, and subsequently having his nose slit by unknown assailants as he staggered home one morning from the Cock Tavern; Buckingham burying his bastard child with public honours in the Abbey—the Court was in ill odour that winter. Men loved to speak of the vices of their rulers, and in that solitary figure, gambling with fate, could see nothing but a sauntering prince—chatting familiarly in the park with Nelly as she leaned over her garden wall above the Mall, or wasting an hour gossiping with the ageing and expensive Cleveland.[11]

Yet all that year Charles drove his team along a road bordered by precipices. Ruler of a turbulent and jealous people, who every day grew more bitterly opposed to France

* The name of this champion of free speech was Sir John Coventry.

and Popery, he was bound to a course whose goal was union with France, a Catholic throne and national toleration. Some of his Cabal hung back : Arlington counselled caution; Ashley made friends with the mammon of righteousness; Buckingham and York, for very different reasons, dared not face Parliament, and urged dissolution. Out of these divergent elements arose one man of fire and iron—Thomas Clifford, a Restoration Strafford—heroic, passionate and reckless. Wedded from boyhood to bold measures, rugged and tempestuous as the Dartmoor from which his ancient race sprang, he stood that year at the King's side, a dark and sinister figure. Yet the gentle Evelyn spoke of him with affection as " a valiant, uncorrupt gentleman, ambitious and not covetous; generous, passionate, a most constant, sincere friend." A Hotspur, ever ready to pluck bright honour from the pale-faced moon, he was the very antithesis of Charles, and therefore perhaps appealed to him the more. On this rough hero the mantle of Minette fell. For those things for which she had pleaded he now urged—monarchy absolute, the ranks of ordered chivalry riding arrogant over traitors, and the Catholic Church at peace once more in an ancient land.[12]

When that May, a bold scoundrel made a nine days' wonder by all but capturing the Crown jewels from the Tower, Charles, who examined him in person, was so struck by his frank and undaunted replies that he could not bring himself to punish him. Perhaps a fellow-feeling for the insane daring of his undertaking, perhaps a premonition that he also must be detected and brought beaten to the bar, touched him. Storm was in the very air that summer. In July—making one of his famous early starts from Windsor and arriving at Portsmouth several hours before he was expected—the King took a naval voyage to inspect his fleets and arsenals. Westwards from St. Helens, gales scattered

BUST OF CHARLES II. IN THE VICTORIA AND ALBERT MUSEUM.

By HONORÉ PELLE.

". . . a sauntering prince—chatting familiarly in the park with Nelly as she leaned over her garden wall above the Mall."

his fleet and kept him long at sea.   As his coach brought him home across the rough Devon roads, war with Holland—avenging Medway, libellous cartoons, unforgotten injuries in Surinam and India—was brewing.   In the North Sea the captain of the little Merlin yacht carried orders to fire at the whole Dutch Fleet if need be, should their admirals fail to strike to the English flag.[13]

For such gathering clouds, Louise's boyish face and delicate love of beauty were all the more appealing.   Charles liked to visit her apartments in Whitehall and sit at his ease talking; he paid her card debts, and of course set every tongue wagging wildly.   Colbert was almost beside himself with excitement when she sickened at his dinner-table, but the ambassadorial hopes were premature.   The nymph was still receding from the satyr, yet observers noted that the pace was slackening.   Among these were Arlington and his virtuous countess.   When the King, after making a progress in the eastern counties—delighting the gentry by visiting their houses and graciously eating a vast number of herrings at Yarmouth—came to rest in October at Newmarket, they invited the little lady to stay with them at Euston.   In this Suffolk palace amid frescoes by Verrio, Roman pavilions and "numerous bathrooms," she received the homage of her sovereign.   Almost every other day he was there, mixing courtship with the joys of Newmarket, where "all the jolly blades were racing, dancing, feasting and revelling," or sometimes with the more sober delights of sermons from Cambridge divines and a visit to the University, where he desired that the speeches might be "few and short, or none." The wildest and most delicious rumours were circulated: he and Louise had been bedded one night, they said, and the stocking flung after the manner of a married bride, though the virtuous Evelyn, who was staying in the house, carefully "observing all passages with much curiosity," was forced to

admit that he had seen or heard of nothing beyond a little
"fondness and toying." Yet the French ambassador was certainly able to testify that when, with the rest of the company
at Euston, the lady visited Newmarket, the King proved a
most solicitous cicerone. And nine months later, the good
man's highest hopes were confirmed, and the ducal house of
Richmond founded. Virtue, duly tempered to meet the needs
of a great occasion, had proved the handmaid of diplomacy.[14]

It was not merely Louise's charms that drew the King
so frequently to Euston; the stately demeanour of his host
hid knowledge of many grave and secret affairs. Louis
was arming and the world shaking, and the time was
drawing near for the fulfilment of promises. Parliament—
a wolf in the lambing season would not have been more unseasonable, with the ambassadors of all Europe waiting with
bribes and tell-tale stories—was prorogued for another year.
Two obstacles stared the Cabal in the face—the peril of war
with France's hereditary foe, Spain, with its consequent loss
to English trade, and the eternal problem of money. The
latter was now so serious—in every dockyard the unpaid
workmen were in mutiny—that Charles had to ask Louis to
forego the clause of the treaty by which an English expeditionary force was to join the French Army. This caused a
crisis in the Cabal, for Buckingham, who had been promised
the command of the troops, was furious and retired in sulks
to his tent. The King, who declined to regard his old friend
as an Achilles, sent for him and told him frankly that he
had no intention of letting his desire for military glory stand
in the way of the public interest, and that in such a matter
he would consider him no more than his dog. Similar sentiments expressed to Ashley and Lauderdale had a sobering
effect on the pirate crew, which now once more bent to the
ropes, as the stern-browed Clifford hauled up the Jolly Roger.
Before 1671 ended, the old Cromwellian ambassador, Down-

ing, left for the Hague with demands as stormy as his own temper.*[15]

The Christmas of 1671 saw all Europe in alarm. Louis was putting into the field a hundred and twenty thousand troops : " a great diminution," wrote one, " is like to befall mankind next summer." Of such tempests, the men of money, so fearful and far-seeing, are the barometers. At that moment, with the English Government indebted to the tune of nearly two and a half millions, the bankers, on which it was entirely dependent, announced that they would advance no more. National bankruptcy had come at last.[16]

On January 2nd, 1672, the Council met in haste to consider the situation : the more grave because money was needed urgently to set out the Fleet. The revenue for the coming year was assigned up to the hilt to the bankers, and the only way to recover it was to suspend payment of their assignments. Yet such a course, though no one could suggest an alternative, naturally outraged the conscience of the Council, and it was left to Clifford, more daring than any present, to force the inevitable. Since the Restoration the necessary expenditure had exceeded the annual revenue by some £400,000 per annum. Additional and grudging parliamentary grants had failed altogether to bridge the gulf: in the past three years these had amounted only to £660,000. No provision had ever been made by Parliament for paying off the pre-Restoration debts, though Charles had somehow contrived to liquidate half a million pounds of these. Under such circumstances the Government, crippled at every point by its poverty and the usurious rates of interest it was forced to pay its creditors, had no further option. If the bankers, who had grown fat on its necessities, now chose to withhold their aid at the very

* The Dutch were to acknowledge clearly in writing the King's right to the dominion of the narrow seas and salute for his flag from all fleets and ships—as well as granting free trade to the Indies and redress for the insulting medals and pamphlets. (C.S.P.D. 1671-2, 42, 81.)

moment when affairs of State most demanded it, it seemed
only reasonable that the consequences should fall on their
shoulders and not the King's. So urged, the Council ordered
a suspension of all bankers' assignments for the space of a
year, provision to be made for their liquidation in better
times and interest at the rate of 6 per cent. to be paid in the
meantime.

The result was an immediate, though somewhat unnecessary panic, for the suspension only directly touched a
few wealthy bankers—the holders of large assignment orders
—and in the upshot not one of them failed. But it is not
in the nature of bankers to endure loss, and they at once took
steps to pass the deficit on to their clients, not only by refusing
all payments but by seizing deposits left in their hands by
private merchants. A commercial panic was only prevented
by the personal intervention of the King. On January 7th
he sent for the bankers and, assuring them that their debts
and interest would ultimately be met in full, requested that
they in their turn should meet their obligations to their clients.
Within a few days, comparative normality was restored in the
city. None the less the crisis had been a grave one and had
left a sting behind it.[17]

Within five days of the suspension, and as its natural
consequence, the Council was able to order an expenditure
of £750,000 for setting out the Fleet. Before the end of
the month a dozen wagons guarded by a troop of cavalry
were winding through the narrow streets of Rye towards
London with the first instalment of the French war
subsidy.[18]

Meanwhile events were moving with great rapidity.
Downing, outrunning his instructions* and refusing even

* Charles wrote to him angrily: " That you may not err in the future, I
have thought fit to send you my last mind upon the hinge of your whole
negotiation, and in my own hand, that you may likewise know it is your part
to obey punctually my orders, instead of putting yourself to the trouble of finding

to accept the Dutch reply to his demands, was back in London by February 6th. Four days before a further *Traité Simulé* was signed with France for the deception of the remaining Protestant councillors. The entire Government was now committed to the alliance. Despite the coming of a Dutch peace delegation and frantic English efforts to avoid a break with Spain, war with Holland was certain. In the maritime ports, where the Dutch were hated, it was eagerly awaited, the seamen actually pressing to sign on in the King's ships. The Cabal, realizing that speed was essential, not only to achieve success but to save itself from financial disaster, acted on the pirate's adage :

> " We must advance or be undone,
> Think this and then the battle's won ! "

and instructed the Portsmouth Squadron to seize Dutch merchantmen to provide the sinews of war. On March 13th Admiral Holmes fell in with a homecoming Smyrna fleet off the Isle of Wight, and—too greedy or impatient to await help —caught, as Arlington said, a tartar. With the timely aid of an English merchant ship, which stood in to share the fight, he captured a few rich prizes, but the rest of his intended booty, defending themselves with the utmost gallantry, reached Holland. Four days later followed the official declaration of war.[19]

In its attack on the wealth and power of Holland, the war was popular enough. But from the start a religious factor embittered the patriotism of the nation. With Louis setting out from Paris to lead his legions to the conquest of Flanders, " all Protestant hearts trembled." Such was the terror of the Catholic King that in Leicestershire mothers refused to let their children go to school, lest he should spirit them away to suck their blood.

reasons why you do not do so." (Charles II to Sir George Downing, 16 Jan., '72, *H.M.C. Rep. 8, Ashburnham*, 6-7.)

In the hopes of uniting the nation and pleasing the Dissenters—who had for long been urging him to use his prerogative to suspend the laws against their meetings—Charles issued on March 15th a Declaration of Indulgence for Tender Consciences, by which the penal laws were suspended, places of public worship promised to Protestant Nonconformists and freedom of worship in their own houses to Catholics. The measure was not a success.   The Catholics were of course delighted, but the dissenting Protestant Ministers, for all their former entreaties, returned only a grudging thanks to the King.   From the moment of the publication of the Declaration, the majority of people became convinced that the war was a cloak to the establishment of arbitrary government and Popery.[20]

At loggerheads from the start with his subjects, the King, who rested upon it his honour, his hopes and Minette's dreams, gave himself whole-heartedly to the prosecution of the war. That spring he was much with his fleet—at Sheerness, at the Nore, at Portsmouth.   " A goodly yet terrible sight to behold," Evelyn saw it in May, " passing eastwards by the straits 'twixt Dover and Calais on a glorious day."   A fortnight later De Ruyter found it watering in Solebay, and at once attacked.   In a ghostly fog, great hulls flashing flame rose out of the darkness; the *Royal James*, drifting with death-huddled decks through the heart of a Dutch squadron, was blown to the skies with all hands; reports as confused and contradictory as the battle itself reached Whitehall.   On the following day the shattered fleets sailed within gun-shot till evening, parting powderless seven leagues from Zeeland, when York, almost blind with smoke, led his charred ships home. A week later the tide brought to shore the fish-gnawed body of an English admiral, the Star of the Garter still adorning his breast.[21]

The battle—though the first account published in the

Gazette was far more gloomy than the facts—dispelled for that year the idea of an English landing on the Zeeland coast. Meanwhile the war seemed likely to be brought to a swift conclusion in a way unforeseen by Charles and his lieutenants, and one by no means pleasing to England. Within a few weeks the French armies had overrun Holland, the whole of Europe watching in amazement the sudden collapse of a rich and famous nation. Then, while Arlington and Bucking-ham—dispatched in haste to the Continent—were endeavour-ing to conclude a peace that would give them the wealth and prestige they needed at home without leaving all the spoils to France, the Dutch people flung off the republican yoke, and young Orange, resolving " to die in the last dyke," let in the sea as his great ancestor had done.[22]

While besieging French armies waited amid the fall of winter for a surrender that never came, their allies in England, disappointed of the rich victory on which all their hopes had been bent, were slipping into ever-deepening difficulties.* The French subsidies proved altogether inadequate for a long war, and attempts to obtain additional money from Louis—first by a sudden display of a Catholicism that had now sunk to a flicker, then by a request for a million pound loan—were alike unavailing. Though the prorogation of Parliament was extended once more, it was a policy of despair. By the end of the year it was plain that a meeting of Houses could be no longer postponed.[23]

When the members met in February, 1673, the King faced them in vigorous mood; only a few days before he had walked by Louise's coach, on " a delicate, clear, frosty day," the whole

* " The King finds himself . . . without money and without credit, his revenues, which consist chiefly of import and export duties, diminishing very much during the war, and his expenses increasing every day by the purchase of arms." (*Colbert's Memoir,* 7 June, '72; *Christie,* II, App. No. II.) The same *Memoir* bears witness to the courage with which Charles and Arlington faced these ever-growing difficulties.

P

way from Whitehall to Hampton Court. Demanding supply
for the Fleet, he told them that he intended to stick to his
Declaration of Indulgence, issued, he added, to secure peace
at home while there was war abroad. But, though the
Commons responded to the appeal to their hatred of the
Dutch—contained in Chancellor Shaftesbury's* famous
" Delenda est Carthago " speech—they made it plain that
supplies for the war would only be forthcoming when the
policy of toleration was abandoned. Within two days they
had voted a resolution that penal statutes in matters ecclesiastical could not be suspended save by Act of Parliament.
Charles—remarking there was no use in a man being angry
to his own hurt—offered to assent to any Act they might pass
for the security of religion, but tried to maintain his suspensory
right. But the Commons were inexorable, and, regardless of
his feelings, insisted on absolute surrender. For a few days
Charles contemplated civil war, saying that, were he to yield
as his father had done, he must suffer the same fate. But
his penniless condition, the complete absence of support even
from his own Ministers—now all but Clifford frightened out
of their wits—and, above all, an urgent entreaty from Louis,
fearful lest a constitutional quarrel should withdraw England
from the war, convinced him of the hopelessness of resistance.
On March 8th, crowned and enrobed, he informed the
Houses that he would withdraw both his Declaration and the
right claimed in it. That afternoon the triumphant members
crowded into the Banqueting Hall to return thanks, subsequently enjoying in his cellars the hospitality of a deeply
humiliated but still good-natured sovereign. Yet even now
they had not finished with him. Before March was out they
were coupling with the Bill of Subsidies, which alone could
maintain the Fleet and save the nation from another Medway,

* Ashley had been promoted to the Chancellorship as Earl of Shaftesbury in
1672.

a Test Act, by which all persons who should refuse to take
the Anglican Sacrament and an oath against the Catholic
doctrine of transubstantiation, were to be declared incapable
of holding public office. The measure would have been
moderated in the Lords, had not Clifford, throwing caution
to the winds, aroused violent suspicion by a passionate speech
against this cruel inquisition. Thereafter all hope of a sane
religious policy was gone, and Chancellor Shaftesbury, hastily
bowing to the tempest, spoke on behalf of the Bill. There
was nothing for it but to give way. At the end of March the
King assented, and the Houses adjourned until October. The
grand design was dissolved, and Minette's dreams faded
as though they had never been: yet they had left a rack
behind.[24]

The sequel came rapidly. In the time of tests* that
followed, it was noted that Clifford did not appear at the altar
to gain his Sacrament certificate. The cat finally came out
of the bag one Saturday in May, when his coach upset in the
Strand, revealing to an amazed public the Lord Treasurer
with a priest in full canonicals. By midsummer the White
Staff had been transferred, at the King's direction, to Sir
Thomas Osborne, a Protestant gentleman from Yorkshire, and
the Duke of York, deprived by the new Act of his command
of the Fleet, might be seen walking in the park in a profound
melancholy. Already men spoke of him as Squire James, and
named the popular young Monmouth, fresh from a heroic
military exploit in France, as a possible successor.[25]

It was a black summer. While De Ruyter fought Rupert
and, by a great naval campaign, saved his country, the most
sinister rumours circulated in London. A forceful pamphlet,
" England's Appeal from the Private Cabal at Whitehall "—
written by a clerk, dismissed from Arlington's office for Dutch

---

* " We are mighty busy here swearing against the Pope." (Sir Thos.
Player to Sir J. Williamson, 29 July, '73, *Williamson*, I, 134.)

intrigues and now in the employ of Orange,—gave form to a general suspicion that the Ministers were in the pay of France. The Army, assembled on Blackheath, and later at Yarmouth, for the invasion of Holland—and so frequently inspected by the King—was said to be full of Papists, hired for the overthrow of English liberties.* Press gangs, Dutch commerce raiders and rising prices all contributed to make the war unpopular. And the whole nation was filled with an evergrowing hatred of its ally—a loathing heightened by the deliberate refusal of a French admiral to support Rupert in the great battle of August 11th, off the Texel. Though the officers of the Fleet were given strict orders not to speak against the French, a captain reported that he could not get half a dozen men to cheer their ships.[26]

As at the time of the Medway disaster, opponents of the administration resented the very existence of the Court and its inextinguishable gaiety. "The Government begins to thrive marvellous well," wrote a City merchant, "for it eats and drinks and sleeps as heartily as I have known it, nor doth it vex itself with that foolish, idle, impertinent thing called business." Men noted the gay little picnics on summer evenings at Barn Elms or Chelsea, with their lanterns on the trees and couples dancing on the green, and Charles so merry upon the water going home; the transmogrification of Louise into Duchess of Portsmouth; the King's chance meeting with Nelly while hunting at Chiffinch's pretty house at Filberds. The more serious activities of his life they missed: the ceaseless Council meetings and visits to the Fleet; his interest in the foundation of a mathematical school at Christ's Hospital to

---

* The necessity of maintaining some sort of discipline by martial law put the people into paroxysms of fear. So Sir William Coventry wrote to Mr. Thynne on July 7th, 1673: "If ever Parliament sit again, whoever shall have sat at condemning any man for life or limb will, I believe, be questioned, this point and matter of money being the only guard the people have against an army they so much dread." (*Longleat Papers*; *Christie*, II, 150. See also *Hatton*, I, 111; *Williamson*, I, 116; II, 59.)

breed merchant officers, and in Wren's final designs for St. Paul's.[27]

It was plain that when Parliament should meet that October, it would be no serene month. It was openly said that the Commons would not vote the King a farthing unless he handed over the control of the war. Everybody spoke of the " great baiting " that was to come : " we are already condemning and acquitting several persons (and those of no mean quality)," wrote one, " as if the next meeting of Parliament should be nothing but a high Court of Justice." One Minister at least, Shaftesbury—" the weakest and wickedest of men," his master called him—had decided that it would be more profitable to be among the baiters than the baited, and was mysteriously consulting with the anti-Court leaders in the Commons. From this liaison sprang the new opposition—the country party as it was called—in due course the Whigs. Every tavern in Westminster, as the time of meeting drew near, was filled with little cabals of politicians.[28]

When the Houses met on October 20th, it seemed to old men that the clock had gone back thirty years, and that the days of angry assemblies brooding revolution were come again. Even before Black Rod had time to summon the members to the Lords, the Commons had passed a resolution against Mary of Modena, the young Catholic bride, chosen, in loyalty to the French alliance, for the widowed Duke of York—the Pope's eldest daughter, as country folk thought her. Fear of a Papist successor was all the more acute since Charles had suffered a fit of apoplexy that autumn, and Shaftesbury was already advancing proposals for a royal divorce. The Queen, poor woman, reckoned on being put away. The King alone gave no inkling of the future, maintaining an impassivity which some attributed to indifference and others to disgust.[29]

A week's prorogation gave breathing space to the Government, but when the members reassembled on the 27th to listen to Charles's request for supply, they saw a chaplet of beads and a wooden sabot under the Speaker's chair, with the French King's arms on one side and those of England on the other. In some mysterious way the English people had grasped the substance of the *grand design*, and it was in such a guise that it appeared to them. Before the month was out, the Commons, after a furious attack on their own Speaker, were debating four great grievances: growth of Popery, a Standing Army, the French League and Evil Counsellors. Behind them lay the power of an angry city, enraged by war prices and religious fear. On November 3rd they voted the Standing Army to be a grievance, and trooped to Whitehall in the afternoon with an address against York's marriage. Next day they turned to consider "evil counsellors."[30]

Lauderdale was in Scotland, sent there by his master to prevent a repetition of the events of '38; Shaftesbury had joined the hunter's pack; Buckingham, tremulous to do likewise, was playing the bluff country gentleman at Cliveden. Only Arlington—fearful though he was for his fine possessions —remained at the King's side. But one counsellor was past the reach of " the mighty terrible Parliament " and the judgment courts of men. From the lonely Devonshire valley of his forefathers, Lord Clifford of Chudleigh, leaving behind all baubles—White Staff, vast pictures of hunted beasts, Court, City and Country, and all the timid hearts that dared not face their destiny—went out to meet his God.*[31]

* The last words of this man, who had followed his faith so blindly and heroically, were: " Well, let men say what they will; there is a God, a just God above." (*Evelyn*, 18 Aug., '73.)

CHAPTER IX

THE FAITHFUL COMMONS

" With our modern system of annual budgets, estimates and supplementary estimates, we are so far removed from this seventeenth-century practice and theory that we cannot conceive it possible. It is this want of proper sense of historical perspective that has produced the accepted Whig view of Charles II's reign— a view which is as mean in its psychology as it is gross and palpable in its ignorance.

" Rough balance sheet as between Charles II and his Parliament

Deficit		How the deficit was made up	
In his ordinary revenue (including interest) Charles was cheated by his Parliament on the whole reign roughly	£4,432,000	Rendition of Dunkirk . .	£290,000
		Queen Catherine's dowry .	180,000
		French King's money . .	742,000
		Bankers' debt . . .	2,000,000
		Crown lands sold . .	1,000,000
In the extraordinary or war revenue Charles was cheated by his Parliament—		Departmental debts and debts at interest resting on the Executive at the death of Charles . .	2,000,000
On the first Dutch war .	1,500,000		
On the second Dutch war			
On the thirty ships . .	100,000		
On the intended war with the French King and the Disbandment . .	180,000		
	£6,212,000		£6,212,000

Even and quit.
Requiescant in pace Rex et Parliamentum suum fidelissimum."
—W. A. SHAW, Calendar of Treasury Books,
Vol. VII, Pt. I.

At the very moment when the Commons were proceeding to the impeachment of Lauderdale, the sound of Black Rod's knocking was heard on the door. On the ninth day of the session, the King, acting on his own initiative—for no Minister at that terrible moment dared give such advice—prorogued the Houses till January. He was beaten, and the causes of that defeat were clear—the old cry of France and Popery, first prompted by his own policy and now raised by men in league with those whose interest it was to divide England against herself. At least one of the little inner ring of Ministers was implicated in a movement which threatened the throne itself. On November 9th the seals were taken from the Chancellor, Shaftesbury. Such action was timely. To Lauderdale, who still stood firm for his master in Scotland, Charles wrote a few days later that some of those who had taken a lead in the recent extravagances were not " so pert in that subject as they were."[1]

With all he had striven for in ruins and the bleak winds of '41 blowing across his realm,* the King had to build again or perish. Politically, he was more lonely than ever—Clarendon, Minette, Clifford, gone; Buckingham and Shaftesbury fled to the enemy; Arlington afraid and compromising. Only, across the water, Louis seemed to offer some dim link with the far-off days of Dover. Yet there was something one-sided about Louis's friendship: he gave money it was true, but the cost of his alliance always outweighed the price, and the fruits of victory invariably remained in his hands. Reluctantly, and very slowly, Charles was beginning to perceive that Minette's brother-in-law was far less concerned for the maintenance of monarchy in England than he pretended.

In Charles's perplexity one thing was certain: he must

---

* " A party in the House would drive the King upon precipices and introduce a Commonwealth once more." (John Wynne to Sir Richard Wynn, 20 Dec., '73, *Wynn Papers*, 408.)

find money. The Fleet was ill equipped, the household
officers unpaid, the roof of the royal mews letting in all the
rain of heaven. The additional cost of the war had proved
at least a million and a half, and the only grant he had
received from Parliament had fallen short of this amount by
several hundred thousand pounds. It was certain that the
Commons—with Spanish and Dutch agents displaying their
purses, and an infuriated country declaiming against Popish
allies and a standing army—would vote no war subsidies, and
that, if the Crown was to be preserved, peace must be made.
In despair for his obligations, Charles placed his plight before
Louis; he could only continue the war if France would bear
the cost: failing that he must seek a separate peace. Louis,
coldly disapproving, offered £75,000—a sum which, in
Charles's condition, was mere mockery.[2]

One group of men alone seemed to offer any refuge—the
survivors of that party which, in the storms of the past, had
stood firm by Church and Crown. "We are not altogether
in despair," one of them had written in the dark days of
the summer, "that the old honest party will weather the
storm, my Lord of Ormonde being in the Cabinet." He,
with the new Treasurer, Osborne, Seymour, the Speaker, and
Henry Coventry, Arlington's fellow Secretary of State, formed
a composite Cavalier group in the Council. Their position
had been strengthened on Shaftesbury's fall by the appointment of another of their party, Heneage Finch, as Lord
Keeper. But their weakness hitherto had lain in their lack
of a leader. Now the hour of need had brought forth the
man. Shrewd, hard and businesslike as the Yorkshire from
which he came, experienced in finance and public affairs,
and with all a country gentleman's distrust of Whig lords
and fanatics, the Treasurer was to prove a match for the best
brains of the Opposition.[3]

The King, though he never loved him, at once recognized

Osborne's ability and sound sense.   Henceforward, though to
do so meant the abandonment of that broad and inclusive
policy in politics and religion to which his heart ever leant,
he relied on him implicitly.   A change was at once apparent.
Before the end of November a proclamation was issued for-
bidding Catholics the Court and putting the laws against
recusants into execution.[4]

The new Minister was set on an immediate peace as the
first means to reduce expenditure and quiet the popular fear
of a standing army; in this he was at one with Arlington,
who was almost beside himself with panic as to what Parliament might do.   The King, who could not easily stomach
the thought of abandoning his ally, insisted on a last despairing
attempt to obtain a parliamentary grant to fit out the Fleet.
But the moment he met the Houses on January 7th, with an
offer to allay suspicion by revealing the text of his sham treaty
with France—an observer noticed that for once he fumbled
in delivering his speech—the storm burst.   Despite all that the
Government had done to prove its Protestantism, the Lords,
assured by Shaftesbury—in daily conclave with the Presbyterian magnates at Lord Holles's house—that sixteen
thousand London Papists were in arms, petitioned that all
Catholics should be banished from the capital.   By January 13th the Commons had passed a vote for the removal of
Lauderdale.   Next day they were about to fall on Arlington
and Buckingham, when the latter, who had been doing his
best to please all parties—" the debauchees by drinking with
them, the sober by grave and serious discourses, the pious by
receiving the sacrament "—begged to be heard and, in a wild
and distracted speech, threw the blame of everything that had
happened, and much that had never happened, on Arlington.
On the 15th the latter was also " run down "; but his fear
fell from him as he underwent that terrible ordeal, and, in
a long, calm and persuasive speech, in which he blamed no

one, yet contrived somehow to hide everything under the cloak of collective ministerial responsibility, completely baffled the House.   Yet though Arlington saved himself, it was " a bloody week of impeachments and accusations " for the Government.   In that impassioned time, honest Secretary Coventry played a notable part, " like a cherubim with his flaming sword, turning it everywhere to defend his master's cause."[5]

With nothing but the sound of angry clamour against Papists and standing armies, it was plain that the war and French alliance must go.   As always in a crisis, the King acted rapidly.   On January 24th, waving prerogative to the wind, he submitted the terms offered for an Anglo-Dutch peace to Parliament.   By these the Dutch conceded the right of the flag, a war indemnity of £200,000, and agreed to a mutual restoration of colonial conquests.   Both Houses recommended the King to treat.   Temple was at once dispatched to the Hague, and by February 9th Charles was able to announce that he had concluded peace.   Only to Ruvigny did he reveal his humiliation, bidding him make his apologies to Louis and assuring him that no pressure whatever should make him withdraw the English regiments serving with the French Army.[6]

Yet the Opposition still remained unsatisfied.   The very peace which it had clamoured for so loudly now became a grievance.   Bills, to bring up royal children in the Protestant faith and exclude the Duke of York from the King's presence, floated before both Houses.   The most crying public need of all, money, was ignored.   Yet by such factious courses, his opponents were playing Osborne's game, for there were many thousands of Englishmen who remembered the ways of their forerunners in '41 and the evil that had followed.   " I find," Charles wrote to Lauderdale, " the country gentlemen begin to understand some of the great leaders."   On February 24th he prorogued Parliament till November.[7]

To Charles it must have seemed at times as though there was no governing this jealous and turbulent people. He had tried to rule by Clarendon's broad and conciliatory policy: by alliance with the High Church, with the Dissenters, with the Catholics and France; all had failed to still his subjects' genius for faction and the obstinate refusal of their representatives to grant him enough money to make his task even barely possible. Their passionate insistence on individual liberty—from the proud Whig lord on his abbey lands to the London apprentice and drayman—made government a perpetual burden. Every action of the Executive, however reasonable or necessary, was regarded with jealousy and suspicion, and the very judges, though appointed by the Crown, preferred to flout it openly rather than give an angry House of Commons or unreasoning populace the least reason to suppose that they favoured the cause of authority. With all this, the individualism of the English was of the most egotistical kind, for the liberty they sought so fiercely for themselves they denied with fury to anyone else—to a Frenchman, a Papist, an Irishman. It was not surprising that it was once rumoured that their easy-going monarch had given up the task in despair and retired, with one of his mistresses and a well-lined purse, to France.

But in truth nothing was further from Charles's mind. On one thing he was determined—never to set out on his travels again, and, if only for that, he was resolved to keep his seat on what was regarded as the most difficult throne in Europe.* And beneath his easy manners and gentle nature,

* " The English Monarchy is made up of three kingdoms, the inhabitants of which vary in their tempers and inclinations. In one thing only they agree, namely in working with strenuous care to reduce the royal authority, and to place it under the dependence of their Parliaments." (Louis XIV to D'Estrades.)

" If Aristotle . . . were to come again to this world he could not find words to explain the manner of this Government. It has a monarchial appearance, as there is a king, but it is very far from being a monarchy." (Cominges to Louis, *Jusserand*, 98, 100.)

Charles hid a sterner purpose and one that deepened as the years passed—to be a king, to resist the encroachments of ambitious aristocrats or ill-informed assemblies, to maintain the just prerogatives of an ancient throne. To this, through all the meanderings of his foreign and religious policy, he was constant.[8]

So long as he remained poor, Charles was the slave of the politicians and the great men who managed them. Long ago his old governor, Newcastle, had warned him to put money in his purse and keep it. Now he had learnt that lesson's truth: "the King," wrote one, "says he would rather be a poor king than no king." As soon as the members had vanished to their country homes, "reproaching one another that they had sat so long upon eggs and hatched nothing," Danby* began his work of making the ends of State meet. Declaring that the Government's expenditure had exceeded the revenue by a constant million a year† since the Restoration, he announced his intention of reducing the Fleet and putting a stop to all salaries and pensions till the seamen were paid. When Louise, in wild alarm like the rest of the Court, explained tearfully to the King that a diamond necklace she had set her heart on could only be bought for ready money, he advised her to make friends with the Treasurer. Ruthlessly the latter proceeded on his course. Without a penny from Parliament to help him, in six months he restored the national finances—which Clifford's reckless spell at the Treasury had almost broken—paying off troops and ships, liquidating the debts that mortgaged the dockyards, and reducing the rate of interest on Government loans from 10 to 8 per cent.[9]

In all this Danby was helped by external circumstances.

---

* The Treasurer was created Earl of Danby in 1674, and is so called in these pages henceforward.

† An overstatement, see p. 221.

It so happened that his rise to power coincided with the commencement of one of those cyclical periods of trade expansion
which occur in every age. During the years 1674 and 1675
England enjoyed unusual commercial prosperity.* Like
everyone else, the Government benefited. The yield in the
Customs, which three years before had only been £160,000,
rose in 1674 to £400,000, the Excise from £300,000 to
£750,000. As a result the Crown, for the first time in the
reign, became temporarily solvent, the revenue rising to
£1,400,000, a sum rather more than adequate for the normal
peace-time expenditure of the State. This unwonted affluence
Charles and Danby used largely to liquidate old obligations.
On July 23rd an order was issued for paying two years'
compound interest to the bankers, who had suffered by the
stop of the Exchequer. In the same way the debts of the
Dutch war, for which Parliament had failed to make adequate
provision, were paid off. In all this the King was true to a
practice which he most honourably endeavoured to follow in
good and evil season—of keeping, to the best of his ability,
faith with his creditors.†[10]

It was only natural that Charles should wish to share his
unwonted prosperity with those whom he felt to have the
strongest claim on his benevolence. Up to the present his
generosity to his mistresses had been tempered by poverty;
now for a brief season it flowered in almost tropical profusion.
Louise got the pearls and diamonds her fastidious soul required
—malicious gossip said in consolation for the infidelities of
her lord, who had been a little promiscuous in his amours of
late. Cleveland, though long passed into the limbo of retired

---

* " Trade flourishes in all our ports. This is likely to be a very happy and
fruitful year in all manner of commerce." " Trade was never better than
now." (*H.M.C. Fleming*, III, 5, 26 May, '74.)

† A year before, in the depths of the financial morass of 1673, he had
somehow contrived to pay the last instalment of a debt incurred by his father in
1641. (*H.M.C. Duke of Hamilton*, 146.)

loves, married her daughters with a profusion of gold and silver lace, paid for, of course, by their kind father. Even the unseeking Nelly, now retired from the stage and chastely established in a house in Pall Mall as a kind of annexe to the reigning Portsmouth, came in for her share of the good times: the French ambassador, who was privileged to see much that was hidden from others, was much impressed by her fine petticoats—their " thorough cleanliness, neatness and sumptuosity." Between her and her magnificent rival there waged a ceaseless war. When the latter went into deep mourning for a French prince to whom she was in no way related, the little Cockney comedienne dressed herself in black from head to foot, in grief, she explained, for the Cham of Tartary.[11]

Though the sums which Charles lavished on these fair creatures were far smaller than was commonly supposed, and amounted to only an infinitesimal fraction of the royal revenue, they had powerful repercussions in the political world. Honest Parliament men, who had little objection to Charles's amusing himself in what was, after all, a national pastime, objected strongly to seeing the royal loves, past and present, preserved as permanent pets at the public expense: it was not Charles's frailty they objected to so much as his generosity. The artistic Louise—whose name Queroalle they abbreviated English-wise to Carwell—in particular aroused criticism, partly by her magnificent tastes, and still more by her rather ostentatious virtue (where Charles was not concerned), and her overwhelmingly distinguished manners. Whenever the King henceforward appealed to Parliament for money, the Commons, egged on in their virtuous passion for economy by the great manipulators, made ill-veiled allusions* to what Shaftesbury called " the chargeable ladies about Court," and shut their purses

---

* See the highly entertaining and altogether misleading mock King's speech which Andrew Marvell, one of Shaftesbury's right-hand men, wrote for the opening of Parliament in April, 1675. (*Marvell, Grosart*, II, 431-3.)

more closely than ever. They altogether missed sight of the
fact that Charles's Court was one of the least expensive in
Europe, and that his affectionate generosity to his bastard
sons—seven of them by now and all ennobled—was no
more costly to the country than the normal brood of younger
princes denied them by a childless queen. As a matter
of fact, Charles contrived to dispose of his offspring at a very
moderate cost by marrying them to suitable heiresses. When
old John Cartwright of Aynho died leaving two little grand-
daughters worth £25,000 apiece, a knowing subject hazarded
a guess that the King would " put in for them for some of
his bastards."[12]

During the summer of 1674, while Charles kept Court
at Windsor, and his people flocked to watch the great August
tattoo which he staged in the meadows beneath the terrace
for the benefit of his young army—a mimic siege of Maestricht
with " great guns fired, mines sprung, prisoners taken . . .
and all the circumstances of a formal siege "—the continent
of Europe shook with the thunder of French armies em-
battled against the great league which Lisola, the Austrian,
and William of Orange were building to throw down Louis.
Dutch agents were already at work stirring up English fears
of France in the hope that Parliament, which was due to
meet in the autumn, would force the King into war. But
Charles, though he had been compelled to abandon his old
ally, was determined not to give way to popular clamour in
a matter in which his honour and good faith were so much
involved. Nor had he reason to suppose that intervention
could be anything but disastrous to himself and his subjects:
he was still paying for the last war, while they were reaping
the rich harvest of being at peace when the rest of Europe
was in arms.* Accordingly in September he told his Council

---

* In June, 1677, Charles told Courtin " that at the bottom England enjoyed
a profound tranquillity and enriched herself, while all the neighbouring states

that he proposed to continue the prorogation of Parliament till the spring.[13]

In the meantime Shaftesbury, set on revenge, was doing his best to stir up trouble and had taken up his abode in the City of London, where he lodged with an old fanatic, entertained vastly and spread alarming rumours about Papists, Irish cut-throats and standing armies. But his hopes of opening the floodgates of rebellion in Scotland and Ireland, by procuring the recall of Lauderdale and Essex, were defeated by the King's steady refusal to part with either; when someone spoke of a rumour that Essex was about to be dismissed, Charles offered to go halves on it. It pleased him that both his Viceroys corresponded directly with him and placed more reliance on him than on his Ministers: one day, when York followed Essex's agent into his bedchamber, he led the latter into a farther room, deliberately shutting the door on his officious brother.[14]

Against the spring session of 1675, both Danby and Shaftesbury prepared all their artillery, while in the background the agents of the warring powers of Europe waited with bribes for the real sovereigns of England. But when Louis offered money for a dissolution, Charles declined it, saying that, though he would not allow his faithful Commons to drive him into war with France, he must give them another trial. Shaftesbury and his somewhat erratic fellow-conspirator, Buckingham—" Alderman George " as his old friend Charles now dubbed him—issued a manifesto to their supporters, calling for a new Parliament. Danby, for his part, was equally anxious to maintain the old one, upon which, unsatisfactory though it was, the hopes of his party rested: its continued existence, he knew, would depend on his ability to persuade

were drained or ruined by the war; and that the English would one day thank him for having kept them by prudence in so happy a state and so advantageous for their commerce." (Courtin to Louis, 21 June, '77, *Dalrymple*, II, 117.)

it to supply the King's needs. He also wrote letters calling
upon "his old friends of the loyal party" to support the
administration by their votes. The party scene was set: the
Whigs and Tories listed against one another, and the age-long
tale begun. Orders were given that members of the House
who held commissions were not to be on the Guard when
important divisions were pending.[15]

Charles himself prepared for the meeting of Parliament in
his own manner, by attending the spring meeting at Newmarket. Here, amid "March dust in abundance and
December ice," he saw a Cambridge don, who elected to
cross the course at a critical moment, knocked over, lost his
money with the rest of the Court when the famous "Lusty."
was beaten, and, riding three hard heats, won the Plate by
sheer good horsemanship. He was thus in excellent humour
when he met the Houses on April 13th, telling them that he
had called them together to secure religion and property, and
assuring them that—though many inducements had been
offered him to dissolve them—he had no intention of obliging
his enemies by parting with such good friends. He then left
it to Lord Keeper Finch to ask for money for the Fleet.[16]

As the Government had taken the preliminary precaution
of issuing a proclamation against Catholic priests—with a
corresponding ukase against Dissenters to please its own
supporters—the Opposition leaders' slogan of 'Ware Popery
fell somewhat flat, nor were they more successful in their
efforts to impeach Danby. But they received decidedly more
support when they fell on Lauderdale, who was almost as
unpopular with Anglicans as with Presbyterians, and only the
King's support saved him. And an appeal to anti-French
feeling, by a demand for the recall of the British volunteers in
Louis's army, all but broke Danby's ranks, the division being
so close that both parties, "thinking themselves wronged in
the reckoning, called one another all the opprobrious names

imaginable, spat in one another's faces, and pulled off one another's periwigs." As for money, far from supplying any, the Commons gratuitously insulted the King by attempting to ear-mark his Customs receipts for the Navy.[17]

Before the brief session ended, Danby counter-attacked with a measure after his own heart, a *No-Resisting Bill* to make State office and membership of either House dependent upon a declaration of the illegality of taking up arms against the King's person—a step tantamount to concentrating all power in the hands of the Anglican party. It naturally appealed to Danby's legions in the Commons, and the King, out of loyalty to his Minister, did his best to ensure its passage in the Lords by attending in person. Shaftesbury, to whom the Act would have meant political extinction, defeated it by precipitating a violent and unseemly quarrel between the two Houses over the privileges of a member of the Commons summonsed before the Lords in an appeal. When most of the counsel in this unhappy case—it is known to students of constitutional history as *Sherley v. Fagg*—had been committed to custody by the angry participants, and the Lords had accused the Commons of " transcendant misbehaviour, breach of privilege, Magna Carta, subversion of government, and other high, provoking and diminishing expressions," the King, after a vain effort to restore peace, prorogued Parliament till October.*[18]

After this kind of thing, or being driven, as he was one evening that June, into a corner of his Bedchamber, while his squabbling Ministers badgered him about Irish affairs—thence pursuing him into the Queen's drawing-room and continuing the argument throughout his supper—Charles was not sorry to escape to sea. He boarded the *Greyhound* yacht at Graves-

---

* " The divell Presbyterian in both Houses does all he can to force the King to dissolve us, and the Lords were never higher but in '42." (Richard Legh, *House of Lyme*, 272.)

Q*

end at noon on June 26th, and at once gave orders to weigh; anchoring that night between the Cant and the Oaze Edge Buoy, he was up at four next morning, firing with his own hands the gun to set his little squadron in motion towards the Downs. Driven far out of his course by westerly gales, with " no other security on board but his own seamanship," he was almost given up as lost by Secretary Pepys and the anxious Admiralty officials at Portsmouth, when he anchored, wet but happy, at dawn on July 1st under Dunnose in the Isle of Wight. Thence, to the infinite disgust of his courtiers, who had " had enough of the sea for this bout," he insisted on returning Thames-wards by the same unquiet element.[19]

Charles spent the remainder of the summer of 1675 at Windsor, a place of which, as the years went by, he grew increasingly fond. While his Queen made alfresco picnics on hot August days in the forest,* he occupied the intervals of fishing, planting and hunting with plans for the October meeting of the Houses. All who opposed Danby were bringing ceaseless pressure to bear on him to dissolve Parliament: Shaftesbury and his " mutineers " because they wanted a new one with a Nonconformist majority; York and the Papist politicians because they wanted none at all, believing absolutism to be the one way to avert their own destruction; " such small things " about the Court as Bab May, Chiffinch and the mistresses, because they did not like the perpetual shortage of money under which the great finance Minister kept them. As anxious as any of these to see the last of the Cavalier Parliament was Louis XIV. That summer his arms had

* There is a charming picture of such a picnic in a letter of Lady Chaworth's of September 7th: " All the Queen's servants treated her by everyone bringing their dish, who then attended her into the forest, and she eat under a tree. Lady Bath's dish was a chine of beef, Mrs. Windham's a venison pasty, but Mr. Hall brought two dozen of ruffs and reeves and delicate baskets of fruit, Mr. Chiffinch, for his daughter's behalf, twelve dozen of choice wine. The Queen wonderfully pleased and merry, and none but herself and servants." (H.M.C. Rutland, II, 27.)

suffered reverses, and negotiations had been opened at Nymegen.   For the moment he was genuinely anxious for peace, but so long as the allies, who wished to break his ambitions once and for all, had any hopes of drawing England to their side, he had small hope of obtaining it.   And so long as Parliament sat, its bellicose anti-Gallicism hung over his head like the sword of Damocles.   Once more, therefore, in September, 1675, he offered money for a dissolution.   But Charles, against all probability, still clung to Danby's ideal of a loyal Parliament that should make proper allowance for the needs of the Crown and country, and would even now only agree to dissolve it if, after its next meeting, it should still insist on war.*[20]

If Louis strove to bribe the King of England, the money-bags of all Europe jingled as the members of his faithful Commons rode towards Westminster.   Beuningen, the Dutch ambassador, took a house close to St. Stephen's; Don Pedro Ronquillo of Spain had instructions to spare no expense in ensuring a refusal of supply unless the King should consent to go to war with France.   To foreigners the constitution of England seemed a heaven-sent opportunity.†

On October 13th the King opened Parliament with the usual financial speech, promising to economize and asking for money to pay off old debts and build new ships.   The session was a complete failure.   The Commons, by a vote of 172 against 165—for which the Spanish ambassador took the credit—refused to make provision for the debts,‡ and, after

---

* As Coleman, the chief wire-puller of the Papist party, put it, Charles's argument was: " If I try them once more, they may possibly give me money; if they do, I have gained my point; if they do not, I can dissolve them and be where I am now." (H.M.C. Westmorland, 37.)

† " I am not able to express how much his Majesty's honour and interest abroad are weakened by some proceedings of the Parliament at home, which they reckon upon, as the French in ancient times were wont to do, as a certain diversion." (Wm. Godolphin to Arlington, 20 June, '75, Arlington, II, 238.)

‡ One member, in a speech deploring the expense of Government, actually blamed Charles for needing more money than Edward III. (Parl. Hist., IV, 746.)

agreeing to build twenty warships, voted only £300,000, a sum altogether inadequate for the purpose. The Opposition then insulted the Crown by proposing that this money should be administered by the Exchequer of the City of London, and thereby all but succeeded in setting up what would have amounted to a rival government. But the climax came on November 11th, when the Commons insisted on tacking to the Subsidies Bill a clause, appropriating the whole of the King's existing Customs revenue to the Navy, and thus denying the Crown even the prerogative of veto. Having thus proved up to the hilt their argument that the continued existence of the Cavalier Parliament could be of no advantage to the King, the followers of Shaftesbury and York joined hands in the Lords to move an address for a dissolution, which was only defeated by two votes. The session ended in a further outburst of Sherley *v.* Fagg, while Shaftesbury thundered against the national grievances of Standing Army and Standing Parliament. On November 22nd the King, having obtained not one penny, prorogued the Houses.[21]

Even after this rebuff, Charles would not despair. At the secret supper-parties in Chiffinch's rooms, at which, unknown to his Ministers, he was wont to acquaint himself with the sentiments of his malcontent subjects, he was urged by Shaftesbury to take the plunge and venture on a new Parliament. But, rather than give himself over to the men of '41, he still preferred to trust to Danby, who believed that, with time and a long prorogation, he could win or bribe a working majority. When the great Achitophel grew insistent, and, from his city throne at John's Coffee-house, industriously circulated libels against the Court, Charles acted firmly: issued a proclamation for suppressing the London coffee-houses, ejected the rebel lords from the Council, and hinted to Shaftesbury that he would be better employed in the quiet air of his native Dorset.[22]

With the opening of 1676, the trade boom of the past two years definitely broke, and the old vista of money difficulties opened anew.   The position was the more serious because, through the interest on the Banker's Debt and the loss of revenue consequent on the sale of Crown lands—authorized by a niggardly Commons, anxious to meet current expenditure out of capital—the King's fixed income had fallen by about £120,000 per annum, while, with the growing development of the nation and its young Empire overseas, the cost of administration had steadily risen.   Tangier alone, with its ceaseless wars against Moors and Algerian pirates, was costing nearly £100,000 per annum—a drain on the Crown for which Parliament made no allowance.   In this plight, while the King wheedled from a rather dubious Louis a subsidy of £100,000 as the price of keeping Parliament prorogued for a year, Danby cut down pensions and rationed the spending departments.   But no economy axe, however sharp, could cut through the difficulties of an administration consistently starved by the legislature, and in this case the axe was blunted from the start.   For Danby's lot was cast, not in the admirable paper world of accounts and figures in which his fine brain so naturally moved, but in the Court of an easy-natured and yielding prince, who found it hard to say no to any man, and harder still to any woman.[23]

A new claimant on Charles's good nature came to England that winter of 1675-6—

> " Mazarin, des amours
> Déesse tutélaire "—

whom fifteen years before he might have made his wife. Niece of the great cardinal, who had dominated his exile, married to a miserable husband whom she had long abandoned for a life of unblushing romance in half the capitals of Europe, she now carried her ripe southern beauty, her wrongs and her

diamond wit to England.   A natural and glorious lover, she
rode to Charles's Court arrayed like a gentleman of fashion,
with half a dozen retainers, a penniless exchequer, and a
most exotic little black page.   Her charms were not in
Charles's nature to resist—nor did he.   Within little more
than a week of her arrival, deeply moved by the tale of her
misfortunes, he was urging Louis to compel her husband to
make her an allowance.   In French circles there was a panic;
her grievances against France were notorious, and it was
whispered that she had been chartered by Arlington and the
pro-Dutch party to win over the King.   Such alarms were
groundless: if there was one insinuation Charles hated more
than another it was that, in political affairs, he could be
swayed by his mistresses.   At the very moment when Hortense's frank pagan beauty and conversation were winning
his heart from the fastidious Louise—impelled by his desire
to redeem his broken faith with France and his old fear of
a Franco-Dutch agreement to partition Flanders behind the
back of England—he concluded a secret treaty with Louis,
by which the two kings bound themselves never to aid each
other's enemies.   Charles—for Danby was too much afraid—
wrote out the treaty and sealed it with his own hands.   " It
will be difficult," wrote the French ambassador, " to conceive
that a King should be so abandoned by his subjects that even
among his Ministers he cannot find one in whom he can
place entire confidence."[24]

In one quarter the coming of Mazarin caused heart-
burnings.   Though to Cleveland—whom Charles had surprised in circumstances which had caused the future victor
of Blenheim to retreat, only very partially clad, through a
window—it mattered but little so long as her annuities were
regularly paid, to poor Louise it was a serious matter.   She
sickened, grew thin and, though the King still wrote her kind
letters and swore he would never abandon her, sought relief

at Bath.   As for Nelly, she was enchanted and went into mourning for the eclipse of her rival.[25]

For Charles the summer followed its habitual course; as he grew older he liked to reduce his overcrowded life to a rule.   April at Newmarket, London for a season, and then in July Windsor, where he spent such leisure as he had in supervising his building operations and making scientific experiments, was his round that year.   Interspersed were occasional visits to the seaports to view the Fleet, and once to inspect two ships, which he had contrived to fit out for the discovery of the North East Passage.   But heavier cares than these lay on his shoulders.   Everywhere an unreplenished Treasury told its tale of hard shifts and discontent.   From Ireland the Viceroy, complaining that his Guard of Battle Axes in their worn-out buff coats looked like a band of bailiffs, wrote warningly that the empty Government coffers were all too reminiscent of the days before the Rebellion of '41.   In England, sunk in commercial depression, the fire-lights of revolution flickered prophetically.   Behind the throne of a too easy monarch, nervous citizens saw the threatening shadow of his brother York, with his known predilections for absolutism, his proselytizing priests and his following of busy, intriguing Romanist politicians.   At the midsummer election of the London Sheriffs, an inspired linen draper of the name of Jenks—said to be " put upon the exploit by a great man turned citizen "—made a long speech about the danger of religion, decay of trade and French influence, and, calling loudly for a new Parliament, passed through the portals of an examination by the Privy Council into the temple of popular martyrdom.   Even an outburst of fires in London was turned to good purpose by the party libellers and dissenting preachers—the authorship being attributed impartially to French and Papist emissaries and the just judgments of God. Everywhere in the country panic, cunningly fomented, sprang

into flame with the midsummer heats; the nation was like
dried bracken in a drought. "I never saw the people in
such fears as they are in," wrote a traveller in the West
Country that July: "they keep guards in all places as in
time of war."[26]

Misunderstood by his people who, through the blindness
of their political representatives, never saw that cruel canker
of poverty which was eating the heart out of the English
monarchy, the King made a lonely figure. His easy courage
and unconcern amazed everyone: "the Parliaments are to
be feared," wrote the French ambassador, "and it is like a
miracle to see a King without arms resist them so long." At
one of the royal supper-parties a drunken courtier hiccoughed
out that soon, when all should be in confusion, he would climb
on to the old King's statue at Charing Cross and watch his
royal master, with Will Chiffinch and the Sergeant Trumpeter,
—"for, by God," said he, " he would have no one else "—
charging the three kingdoms.[27]

Yet Charles could never be quite as alone as politicians
and foreigners thought him. For, to the heart of the English
common people, there was something very appealing in their
all too human King. Supping with the jockeys at Ned
Griffin's; offering a man, who had stood on his head on
the top of a steeple, a patent to prevent anyone doing it but
himself; loving to see, and be seen, at cock-matches, horse-
races and plays, "where he never failed to warm the heart
of every spectator," he was the very embodiment of a nation
which, when it could forget religion and politics, was the
best humoured in the world. He delighted to give and take
a jest; would receive visits at all hours of the day, even from
fools and madmen, and, "in a word was so pleasant a man
that no one could be sorrowful under his government." At
a Guildhall banquet, the loyal Mayor, Sir Robert Viner,
overcome with the joy of his company and the perpetual

warmth of drinking his health, grew a little too familiar. The King, who well understood how to extricate himself from such difficulties, with a hint to the company to avoid ceremony, stole off towards his coach. But the Mayor followed him and " catching him fast by the hand, cried out with a vehement oath, *Sir, you shall stay and take t'other bottle*. The airy monarch looked kindly at him over his shoulder, and, with a smile and graceful air,* repeated the line of the old song:

> ' He that's drunk is as great as a King,' "

and suffered his host to lead him back.[28]

As the year 1676 drew to a close, all eyes turned to Flanders. A flood-tide of French victories had reversed the European situation. On November 5th Charles, taking Courtin secretly into his Closet, told him that he had good news and that the peace, so long desired by Louis, was in his hands, for the Dutch were now beseeching him to procure it. Having about the same time obtained from Louis a favourable commercial treaty, by which to appease his subject's anti-Gallic feelings, Charles seemed at last in sight of the goal of his foreign policy since 1674—a pacification of Europe which, while safeguarding English trading interests, should secure to France terms as favourable as those she might have obtained had he not been forced to abandon her.[29]

But it was never in Louis's nature to be satisfied. The close of the old year, that saw a cheerful Charles driving his sledge on the ice in St. James's Park, saw the French King arming for a new campaign. To secure his flank he offered his cousin a further £100,000 if he would prorogue Parliament for another year. This Charles refused to do; he

---

* " For I saw him at the time and do now," observed the narrator, writing over thirty years after. (*Spectator*, No. 462.)

was over a million in debt, and the state of public opinion
made an early meeting of Parliament more than advisable.
Though Shaftesbury and his crew of "mutineers" were
doing their best to rouse the country with the old grievances of France, Popery and a Standing Parliament, Danby
was still working hard to give his master a majority in the
Commons.[30]

In these efforts, Charles used all his arts of persuasion to
aid his Minister. When that honest but greedy Yorkshire
member, Sir John Reresby, reached London for the opening
of Parliament, he was delighted to receive an intimate invitation from his sovereign, who most graciously informed him
of his intentions and difficulties. "I know," explained this
confiding sovereign, "it is said I intend the subversion of
religion, that I intend to govern by an army and arbitrary
power, to lay aside Parliaments and to raise money by other
ways. But every man—nay, those that say it the most—
knows it is false. There is no subject that lives under me
whose safety and well-doing I desire less than my own, and
should be as sorry to invade his property and liberty as that
another should invade mine. Those members," he added,
"that pretend this great zeal for the public good are of two
kinds, either such as would subvert the Government and bring
it to a Commonwealth again, or such as seem to join with that
party and talk loud against the Court, hoping to have their
mouths stopped by places or preferments."[31]

On February 15th the King opened Parliament. Scarcely
had the Chancellor sat down but the Opposition lords, all
"in great bravery and liveries of blue," made a serious
blunder. For some weeks they had been flooding the
country with pamphlets to prove that, under an old act of
Edward III's, a Parliament that had not sat for over a year
was *ipso facto* dissolved. Buckingham, Shaftesbury, Wharton
and Salisbury now rose in turn to argue, by no means gently,

this interesting constitutional point.   But no public body likes
to be told that it does not exist, and, instead of winning support for their thesis, the malcontent lords found themselves
violently attacked for outraging parliamentary dignity and
privilege.   When they refused to apologize or withdraw,
their fellow-peers ordered them to the Tower.[32]

In the Lower House the Opposition fared no better.   On
February 21st, inspired by a great speech of Pepys's on the
services of the Stuart Kings to the Navy, the Commons, by
a majority of thirty-four, voted £600,000 for building ships
—a sum only £200,000 less than the Admiralty demanded.
On March 5th they refused the Opposition's motion to tack
an appropriation clause to the Subsidies Bill.   For a moment
it seemed as though Danby's policy had triumphed and that
at last Parliament was going to do that which alone could
make a strong national Government possible.[33]

The news from abroad broke all.   The spring campaign
in Flanders opened dramatically; Valenciennes, Cambrai and
St. Omer fell to the French armies.   The Opposition leaders,
aided by a golden shower from the allied ambassadors,
roused an alarmed Parliament to address the King to " fall
to the interest of Europe."   Louis did nothing to make
Charles's position easier, for, fearful of any agreement that
should make a national war policy possible, he was now bent
on stirring up trouble in whatever quarter he could.   With
such intentions he sent Barrillon, who was to succeed Courtin
as ambassador, to London.   Corrupted by the agents of every
power in Europe, the politicians, when they met after the
Easter recess, were factious to a degree, addressing Charles to
enter the war—as urged by the agents of the allies—and
flatly refusing him money to do so—as by those of the French.
In the presence of the Dutch ambassador, an angry King
tossed his handkerchief in the air, remarking: " I care just
that for Parliament ! "   On May 28th he closed the session

by a brisk reply to the Commons' claim to dictate the nation's foreign policy, observing that the prerogative of making war and peace was so essential a part of monarchy that, if he surrendered it, no one would any longer believe that the sovereignty of England rested in the Crown.[34]

CHAPTER X

THE PATRIOT KING

" Never was patriot yet, but was a fool."
—DRYDEN.

SOMEONE had spoilt his game, and it did not take Charles long to realize that it was Louis. The latter, pursuing his campaign in Flanders in the belief that he had spiked England's guns, empowered Courtin to offer his good-natured cousin £100,000 for a dissolution. But Charles had at least got some money from Parliament for his fleet, and, if Louis chose to bribe his subjects behind his back, he would show him that in the game of political intrigue he could still teach him something. Besides, he wanted peace in Europe: the constant strain which Louis's conquests imposed on the loyalty of his people was wearing. He therefore informed Courtin that he must have twice the sum offered.[1]

Within a few days of the adjournment of Parliament, there arrived in England one Bentinck, on behalf of the Prince of Orange. The latter, alarmed by the French successes in Flanders and the recrudescence of republican activity in Holland—a complaint curiously similar to that which afflicted the English monarchy—was contemplating an idea raised by Arlington three years before—a marriage with his cousin, Mary of England, York's eldest daughter. Charles and Danby, angry with France and seeking some way to escape from the everlasting suspicion of their people, welcomed Bentinck with open arms. Such a match would strengthen

255

the House of Stuart in both countries, give it perhaps a
Protestant heir, and bring peace to Europe. If Mary's stubborn
father thought otherwise, that could not be helped: "God's
fish," said Charles, "he *must* consent."   It was secretly
resolved that when the summer campaign was over, Orange
should visit England.[2]

Meanwhile Charles continued to fool Louis to the very
top of his bent.   While Danby always raised the sum asked,
and the stupid York reduced it, the conferences with Courtin
continued until July 26th, when Charles had brought the
wretched ambassador to the highest point to which his
instructions would allow him to go and obtained the promise
of two million livres (£150,000) as the price of an adjournment
till the following April.   Even now Charles had not quite
done, and, by pretending to have mistaken the currency
medium when the time for payment became due, managed
to screw an additional £50,000 out of Louis.   When a much
perturbed ambassador complained to him, Charles was all
arithmetical innocence and confusion: "For God's sake, do
not speak to me of this affair," he exclaimed; "go to the
Treasurer and do as you and he shall understand the matter;
as to myself, I am driven to despair whenever it is mentioned
to me!"   When the ambassador pointed out that to do so
would not solve his troubles in the least, since Danby was
adamant in his insistence on his extra pound of flesh, Charles,
fuller than ever of apologies and regardless of etiquette,
conducted him to the door and opened it himself.[3]

In August, while his cousin of France and his cousin of
Orange fought, marched and counter-marched across Flanders,
the King of peaceful England spent a fortnight at sea.   Sailing
at dawn from the Downs on the 7th, he encountered such a
succession of blustering western gales that the waiting people
of Plymouth thought him drowned, and, when his three little
yachts dropped their anchors under St. Nicholas Island at

dawn on the 16th, the joyful news brought them all out of their beds. At six o'clock he weighed and came into port, while the guns of the Island and Mount Batten thundered salutes. The Mayor and Aldermen greeted him at the citadel, whence this indefatigable monarch, after hastily changing his linen, walked and rowed all round the fortifications. On his return he wrote dispatches until dinner, received and knighted the leading gentry and officials, and spent the evening shooting at Saltash. After two such days, expressing the greatest delight at all he saw, and promising to build himself a house in the town, he sailed again for the Downs.[4]

At the end of September Charles went to Newmarket, to race, beagle and hawk and sup with his friends, the jockeys. On October 10th he was joined by Orange. The cold, haughty young Dutchman seemed a trifle out of the pace of the merry little town, but his uncle allowed him to waste no time. On October 21st, back in London, Charles was able to announce the engagement of his nephew and niece. The whole country, long haunted by the terror of a Catholic succession, dissolved in bells and bonfires; judges, clergy, aldermen processed to Whitehall to congratulate the happy pair, and as far north as Edinburgh, where the Cross was hung with green bows and oranges, the magistrates in scarlet robes scattered sugar plums among the revellers.[5]

Though the King sent to young Rochester to beg him to return to London to dispel the clouds of Dutch dullness which emanated from his nephew's attendants, he contrived to make the wedding—which took place on the night of November 4th—a jolly affair, bidding the bride, whom he gave away, make haste lest her Catholic stepmother should have a son before her, and concluding the festivities, as he drew the curtains on the young people, with a " Now, nephew, to your work; hey! St. George for England! " A few days later he had concluded a treaty with the bridegroom for the

R

security of the Netherlands and pacification of Europe. "You will think we have been quicker than ordinary," wrote Seccretary Coventry, " that a Prince should come and woo, marry, bed and carry away the Princess Mary in a month's time."[6]

Of course there were some who were not pleased. The faction leaders had small use for an alliance which took the sting out of their *No Popery* cry, and did their best to attribute the whole thing to French designs.* The French were even less pleased. In a long interview with Barrillon, Charles tried to show that the match was his sole means of continuing his alliance with Louis and of allaying the suspicions of his subjects, who, terrified by his brother's avowed Catholic policy, believed the Court to be taking measures with French aid to change their religion. But when Lord Feversham arrived in France, bearing proposals for a European peace agreed by Orange and an intimation from Charles that, as he had looked without jealousy on the advance of French power for so long, it was time for his cousin to do something for him, and accept what were, after all, highly advantageous terms, Louis was furious. The success of his armies had increased his ambition, and he now felt, that if only England could be kept from interfering, he might obtain frontiers that would secure France from invasion for all time. He therefore refused Charles's mediation, stopped his subsidies, and prepared for a new campaign both in Flanders and at Westminster.[7]

Before the end of December it was plain that Charles meant business. As though to emphasize the break, Portsmouth, who had just recovered from a dangerous illness— according to her confessor through the intervention of the Virgin Mary, and according to Charles through the efficacy of his medical drops—left for the waters of Bourbon. The

---

* By November 16th, an Essex parson (an old Puritan) was recording in his diary: " Heard that the city was alarmed that the Papists plotted a massacre; was the marriage a pillow to lull us asleep? " (*Josselin*, 172.)

English forces were mobilized, envoys dispatched to the allied governments to plan a joint campaign in Flanders, and Parliament summoned to meet on January 15th. Before it could do so, Louis was hastily offering money again. Charles, who was still anxious to avoid war if it were possible, adjourned Parliament for another fifteen days, and replied that he would be glad enough of Louis's money, provided that the latter would agree to a treaty that would satisfy the Confederates. On this point all further negotiations broke down. On January 28th Parliament was allowed to meet.[8]

Yet Charles fully knew how bold a step it was to break with Louis, for he had no money and few troops, and his kingdom was divided. He had small hope that the party managers, who had used his friendship with France to such advantage against him, would now support him; on the contrary they were already whispering that all the noise of war was but to get money out of Parliament. From Ireland and Scotland came tales of armed multitudes and the godly preachers, who ever preceded rebellion, busy at their work. Signs and portents in the skies foretelling the fall of thrones; inspired prophetesses dreaming of cellars full of knives and armed men with torches and pole-axes in London streets; demagogues crying to excited multitudes that " kings and prelates were the murderers of Christ "; it was not difficult to guess whence these springs came and whither they flowed.[9]

Against these time-honoured arts of revolt, Charles fell back once more on his dream of a united nation, in which no divisions of creed or faction should impede the course of government. At Nelly's candle-lit supper-parties he mixed with others than those who officially supported him : once that winter he asked the daughter of an Opposition peer, whom he met there, how her father was, and declaring him to be the best of men, exclaimed, " Come, let's drink his health," and so did. In such society he would listen to his old crony,

R*

Buckingham, mimicking his Ministers, or to Bowman's lovely
voice singing

" The glories of our blood and state
Are shadows, not substantial things "

so movingly, that once afterwards young Rochester, with some
others of the merry crew, staggered out into the Privy Garden,
and there throwing his arms round the King's favourite dial—
esteemed the rarest in Europe—cried out:

" Sceptre and crown
Must tumble down

and so must thou! " and flung it down.   When Danby
protested at his all too inclusive company, Charles replied that
he would not deny himself an hour's divertisement for the
sake of any man.[10]

As in his pleasures, so in matters more spiritual he was
anxious to broaden the basis of his policy.   That December,
to the disappointment of the Anglican highflyers, he raised
to the vacant see of Canterbury, Dr. Sancroft, Dean of St.
Paul's—a man so humble that he had once before declined a
bishopric for the lowlier task of rebuilding London's cathedral,
and so gentle that he could be trusted not to persecute.   When
Chiffinch led him to the royal presence, the good man protested that he was unfit for so high a post, until Charles ended
the argument by explaining that there was no choice in the
matter, since he had already given his deanery to someone else.[11]

In his opening speech to Parliament on January 28th, the
King appealed for a united nation to save Europe.   But
Louis had been before him, and had authorized Barrillon—
to aid whom he sent the Protestant Ruvigny, a near relation
of Lord Russell's, most influential of the Whig leaders in the
Commons—to meet the overtures of the Opposition leaders for
money and moral support.   The new alliance was quickly
concluded. Both parties had the same aim—to prevent Charles
from obtaining from a patriot House of Commons the where-

withal to free himself from the dual subjection in which he
stood; both one overwhelming fear lest English King and
people should be at last united.*   To declare that Charles's
withdrawal of his troops from France was part of a design
to enslave England, that his war policy was a mere blind for
money, that Popery and massacre were intended by means of
a standing army, became now the Opposition programme.
With the aid of French money, the Grandees guaranteed to
prevent Charles obtaining the sinews of war; when he had
been forced back into Louis's arms, the latter was then to advise
him to dissolve the existing Parliament for a new one and so
play into their hands.   In the meanwhile every effort was
to be made to provoke rebellion in Scotland and Ireland,
and, as a preliminary step to secure, by bedchamber intrigue
or parliamentary address, the removal of their viceroys.   It
was an old game which some, still living, had played in the
far-off days of '39 and '41.†[12]

As soon as the session opened, the elaborate farce began.
The Opposition leaders could not openly oppose a war, which
they had so long demanded, but, by denying any grant of
money until the King should agree to reveal his foreign
policy, and then by attaching conditions incompatible with
monarchy to the Subsidies Bill, they believed that they would
be able to drive him back into the arms of Louis.   When
Charles's frank declaration on his foreign policy won him a
vote for ninety ships and thirty-two regiments and a promise
of a nominal million for supplying them, they added a popular
clause against the importation of French goods, which deprived

---

* " The whole nation being in one way of thinking." (Conversation of
Shaftesbury, Russell and Holles with Barrillon: Barrillon to Louis, 11 April, '78,
Dalrymple, II, 167.)

† " There is yet living in France one Monsieur de Montreuil, who was
resident with the rebels in Scotland many years together during the troubles
of the late King; and there be some old enough to remember the negotiations he
had there with which they were perfectly acquainted." (J. Brisbane from Paris
to Danby, 18 Dec., '77, H.M.C. Lindsey, 391.)

the Crown, through the loss of Customs revenue, of as much
as they had given, and effectively delayed the passing of the
Poll Tax by which the grant was to be raised.* All the while
Louis's legions were sweeping across Flanders. At a levée
at the end of February Charles told Reresby that, unless the
money bill was dispatched soon, the French King would have
finished his business.[13]

Though his drums were beating to arms and men raising
as fast as possible, Charles was finding mysterious difficulties
put in his way by the very allies, who for so long had urged
him to come to their aid. Orange, as ever, remained true
to the purpose of his life—the defeat of French ambition—
but the Dutch republican deputies, inspired by the same golden
source as their English brothers, were now demanding peace
on terms far inferior to those agreed a short while before.
While England, at great loss to its trade and the King's
revenue, forbade French commerce, the Dutch continued
openly to trade with the enemy. From the Spanish authorities in Flanders came similar obstructions, and for several
weeks Charles was unable to send the Guards to Orange's
aid in Flanders, owing to the Governor of Ostend's refusal
to allow them to land.[14]

Charles had not found much advantage in "falling to
the interest of Europe," as he had been so long addressed to
do. The most that he could hope from the war grant was
£300,000, which was set off by the loss of the Customs on
French goods, and he had already exhausted his overburdened
credit by raising money on his own to equip the Fleet.
Meanwhile furious attacks on his honour and intentions
were being made by the Faction.† He was under no delusion

---

* " And thus they go on, contending and disputing every particular step
that is made, having a greater number of able and contentious speakers, though
they are outdone in votes." (Sir R. Southwell to Ormonde, 9 Feb., '78, H.M.C.
Ormonde, IV, 399.)

† Pepys's words, spoken in the House in defence of his master against an

as to what his enemies intended; when Reresby, who had been voted out of his seat on an election petition, told him of the shout with which the Opposition members had halloed him from the House, Charles observed that they would still more willingly halloa him out of his kingdom.[15]

Insulted and humiliated by the politicians, betrayed by his new allies, committed to vast expenses, yet granted scarcely a penny to meet them, it was not unnatural that Charles should take steps to secure his retreat.   After receiving from Orange, who was faced by the same combination of French gold and factious deputies, an anxious intimation of his desire for peace, he secretly approached Louis with an offer to procure favourable terms from his allies in return for a three years' subsidy.   But Louis's demands, backed by his conquering arms, were too high, and Charles, though he was ready enough to obtain money for doing what it was his business to do in any case, would not abandon Orange. Maddened by the perpetual circle of penury and intrigue in which he found himself held, and worn out by a ceaseless round of interviews, dispatches and Council meetings, even Charles's temper showed signs of strain.   Once that spring he spoke with anger of some domestics who had served him ill, and even threatened them with dismissal—a thing almost unknown in his palace.   Yet such ill humour never lasted; and, though forced to forego his customary holiday at Newmarket, he contrived to obtain a little amusement— if only from the contentions of two noble ladies, who provided laughter in that captious time by throwing candlesticks at each other and then petitioning the House of Lords for

ill-tempered and baseless attack, have been substantiated by the publication within comparatively recent years of the *Calendars of Treasury Papers,* which show how religiously Charles applied his all too scanty grants to the maintenance of England's Navy. He was speaking the bare truth when he said: " There has not been one penny of it spent but towards a war with the French King. If there has been a ' cheat ' it is on the King's side, who has debarred himself of all of it." (Debate of 11 May, '78, *Parl. Hist.*, IV, 975-6.)

redress. Charles took care to be present and begged that he might be allowed to judge of the damage done to one fair combatant's knee.[16]

On April 29th, when the Houses met again after a brief recess, they were greeted by an extraordinarily frank speech, outlining the diplomatic and domestic difficulties of the Government and appealing for support and a vigorous policy to save the Netherlands. It might as well have been spoken to the stones of Westminster Hall. Well fortified by Barrillon and Ruvigny, the Commons were in fine fettle: refused to give money until religion was secured, and bellowed *No Popery* to the skies. To add to the confusion they voted that the form of the King's alliance with the Dutch was inconsistent with the safety of the kingdom, attacked the Army as a threat to the liberty of the subject, and finally fell upon the Ministers. In weather hot as August, tempers grew as warm: when Harry Savile, one of the King's household officials, after having out of personal animosity spoken in the House against the hated Lauderdale, appeared as usual at the royal *coucher*, Charles, instead of the "innocent puffing and spitting" which was his normal expression of displeasure, turned white with passion and resentment. A day or two later, despite Danby's desperate attempts to rally the Court party—whipping up the aged, the sick and the halt—the Opposition carried an address to the King to dismiss Lauderdale. Charles replied curtly that he preferred not to give it the answer it deserved, and on May 13th prorogued the House for ten days to cool their heels.[17]

Louis and the Opposition had won their game. Though Charles had poured his little army into Flanders and done his best to fall to the interest of Europe, he had been checked at every move.* With debts piling up, the Scotch Coven-

* " What return you gentlemen of the House of Commons made me, and whether it was suitable to the end I intended (which was the saving of Flanders) I leave it to yourselves in cold blood to consider." (King's Speech, 23 May, '78.)

anters again in arms, and civil war imminent in England, it was time to look to his own interests. He therefore warned Orange that it would be impossible for England to do anything by arms, and advised him to secure the best peace he could.* Before the end of May Charles had agreed to Louis's proposal that he should stand neuter if the allies had not accepted within two months the terms which France was then offering at Nymegen. He refused to sign any treaty to disband his levies or dissolve Parliament—as Louis, true to his English confederates, demanded—but obtained from Barrillon a promise of six million livres (about £450,000) payable whenever he should do so. Once more he had been driven by his faithful Commons into the arms of France.[18]

Yet one last attempt to secure a national and independent policy Charles made. When the Houses met on May 23rd, in a clear and resolute speech he urged them not to drive him to extremities, which must end ill both for him and them and, worst of all, for the nation. The Chancellor, following, asked what instances of arbitrary government in the whole reign the Opposition could offer to justify its jealousy of the Crown, and what nation in Europe could rely on England, when England was no longer itself. The appeal fell on deaf ears, for three days later, when news came that hostilities on the Continent had been suspended for two months, the Commons, without considering for a moment the effect of such action on the negotiations at Nymegen, voted an immediate disbandment of the Army. They thus did for nothing what Charles had refused to commit himself to doing unconditionally for six million livres. A few days later they rejected Danby's request for a grant to bring the

---

* " There will be no possibility of carrying on the war now that the factious party in the House of Commons does prevail; it is necessary for me to say this to you, that you may take your measures accordingly, and you must expect to hear of great disorders: they are not to be avoided." (York to Orange, 7 May, '78, Dalrymple, II, 209.)

Crown revenue up to the ordinary peace-time expenditure of the State, on the grounds that to do so would reduce England to slavery and wooden shoes.[19]

The natural result of such precipitate behaviour was that Louis raised his terms and refused to restore the captured Flemish towns, giving the claim of his ally, Sweden, as excuse. At the same time Luxemburg's great army moved towards Mons. "If the French King," wrote Secretary Coventry, " should publish his design to conquer Christendom under his hand, he could not reveal it better than by this last proceeding." Charles at once informed the Lords, urging that the disbandment should be suspended, and the English forces in Flanders strengthened. In this he acted with real courage and independence, for by so doing he sacrificed all hope of financial aid from Louis, without the least certainty that his subjects would support him. But he did not care to let France flout him, and was genuinely anxious to preserve as much of his little army as he could. To the author of *The Growth of Popery*, answered about this time by a spirited little pamphlet entitled *The Growth of Knavery*, the recruits encamped on Hounslow Heath constituted a " dark, hovering army," threatening massacre and despotism. But to Charles, who loved to watch them at their drill, and added to his difficulties by pledging his ruined credit to maintain them, they were a source of perpetual pride and interest. Throughout his whole reign, in the face of poverty and every discouragement, he always contrived somehow to keep a few regiments in being, and to him, as much as to any man, belongs the honour of having created that regular army, which a generation later was to humble the pride of Louis and build the walls of Empire. In so doing he had to contend with the disapproval of his subjects, who, remembering Cromwell's major-generals, regarded a soldier as an object of hatred and ridicule; a Suffolk baronet, who appeared at a levée in the uniform of the Guards, was laughed out of Court. To the witty Harry Savile, the military zeal of that summer seemed merely an interference with the more serious business of love. " A true good fellow like a kingfisher can only breed in calm weather," he complained; " the continual noise of horse, foot, dragoons, cuirassiers, grenadiers, guidons, aides-de-camp, and a hundred such words repeated ten thousand times a day in Whitehall Gallery, have frighted away even the thoughts of the least indulgence to a man's pleasure."[20]

Yet this time Charles did not appeal altogether in vain, and a sudden wave of patriotism for once proved too strong for his enemies. On July 15th a weary and jaded House of Commons, after having voted what was thought a reasonable provision for the new emergency—though in reality the King was left no better off—was prorogued for the summer vacation. While reinforcements were hurried off to defend Mons, Temple was sent post-haste to Holland to conclude a league between the two countries against Louis unless their terms were immediately accepted. " The King," he wrote, " is once more at the head of the affairs of Christendom." A few days later Louis, pressed by his friends at Westminster, who now saw all that they had most feared come to pass—a united nation following a patriot King to war—gave way. On July 31st peace was signed at Nymegen. A posthumous battle between Orange and Luxemburg before Mons, in which the English levies won some glory, revived for a few further weeks the talk of war, but by the beginning of September Louis had again yielded. Thus, at the eleventh hour, a general pacification of Europe was secured, which, while giving to France that secure north-eastern frontier which is her eternal need, assured to the allies—so long as they remained united—the preservation of the Netherlands.[21]

CHAPTER XI

THE POPISH TERROR

" What stratagems and devices, what ways and means, will not disaffected persons find out to blacken a government they have a mind to overthrow."—ROBERT FERGUSON, the plotter.

SURPRISED and pleased at his success, Charles betook himself in August to Windsor. Here—for Windsor, as the Clerk of the Council wrote, was " a charming place "—there was little business, a great deal of hawking and fishing, and, for Charles, a touch of ague. But across the Channel the French King was not pleased, and sought eagerly for a chance to make his anger felt. With Scottish Covenanters in arms, and the English Grandees fuming under their defeat, he had not far to look. While the Duke of Buckingham paid a mysterious visit to Paris, Louis gave Ambassador Barrillon orders to do " everything possible to make troubles for the King of England." Above all Danby, who had proved himself the sworn foe of France and republican alike, was to be brought to the ground.[1]

Throughout the hot summer of 1678 omens of coming storm had been observable. Wiseacres remembered the events of thirty years back; as in those days, the first clouds came from Scotland and Ireland. There, as one Anglican divine wrote, covenanting preachers, mysteriously paid and inspired, rode " up and down the country like martial evangelists with sword and pistol, as if they came, not to prate down, but storm our religion." Old Ormonde, watching the course of events, admitted his anxiety; " better," he wrote, " a thatched house in Ireland or a grave anywhere than the Louvre or Palais Royal."[2]

Yet all this would not have stirred the people, had not an overmastering fear gripped their hearts. Ever since the Gunpowder Plot, Englishmen had been afraid of red cardinals and black priests, of racks, fires and midnight massacres, of all the devilries of a mighty Church against which their forefathers had rebelled, and which ever—so they had been taught from the cradle—plotted to enslave them. Instinctively they felt that some horrible attempt against their faith was being planned. Their eyes travelled to the English Colleges beyond the seas, where young men of their race were bred up by " that subtle people, the Jesuits," to trouble their Israel; to the almost daily conversions among the great at Court; to the pageant-like display of hated rites in the Chapel of the Savoy and the French Embassy, and the mysterious comings and goings of Romish emissaries; above all to a Catholic Queen and a busy, zealous, pragmatical successor, bent, as all believed, on the overthrow of the national liberties and religion. Among the Grandees, this unreasoning terror was transmuted to a more subtle fear—that the broad abbey lands they owned might revert to the ancient Church. With the brushwood dry and crackling, all was ready for a conflagration, should Louis, Shaftesbury or blind chance set a match.[3]

On August 13th, a day before the King went to Windsor, he was stopped in the park and warned of a Catholic plot against his life—the discovery of a certain Israel Tonge, a hair-brained meddlesome clergyman, and Titus Oates, a renegade Jesuit novice and son of an Anabaptist preacher. Charles, who was used to such tales, merely referred it to the Treasurer. But when in September he returned to London on his way to Newmarket, he learnt that Tonge was still making discoveries at the Secretary's office, where the clerks, a little wearily, supposed that he was after a deanery. The stories were so insistent that, on Saturday the 28th, the Council took the matter into consideration. Tonge was sent for, and a mysterious bundle of papers, importing a Jesuit conspiracy, opened. In the afternoon the original informer, Oates, was examined, and as this strange creature—with neckless head and mouth set flat in the centre of the circle of his low brow and vast chin—told his story, the Council sat amazed. Gradually the wondrous tale unfolded: the Pope, the French King, the General of the Jesuits, the Provincials in England, Spain and Ireland, the Archbishops of Dublin and Tuam, and the Rectors of the Jesuit Colleges, linked together in a mighty plot to kill the King, set up the Duke of York, plunge Ireland in blood, impose Catholicism by the sword, and destroy English commerce; the four Irish ruffians who were to do the bloody work at Windsor, the Lancashire incendiaries to fire London, and the three thousand cut-throats to massacre the sleeping citizens; the poisoners in attendance, who included Wakeman, the Queen's physician, and Coleman, the Duchess of York's Secretary. It was a horrible conception, and one well attuned to Protestant fears. The Council sat till midnight, and again all Sunday. "If he be a liar," wrote Secretary Coventry of this ominous witness, " he is the greatest and adroitest I ever saw, and yet it is a stupendous thing to think what vast concerns are like to depend upon the evidence of one young man who hath twice changed his religion."

The King himself was under no delusion. Cross-examined as to how he came into possession of all this evidence, Oates, holding up his hands, declared that, by God and His holy angels, he had gone among the Jesuits solely to betray them. As his confidence grew, he became more specific; named five Catholic peers, Arundell of Wardour, Powis, Petre, Stafford and Bellasis. When he added that the last, who was bed-ridden with gout, was to be Commander-in-Chief of the Papist army, Charles could not help laughing. Yet certain of the charges bore the impress of an inner knowledge, not easily obtainable by the son of an obscure Anabaptist preacher.[4]

While Charles showed his unconcern at the alleged threat to his life by proceeding to Newmarket, the Council continued to examine the evidence, which every day grew in length and wonder. By October 5th informations were coming in from every quarter, and the outlines of the plot were already, by some mysterious means, familiar to the whole kingdom. Even those least likely to be moved by the tale were impressed when the Council started disarming Papists and arresting persons accused by Oates. The discovery—an ill-fated stroke of Danby's to smash once and for all his Catholic rivals—of a long and wildly indiscreet correspondence between the French King's Confessor and Coleman,* did much to strengthen credence in the plot. But it was not till the middle of October that the passions and fears of the people were fully aroused. A popular magistrate, Sir Edmund Berry Godfrey—a man of strange and melancholy appearance, and though a strong Protestant a personal friend of Coleman's—to whom Oates had recently made depositions, went out, saying he would be home to dinner, and completely vanished. Before evening it was rumoured throughout the town that he had been murdered by Papists. Five days later his body was found in a ditch on Primrose Hill, with his own sword through it. Medical examination showed that he had been previously strangled, and that for two days before his death he had eaten no food. The inference—though few drew it—was that he was murdered some time after the first report, so sedulously spread, of his assassination.[5]

At this fresh piece of news all Protestant hearts dissolved in terror. It seemed to confirm all that Oates had said. The wildest rumours spread like fire: of cellars full of cutlasses, of

---

* Charles had some time before ordered York to dismiss this meddling and indiscreet servant. (*Hatton*, I, 138-9.)

French legions sailing Kentwards, and Papist armies marching underground. A massacre was universally expected. Lady Shaftesbury, duly instructed by her lord, never walked abroad without a loaded pistol in her muff, and everywhere terrified ladies followed her example. Everything that was reported against the Papists was immediately believed, regardless of probability, even to the story that a troop of monks had arrived from Jerusalem expressly to sing Te Deum for the success of the plot. Most ominous of all, the mob, afloat since the day of Godfrey's disappearance, marched through London, exposing the murdered man's body in such angry fashion that, as one observer recorded, had anything Catholic appeared—even a dog or a cat—it had gone to pieces in a moment. All over the country the blood-hounds began to bay. Anyone who bore the least resemblance to a priest was hustled to jail to await trial for life; anyone with a cock-and-bull tale of a plot was believed and rewarded. Thus that Protestant apprentice, Eli Thomas, after spending his afternoon viewing a hairy girl in Moorgate, could earn pay enough for his liquor by pretending he had seen a French Papist, kicking the ceiling with his foot, in a Moorfields tavern.[6]

Charles still remained incredulous. When Oates appeared before the Council to give evidence against a knot of poor Jesuit priests, he examined him closely, and several times caught him tripping. Relying on the popular belief as to the Spanish appearance, he asked him what manner of man was Don Juan, and, when Oates answered tall and black, fell into a laugh, for he happened to be short and red-headed. Again, when Oates spoke of the Jesuit College in Paris, Charles asked him where it was, and, when he replied near the Louvre, observed that he was as much out as if he had said Gresham College stood in Westminster. But all this did nothing to shake the popular belief in Oates. So long as he could, Charles refused to leave the accused prisoners to the fury of a jury. Yet he saw clearly now that he was faced by something very sinister—a story so well attuned to popular fears that the nation in its existing mood must almost certainly believe every word of it, and at once suspect anyone who did not do likewise. He knew that Oates was in daily conclave with the agents of the great Lords and politicians who, from their Green Ribbon Club at the King's Head Tavern, controlled the City, and already guessed the course the tempest must take. If he set himself openly to discredit the plot, far from succeeding, he must be drawn into open conflict with the whole mass of his people, and so fall into the hands of his enemies.*[7]

Therefore when Parliament met on October 21st, Charles, after his usual fruitless appeal for money to pay for the Fleet and Army and to meet the anticipations on the revenue, referred guardedly to the plot. " I now intend to acquaint you (as I shall always do with anything that concerns me) that I have been informed of a design against my person by the Jesuits, of which I shall forbear my opinion, lest I may seem to say too much or too little. But I will leave the matter to the law, and in the meantime will take as much care as I can to prevent all manner of practices by that sort of men, and of others, too, who have been tampering in a high degree by foreigners, and contriving how to introduce Popery amongst us." By the last he indicated his very real displeasure at Coleman's foolish letters, which revealed, not an assassination and revolutionary plot of the Oates variety, but a long planned design to subvert the national religion.† The rest he left to the members.[8]

It at once became obvious that Oates was a favourite of

---

* Witness Ralph Montagu's delight at Wakeman's acquittal in 1679: " For it is much better for us Mutineers." (*Blencowe*, 34.)

† A few days later the King told Reresby that though he did not believe one word of the plot, or that there was any design on his life, it was plain from Coleman's letters that there had been a design to introduce Popery. (*Reresby*, 23, 25 Oct., '78.)

theirs. On the very first day of the session he was before them, " swelled up to a high pitch of vanity and insolence," and making statements, far bolder than he had hitherto dared, against the Catholic peers. This Tribune of the people now came in for a golden time. His lightest word was law, his accusation of any man tantamount to immediate imprisonment, and his claim to be the saviour of the nation universally accepted. An old stone found at Oatlands, engraved with the sibylline words, " Oats shall save this land from destruction," was held to be proof positive of his sublime mission. To the people this arrant scoundrel had become a kind of male Joan of Arc. At the urgent request of Parliament, he was given apartments at Whitehall—where he could the better secure the life of his sovereign—a pension of £1,200 per annum, and an armed bodyguard.[9]

Nation and Parliament alike were now in a state of stampede. The overmastering passions were fear* and a furious desire to find victims. Anyone who cast doubt on the credibility of Oates, or spoke on behalf of those he accused, was in danger of his life. The Commons petitioned that all Papists should be disarmed, banished ten miles from London, and confined to their homes; the King, who steadily refused to play into the hands of the plot-makers, and was resolved that, if there were eggs to be broken, they should break in their pockets and not his, did as they requested, and issued the necessary proclamations. Only in private did he continue to state his conviction that the whole plot was an artifice.[10]

The plans of the great contrivers soon became all too apparent. A Bill was immediately introduced and carried in both Houses to exclude Catholics from sitting in Parliament.

* " It is now doubted the matter will not be thoroughly canvassed, and some money being well placed, we shall be contented with the hanging of three or four inconsiderable fellows, and some law against Popery, which will keep our throats from being cut a month at least." (H.M.C. Kenyon, 108, 31 Oct., '78.)

Its real purpose was shown by the fury of its promoters at an amendment, which Danby succeeded in carrying by two votes in the Lords, to exempt the Duke of York—since the discovery of Coleman's letters the most hated man in the country —from its provisions. Fear of revenge, should he ever come to the throne, as well as dread of Popery and loss of property, were driving even moderate Protestants along the republican path. Their leaders had no scruples in beckoning them on: before the session had begun Buckingham had asked the French ambassador for money to arm the Londoners. On November 2nd the spear-head of the attack on York was driven home by Shaftesbury, who declared in an impassioned speech that the only way to save the country was to dismiss him from the Council. At this the King, after persuading his brother to withdraw from the chief Committees of State, came down to the Lords and announced that he was ready to join in all that would establish a firm security for the Protestant religion, provided that the lawful succession of the Crown was not impeached. The effect of this timely action was parried by two startling rumours which were at once circulated—that Monmouth was to be recognized as heir apparent, and that Shaftesbury had been sent to the Tower. " If I should write you all the news and malicious stories that are told," York informed Orange, " instead of a letter, you should have a volume from me."[11]

Meanwhile the baying of the blood-hounds continued. In the city the alarm was such that two thousand men were maintained day and night in arms, and the Governor of the East India Company sent his wife and children away for fear of a massacre. The whole country was searching for priests and hidden arms.* It was a wretched time for Catholics: the

---

* Surveyor Christopher Wren was kept particularly busy looking for prospective Guy Fawkes under the cellars of the Houses of Parliament. (*H.M.C. House of Lords*, 1678-88, 16.)

S*

best advice a friendly Westmorland Justice could give one, a wealthy widow, was to marry a Protestant, who could protect her person and property, as quickly as possible. Meanwhile a Chepstow horse-thief named Bedloe appeared before the House of Commons with wonderful revelations about Godfrey's murder, which he declared had taken place in the Queen's Palace of Somerset House; for him, as for Oates, a free pardon, State apartments and a pension were at once forthcoming. The King alone remained unimpressed, and expressed somewhat forcibly his opinion that Bedloe was a rogue. Though he was resolved to let the national flood run its course, he did what he could to mitigate its terrors, had Father Huddleston expressly exempted from the proclamation against priests, and refused to dismiss from his pay several humble Catholic officers who had long served their country. When the Commons, on discovering this, summarily dispatched the Secretary of State, who had signed their pay warrant, to the Tower, the King sent for them and informed them that he would be more civil to them than they had been to him, for, though they had put one of his servants in the Tower without acquainting him, he would now let them know that he proposed to let him out again.[12]

But his enemies were ready with a new blow. A few weeks before, Oates, who continued to make fresh discoveries every day, had accused Mazarin of complicity in the plot;* now, emboldened by the support of the Commons, he made a loftier flight. On Sunday, November 24th, he accused the Queen in the Council of having been privy to a scheme of her physician, Wakeman, to poison her husband. If the great men who had set him on trusted to Charles's indifference to his wife, they found they had overreached themselves. Charles was furious. He had Oates clapped up, and it took all the

* " When he will make an end of accusing people the Lord knows." (York to Orange, 29 Oct., *H.M.C. Foljambe*, 123.)

clamour of the Commons to get their precious saviour at large again. Before they could do so, he had been detected in a manifest lie, for having been sent by the King to identify the rooms in which he had heard the Queen consent to the murder, he had displayed an entire ignorance of the place.[13]

Catherine put a brave face in public on this infamous charge, but in private she never ceased to weep at being accused of wishing to murder the man she loved. In him she found an unflinching protector. The attack roused all his chivalry, and he turned to fight. " They think," he said, " I have a mind to a new wife; but for all that I will not see an innocent woman abused." To Burnet, who had once before been Buckingham's emissary to persuade him to a divorce, he spoke out his mind freely, saying that, considering his faultiness towards her, he thought it would be a horrid thing to abandon her.[14]

His courage saved her, and, for a moment, stayed the flood. On November 29th the House of Lords, following his lead, rejected by eight votes a proposal to concur with the Commons in an address for her removal. Throughout the country honest and loyal men, for the first time since the panic began, paused to reflect. At Christ Church, when a foolish chaplain deliberately omitted the Queen's title of " Most Gracious " from morning prayer, the Fellows of the College waited on him afterwards and compelled him to drink her health. Yet, if the best of his subjects were still ready to rally to his side in a clear cause, Charles knew well that he was fighting a rearguard action. His enemies were too well led to let the national terror, on the continued existence of which their possession of the political initiative depended, flag for a moment. A never-failing stream of discoveries* and

---

* " More discoveries every day of the plot, and I confess I am entirely convinced that there was a most desperate design." (Coventry to Ormonde, 14 Jan., '79, *H.M.C. Ormonde*, IV, 303.)

mysterious murders* kept the tide of panic at a flood. Those
who were not frightened by the sham plot could be terrorized
by the real one: the scowling Oates, from whose presence
honest men drew back as "from a stench from hell," had
only to growl his famous threat, "You're a Yorkist, I'll
remember you for it," for opposition to crumble away; for
behind that blood-stained and accusing finger lay the powers
of Parliament, packed juries and frightened judges, and the
howling mob.[15]

Yet though Charles was retreating in the face of overwhelming force, he was ready, as he proved again and again,
to fight for essentials. At the end of November the Houses
presented him with a Bill for placing the Militia under
parliamentary control—the very demand which had precipitated civil war in '42. For the first time in his reign,
Charles used his power of veto: he would not, he told them,
let that command pass out of his hands for even half an hour.[16]

Urged by France the Grandees prepared a further assault.
Louis had given them word that two things must go—the
Army and Danby. On November 25th the King made a last
appeal to the Houses for money to maintain his troops in
Flanders until the final terms of the European pacification had
been accepted: they replied that they must be disbanded at
once. Having received not one penny to support them,
Charles had no option but to agree. A day or two later the
politicians fell upon the Ministers. But their great blow was
withheld till the third week of December and then came
straight from France. A little while before Montagu, who
had been dismissed for misconduct from his ambassadorship at
Paris and was now seeking revenge, had suggested to Barrillon
the production in Parliament of a confidential letter sent him
that spring by Danby, referring to Louis's offer of money

---

* "Someone or other is murdered every week, and the malefactors cannot
be found." (Anglesey to Ormonde, 23 Nov., '78, H.M.C. Ormonde, IV, 243.)

for a favourable peace; this letter, he thought, divorced from its context, would sweep the House off its feet and render an impeachment certain. In return, since such a breach of confidence would infuriate Charles and alienate honest men, Louis was to grant Montagu a large pension. A little doubt-fully—for the due consideration of other letters in Danby's keeping might have blasted the whole design—Barrillon agreed, the popular leaders were informed and a seat in the Commons procured for Montagu. On December 16th, after a fruitless attempt on Danby's part to anticipate matters by seizing the ex-ambassador's papers on a charge of secret corres-pondence with the Papal Nuncio, the mine was sprung and the fatal letter read in the House. At once the members of all parties were in a flame, and, by a substantial majority, articles of impeachment were voted. But in the Lords the attack received a check, the peers refusing to commit until the articles of treason were better grounded. The result was a furious duel between the two Houses. Taking advantage of this temporary lull, the King on January 30th prorogued Parliament—which had sat steadily through the Christmas holiday—till February.[17]

The dying year saw also the first impeachment of the Catholic peers, the trial of Coleman and the Jesuits, and the indictment of three wretched servants of the Queen, charged with Godfrey's murder. The prorogation saved the peers, who remained in the Tower, but nothing could save the others, who were tried by terrorized judges while the mob yelled with joy at every word spoken by the witnesses for the prosecution. The King himself did his best for those accused of Godfrey's murder, by cross-examining the Crown witnesses for days at a stretch in the Privy Council, but, though he shook the evidence to pieces, it made no impres-sion on a nation almost mad with terror. More he could not do: had he insisted on exercising his right of pardon, with the mob up and the City armed, revolution must almost certainly have followed. His only way of maintaining peace was to follow his declared plan and " let the laws take their course." " Let the blood lie on them that condemn them," he said, " for God knows I sign with tears in my eyes."*[18]

∽ Alone, vilified, driven on every side, Charles remained calm and patient. This middle-aged roué, who liked to be easy and see those about him so, was now fighting almost single-handed against an utterly unscrupulous caucus and a maddened populace for the preservation of English monarchy and of decent dealing in public life. To that contest he brought a cool courage, a temper that to the outer world remained imperturbable and a skill in gauging the deepest designs of his adversaries that amounted to genius. One asset he still retained—his personal popularity with the people, which all the foul defamations, scattered about a credulous City and nation by intellectual republicans to whom a king was merely a contemptible idol,† could never altogether obliterate. Yet the odds against him were tremendous. At the New Year he was so poor that he confessed to Barrillon that he would have to withdraw his ambassadors from the Continent. The unpaid troops were being disbanded, furious with a Government which thus threw them on the world.

* Yet, despite the entreaties of his whole terrified Council, he reprieved one of Godfrey's murderers, and refused for weeks to sign the death warrants for three condemned Jesuits. (*H.M.C. Ormonde*, IV, 492 *et seq.*)

† The republican attitude towards the King was never better summarized than in the brilliant and scornful lines with which Marvell recalled the Restoration:

" Of a tall stature and of sable hue,
    Much like the son of Kish, that lofty Jew;
    Twelve years compleat he suffered in exile,
    And kept his father's asses all the while.
    At length by wonderful impulse of fate,
    The people call him home to rule the State:
    And, what is more, they send him money, too,
    And cloath him all from head to foot anew!
    Nor did he such small favours then disdain,
    Who in his thirtieth year began to reign."

The City, since the prorogation of Parliament, was in the utmost consternation: it was whispered that, had the Houses sat a few days longer, the whole plot would have been revealed, and that they had been dismissed on the tearful entreaties of Portsmouth, who had assisted at the murder of Godfrey and spat on his dead body. Until the King quieted public opinion in some measure by a reassuring address to the Lord Mayor, the London shopkeepers threatened to close their shops and suspend all business. The wildest rumours passed from the coffee-houses, where the Lords of the Green Ribbon congregated, to taverns and street corners: Shaftesbury was to be murdered, troops quartered in the city and forty thousand French cut-throats to take ship at Dunkirk. Outside Newgate the mob howled daily for the execution of the condemned priests.[19]

In despair the King turned again to France; the humiliation of having to do so, great though it was, weighed but little against the far greater evils of civil war or the surrender of his crown. But the gates were closed. Louis, who had England trepanned before him, was true to those who had done the trepanning. It was made plain to Charles that he must live now, as he had lived in the days of exile, on his wits alone.[20]

To save Danby, the King took the plunge he had so long dreaded, and dissolved the Cavalier Parliament. On January 24th he informed the Council of his resolution. Writs were at once issued for a new Parliament to meet in early March. For the first time in eighteen years the country awaited the delights of a General Election.[21]

In the anxious weeks that followed, the King preserved his outward calm, declaring that he would give the people all imaginable freedom in returning whom they chose. But those near him noticed that he bit his nails to the quick—so much so that his thumb festered and he could obtain no sleep for pain. Out in the country his enemies made no disguise of their determination that the elections should go as they intended. To the usual flood of guineas and beer was added a shower of abuse for all those suspected of leanings towards Church and King. Papers, containing fiery extracts from the Bible against choosing bribe-takers, pensioners and Papists, were passed about from hand to hand, and in Bedfordshire Lord Russell and his crew gave out that their opponents did not believe in the plot—a damning imputation. Even a ghost was sent electioneering. One Sunday morning, it was rumoured in the Green Ribbon Club-rooms, a prodigious darkness had overspread the sky and, in the midst of it, the murdered figure of Godfrey had appeared beside the altar in the Queen's Chapel. Everywhere Presbyterians, Independents, and Republicans swept the polls. When the final result was known, Danby's old Guard—who had once proudly flouted " a fanatic crew that will oppose all things that are just and good, for blessed be God, we outnumber them! "—had shrunk from a hundred and fifty to barely thirty.[22]

Charles had to recast his plans, and do so quickly, for his opponents now held all the best cards. Either the victorious Shaftesbury would use a new attack on York to destroy monarchy altogether, or—as Ormonde in the less troubled air of Ireland thought—alter the succession, break the Anglican monopoly and place the control of public finance, Militia and Navy in the hands of the oligarchs who now controlled Parliament and the constituencies. In either case the weakest point in Charles's armoury was his brother's Catholicism. Therefore, while the Court was still reeling from the result of the elections, he made a last attempt to convert his brother; but neither his own politic entreaties nor the more celestial arguments of Canterbury and the aged Bishop of Winchester could move York from his unswerving purpose. There was therefore nothing for it but to try to save the succession at the price of the successor. Within a week of the final election results, Charles had commanded his brother to leave England; his reasons for so doing, expressed in the form of an affectionate letter, were at once published, to the universal delight of simple, loyal folk.* At the same time, to make it known that he would have no tampering with the legitimate succession, he declared publicly in Council that he had never married any other woman but the Queen.   Certain of the Opposition chiefs had for some time been hinting that Monmouth might be legitimatized, to which his father replied that, love him as he did, he would sooner see him hanged; now they began to insinuate that he *was* legitimate.   Finally, on the day before the meeting of Parliament, Charles announced that Danby, whose services he rewarded with a warrant for a marquisate, should lay down his office at the end of the quarter.   Thus prepared, he awaited his foes.[23]

When the Houses met on March 6th, though approving hums greeted the King's reassuring remarks about the steps he had taken to guard against Popery, it was made manifest that the Grandees had their new flock well in hand.   The first skirmish was over Charles's refusal to accept the Speaker chosen by the Commons, an undoubted Crown prerogative which his opponents decided to challenge.   In this they were defeated, for the King, feeling himself on firm ground, refused to budge an inch, and on each successive appearance of their protesting delegations, returned only this brief answer : " You do but lose time, go back and do as I have directed you." After a week, their masters wishing to get on with other and

* Thus from the White House, East Claydon, Mun Verney wrote to his convalescent father : " That the distemper should leave you, and the Duke of York England, much at the same time is a mercy, which makes me merrily and trebly sing *Gaudiamus and Haleluia*, and I pray that the one be never suffered to trouble you more, nor the other this nation again, and so God bless our good King Charles, in whom I hope there is no guile." (*Verney*, II, 330.)

more serious business, the Commons gave way.   Then the
storm fell.   The frightened Danby, who saw his head on the
block, pressed the King to take the White Staff from him
without delay.   Charles did so, but, despite his own necessities,
insisted on his accepting a grant of money.   In doing so,
he was adding to his difficulties, but he meant to show
that faithful service to the Crown would be rewarded, at
least in one quarter.   In the Lords, Danby's enemy, Halifax,
declaring that he did not believe it possible that such a traitor
could be rewarded, looked as he spoke straight at Charles,
who was standing by the fireside.   " My God," the King was
heard to exclaim, " how I am ill treated, but I must bear
it and keep silence."   Meanwhile, before the " hard-hearted
Commons of England," Bedloe and Tonge performed
prodigious exercises, accusing Danby of concealing the plot
and tampering with their sacred evidence.   On the 22nd the
King, to cut short the impeachment, appeared in the Lords
and told the members that he had pardoned Danby and
would, if necessary, do so ten times over.*   After that, chaos
broke loose, for the Opposition, prompted by its French pay-
masters, was resolved to have Danby's blood.   On April 14th
the Lords, by three votes, agreed with the Commons for an
Act of Attainder.   To avoid this, Danby surrendered himself
to Black Rod and was committed by his fellow-peers to the
Tower.   As he went down the river, the mob flocked to the
waterside, yelling and holding up halters.[24]

Before Danby was down, the Opposition had made it
plain that it was no mere security against Popery that was
sought.   That was but the handle: the aim was avowedly
the old one of '41—" Reformation ! "   Nor were the weapons
different: armed Covenanters in Scotland, the rabble loose in

* " I will give it him ten times over, for I will secure him in his person and
fortune, which is no more than I commonly do to my servants when they
quit my service, as the Duke of Buckingham and my Lord Shaftesbury well
know."   (King's Speech, 22 March, '79, *H.M.C. Lindsey*, 404.)

London, and the City magistrates refusing to tame it, since, as one worthy constitutionalist declared, the noise of its roaring would do more to persuade Whitehall than all the fine speeches in Westminster. But two factors which had contributed to the fall of monarchy in '41 were now lacking. The interference of the mob with the freedom of parliamentary debate and administrative action was checked by the presence of " some naughty Guards, which the King had always in good order," and whom he still contrived somehow to pay and keep together; how much their presence was resented by the Grandees is shown by the Commons' resolution of April 1st that all military forces, including Guards, were illegal. The other was rebellion in Ireland, which was now made impossible by the presence of Ormonde. The Bishop of Oxford hit the nail on the head when he wrote to the latter: " Although everything about us threatens confusion and ruin, we may entertain hope that God has mercy still in store for us, in that he has raised up a person of your Excellency's zeal and love to religion to stand in the gap, and, by supporting one of the three kingdoms, exceedingly contribute to the stay of the others." The Opposition knew this only too well. When Ireland was mentioned in debate, Shaftesbury shook his head and said he did not like the management of affairs there. Coffee-house rumours were started to discredit the Viceroy: he was whispered to be in league with the French, and planning a second Irish rebellion and massacre. But old Ormonde only wrote: " I am here in my old station, pulled at on all hands. Time was when I was believed to be an enemy to French and Papists: now I am said to be absolutely at their service. But I feel myself just as I was."[25]

Now the ground was prepared for the great attack; once more Popery was to be the handle. Everyone who opposed the great designers was labelled Papist; honest Edward Cooke declared that were Christ Himself on earth again there would

be those who would brand Him with that fashionable calumny.*
On April 3rd the Commons brought in a Bill against Popery
of such length that the very reading of it took over an hour.
On Sunday, 27th, they voted that the only way to preserve
the King's person was to prevent the succession falling into
the hands of a Papist, and that the Duke of York was the
cause of the plot.   At the same time the Ministers were once
more fallen upon.[26]

Again Charles parried.   On April 20th he declared that,
to quiet all fears of evil counsellors, he would have no more
cabinets and reduce the Privy Council to thirty, reconstituting
it on a new model suggested by Temple and Sunderland, by
which wealth and land were mainly represented.   To direct
the Commons' factious dislike of all government against their
own leaders,† he filled the Council with Grandees, and made
Shaftesbury President.   To York, looking anxiously on from
Brussels, it seemed as though a republic was already established.   But to one whose loyal father had been omitted from
the new list of counsellors, Charles explained: "Doth he
imagine I left him out because I did not love him?   He was
left out because I do love him.   God's fish, they have put a
set of men about me, but they shall know nothing; but this
keep to yourself."   On April 30th he once more offered
expedients against a Popish successor, promising to agree to
any Act that would deprive a Catholic king of the power of
ecclesiastical nomination or of appointing a co-religionist to any
office of State.   One thing alone he would not do: consent to

* " . . . French and Papists, two terms of art in every malicious mouth,
completing revenge on whomsoever either can be pinned, and considering the
easy credulity of this uncharitable age, it seldom fails to stick." (Colonel Ed. Cooke
to Ormonde, 29 March, '79, *Ormonde*, V, 7.) Or as Pepys, hounded from his
task of " encompassing Britain with wooden walls," put it: " Whether I will or
no, a Papist I must be." (*Tanner, Pepys Corr.*, I, 6.)

† " No sooner doth any man get the least employment but a hundred others are
immediately contriving to turn him out, so that here will be nothing but
tumbling down one another till they all come to the bottom of the hill." (Lord
Conway to Sir G. Rawdon, *H.M.C. Hastings*, II, 387.)

the alteration of the lawful succession. But still his foes were dissatisfied, for the hated York would still succeed, and the limitations were not to take place until after Charles's death.[27]

After a brief May-day interlude, in which King, Lords and Commons mingled together at Hampton Court to watch a greyhound match,* the dusty battle was joined again. On May 8th the Commons voted an address for the removal of Lauderdale from Scotland; on the following day an angry King announced to the Houses the news of the barbarous murder in that country of Archbishop Sharp by Covenanters. On the 22nd, as the weather grew hot and sickly, the Bill for changing the succession of the Crown and disabling the Duke of York from succeeding passed its second reading by a majority of ninety-two. That night the Whig Club at the King's Head, Temple Bar, was illuminated by an enormous bonfire. Alone, almost defenceless, his household officers unpaid and clamorous, the garrisons without stores, and open rebellion imminent,† the King seemed to have no alternative but surrender. Yet a night or two later, a visitor to the Palace was amazed to see him looking so cheerful amidst his troubles, and heard him say that he would stick to his old friends. And though scarcely anyone believed it possible, he did so. On May 26th, while a vast crowd awaited the trial of the five Catholic peers in Westminster Hall, he came down the river and, after passing a batch of Bills which included the famous Habeas Corpus Act, prorogued the Houses, who were once more in angry altercation with one another, till August. As he returned to Whitehall he observed that he had freed himself

---

* " . . . The Hampton Court Olympic, where the King honoured the pastimes with his presence, and thousands followed his example, so that the breadth of the paddock was fain to be divided with stakes and ropes." (Colonel Ed. Cooke to Ormonde, 30 April, '79, *H.M.C. Ormonde*, V, 75.)

† " Unless something very vigorous be done within a very few days, the monarchy is gone." (York to Orange, 1 June, '79, *H.M.C. Foljambe*, 131.)

from a burden that weighed upon him, and that those who fancied that want of money must drive him to extremities were mistaken. "I shall find means to pay the Fleet and manage economically," he added; "it will be difficult and uncomfortable for me, but I will submit to anything rather than endure the House of Commons any longer."[28]

CHAPTER XII

THE FIGHT FOR THE SUCCESSION

" Thus have I seen a King at chess,
    His rooks and knights withdrawn,
His Queen and Bishops in distress,
Shifting about, growing less and less,
    With here and there a pawn."

THOUGH Shaftesbury was furious, and tried to march the
'prentices on the Palace, all, "with much ado, was kept
quiet." With Parliament out of the way, the white heat of
the plot began to cool a little. Outside London, sensible,
reflecting men paused, as Charles had foreseen they must, to
ask themselves whether they had not been befooled, and what
kind of a picture their country presented to the rest of the
world.* And in the quiet that succeeded the clamour of
Westminster, England became more like itself. A little while
before Ormonde had commented on the strange change that
had come over that good-humoured, sport-loving country:
"In all your letters I find not one word of horse, hawk and
hound." Now in the shires men turned again to the
traditional ways and pastimes of their fathers. It was the
first sign of returning health.[1]

But the King had a long road to travel yet, and he knew
it. Though he strictly retrenched his household expenses, he

---

* "I much fear that this business at last will appear very foul and render us
odious and contemptible through all Europe." (Humphrey Prideaux to John Ellis,
29 July, '79, *Prideaux*, 70.)

T

resisted the attempts of his new Ministers to disband his
Guards, and replied to a proposal to send some of his scanty
troops to Tangier that, though he loved Tangier well, he
loved himself better. On July 9th came news that seven
thousand Scottish Covenanters were in open rebellion. When
Russell—whose party had done its best to bring it about*—rose
dramatically in Council to lay the blame on the hated
Lauderdale, Charles observed quietly : " Sit down, my Lord,
this is no place for addresses." Monmouth—chosen to
conciliate moderate Protestant opinion—was dispatched as
Commander-in-Chief to Scotland, and a fortnight later the
King, who had been prevented, much to his disgust, from
proceeding to Windsor, was able to announce the defeat of
the rebels at Bothwell Bridge.[2]

Meanwhile the plot pursued its weary course. All June
the Judges were busy trying men for their lives. The City was
still frenzied, and the slightest opposition to the popular
clamour for blood at once denounced as " a plot to stifle the
plot "; and when the King argued in Council against the
iniquity of allowing the law to destroy the innocent,† his
terrified Ministers opposed him to a man. On one point,
however, he insisted on fighting. Wakeman, the Queen's
physician, was awaiting his trial; as before, rumours were
spread about that his mistress was implicated in the conspiracy
to poison the King. But though the pack, set on by those
who thought to change the succession, howled against her,
she was secure in the protection of him that " feared no
colours nor was sensible of any danger." Before the trial,

---

* See (inter alia) the republican Algernon Sidney's commentary. " . . . The
discourses I have heard very often of late of those who every day expected some
such thing persuades me to believe it is not fallen out by chance." (Sidney to
Savile, 9 June, '79, Sidney, 90.)

† " . . . After he had had a little advice, kept it pretty well to himself."
(Blencowe, 13 June, '79.) " The business at Council was to reprieve Langhorne,
wherein the King took great pains, which troubled all those that were concerned
for him." (Blencowe, 27 June, '79.)

Charles had the informers summoned before him and, after several hours cross-examination, obtained a reluctant admission that they had said all they knew against his wife. " There is nothing," wrote Catherine to her brother, " that concerns me more than to tell you how completely the King releases me from all trouble . . . by the care which he takes to defend my innocence and truth. Every day he shows more clearly his purpose and goodwill towards me, and thus baffles the hate of my enemies. . . . I cannot cease telling you what I owe to his benevolence, of which each day he gives better proofs, either from generosity or from compassion, for the little happiness in which he sees I live."[3]

At the end of June he took her to Windsor, spending his first day there showing a guest the improvements he was making in park and castle—the stately Court, now nearly finished, with Gibbons' copper statue riding in the midst, and the frescoes Verrio was painting in St. George's Hall. Here, while he awaited the result of Wakeman's trial and amused himself by fishing—a form of quiet in which he had come to take great delight—he laid his plans for the future. Early in July, having obtained the collaboration of the more moderate of his new Ministers—Halifax, Essex, Sunderland and Temple—he announced to a dismayed and protesting Council his intention of dissolving the existing Parliament and calling a new one for October.[4]

His courage was rewarded, for on July 18th Wakeman was acquitted, Chief Justice Scroggs plucking up heart and turning fiercely on the informers, whose testimony was proved to be manifestly and criminally perjured. The effect was electric; it divided the nation straightway into two halves, those who saw that they had been deceived, and those who blindly persisted in believing. The latter howled terribly; a simple country mayor expressed their view when he protested that, had Wakeman been innocent, he would never have been tried.

T*

" If Oates and Bedloe are not to be believed in all they say,"
declared one of the great leaders, " and the Queen be not a
traitor, our business is at an end." Therefore, while the mob
flung a half-hanged dog into the Chief Justice's coach, Shaftesbury solemnly complained of him in Council.[5]

The King took his measures. He sounded Barrillon as to
the possibility of French aid, but negotiations broke down
when Louis demanded a dissolution of Parliament for three
years. This Charles refused, for he knew that he could never
secure an adequate revenue save by parliamentary aid, and he
still had some hope of the new elections. But a small,
scattered and highly corrupt electorate was not to be won
without considerable resources and a high degree of organization, and in these the King was immeasurably inferior to his
enemies. Denouncing Wakeman's acquittal as a Court plot,
the Exclusionists again swept the polls with all the clamour
of a great and powerful party.* Even in the royal borough
of Windsor itself, the hallooing of the mob disturbed the
King's fishing.[6]

At the beginning of August Charles made a sea voyage,
viewing the coast defences from Woolwich to Portsmouth,
where fever was raging in the crowded streets. On the 21st,
back at Windsor, he played a long, hot game of tennis, and,
after being rubbed, walked in the cool of the evening beside
the river. Next day he was taken sick with a shivering ague
and high fever. On the 23rd his life was despaired of. All
night he lay tossing up and down, calling in a quenchless
thirst for wine and water.[7]

The consternation of the nation was indescribable.† The

* As in former times the pulpits were requisitioned by the politicians: the
Puritan vicar of Earles Colne, who a few weeks before had deplored the defeat of
the Scottish rebels, recording in his diary: " The choice of Parliament men at
hand: I publicly stirred up people to chose." (*Josselin Diary*, 177.)

† " Good God! what a change would such an accident make! The very
thought of it frightens me out of my wits." (Harry Savile, 11 Sept., '79, *Blencowe*,
I, 141.)

republicans were ecstatic : they thought all things their own. But the loyalists and moderate men, who loved peace, and the mass of the people, who did not rightly comprehend the great designers, were in terror : all the worst things the plot had threatened seemed now at hand. In the Council itself, where a split had already occurred, the ruling moderates— Halifax, Essex and Sunderland—terrified by the all-consuming power of Shaftesbury, sent a secret message to York at Brussels, bidding him hasten to England before it was too late.[8]

But those who counted on confusion did not reckon with the King's calm temper, which did more for him than all the ceaseless bleedings of his physicians.* By the 25th the fits were losing their rigour and he was able to sleep a little : by the 29th he was reported out of danger. On that day he noticed the anxious Chief Justice in his Bedchamber—which throughout his illness had been crowded almost to suffocation with inquirers—and called out to him to pluck up heart, for he was resolved they should stand or fall together. When York arrived at Windsor on September 2nd he was greeted by a cheerful convalescent, who had already exchanged gruel and water for mutton and partridges, and was talking to his indignant doctors of his intention of going to Newmarket.[9]

In the general relief at his recovery, York's return aroused so little protest that Charles felt he could take a bolder step. Though, in view of the election results, his brother's continued stay in the country was plainly undesirable, the occasion seemed ripe for an indication that the Government would defend the legitimate succession. Accordingly Monmouth was also ordered abroad. It proved the easier to persuade the King to this, since for once he was exceedingly angry

---

* " The King has contributed much to his recovery by that extraordinary calm temper that he has showed in all his sickness; and in those fits, which are of great pain and uneasiness, he never changed from that calmness he had in health." (Sir Robt. Howard to Ormonde, 27 Aug., '79, *H.M.C. Ormonde*, V, 194. See also *Add. MSS.* 25124, f. 205.)

with his beloved son—partly on account of his intrigues with
the republican politicians and partly because of certain amorous
advances he had been making to his sister-in-law, the child
Duchess of Southampton.   Not till he had seen the rival
claimants depart, the one to Brussels and the other to Holland,
did Charles feel free to proceed to his promised convalescence
at Newmarket.   Here in the sweetest air of England, all was
gaiety and merriment, so that a courtier, used to the alarms
of London, could not believe he was in the same country.[10]

Early in October the King's brief holiday ended.   Shaftesbury, disquieted by the news that secret permission had been
given York to remove from Flanders to Scotland, had summoned the Council to consider the matter.   On his return,
Charles at once took the offensive, rated Shaftesbury soundly,
told him that he knew of nothing to hinder his brother from
going into any part of his dominions that he chose, and gave
the latter, who had been driven by storms into the Suffolk
coast, leave to stay for a few days in London on his way
north.   On October 13th he informed his Council that he
proposed to prorogue the new Parliament till January at the
very least.   On the same day he dismissed Shaftesbury.[11]

A state of almost open war henceforward raged between
Charles and Shaftesbury.   The latter, crippled in body and
in perpetual pain—

> " restless, unfixt in principles and place,
> in power unpleased, impatient of disgrace,
> a fiery soul, which working out its way
> fretted the pigmy body to decay "—

set up his banner at his old headquarters in Aldersgate Street.
Here, amidst a staff of green-ribboned politicians, informers,
and rumour-makers, he prepared a new thunderbolt.   For
some time the informers' accusations had been growing
more and more unbelievable; a mighty effort was now made
to revive the old pious faith by the exposure of a Catholic

conspiracy to "fasten the plot upon the Presbyterians." On October 26th Oates preached before an enormous congregation in Foster's Lane, and next day the great "sham plot" of the Meal Tub burst on an angry town. A packet of forged letters was conveniently discovered in a tub of meal, and one Captain Dangerfield (alias Willoughby)—"an artist in all sorts of land piracy"—who had been set up to decoy certain unwary dames of the Papist party into the concoction of a sham Presbyterian plot, turned King's evidence and exposed the whole affair. Dangerfield was at once promoted to the glorious company of pensioned informers,* and York and the lords in the Tower denounced as hidden manipulators, guilty of the horrible offence of conspiring " to scandalize Dr. Oates and Mr. Bedloe and render them persons of no credit." The Popish Plot was on its feet again.[12]

Thus strengthened, Shaftesbury endeavoured to force the King's hand. He first tried to play on his love for Monmouth and his known inclination for peace. On November 2nd and the next two days, the intermediary, Justice Warcup, had several long talks alone with his sovereign in his Bedchamber; Charles admitted that he could not believe ill of Monmouth, and at the end of the first interview clapped Warcup kindly on the shoulder. But when the latter, in a burst of enthusiasm, mentioned the pious Oates's offer to have him prayed for in the Nonconformist congregations, Charles replied that he would not have God mocked and bade him tell Oates to stick to his own business and speak truth. Nor would he consider for a moment Shaftesbury's dangled bribe that he should agree, in return for a grant, to leave all matters concerning the Queen, York and the succession to Parliament.[13]

On November 17th—the anniversary of Elizabeth's acces-

---

* The informers had even tried to coax the King into the affair, by offering to give evidence against their employers, but he told their intermediary that, though he loved to discover plots, he never cared to create them. (*E.H.R.*, 40, *Warcup Journal*, 23 Oct., '79.)

sion day—Shaftesbury paraded his power, his brisk boys laying an effigy of Sir Edmund Berry Godfrey at the doors of Somerset House, and a hundred thousand people marching in procession through the streets of London, with infinite clamour, behind images of Pope, Devil and surpliced choristers. Charles grimly watched the spectacle from a goldsmith's window. About the same time there appeared, amid a burst of other libels, a widely circulated tract entitled " An Appeal from the Country to the City," which, after an incendiary appeal to all the worst fears and passions of the ignorant,* insinuated that York was the author of the Fire of London and that nothing but the succession of Monmouth could save the people from massacre. This was followed at the end of November by the reappearance of Monmouth himself. Almost before he arrived, the London bells were ringing for his return and pamphlets announcing the fact selling in thousands in the streets. But the King, furious at this attempt to nominate his successor, ordered his son to leave Whitehall, and deprived him of his commands. In the city, to which Monmouth retired, the people acclaimed him incessantly, rising up and cheering him even as he went to take the sacrament, while all the great world, believing his victory assured, paid him court. Even Nell Gwynn turned traitor and supped with him nightly; when the populace, seeing her gilded coach, took her for her Catholic rival, she popped her head out of the window and cried: " Be silent, good people, I am the *Protestant* whore! " None the less, with her usual impartiality, she christened Monmouth " Prince Perkin."[14]

Defeated for the moment in his attempt to impose Mon-

---

* " Imagine that you see the whole town in a flame, occasioned this second time by the same Popish malice which set it on before. At the same instant fancy that amongst the distracted crowd you behold troops of Papists ravishing your wives and daughters, dashing your little children's brains out against the walls, plundering your houses and cutting your own throats." (" Appeal from the Country to the City," *Parl. Hist.*, IV, App. No. ix.)

mouth on the King, Shaftesbury concentrated his efforts on forcing an early meeting of a Parliament in which he must necessarily hold all the best cards. But the King was convinced that such an assembly was intended only to lead a revolution and told Essex that, though he would be glad to meet it when the violence of the times wore off, he proposed till then to live upon his revenues. For a time Shaftesbury thought of assembling the Commons in the city as a kind of private national Council of his own, but, by December, he had fallen back on the happier device of using his party organization and the general fear of Popery to manufacture monster petitions for an early meeting of Parliament. In this way the maximum amount of publicity was obtained for his programme, while all opposition was stigmatized as interference with the freedom of the subject.* The art of petitioning was simplicity itself. " Observe," wrote the Clerk of the Council, " how the plot begins to foment. There are printed here in one form a multitude of petitions, dispersed into the several counties and confided to certain gentlemen therein to go from parish to parish and, not only to gather hands, but to set down those that refuse, that their good qualities may in convenient time be made known." The general impression given was that it was not safe to refuse. Yet there were many loyal men who did so. When the politicians visited the organist of Salisbury with their roll, he answered that, since he understood nothing but music, the only thing he could do for them would be to set a tune to it.[15]

Shaftesbury, counting on the King's utter poverty, employed all about him to persuade him to abandon his wife and brother to Parliament. Attending the Palace with a

---

* One of Shaftesbury's allies, Lord Essex, had expressed during his Viceroyalty of Ireland five years before, his views on petitioning: " Such petitions can only serve to manifest the factious and seditious spirits of those who promote them, to raise tumults and disorders in the city and discontent against his Majesty's Government." (20 March, '74, Essex, I, 189.)

petition, he told the courtiers that, though now they had
neither meat nor money, if their master would give way they
should have both, and new wenches too, if their old ones
would let them.   Such efforts only made the King more
resolute.   Before the year ended, in spite of all his Council
could say, he announced his intention of continuing the prorogation till the following autumn and, when the timid
Chancellor, Nottingham, protested, told him that if he said
any more he would rise from the chair.   In the burst of
wild petitioning that followed, Charles remained calm and
firm.   When Gilbert Gerard, heir of an old loyal house,
appeared at the head of one delegation with Oates, Bedloe
and the sons of two regicides, Charles replied that he was
sorry to see one of his name in such company.   To the Essex
petitioners he remarked that he remembered '40 and '51, on
which their spokesman, an old rebel, answered that he remembered '59 and '60.   But he was more genial towards the
Berkshire petitioners who arrived on the same day; and, after
expressing regret that his neighbours should meddle with his
business, added pleasantly: " We shall agree better over a cup
of ale when we meet at Windsor."[16]

It was " a crazy time everywhere," especially in London.
" Our world here," wrote the great Lord Halifax, who was
now grown weary of the ways of his old ally, Shaftesbury,
" is so overrun with the politics, the fools' heads so conceited,
and the knaves so busy, that a wasp's nest is a quieter place
to sleep in than this town. . . . I confess I dream of the
country as men do of small beer when they are in a fever."
Everyone supposed Charles lost: he appeared to be completely
forsaken, his very person surrounded by strangers.   " The
King," wrote one, " seems to have staved off the evil day
as far as he is able, and now I fear it will come upon him
with the utmost calamities we can apprehend: he seems
to all ends and purposes an undone man."   Gone was the

brilliant Court of old days, the pensions and salaries unpaid and " scarce bread for the King's family." It seemed miraculous to many that the Government could subsist at all. But Charles was at last fulfilling an old prophecy of William Coventry's, who had told him twelve years before that rather than be a poor King, he had better eat bread and water and discharge all the idle company about him, and that he must do so in the end.[17]

He had seen worse times; he could make shift for the present and trust his foes to throw their cards away before the game was done. " God be praised," wrote Lord Bruce, " he was endowed with a great temper of mind and of kingcraft and knew men to a hair, and usually said, *Give them but rope enough and they will hang themselves.*" Therein lay his salvation. Before January, 1680, was out, Lord Russell and three other of the Exclusionist Councillors tried to force his hand by threatening resignation. " With all my heart," he answered, and they went. About the same time orders were issued for purging the Commissions of Peace of malcontents, and York was given temporary permission to return from Scotland. Charles, though he was careful to forbid any indiscreet celebrations, greeted him with affection. There succeeded a period of quiet.[18]

In his government of the country the King was now aided by a triumvirate—two young Treasury Commissioners, Lory Hyde and Sidney Godolphin, and the new Secretary of State, Lord Sunderland. Hyde was as much an exemplar of the new and laxer school of Cavalier as his father, Clarendon, had been of the old; Godolphin, a perfect colleague, servant and administrator—" never," Charles said, " in the way and never out of it." Sunderland was a less certain quality—young, brilliant, handsome, to be proved by time a double-dyed traitor, he was the glass of fashion by which all the coxcombs of England learnt to dress. His famous drawl,

" Whaat maatters who saarves his Maajesty, so lang as his
Maajesty is saarved," was the model for the aspiring Oates's
" Aye, Taitus Oates, accause Catherine, Queen of England,
of Haigh Traison." As this cautious ministry, by conducting
a vigorous campaign against priests, made it difficult to raise
the cry of Popery, the Opposition fastened on its youth and
inexperience to bring it to ridicule.

> " Clarendon had law and sense,
>   Clifford was fierce and brave;
> Bennet's grave look was a pretence
> And Danby's matchless impudence
>   Helped to support the Knave.
>
> But Sunderland, Godolphin, Lory,
> They'll appear such chits in story,
> 'Twill turn all politics to jests,
> To be repeated like John Dory,
>   When fiddlers sing at feasts."[19]

But the real head of the ministry was the King, and his
foes could not count on any inexperience in that quarter. He
was winning popular opinion, not only in the country but in
their own stronghold, London. In March he supped with
the Lord Mayor, sitting next to the Lady Mayoress—" all
over scarlet and ermine and half over diamonds "—and when
the Aldermen had drunk his health on their knees, wishing
all hanged and damned that would not serve him with life
and fortune, they insisted on escorting him home at two
o'clock in the morning. Something in the courage and
originality of their King appealed to the younger generation;
and there was some talk that spring of the apprentices burning the Rump on Restoration Day—a proposal promptly
magnified by the Faction into a design for the long advertised
Popish massacre. At any moment a flood might set in for
loyalty. In Quarter Sessions and country market-places,
men were already joining together to declare their abhorrence

of seditious petitions.   If the petitioners were the first Whigs, the abhorrers (as they were called) were the fathers of the Tories.   Their attitude was best summarized by the Lancashire Justice who remarked that the nation was divided into three parts—knaves, fools, and wise men; that the former made plots, the second believed them, and the third believed them not.[20]

Once more Shaftesbury prepared a new assault.   On the last day of March the King was brought hurrying back from Newmarket by the tale of an Irish plot.   Once more the old story of massacre and fire shook the hearts of honest citizens, substantiated by the strangest witnesses that ever obtained credence from English juries.   A stream of ragged, be-brogued Irish cow-stealers and jail-birds, "hearing that England was disposed to hearken to good swearers," poured into the country.   Their real business, apart from making Protestant flesh creep, was to discredit Ormonde, without whose removal nothing could be done in Ireland.   The Opposition hoped that, stung by insinuations and threats of impeachment, he would resign; but the old Cavalier assured the King that he was only the more resolved to serve him with all the vigour time had left him and all the faithfulness time could not take.*[21]

Meanwhile Shaftesbury took a further step in his campaign.   In April a rumour began to circulate of a mysterious box, found in the possession of the old Bishop of Durham (who, being dead, could not deny it), which was said to contain evidence of Charles's marriage during exile with Lucy Walter.   It became so persistent that the King was forced to

---

* " My first reason is that the Crown and my bountiful master are too apparently threatened for a man that pretends to honour and gratitude to make a voluntary resignation. . . . The next is that I have a little stomach left yet that rises at the thought of giving some men their will just when they would have it of me." (Ormonde to Henry Coventry, 14 April, '80, *H.M.C. Ormonde*, V, 304.)

issue a public declaration in denial. Yet, as it was just the
kind of romantic rumour which appealed to the common
people, the tradition of handsome, Protestant, disinherited
King Monmouth took root in many a simple English heart.[22]

Ever since his illness of the past autumn Charles had been
in poor health.* Two country girls, who had visited his
Court that winter, reported him as silent and sad, and looking
so ill that it grieved them to see him, though in the same
picture they painted his Queen as brisk and well, and his
little son, the Duke of Richmond, playing before him as he
came into the antechamber. During the summer of 1680,
to save the expense of Whitehall, Charles moved his household to Windsor. Here in May, after leaving off his waistcoat, shaving his head, and then walking in the dawn mists
beside the river, he was attacked again by his old enemy,
ague. Once more he was seized with violent fits, and his
lips broke out; the physicians, in alarm, prescribed the new
Jesuit powder—quinine from the Peruvian bark—and by a
quaint irony the Papist cure saved his life. The rest of the
summer he remained at the Castle, living very privately and
passing his days fishing or walking in the park. The quiet,
inanimate things beside the river, and the fish between the
shadows and the sunlight, were not in the power of politicians
to take from him. He still seemed depressed, but his old
health promised to return, if only, as a courtier wrote, he
could be kept from fishing on days when a dog would not
be abroad.[23]

This quiet time was attended by a whole burst of acquittals,
the Judges both on the Assizes and in London plucking up
courage to cross-examine the Crown witnesses—an event
always attended by the collapse of their evidence. Through-

---

* He suffered much from ague, and for a time had tried to live on milk: it
is refreshing to find the faithful Chiffinch, now grown sadly frugal, at last expending
£13 18s. 8d. on some Saragossa wine for his use. (*Secret Services*, 15.)

out the prolonged battle, the King had rested his policy on an unswerving respect for the forms and processes of law— he would leave, he constantly declared, all to the laws. To be victorious he only needed to wait till subsidence of the panic made the law once more an instrument of justice. The incredulity which attended the depositions of some of the new Irish witnesses—men such as the informer who told Justice Warcup that he could do anything with his pen but that he could not speak—warned Shaftesbury that the rich veins of the plot were becoming exhausted. He therefore devised a new method of attack—to turn the natural course of justice by packing the juries with party men, and so make the Judicature as subservient to his will as the Legislature. The key to the juries was the Sheriffs and Corporations, and on these Shaftesbury, with matchless skill and daring, now fell. In a riotous and prolonged election that summer he secured the return of two republican Sheriffs, Cornish and Slingsby Bethel, for the City of London. The victory ensured that every London jury, so long as there were twelve men left in the city of his way of thinking, would return whatever verdict he chose.[24]

Now, as before, the King's necessities, added to by the complications of foreign affairs, gave Shaftesbury his chance. In June news had come that Tangier was in peril: Charles had dispatched men and supplies in haste to save it, but the drain on his impoverished finances left him near breaking-point. The same determination to serve the external interest of England, even when he could barely maintain his throne, led him that summer to strengthen his alliance with Orange against a new threat of French expansion. Once more, for a moment, Charles seemed about to appear at the head of a great European league to stem the ambitions of Louis. But he could not do so without money and parliamentary help. As soon as Charles showed that he intended to meet his new

Parliament, Barrillon, slapping his vast insolent thighs and heavy with bribes, marshalled his legions.*[25]

The combatants girded on their armour. In the city— now by the election of the fanatic, Patience Ward, as Mayor, almost a rebel stronghold—Monmouth, after an August progress in the west, was greeted by the rabble with royal honours. It was a fine time for " Mutineers." The drunken Whig, Lord Lovelace, at a public banquet, flung his cap in the air and shouted he was for a Protestant Duke, no Papist, and, God damn him, he was for the Protestant religion! A few weeks before the Houses met, a final contingent of fourteen Irish plot-discoverers arrived, and, after dining with Oates, were ushered into the mighty presence of Shaftesbury. Far away at Newmarket, Pepys was taking down, at the dictation of his sovereign, the tale of that miraculous escape of twenty-nine autumns before.[26]

On October 21st, after packing his unpopular brother off to Scotland to be out of harm's way, Charles greeted his fourth Parliament. In a remarkable speech he referred to the necessity of saving Tangier, and to the league which he had concluded with Spain and Holland " for the safety of England and repose of Christendom." After promising to concur in any measures for the security of religion, consistent with the preservation of the legal succession, he concluded with a passionate appeal for unity:

" But that which I value above all the treasure in the world . . . is a perfect union among ourselves. Nothing but this can restore the kingdom to that strength and vigour which it seems to have lost and raise us again to that consideration which England hath usually had.

" All Europe have their eyes upon this assembly, and think

* In the previous year, the republican Sidney had written: " I am confident . . . that, if the Parliament had met, neither this nor anything that is like to engage us in any war, would have been endured by them, nor that they would have given a penny towards it." (Algernon Sidney to Harry Savile, 29 Oct., '79, *Sidney*, 151-2.)

their own happiness and misery, as well as ours, will depend upon it.* . . . Let us therefore take care that we do not gratify our enemies and discourage our friends by any unseasonable disputes. If any such do happen, the world will see it was no fault of mine; for I have done all that was possible for me to do to keep you in peace while I live and to leave you so when I die."[27]

But while Monmouth swaggered in the Lords with a crowd of gentlemen walking bare-headed before him, the Commons treated his father's appeal for unity with contumely. Russell at once rose to declare the absurdity of considering trifles when every Protestant life in the country was in peril. Then the nature of that Parliament was revealed as its members fell upon their enemies. They voted the abhorring gentlemen of the provinces to be betrayers of the national liberties—imprisoning without trial such of them as they could lay their hands on—expelled one of their members for having expressed disbelief in the plot, and attacked the Judges who had dared to acquit those accused by the informers. In this they followed the old and worn ways of '41; their purpose was to prove that no man could safely oppose them or pin his faith to the King: already they had frightened half the Court, including Louise and Secretary Sunderland, out of their loyalty. It was for Charles to prove them wrong. "I will stick by you and my old friends," he told Reresby, "for if I do not, I shall have nobody to stick by me." Seeing one day the Lord Chief Justice—who was threatened with impeachment—sitting pensive on the Woolsack, he sat down beside him and bade him be of good comfort, since he would never forsake his friends as his father had done. When the Commons waited on him with the usual address for the removal of his Ministers, he put it in his pocket and walked away without a word.[28]

* Orange thought so too, for on November 12th he wrote to Secretary Jenkins: "May God make people wise and moderate, for surely on this meeting of Parliament depends the good or ill fortune of all Europe." (*Dalrymple*, II, 373.)

On November 4th the Exclusion Bill received its first reading in the Commons, only three members—Hyde, Seymour and Secretary Jenkins—daring to speak against it. It was determined that as soon as it had passed both Houses, the mob should march on Whitehall. On Saturday, 15th, the impetuous Russell, with his delirious supporters swarming after him, carried the Bill red-hot to the Lords. There, while the King watched the fate of his kingdom swaying in the balance, and Shaftesbury, Essex and Monmouth spoke for the measure, Halifax rose to defend the ancient laws and peace of England. Though Sunderland had abandoned his master and was plotting to bring over Dutch Orange, this fastidious aristocrat, who once declared that he " would rather die than see a spire of English trampled down by a foreign trespasser," chose the better side—

> " Nor chose alone, but turned the balance too,
>   So much the weight of one brave man can do."

Sixteen times he spoke in the course of that terrible afternoon, and it was nearly midnight when the Bill was thrown out by thirty-three votes, and a group of tired loyalists sat down to supper at Lord Conway's.[29]

The Commons were not prepared for this. Next day, when they assembled, they sat looking at each other for nearly half an hour in silent consternation. Then they fell with fury on all who had dared oppose them: Lords, Ministers, Judges. But when they voted an address to remove Halifax, the King stood firm. Let them do what they would, he declared, he would not part with any of his officers at the request of either House; his father had lost his head by that compliance, as for him he would die another way.[30]

One victim the angry hosts obtained. On November 29th the Catholic Lord Stafford was brought from the Tower to Westminster Hall to take his trial for treason by his fellow-peers.   Hated even by his own relatives, so nervous that he was commonly reputed a coward, and old and ailing, he seemed to the promoters of the plot an easy victim, and it was hoped that he would save his life by offering to give false evidence against York and his fellow-prisoners, and so restore popular belief in the plot.   But in this they were mistaken.   Throughout a trial which lasted nine days—which the King watched, grim, silent and motionless, from his box—though denied all help of counsel and even the common justice of cross-examining face to face his foul accusers, Stafford remained constant to his creed and honour.   On December 7th he was found guilty of treason by fifty-five votes to thirty-one, and the axe was turned towards him.   Charles was deeply concerned, but, fixed immovably on his policy of leaving all to the laws and letting justice, such as it was, have its course, he could do no more than reduce the poor old man's sentence to beheading.   In the House Russell spoke furiously for his full pound of flesh—hanging, disembowelling and quartering; and the London Sheriffs gratuitously insulted the King by inquiring whose orders they were to carry out—his or the Commons'.[31]

That stormy year went out with the rumbling of coming thunder.   Evelyn, watching the blood-red comet that hung over the night skies, recalled a similar portent that had appeared during Strafford's trial forty years before.   Shaftesbury and the Commons, resolved to bring the King to his knees, passed a passionate resolution that whoever should advance him money was a national enemy, and prepared plans for a Party Association, into whose hands the principal fortresses of the kingdom should be placed.   Stafford died on Tower Hill " like a Roman "; Halifax remarked to his Yorkshire neighbour, Reresby, that if it came to war, they two must go together; and Monmouth and the republican Lords marched from Wapping to Soho amid a vast tumult of

u*

Wapping seamen. But still the King kept his peace and his calm, smiling impassivity. Going to bed on Christmas Eve, he talked for some time of the cheat of those who pretended to be more holy than others, said they were generally the greatest knaves, and, for proof, mentioned several eminent contemporaries. He was over two hours undressing himself that night, and seemed extremely free from any trouble or care, though most men supposed he had no alternative but surrender or civil war. So he awaited the coming of Christmas. His prescient, experienced mind, so quick to sense the self-seeking motives underlying all politics, already saw far out the white surf-lines that denoted the turn of the tide.[32]

For the pace at which Shaftesbury, tortured by physical pain and tense with anger, was driving his team was too fierce to last. On January 8th he told Justice Warcup, who he little guessed was in almost nightly consultation with the King, that he would draw a line around the Palace, and that Charles should suffer as his father had done. Two days later the Commons resolved that whoever should advise a prorogation was a betrayer of the kingdom, a promoter of Popery and a pensioner of France. In the midst of these proceedings Charles appeared in the Lords and prorogued them without further ado. A week later he informed the Council of his decision for an immediate dissolution. When Shaftesbury, silenced as he attempted to protest, asked leave to withdraw, Charles replied that he could not have made a request more easy for him to grant.[33]

On January 19th writs were issued for a new Parliament to meet, not in London, but in that loyal " retreat of Kings in time of war and pestilence "—Oxford. To the Exclusionists, who counted on the support of the mob to overawe the Palace, no step could have been more unwelcome. A further burst of petitions, demanding that the Houses should meet at Westminster, at once descended on the King. When one signed by ten peers was presented by Essex, Charles replied with scorn that he looked upon it only as the opinion of so many men, and deprived him of his Lieutenancy of Hertfordshire. A vigorous purge of malcontent Lords from Council and Household proved to all that he meant to stand firm.[34]

That January several persons going from Eynsham to Abingdon saw above the rising sun the representation of a crown. It was an omen. For secretly the King was taking measures to secure a throne for himself and peace for his people. Since the defeat of the Exclusion Bill a horrible fear had begun to haunt Louis: what if Charles should defeat his foes by sacrificing the legitimate succession, not in favour of Monmouth, but of Orange, and so unite all England in league with Holland against France. It was a fear which York, who pinned all his hopes on France, took care to foster. Before Christmas Barrillon was assuring Charles that Louis would stand by him with such financial help as would make it possible to defend the legitimate succession.[35]

This time nothing definite was asked of the English King: it was understood that in return for a modest subsidy, and a French undertaking not to attack the Netherlands,* he should gradually withdraw from the alliance against France, and if Parliament still insisted on exclusion, dissolve it. Charles well knew that if he remained constant to the cause of English monarchy, he must in the end do both these things, whether Louis offered money for them or not. Yet, before he agreed, he resolved to make one last attempt to obtain concord with his Parliament, money for Tangier and the Fleet, and an

---

* " So in July, 1681, Charles, assuring Barrillon that he would not enter into any commitments that might displease Louis, added: ' *It being always understood that he is not to attack the Low Countries; you know that that is the foundation of our union.*' It is curious how historian after historian has ignored this simple but eloquent fact." (*Dalrymple*, II, App., Part I, 9.)

independent policy abroad; and, though he would never surrender the legitimate succession, offer such expedients against a Popish successor as would satisfy every reasonable man. If that proved unavailing, he must fall back on Louis. To be ready for eventualities, he asked Hyde to prepare an estimate of the annual Treasury deficiency, and, in the Queen's bedroom, hidden between the bed and wall, discussed with him and Barrillon preliminary details for an understanding. So secret were the conferences that even Louise knew nothing of them.[36]

In the utmost quiet—his household and garrisons reduced, his table cut down and the royal mews sold—Charles awaited the coming of Parliament. One evening towards the end of January, some country gentlemen had been dining together in Chiffinch's rooms when, about candle-lighting, the King unexpectedly joined them. He told them he had come to drink a glass of wine with them, and that it should be to the happy meeting of his Parliament at Oxford, where, he said, he would go as far as any man for the preservation of the Protestant religion as by law established and the utter extirpation of Popery. Whereupon loyal Sir Thomas Vernon cried out: "Amen, and Presbytery too." "With all my heart!" replied the King.[37]

As anticipated, the elections went against the Government; "the Russell Faction was like a spring at full moon."* Pamphlets were circulated urging Englishmen to save their sons from slavery and their daughters from rape by "hellish French and Popish miscreants"; filthy songs like "Macninny" and the "Raree-Show," bespattering Charles and York, were bawled about the city; and old Commonwealth men appeared in remote country towns to urge the electors

---

* "All are very well pleased," wrote the agent of one of Shaftesbury's candidates, "but the tap must keep running day and night." (Will Bennett to Col. Bennett, 25 Feb., '80, *Pythouse Papers*, 95.)

to send them to Oxford with armed escorts. A new plot —Irish this time, and implicating not only York and the Queen, but even the King—was unearthed. But Charles, who, in his nightly conferences in Chiffinch's rooms, kept his cool hand on the pulse of London's underworld, was growing used to dealing with plots, and this time the conspirators obtained more than they had bargained for. The accused Fitzharris, who, according to plan, was to have turned King's evidence at the right moment and then made dramatic revelations to Parliament, was promptly placed out of reach of that body by being committed to trial before the Court of King's Bench, while his capacity for making incriminating confessions was seriously cramped by Charles's flat refusal to grant him the usual pardon in advance for his evidence; he should not have it, he declared, if twenty Parliaments addressed him for it.[38]

Now the Faction strained every nerve. Shaftesbury's "brisk Protestant boys"—in other words the hot rabble of the eastern suburbs—were mobilized, while attempts were made to indict the King's Guards as armed rioters and kidnap them as they walked the streets. In Paris there were rumours that Charles was poisoned and besieged in the Tower. But as a matter of fact Shaftesbury was already losing ground in the very capital which it was his boast to rule. He was sure of Wapping and Southwark, he told Warcup, but " the damned city flags and falls off." The wealthier merchants, the honest shopkeepers, all those who loved to kiss their lady Peace at home, were growing alarmed; railing at priest and Court was one thing, revolution another.[39]

The King took his measures calmly; made the guns of the Tower safe from assault and posted his Guards along the road to Oxford. Before he left, the volunteer officers of the London Artillery Company waited on him to beg his advice in the choice of a new captain; he answered that he himself would be their leader. On March 12th he set out for Oxford, spending a week-end at Windsor on the road. As his coach rumbled through the wooded Chilterns, the gentry flocked in hundreds to greet him. At the entrance to the city, the Corporation and University met him with speeches. " You," so ran one, " are the blessed father of your country and under the shadow of your royal protection we enjoy all our rights, religious and civil." All next day he received the Oxford-shire squires; only in the evening was he able to escape from Christ Church and weary his courtiers in the meadow walks.

On the 17th Charles was early abroad. At Witney he watched Chiffinch's little black beagles run a hare; then cantered with his hawks towards Burford Downs, where all afternoon the jockeys rode races before him. Next day, after a night at Cornbury, he went hawking over the high Cotswolds towards Oxford, taking coach at evening at Campsfield.[40]

During the week-end, every road into Oxford was packed with members and armed retainers, every hat a flutter of blue ribbons and " No Popery! " badges. On Monday, March 21st, while the King was opening Parliament, Mon-mouth rode in over Magdalen Bridge, with Lord Grey of Werke on one side and Sir Thomas Armstrong on the other, and hundreds of shouting roughs, armed with leaden flails for cracking Papist and other heads,* running behind.[41]

In his speech, the King declared his willingness to offer expedients or agree to any measure against a Popish successor that did not alter the legal descent of the Crown. But, he

---

* " Listen awhile and I will tell you a tale
  Of a new device of a Protestant Flail,
  With a thump, thump, thump a thump
       Thump a thump, thump!
  This flail it was made of the finest wood,
  Well lined with lead and notable good
  For splitting of brains and shedding of blood," etc.
        —STEPHEN COLLEGE, " The Protestant Flail."

warned them, "I, who will never use any arbitrary government myself, am resolved not to suffer it in others. . . . It is as much my interest, and it shall be as much my care as yours, to preserve the liberty of the subject, because the Crown can never be safe when that is in danger; and I would have you likewise be convinced that neither your liberties nor properties can subsist long when the just rights and prerogatives of the Crown are invaded, or the honour of the Government brought low. . . . I must therefore earnestly recommend to you to provide for the Religion and Government together, with regard to one another, because they support each other; and let us be united at home that we may recover the esteem and consideration we used to have abroad. I conclude with this one advice to you, that the rules and measures of all your votes may be the known and established laws of the land, which neither can, nor ought to be, departed from, nor changed but by Act of Parliament. And I may the more reasonably require that you make the laws of the land your rule, because I am resolved they shall be mine."[42]

But the real issue now was the future of the English monarchy. On the morning of the 24th, before the House of Lords was seated, Shaftesbury passed to his sovereign a paper stating that the only expedient to avert civil war was to recognize the pawn, Monmouth, as his successor. Charles glanced at it; he would be glad, he said, to have a son whom he loved to succeed him, but neither for that inducement nor any other, would he do a thing so contrary to justice, law and his own conscience as to deprive his brother of his legal right. Shaftesbury replied insolently that it was the first time a Court conscience had prevented a man from doing a thing so much to his own interest. "My Lord," answered the King, "let there be no self-delusion. I will never yield, and I will not be intimidated. The older I grow the more steadfast I become, and I will not stain my reputation in the little time that perhaps remains for me to live. I have reason and law in my favour; well-minded people are on my side; and there is the Church which will remain united to me. My Lord, she and I will not be divided."[43]

That day the King's friends in the House offered his expedients: York was to be banished for life, and his sons educated as Protestants; on Charles's death the Government was to be vested in the regency of Mary of Orange, or, after her, of Princess Anne. Some thought that more than was safe had been yielded, but, if so, the King knew his opponents better than they. Blinded by faction, the Commons refused every offer and fell furiously on York.[44]

Before the new Exclusion Bill could be introduced in the Lower House, its members had plunged into a violent quarrel with the Lords. Wishing to rescue their new informer, Fitz-harris, from the perils of the Common Law and to secure for the revelations, which he was expected to make, a suitable audience, they tried to impeach him. But the Lords, to their fury, rejected the impeachment on the ground that Fitzharris was already indicted before the Court of King's Bench and must receive the ordinary form of trial by his own peers.[45]

It was now plain to Charles that it was hopeless to expect anything reasonable from these angry men. The alternative was a policy of peace, acquiescence in French continental policy and rigid economy—inglorious, no doubt, but better than surrender or civil war. He had given his foes as much rope as they could ask: it was time to give the noose a jerk. On Sunday afternoon, March 27th, he consulted his Council in the Chancellor's rooms in Merton: all agreed to a dis-solution, nor was there one false or babbling member. That night the royal coaches were sent a stage out of the town on the road to Windsor.[46]

On Monday morning—the day fixed for the introduction of the Exclusion Bill—the King walked down to the Lords in ordinary clothes, his crown and robes following in a sedan chair. After he had donned them, he took his seat on the throne, while Black Rod was sent to fetch the Commons. They crowded in, shouting and bawling, imagining that the King was about to surrender. Then he rose, spoke a few sharp words, and commanded the Chancellor to dissolve them. With amazed and dreadful faces they heard their doom.* But Charles, with " a most pleasing and cheerful countenance," laid his hand on the shoulder of a young member, who was helping him to disrobe, and observed: " I am now a better man than you were a quarter of an hour since; you had better have one King than five hundred."

As soon as he had dined, he entered Sir Edward Seymour's coach and drove swiftly out of the city, reaching Windsor late that night. Before ten next morning he was at Whitehall, where old Lord Craven, keeping watch with the Guards, reported that all was quiet. Two days later the secret treaty with France was concluded. There were no definite conditions named save that Louis was to pay a subsidy of roughly £400,000, spread over the next three years.† With this modest aid to his revenues, Charles could make shift to live.[47]

* " Though I have seen the distractions and dejections of routed armies (a prospect dismal enough), yet nothing ever equalled this day in this place at the surprising dissolution of Parliament." (Colonel Ed. Cooke to Ormonde, 28 March, '81, *H.M.C. Ormonde*, VI, 9.)

† For the responsibility for this treaty see Barrillon's letter of Sept. 22, 1681, to Louis asking for a continuance of funds for bribing the Opposition chiefs: " Your Majesty knows how much the cabals in opposition to the Court are necessary to keep the affairs of England in a state convenient for your Majesty. The correspondence I have with them . . . is perhaps the best and most certain means to prevent the King of England changing his conduct to your Majesty." (*Dalrymple*, II, App., Part I, 30.)

CHAPTER XIII

THE FIGHT FOR THE BOROUGHS

" The Lion and the Unicorn were fighting for the Crown;
The Lion beat the Unicorn all round the town."
—*Old Song*.

THE King had taken the tide at the ebb. No outburst followed the sudden dismissal of the politicians, but instead, for some weeks, a quiet, as though all men were a little out of breath. Yet the battle was only in suspense, and none knew whether the King could hold the political initiative which, after four years, he had so dramatically regained. Then, while the iron was still hot, Charles struck. On the advice of Lord Chief Justice North, the Government, which, since the expiring of the Licensing Act in 1679, had been without the means of combating an unceasing campaign of libel and misrepresentation, now turned on its enemies with counter-writers of its own to answer each new lie as it appeared. On April 13th the first number of the Tory *Observator* was issued, under the editorship of old Roger L'Estrange. The plan was completely successful; the country was swept by a tornado of angry pamphlets, but they were no longer on one side only, and within a short while the sharpest weapon of the enemies of the Crown had been blunted.[1]

At the same moment the King made a personal appeal

to the nation. Early in April he published a Declaration,* setting out the aims of his enemies and the methods they had pursued, which was read in every church in England. Its effect was electric. Coming at the very moment when the King's superb tactics and the violence of his opponents had set all men thinking, it dissipated the last mists of the Popish Terror and established direct contact between throne and people. From every town and county in England, including many which had returned Whig members to the last Parliaments, a shower of loyal addresses, expressing abhorrence of those who had sought to plunge the nation into civil war, descended on Windsor, where, at the end of April, Charles, much to the distress of his physicians, had for economy's sake moved his Court.† He accepted them, as an eye-witness wrote, " with a most joyous and gracious countenance," keeping open hospitality for the loyal folk who brought them. To him, after all he had suffered, this sudden demonstration of loyalty—" the stout fidelios of the strenuous, brisk and valiant youth of this your now much deluded nation "—was as warming as the unbroken sunshine of that wonderful spring.[2]

It was not thus that his opponents witnessed the union of the King and his people. The Common Council of London voted its astonishment at the " untimely dissolution of Parlia-

---

* " . . . We ask'd of them the supporting alliances we had made for the preservation of the general peace in Christendom; we recommended to them the further examination of the plot; we desired their advice and assistance concerning the preservation of Tangier; we offered to concur in any remedies that could be proposed for the security of the Protestant religion, that might consist with preserving the succession of the Crown in its due and legal course of descent : to all which we met with most unsuitable returns from the House of Commons; addresses, in the nature of remonstrances, rather than of answers; arbitrary orders for taking our subjects into custody, for matters that had no relation to privileges of Parliament; strange illegal votes, declaring divers eminent persons to be enemies to the King and kingdom, without any order or process of law, any hearing of their defence, or any proof so much as offered against them." (From Royal Declaration, 8 April, '81, Echard, 1007.)

† Colonel Ed. Cooke wrote to Ormonde on April 30th, 1681, that the word " thrift " was always in the King's mouth. (H.M.C. Ormonde, VI, 51.)

ment " and the Grand Jury of Middlesex—the nominees of
the republican Sheriffs—tried to indict the loyal Address of
the City of Norwich as a " scandalous libel." " The angry
party," wrote stout old Secretary Jenkins, " hath threatened
his Majesty's Declaration with bloody answers; if they do
there is one good way left of replying to them, which is not
by reasoning, but by doing well and worthily."[3]

But, though the King was now determined to destroy
those who had tried to break his throne, he had no intention
of resorting to force.   He had triumphed by law, and with
that weapon he would finish the contest.   Undressing himself one evening he told the gentlemen about him that the
laws should have their course and, whatever his own private
opinion might be, he would govern himself solely by them.*[4]

The first brush in this new battle centred round the far
from pleasant persons of the paid informers.   When, a little
before the meeting of the Oxford Parliament, Shaftesbury
had threatened to produce an affidavit laying Godfrey's
murder on the King, the latter had replied by refusing to
issue any more pardons to witnesses in advance.   This—once
Parliament was out of the way and the Common Law free
to run its course—dried up, as though by magic, the flow of
incriminating perjuries; even the sturdiest of Oates's school
were not prepared to hang themselves.   Such indeed was the
lot of Fitzharris, who, despite all Shaftesbury's efforts to
rescue him, was caught in the very gin he had set, and tried
for his life.   With the administration of that iron law, the
King, as ever, refused to interfere, whether it struck at friend
or foe.   On the same day as Fitzharris died, perished also
Plunket, the Catholic primate of Ireland and the last of
Shaftesbury's victims.[5]

With their profession threatened, many of the informers

* " Indeed, it was a great happiness to his people to live under so just and so
gracious a Prince," was Reresby's comment. (*Reresby*, 20 April, '81.)

turned to the new masters of the State, hoping to receive from them the same reward for perjury as from the old: it was strange, Charles observed, how all his acquaintances kept a tame rogue.   These honest witnesses were quickly disillusioned. The Government would give no money for discoveries; Secretary Jenkins told the entrepreneur, Justice Warcup, that " they were for truth, not designs "; and the King himself cautioned one of Shaftesbury's turncoat informers to stick to the truth.   Within a fortnight of the dissolution most of the tribe of " Mac Shams " had been deprived of their salaries.[6]

Yet what was true, the Government tried to elicit: the bottom of the plot should be seen at last.   In that grim search the King himself took the lead, rising at five to examine witnesses in Council and sternly answering the informer Everard—who hesitated to say what he knew for fear of " the mighty terrible Parliament "—" The law will secure you against Parliament and me whilst you do right."   During the early months of the summer of 1681, several significant facts became known to the Government: that an armed rising had been planned to take place at Oxford, that Shaftesbury had been guilty of suborning witnesses, and that Lord Howard of Escrick had set on Fitzharris to accuse the King of Popery. In June Howard was sent to the Tower on a charge of High Treason.   A fortnight later, at six on the morning of July 2nd, the King arrived suddenly in London from Windsor.   All that day Shaftesbury—taken from his bed and his papers seized—was closely examined* by the Council.   As afterwards he passed out on his way to the Tower, the pious Oates—asking him how he came into Lob's Pound—offered to visit and pray with him.   In the cool of the evening, Charles drove back to Windsor.†[7]

But if the King had justice and, at last, public opinion

* Halifax told Reresby that there was sufficient evidence to hang him.
† The effect of Shaftesbury's arrest on educated public opinion may be seen

on his side, the Faction commanded the London juries.   At
the City elections on June 24th, Shaftesbury had again secured
the choice of such Sheriffs—so Lord Arran told Ormonde—as
would ensure " that no Bill of Indictment would ever be found
against any of their party."   The King's advisers knew this
so well that, rather than face the ignominy of the Grand
Jury throwing out the Bill, they withdrew Lord Howard's
prosecution.   How right they were was shown on July 8th
when, at the London Sessions, a Bill of Treason against
Stephen College, the "Protestant joiner"—author of the
obscene and libellous "Raree-Show" ditty*—was thrown
out by a packed Grand Jury, whose foreman was College's
closest intimate and fellow-conspirator.†[8]

Outside London the attempt of the Whig leaders to make
the law a piece of party machinery was not well received.
As the attempt to seize the King's person, of which College
was accused, had been planned for Oxford, it was decided
to remove the trial to that city.   There, despite every effort
of the Republicans,‡ the Grand Jury found a true Bill, and

from an Oxford don's letter of July 5th, 1681: " We are much surprised
here at the news of Shaftesbury's commitment. I hope now all the roguery will
come out. I wish it be not more than will be to our advantage to know,
for I mightily suspect that the old knave hath been guilty of many subornations
in the management of the Popish Plot, which will be mightily to our disgrace
should it prove so, and would give the Papists such an advantage that they would
carry all things before them. . . . If so, it is a very bad business, and all Englishmen
that go into Popish countries will be sufficiently told of it." (*Prideaux*, 87.)
   * " Apt songs were fitted to these exquisite pieces of wit which this sanctified
crew used over their cups to troll in scurvy tunes, and all come in at the chorus."
(North, *Lives*, III, 159.)
   † When the Ignoramus was returned, Monmouth and the Exclusionist Lords
present shouted their approval, the rabble without joining in at a given signal
from the gallery. (*H.M.C. Ormonde*, VI, 96.)
   ‡ I use the term " Republican " in preference to " Whig," because it was
thus Shaftesbury's followers appeared to their contemporaries in the years 1680-3:
even their ally, William of Orange, spoke of them in 1688 as " The Commonwealth party." (*H.M.C. Spencer*, 15.) Only after the Revolution did the term
" Whig " begin to take on its present respectable meaning, when those who bore
it did their best, very successfully, to forget the republican principles of their
predecessors.

in August, College—taken by barge to Kingston and thence
with a troop of cavalry across the Chilterns—was tried and
sentenced to death.   In the provinces at least the King could
look for justice.[9]

In the midst of these distractions, Orange—alarmed by
Louis's new policy of persuading his smaller neighbours
towards the Rhine to declare for union with France—arrived
in England to persuade his uncle to go to war.   But Charles,
who had not forgiven him for his intrigues with the Opposition
during the Exclusion Bill, and was, in any case, in no position
to break his secret agreement with Louis, was not helpful.
When his nephew urged him to obtain war supplies by calling
a Parliament, he asked him whether he was in favour of
Exclusion or the Expedients of parliamentary control of
Militia, Fleet and Judiciary?   William, who well knew that
one day he might inherit the English Crown, declared he
abhorred both, on which Charles asked whether he could
suggest any other way of securing money from Parliament?
To such a conundrum William could only reply that he did
not know England and ask for permission to consult his
friends.   But when this took the form of accepting an invitation to a City banquet given by the leaders of the Faction, he
was promptly recalled to Windsor.   Early in August Orange
returned to Holland, a sadder but wiser man.*[10]

His guest gone, the King enjoyed his usual sea holiday.
On August 17th, taking coach to London, he joined his yacht
at Greenwich.   To young Lord Bruce, whom he took with
him as one of the pages in attendance, we owe a charming
picture of the voyage.   " It cannot be expressed," Bruce wrote,
" the satisfaction we had by eating twice that day with the
King, who was all mirth and of the most pleasing conversation,

* " The Prince of Orange is returned, as the discontented party says not well
satisfied with his negotiations here, but this advantage he hath had . . . that he
hath clearly seen the hands of both sides playing our great game." (Arlington
to Ormonde, 6 Aug., '81, *H.M.C. Ormonde*, VI, 124.)

X

and, if we played any game, he would come and sit by us."
At the Nore Charles inspected the squadron he was sending
to the Mediterranean against the Algerian pirates who preyed
on his people's commerce. Thence he went on to view
fortifications at Chatham and Sheerness, where, to his great
joy, he received news that a loyal Scotch Parliament had almost
unanimously affirmed his brother's right of succession to the
throne.[11]

All who saw him that autumn were struck by the King's
determination. " His Majesty is as well as ever I knew him,"
wrote one, " and full of resolution not to be any more hectored
by the Whigs, which gives great heart to his friends." On
his return to London at the end of August, he proceeded
vigorously with the intended prosecution of Shaftesbury, whose
friends, in the heat of the pamphlet war which was still
raging, were doing their best to suggest that the evidence
against him was suborned. Charles treated such insinuations
with contempt. " At Doomsday," he observed, in the terse
phraseology of an old proverb, " we shall see whose arse is
blackest." When Shaftesbury, growing alarmed, made overtures for peace, asking for a ship and leave to depart to
Carolina, he was grimly referred to his remedy at law. Those
who had been so relentless but a few months before, now,
when they were met with steel of their own quality, began to
speak hopefully of a new Act of Indemnity—and " damn all
the witnesses on both sides ! " But only to those who yielded
and confessed their error did the King show his wonted
mercy.*[12]

On September 8th Charles departed to Newmarket for his
autumn vacation. Here he remained, in excellent health, for
over a month, coursing, watching races and cock-matches,

* When the mutineer Lord Huntingdon craved his forgiveness, he gave him
his hand to kiss, saying that, though he would never capitulate to his subjects,
he knew how to show mercy when he found they were convinced of their faults.
(H.M.C. Ormonde, VI, 204, 18 Oct., '81.)

and delighting most of all in hawking. Once, to please the Queen, he visited Cambridge, where he was received by the Vice-Chancellor and the Heads of Colleges, "in their formalities, the bells ringing, conduits running with wine, and such other public demonstrations of joy," and presented with a vast number of Latin addresses and a folio Bible.[13]

Yet even at Newmarket the clamour of battle followed him. On September 13th, as he walked on the heath, he was accosted by the Whig Mayor* and Councillors of Oxford, who had come (at the expense of their fellow-townsmen) to petition him to waive his right of rejecting a newly appointed town clerk of republican views. The King was not at all pleased to see these western Boanerges, and told them to wait on Lord Conway, the Secretary of State, for an appointment. But they had their revenge, for at that moment Nell Gwynn happened to pass by, with an all too familiar: "Charles! I hope I shall have your company at night, shall I not?" With this story they made great work when they got home, informing all and sundry that they had often heard bad things of the King before, but now their own eyes had seen them.[14]

The move of the Oxford townsmen was no mere local manœuvre, but part of a great concerted plan to capture the control of parliamentary returns and the administration of justice in every borough in England.† In the widespread

---

* Of the election of this worthy—" a very silly, pragmatical rascal . . . much given to speech-making "—Dr. Prideaux, of Christ Church, gives an interesting account: " We have gotten here a very odd fellow, mayor of the town, who seems to have been put into the office on purpose to serve the Presbyterians as there be an occasion . . . in which office he acteth to the utmost folly of fanaticism, molesting both the University and town, talking against the King and Government with the utmost malice. Trenchard and Vaughan " (two leading Exclusionists) " coming here about the time of his election and being in frequent conference with him, I believe it was by their influence he was chosen, as being a man very fit to be subservient to their designs. These rogues have designs going on." (*Prideaux*, 80. See also Wood, *Life and Times*, II, 463.)

† " I find they are animated chiefly by the Faction at London, who design this as a leading chard to all the other cities in England; for, at the King's coming in, they all taking out new Charters, had them with the same limitations as to the

324 KING CHARLES II [1681

confirmation of town charters that had followed the Restoration, clauses had been inserted, securing to the Crown the right of approving the chief permanent municipal officials; the Faction was now seeking, with Oxford as a test case, to have this check on its further operations removed. How powerful this attempt was, events that followed the King's return to the capital in October proved. As the commencement of the Legal Term approached, the appearance of the London and Middlesex jury panels excited universal wonder: "the most strange that ever were," wrote Secretary Jenkins; "on a panel of fifty, scarce were four that went at any time to church. They are so obscure most of 'em, as never to have been in the freeholder's book, so that the King cannot hope to have justice from them in his own Courts." On October 18th a Bill of High Treason against Rous, the manager of the Wapping mob, was thrown out with every mark of insult by a Grand Jury at the Old Bailey. It was not strange that the King—walking that evening in the park—appeared more serious and concerned than the greatest business usually made him. "It is a hard case," he said, "that I am the last man to have law and justice in the whole nation."[15]

But Charles had no intention of allowing his adversaries to regain their lost initiative. He told the Judges that the handle of the plot was broken, and that they had nothing to fear by doing their duty, and bade them put the laws against the Dissenters into execution; every subject, he added grimly, should have the full benefit of the law, even though the Crown was denied it. That autumn he made a clean purge of his household; even the saintly Oates was sent packing pensionless from Whitehall. His resolution was rewarded by a great

Recorder and Town Clerk; and if Oxford should carry it against the King, you shall find none will allow it him, which will be as great a diminution to the King's prerogative as hath happened in any King's time except the last, when the crown itself was taken away." (Dr. Prideaux to John Ellis, 4 Oct., '81, *Prideaux*, 104.)

triumph—the election of a Royalist merchant, Sir John Moore, as Lord Mayor—a man so nervous and retiring that the Faction had hardly troubled to oppose him.　On October 29th the King dined with this magistrate, receiving a tremendous ovation as he rode through the city streets.　In his speech, studiously ignoring his foes, the Sheriffs, he turned with kindness towards the citizens and declared that, so long as the honest men of the city stuck to him, and the law was on his side, he did not doubt to be too hard for those that endeavoured to divide him from his people.[16]

In November, as the time of Lord Shaftesbury's trial drew near, both parties braced themselves for the test.　Everywhere quiet country folk anxiously awaited the result.*　A week before, the Faction, to show their strength, paraded the London mob in the great Protestant Saturnalia of Elizabeth's accession day.†　As it grew dark, the streets filled with people, until about eight o'clock every throat broke into thunder as, carried high above the heads of the crowd, the famous pageants swept down the streets: the murdered Godfrey before; the Pope, attended by Devils, Cardinals and Jesuits; and Cavalier gentlemen with halters round their necks and an attendant booming through a stenterophonic tube the word " Abhorrers! "　Last of all came a sledge with a single fine gentleman on it, whom some supposed to be the King of France, some the Duke of York, and others the editor of the *Observator*.　At Temple Bar the Lords of the Green Ribbon Club sallied out on to the balcony of the King's Head Tavern, with wigs aslant, pipes in mouths, merry faces and diluted throats, to encourage the

* " I hear Lord Shaftesbury is to be tried speedily; if he meets with a wilful Ignoramus Jury, I fear 'twill prove the greatest occasion of mischief." (Peter Shakerley to Sir Geoffrey Shakerley, 20 Nov., '81, *Shakerley MSS.*)

† " All our streets shine with Popes and bonfires, and our bells are solemnly jangled to express all possible respect to her memory. . . . My girl is just now come in from seeing the Popes and the show, and her tongue does so run with the story that she puts an end to this." (Charles Bertie to Lady Rutland, 17 Nov., '81, *H.M.C. Rutland*, II, 60.)

caterwauling mob. Then the procession turned northwards to the final orgies over the bonfires of Smithfield. But the riot was far greater on the 24th, when the rabble swarmed into the Old Bailey, hooted down the Judges, and, so soon as the packed jury had returned its Ignoramus to the Bill against Shaftesbury, stoned the witnesses for the prosecution along the Strand. That night the town was full of bonfires, and the mob forced the passers-by to pledge its leader's health in kennel-water.[17]

But Charles had resolved that if Shaftesbury must be free, it should be, as he put it, with a bottle at his tail. He therefore published the evidence against him, with a form of an Association, found among his papers, binding its subscribers to destroy all who opposed Exclusion and give implicit obedience to the commands of the existing Parliament, whether dissolved or not. Once again Charles found that the policy of giving publicity to his opponent's intentions brought popular opinion to his side. A new flood of abhorring addresses poured in from the outraged provinces, stirred to the core by the realization of how near to civil war the politicians had driven the country. But someone else besides Charles chose that autumn to affix a bottle to Shaftesbury's tail, where after a lapse of two and a half centuries it still remains. Caught in the quick-silver of the poet's mirror, the false Achitophel lives for ever.

> " A name to all succeeding ages cursed;
> For close designs and crooked counsels fit,
> Sagacious, bold and turbulent of wit. . . .
> In friendship false, implacable in hate,
> Resolved to ruin or to rule the State."[18]

While England was torn by the battle of the juries, the ambitions of France continued to alarm Europe. In the autumn Louis, on an invitation from its inhabitants, had seized Strassbourg; by November he had gone further and was

laying claim to Luxemburg.   But though Charles, urged by
Orange, hinted that under certain circumstances he might be
forced to call a Parliament and ask for supplies—and even
succeeded in obtaining an additional grant of £75,000 from
Louis as the price of not doing so—war was out of the
question.   The leaders of the Opposition had secretly promised
that, if the Government raised a finger against France, they
would quickly put it into a condition of utter powerlessness;
and somewhere in France was secretly printing a book revealing the full story of the Treaty of Dover—ready for publication should Parliament meet.   Charles knew that he was in
no case to defend Spain or Holland when his own throne
was threatened.   " There are devils who intend my ruin," he
told Barrillon.[19]

Before the old year ended the King attacked the Faction
in its own stronghold.   While he proceeded to undermine its
supremacy in the boroughs by ordering the enforcement of the
Corporation Act—which for many years he had allowed to
remain in abeyance—his Law Officers prepared their artillery
against the City of London.   Within two days of Shaftesbury's
acquittal, it had been resolved to proceed against the City
Charter with a writ of *Quo Warranto*.   The effect of the
King's determination was apparent in the December elections
for the Common Council, when no less than eight of Shaftesbury's Ignoramus Jury lost their seats.   A strong reaction
was setting in for monarchy; some of the better-to-do and
more peaceful London citizens, sickened by the excesses of the
politicians, formed a loyal club, which grew that winter like
a snowball.[20]

Fortune was at last beginning to smile on Charles.   With
it returned his good humour; when at the New Year an
embassy from Morocco presented him with two lions and
thirty ostriches, he observed that the only appropriate return
the resources of England would enable him to make would

be a flock of geese. Loyal addresses poured in from every side, and before the spring many towns were voluntarily offering to surrender their old charters for new ones, giving the Crown the right of veto in the election of municipal magistrates. Abroad a diplomatic victory much eased the King's affairs, Louis having responded to his representations by agreeing to withdraw his claim to Luxemburg provided its fortifications were razed.* Charles was still very poor, but that did not prevent him from making a generous provision for those who had served England, repurchasing from the Royal Society, to whom he had originally given it, the site of Chelsea College, and laying, that February, the foundation-stone of Wren's great hospital. It was not an ignoble legacy for an impoverished King to leave to posterity.[21]

At the winter's end, giving his Judges their instructions for the Circuit and bidding farewell to Louise, who was going abroad to drink the Bourbon waters, Charles jolted over the cobble-stones in time to see the dawn lighting the hedges on the Newmarket road. He was in a charming mood that March: " so much pleased in the country, and so great a lover of the diversions which that place did afford, that he let himself down from Majesty to the very degree of a country gentleman. He mixed himself amongst the crowd, allowed every man to speak to him that pleased, went a-hawking in the mornings, to cock-matches in afternoons (if there were no horse-races), and to plays in the evenings, acted in a barn and by very ordinary Bartholomew Fair comedians." It was significant that the press of country people to see him was more than usually great.[22]

Before he returned to London, Charles was rejoined by the Duke of York. The good offices of Louis XIV and

---

* " His Majesty's affairs have had very good success in all places. . . . The removing of the blockade before Luxembourg by the French was one great step towards our repose and quiet." (Lord Conway to Sir George Rawdon, 6 May, '82, *H.M.C. Hastings*, II, 392.)

Portsmouth, both of whom now had excellent reasons for wishing to be on friendly terms with the future ruler of England, had contributed to this victory of Charles's natural affection for his brother over his equally strong desire to keep out of England one who aroused such violent antagonisms. York's return was not attended with those ill results which Halifax, who never liked him, had foretold. It was true that when, in April, he attended the Artillery Company's Feast in the city, there was no great enthusiasm—save for half a dozen paid boys running after his coach crying, " Bless him "—but on the other hand there was no adverse demonstration, and a Whig attempt to hold a rival banquet for Monmouth was easily suppressed. Indeed the City seemed to have fallen into an easy quiet,* and proved more interested that spring in the visit of the Bantam Ambassadors—another manifestation of Charles's far-spread commercial activities—and the April floods that came down so fast at Fleet Bridge that they drowned a whole drove of hogs and filled the streets with an argosy of floating cradles, tables and hogsheads of beer.[23]

But when in May, York, making a farewell visit to Scotland, all but solved the succession problem for ever in a shipwreck on the Lemon Oare, a strong tide of popular feeling set in in his favour. A new sentiment sprang into being, based on the constancy of his political attitude,† that York had been all the time right—the one strong man who had set his face against anarchy and republicanism from the first. When he returned to London on May 27th, the fickle

* " The City is at this time very quiet, the restless spirits, which are not near so many as they would be thought to be, are indeed working to unsettle men's minds in order to disturb the peace, but the wealthier sort among them know when they are well." (Jenkins to Ormonde, 25 March, '82, *H.M.C. Ormonde*, VI, 353.)

† For the strength and consistency of that attitude, see the remarkable series of letters written by York to George Legge (afterwards Lord Dartmouth), printed in *H.M.C. Dartmouth*, I, 30-49, 53-5, 56-74.

crowd, who had howled at his name a few months before, was singing:

> " The glory of the British line,
> Old Jimmy's come again."[24]

Charles, who had caught a slight chill playing tennis at Windsor, came up to London to welcome his brother home. It was a hot day and, returning in the evening, he opened all the windows of his barge and fell asleep. Next day, at service in St. George's Chapel, he was seized with a shivering fever. It was during his subsequent convalescence that old Lord Ailesbury, appearing at his levée with an unusually smiling face, explained on his master's inquiry that it was due to his joy at the royal birthday. " I know, my Lord," said Charles, " your great and good heart towards me and the Crown, but is there nothing else that causes it? " When Ailesbury at last admitted that a grandson had been born to him that morning, Charles called out cheerfully: " And my godson; God's fish! there is another chip of the old block! " And it was all his doctors and the beseeching father and grandfather could do to prevent him attending the ceremony in person.[25]

Prosperous gales were now fanning the King's sails; there was no doubt that his enemies were beginning to break. But before they finally did so, there was a great fight to be fought for the control of London and the freedom of the juries. A further outrageous Ignoramus had recently concentrated public opinion on this problem.* To foreigners it seemed as though in the government of London, the monarchy was challenged by a rival republic. Therefore, while the City authorities put in a plea of two hundred sheets to the royal *Quo Warranto*,

---

* " There were two verdicts given by an Ignoramus Jury at Guildhall upon two indictments against a couple of Whigs, that all the standers-by stood amazed to see that, upon the fullest and clearest proofs imaginable, the jury brought them in not guilty." (O. Wynne to Lord Preston, 18 May, '82, *H.M.C. Rep. 7, Graham of Netherby*, 352.)

the King began a new assault—this time on the very bastion of the republican fortress, the London Sheriffs. The Lord Keeper had persuaded his brother, Dudley North, a brave and honest merchant recently returned from Turkey, to stand as a candidate, and the loyal Lord Mayor employed the old custom—disused during the Civil Wars but since revived—of nominating him as one of the two Sheriffs by drinking his health at the Bridgehouse Feast. The Republicans, having failed to hector North into withdrawing his candidature— threatening him with every kind of evil, from hanging upwards, if he should dare to oppose them—made a mighty muster in the Guildhall at the June elections, and, by refusing to allow their opponents to enter the hall to poll and yelling the Lord Mayor down, forced the latter to declare the election adjourned. Thereupon the old Sheriffs, without the slightest legal authority, conducted the poll themselves and, after a riotous meeting, declared the republican candidates, Papillon and Dubois, elected. For this they were committed by the Council to the Tower.* On their release under Habeas Corpus a few days later, they again proceeded to declare their nominees elected, counting the heads of a packed hall of Dissenters, who by the Corporation Act had, in law, no votes at all. But, in spite of threats, the Lord Mayor remained firm and held a further and legal poll, which resulted in a substantial majority of qualified votes for North and Box, the Tory candidates. It was as though an axe had been laid to the root of a dangerous tree.[26]

Though these hot and dusty proceedings brought the King to London more often than he cared for, they did not prevent him making a voyage at the end of June down the river. He missed Louise, who was returning from France, and ran into

* They were conducted thither in their coaches through the heart of the city, attended by only four Yeomen of the Guard. (*Luttrell*, 26 June, '82.) An observer recorded: "They went through the city neglected like dogs." (John Drummond to the Duke of Queensberry, 26 June, '82, *Buccleuch*, II, 104.)

storms, which kept him busy and happy, handling the sails
and taking his turn on deck like a common seaman. He was
several times at sea that summer—much pleased with a new
yacht which he christened *The Fubbs* in honour of his old
sweetheart, who had grown quite plump during her holiday.
But most of all now he delighted in hawking, and at the end
of August, making a State visit to Winchester to watch some
races, was so pleased with the sport the open Hampshire
Downs afforded that he resolved to return there every year.[27]

Meanwhile Shaftesbury strained every nerve to rally his
declining forces. Ever since the beginning of the year his
agents had been busy at their work; now, with the approach
of Michaelmas, when the new Tory Sheriffs must take office
and his right of vetoing prosecutions come to an end, he
sought desperately for some last chance to put the nation
in a flame. A revolution was now his only hope. But
the Government gave him no opening. His vaunted ten
thousand " brisk boys," the great race for the seamen and
watermen on Greenwich Heath, the riotous autumnal progress
of Monmouth, were alike unavailing. On September 29th the
new Sheriffs took office, and Sir William Pritchard, another
Tory, was elected Mayor.[28]

Without awaiting the recount of the poll, which the despairing Republicans demanded, the King, taking the Queen
" a'racing with him," proceeded on his holiday to Newmarket.
On the night before he left he wrote a note to his seventeen-
year-old daughter, the Countess of Lichfield.*

" I have had so much business . . . that I hope you will not
think that I have neglected writing to you out of want of kind-

---

* She was a daughter of Cleveland, but in character strangely unlike her
mother, for she was a pattern of modesty and wifely virtue. The monument to
her and her husband in Spelsbury Church, Oxfordshire, records: " At their
marriage they were the most graceful bridegroom and most beautiful bride, and
till death they remained the most constant husband and wife." Hearne mentions
an arm-chair on which she was wont to sit and tickle her father's bald pate as he
slept after his dinner.

ness to my dear Charlotte. I am going to Newmarket to-morrow and have a great deal of business to dispatch to-night, therefore I will only tell you now that I have five hundred guineas for you . . . and so, my dear Charlotte, be assured that I love you with all my heart, being your kind father.

" C. R."

When he returned to London three weeks later, his victory was almost complete. His enemies were even robbed of the hope that, having obtained the Sheriffs he wished, the King would make the mistake of uniting their party by acts of extreme severity. A regular landslide to the royal side occurred. " The Whigs come over to us daily," wrote a Tory; " you can hardly find six at High Exchange in the city . . . Sir Thomas Player, being £17,000 in arrear of Orphan Money in the Chamber of London (which money, it is thought, they have spent to carry on the good old cause) is absented."[29]

Shaftesbury himself remained till November, intending —after an unsuccessful attempt to rouse the mob on Guy Fawkes Day—to make one last bid for revolution on Elizabeth's accession day. Some were for posting the Guards in the city, but the wise King, remarking that he " did not love to play with his Horse," left it to the Sheriffs to take their own precautions. When the great night came, the latter, with their blue caparisoned attendants, patrolled silent and deserted streets. Only about three in the morning did they discover in a back-yard near Bishopsgate, " a parcel of equivocal monsters, half-formed like those fabled of the mud of the Nile: legs and arms scattered about, heads undressed and bodies unheaded! " The insubstantial pageant had faded. A few days later Shaftesbury, a dying man, fled from England to lay his bones in the great republic he had once sought to destroy.[30]

The climax did not come till the next year. In March,

1683, the victorious King paid his usual visit to Newmarket
—a very quiet one, for he was beginning to age a little now,
and though he would still walk ten miles on the heath of a
morning and watch as many horse-races and cock-fights as
the place afforded, he saw little company and was generally
in bed by nine.   On the evening of March 22nd a careless
groom smoking and a strong wind met together, and next
morning Newmarket was a rubble of charred house timber,
coaches and horses.   Had the fates decreed otherwise, the
royal coach, outdistancing its guards as usual, would have
rumbled Londonwards a few days later than it actually did;
and at the Rye House near Ware, this tale would have ended
with a cart of hay blocking the highway, the rattle of musketry
from the ditch below the causeway, and, while waiting horsemen galloped Londonwards to rouse the City and proclaim
Monmouth, England's Majesty and his brother lying dead
on the road with a dozen bullets through their bodies.[*31]

Whispers of something untoward reached Charles on his
return, but these he dismissed as idle gossip, and it was not
till June, when he was on the verge of his final triumph over
the City Charter, that he discovered how near he had been
to death.   On the 12th of that month one of the conspirators,
an Anabaptist oil merchant called Keeling, sought an interview with Jenkins.   That official, who was always inclined
to be suspicious of confessions, dismissed him, imagining from
his countenance that this queer informer, who seemed an
honest man, was subject to visionary frenzies.   But when
Keeling reappeared next day with a substantial brewer, who
confirmed all that he had said, the Government could no
longer ignore the existence of a widespread and dangerous conspiracy.†   The affair was a little difficult to probe, because the

---

* At that very moment, rumours were already circulating in Scotland that the
King was dead. (*Aberdeen Letters*, 101.)

† " The discoverer is a substantial citizen, zealously factious and active in
the Whig party. . . . He says it was remorse of conscience and horror of so

witnesses, though ready enough to admit their own guilt, were unusually reticent in accusing others, and Charles, who examined them in person, being anxious to avoid any suspicion of subornation, refused to suggest names. But gradually two plots were unravelled from the tangled tales—one to murder the King, concocted by an old Cromwellian officer, a rascally lawyer and a knot of fanatics, and a far more ambitious plan, canvassed by Monmouth, Russell, Essex and the Whig Grandees, for seizing Whitehall, calling the country to arms and establishing either a dogedom under the weak Monmouth or an aristocratic republic. Somewhere between these two plans and linking them, flitted the evil and ominous forms of Shaftesbury's henchmen—Howard of Escrick and Sir Thomas Armstrong, and that stranger and more moving figure, the sworded preacher, Ferguson. On June 23rd warrants were issued for arresting the principal conspirators. But those who knew the King best noticed that he was extremely reluctant to bring Monmouth within the net of justice. Setting his watch one morning by the dial in the Privy Garden, he called to young Lord Bruce, whom he loved and trusted, and bade him go down to his native Bedfordshire and arrest his rebellious son at Toddington. When Bruce, divining his master's secret wishes, spoke of the difficulty of doing so, the King, giving him a look of infinite affection, bade him come for orders some other time, and never spoke of the matter again.[32]

The prisoners were not kept in suspense. On July 12th a Grand Jury—in which all attempt at packing had been scrupulously avoided—found true Bills against twenty-one persons, including Monmouth, Grey, Russell, Essex and Armstrong. Howard, who had turned King's evidence, was

bloody a fact . . . that moved him to repent and discover and we are charitably to believe him, though the fear of some of the conspirators being beforehand with him might have some share in his conversion." (Ormonde to Arran, 22 June, '83, *Ormonde*, VII, 51.)

exempted.   Next day Russell was convicted of High Treason. Before the result was known, Essex, steeped in the stoical principles of the Roman republicans, had cut his throat;* the King, who was inspecting some repairs, was himself in the Tower at the time the tragedy occurred—a fact afterwards used by his enemies to insinuate that the prisoner had been murdered.[33]

In the week that followed desperate efforts were made to secure Russell's pardon—even to offers of large sums of money. But Charles was inexorable: he would not, he said, purchase his own or his subjects' blood at so dear a rate.   Yet he commuted the sentence to beheadal, observing that the courtesy which Russell had endeavoured to withhold from the innocent Stafford should not be denied him, and let him know before he died that his forfeited estates should revert to his widow. On July 20th three of the lesser conspirators were drawn on the sledge to Tyburn, where—confessing their guilt—they paid the penalty of their own folly and that of many other men.   Next day Russell, with a fortitude and dignity that went far to redeem the bitterness and faction of his public life, mounted the black-draped scaffold in Lincoln's Inn Fields amid a silent crowd.[34]

*" My Lord of Essex," commented the King, who was deeply moved, " needed not to have despaired of mercy, for I owed him a life." (*Echard*, 1033.) Essex's father had died on the scaffold for Charles I.

CHAPTER XIV

AUTUMNAL FORTUNE

" Forgiving, humble, bounteous, just and kind :
His conversation, wits and parts,
His knowledge in the noblest useful arts,
Were such dead authors could not give,
But habitudes of those who live. . . .
His apprehension quick, his judgment true;
That the most learn'd, with shame, confess
His knowledge more, his reading only less."
—DRYDEN.

ON the day that the executioners cut off Russell's head, the University of Oxford struck a mightier blow at the principles for which he died.   In solemn conclave assembled, the Doctors and Masters issued their ukase against the theory that authority is derived from the people and may be seized by their representatives.   Before all eyes they burnt the books—Milton, Hobbes, Dolman and many others—which contained such doctrines, declaring them " destructive to all government, both of Church and State."*   In their place they set out, for the comfort of a generation of country squires and parsons, now thoroughly aroused by the spectre of anarchy, the principle of passive obedience—" that most necessary doctrine, which, in a

* " We further decree that the books which contain the aforesaid propositions and impious doctrines are fitted to deprave good manners, corrupt the minds of unwary men, stir up seditions and tumults, overthrow states and kingdoms, and lead to rebellion, murder of princes and atheism itself." (Decree of the University of Oxford, 21 July, '83, *H.M.C. Kenyon*, 163-6.)

manner, is the badge and character of the Church of England, of submitting to every ordinance of man for the Lord's sake, . . . that we may live a quiet and peaceable life in all godliness and honesty."[1]

But while the wise men of Oxford were declaring kings divine, Charles was conscious that they were all too mortal. Not that he would admit that he was growing old; he still played tennis each morning with Feversham, Godolphin and John Churchill—the finest players of their age; still delighted in the same easy conversation and caustic commentary on the passing world. " Walk with me, hunt with my brother, and do justice to my niece, and you will never be fat," he told stout Protestant Prince George of Denmark, whom he had brought to England to marry the Princess Anne. Yet, for all the passionate addresses of loyalty that still poured in on Whitehall, he was glad to escape in August to Windsor; it was only here, amid the willows and water-meadows, that the world never changed. It was very quiet: a day's buck-hunting in the forest, a game of basset at the Queen's or crimp at the Duchess of Portsmouth's, or the wonders of the great water-engine Morland had built for the Castle, were the chief recreations the place afforded. Hence at the end of the month Charles moved his family to Winchester. Every day he rode out at dawn on to the Downs to follow his hawks, cantering lazily with his red-coated falconers across the sea-like turf. Wren was building him a palace on the hill above the town where the old castle had stood—a graceful, classical structure with a marble portico and colonnaded wings, and a cupola above, whence a King, who loved the Fleet of England, could see his men-of-war riding at Spithead. When it was finished, Charles told his guests, its tall windows would look down an avenue, two hundred feet wide, with noble houses on either side, and the long cathedral and the skyline of the Downs to close the vista. Here, in a capital worthy of his empire, he would spend his declining years, and future kings should call him blessed.[2]

In September he took a sea change, driving out early one Wednesday morning on the Southampton road, with Prince George and the Duke of York to bear him company. His yacht landed him at two o'clock that afternoon at Portsmouth, where he walked round the fortifications, examining every gun and bastion with the greatest care, and giving instructions for building a new mound. Later he crossed to Gosport to show the Prince his flagship. Supper ashore with Louise, who had come to see the Castle, ended the day, after which Charles returned to his yacht for the night.

He was up at dawn on Thursday to visit Southsea; saw the Hospital, Guise Mount, the Round Tower and Blockhouse Point, and delighted the port officials by the thoroughness with which he inspected every detail. The rain intervening, he was, however, unable to show Louise her Castle. The visit ended at seven next morning, when his yacht weighed anchor for Southampton. After renewing memories of old wars by a call on Robin Holmes in the Isle of Wight, Charles rejoined the Queen at Winchester on Saturday night, just in time for the official thanksgiving celebrations for his delivery from the Rye House Plot.[3]

With his ever-growing love of country pastimes, the King lingered at Winchester as long as he could, and was only driven Londonwards at the end of September by the vexed problem of the City Charters. A little while before, it had seemed as if the Londoners would surrender their Charter without resort to legal process, but other counsels having prevailed, the Attorney-General entered the judgment of seizure, which had been suspended since the summer. Charles at once restored the Charter,* with certain safeguards prompted by the

---

* On June 18th Ormonde had written: " I know the King does not intend to raise any profit to himself or to lessen theirs; but I believe he will endeavour to

recent interregnum of law, the chief of which was a clause giving him a right of veto in the event of the election of a hostile Mayor or Sheriffs.   In other respects the liberties and financial privileges of the City remained unimpaired.   The King of England—in the words of the new Chief Justice, Jeffreys—was King of London at last.   If in following the high and narrow road of law to make himself so, he had procured some infringement of the liberties of Englishmen, it was only because such liberties, in unworthy hands, had degenerated into licence and threatened the very basis of society.*⁴

Having nominated the old Lord Mayor to continue in office until the new Charter was ready, the King stole a week from October at Newmarket—crowding as many as seven races into a single day to make up for the unwonted shortness of his stay.   Perhaps he felt that his troubles were at an end. But the Gods had other darts than those of politics with which to wound Charles's heart.   The death of his insane brother-in-law, Alfonso of Portugal, scarcely distressed him, but it was another matter when a foreign visitor, the Grand Prior of France—the slayer of no end of ladies—started making love to Portsmouth.   Though the easiest of lovers and rivals, Charles was past the age when he could unconcernedly see someone he cared for made the object of scandal, and if Louise was in one sense a standing scandal, that was all over now. So the Grand Prior was given twenty-four hours to clear out of England, and when he had the impudence to claim the native impunity from arbitrary arrest, Charles informed him that Habeas Corpus did not run for French subjects, and he

reduce their power, so that it shall not be able to hurt the Government, their fellow-subjects and themselves.'' (*H.M.C. Ormonde*, VII, 49.)

    * '' For what in the name of Justice had the Government to do when Ignoramus was mounted *in cathedra* and there was a declared stop put to all State criminal law. . . . It is an unparalleled error of politics in the people, when they think to deprive their Government of the power of punishing capital offences by law.'' (*Examen*, 629.)

went, *The Fubbs* yacht, for luck's sake, wafting him over to Dieppe.[5]

The loves of his youth had left to the King a legacy of responsibilities, and therein lay tragedy, for of all his handsome sons he loved his first-born, Monmouth, best. He, alas—unstable as water—had been swayed by the flattery of false friends to claim his uncle's birthright and, in so doing, become partner in a conspiracy to overthrow his father's throne. Charles would never believe that he had ever known anything of the lower and baser plot to take his life, but others were not so certain. " It is horrible," wrote Ormonde, " to imagine the Duke of Monmouth should have the least suspicion of it, and not immediately, and before he had slept upon it, quit the whole party and run himself out of breath to tell the King his fears." With good men thinking thus, how could Charles find a way to pardon this foolish, impetuous, beautiful son he loved? Truly, out of his pleasant vices, the just Gods had made a whip to scourge him.[6]

Somehow he must find a way, for if before he did, his unforgiving brother should succeed him, Monmouth was a doomed man; nor, in the years that were left him, could he bear to keep him in the outer darkness to which his vanity and folly had banished him. Among those nearest the throne was the great trimmer, Halifax, now Lord Privy Seal. Anxious to balance the growing influence of York and the Tory extremists, he took it upon himself to act as an intermediary between father and son. In this—though the influence of Louise, who had a son of her own, was not friendly—he was zealously aided by the childless Queen, who loved Monmouth. Secretly a reconciliation was arranged. Before it could be effected, the prodigal was to admit his share in the conspiracy, for otherwise people might suppose that his pardon proved that there had never been one at all, and beg forgiveness of his injured uncle, for only so could

the gratification of natural affection be reconciled with justice.
To all this Monmouth agreed.   Twice that autumn he saw
his father; once, leaving Whitehall wrapped in a cloak, he
was recognized by an officer of the Guards, who rushed
impetuously to tell the King, and only got for his pains a
disdainful, " You're a fool; James is at Brussels! "[7]

The date fixed for the return was November 24th; on that
day Monmouth—" an apparition " to an astonished world—
surrendered himself at the Secretary's office, and, begging to
see the King and York, made his submission.   Next day his
pardon was made out, and he was received at Court.*   The
King made no attempt to hide his happiness: everyone noticed
it.†   Coming that evening as usual into the Queen's circle,
he touched Lord Bruce, who was playing at cards with
Catherine, on the shoulder, and bidding him give his cards to
another, thanked him warmly for his friendship to his son,
who he said had now confirmed Lord Howard's testimony
against his fellow-conspirators.   But, he added, as he had
promised that he should not be called to give evidence, the
prisoners in the Tower should be bailed.   The hatchet was
to be buried.[8]

But moderation had never been an attribute of the
Faction's.   Within a day or two, its devotees were proclaiming that Monmouth's pardon proved that there never had been
any plot or conspiracy, and that the King's judges were no

---

* " . . . The Duke of Monmouth on Saturday last came and delivered
himself up to the Secretary, and desired he might speak with the King and
myself alone; so soon as the Secretary had advertised his Majesty, he went down
to the Secretary, taking me along with him, where the Duke of Monmouth,
after having asked his Majesty's pardon in the humblest manner possible, and
owned his knowledge of the whole conspiracy, except that part of the assassination, asked pardon of me also, and said as much to me upon that subject as I
could expect of him, with all the promises of his good behaviour for the future a
man could say."   (York to Orange, 27 Nov., '83, *Dalrymple*, II, App., Part I, 64-5.)

† Monmouth himself recorded in his diary that his father pressed his hand
as he had only done once before—on his return from his first campaign.   (*Welwood*,
App., 322.)

better than murderers.   When Monmouth's confession before
the Council was made public in the *Gazette*, his former friends
surrounded him with insinuations that he was betraying them
to an unscrupulous and unforgiving enemy.   Once more he
vacillated.   To anchor his wavering actions and save him from
himself, the King caused him to sign his own statement.   But
despite his father's repeated promise that it should not be used
to harm any man, Monmouth was persuaded by two of his
old associates, Trenchard and Hampden, that what he had
signed would hang them.   Next day he asked for his declaration back.   Charles in a passion returned it, bidding him go
to hell.[9]

Once more the Faction had closed a door in the King's
face, but its victory was a Pyrrhic one.   On the same day that
Monmouth left Whitehall, Algernon Sidney, sentenced a few
days before, was sent to the block.   The Government could
no longer show any leniency without appearing to admit the
non-reality of the plot.   " I suffer," Sidney declared, " for the
righteous cause," but Chief Justice Jeffreys told him that what
he so described, the law called High Treason.   On the
scaffold the ironical old republican showed " all the indifferency
imaginable," and died after the high Roman fashion he had
made his life's star, leaving behind a great tradition and a last
and highly libellous paper in the hands of the Sheriff.[10]

A season of unprecedented cold followed; even the King,
whose superb physique gave him joy in all seasons, complained of it and of an aching pain in his side.   The New
Year dawned on a snow-bound England—all communication
stopped, the sea frozen for two miles from the shore, and the
Thames a thoroughfare of ice.   Here the Londoners built
themselves a city of booths, so that, as the pale wintry sun
broke through the fog pall, Charles, looking down the river
to the rising height of St. Paul's, could see his ruddy-faced
subjects at their sports on the ice—bull-baiting and ox-roasting,

plays and interludes, and coach races. But behind the gabled, snow-crowned houses that curtained this rough, cheerful scene, the poor, in fireless courts, were fed in that starving time by the generosity of a sovereign who, whatever his failings, never forgot his people in the day of their need.[11]

Three years had now elapsed since England had seen a Parliament, and some of those about the King—notably Halifax and Ormonde—urged that he should rely on the change in public opinion to honour the old Triennial Act and call one. But York was bitterly opposed, and Charles himself felt little enthusiasm for reassembling that house of talkers, from which he and his father had suffered so much. He was at peace at last and his people united, trade was flourishing, he was beginning to make both ends meet: why should he venture on seas that had proved so often dangerous for the sake of a dubious and theoretic good? So long as Louis paid his modest subsidy, he could manage without calling on his people for new taxes—they were the richer so and he the more at ease. He wanted no more; when it was hinted that he might make himself an absolute ruler, like one of those Eastern potentates of whom his subjects read in their Bibles and feared so unreasoningly, he answered: "Nonsense! A King of England that is not a slave to five hundred kings is king enough."*[12]

To his people, the last years of Charles's reign brought a wonderful prosperity.† While Europe was plunged in war, they remained at peace, both with themselves and their neigh-

---

* He once told Lord Essex that "he did not wish to be like a Grand Signior with some mutes about him, and bags of bowstrings to strangle men as he had a mind to; but he did not think he was a King as long as a company of fellows were looking into all his actions and examining his Ministers as well as his accounts." (*Burnet*, II, 3.)

† It had not been so during the brief periods when the politicians at Westminster had ruled. "They like a flood break down all," honest John Verney, the Turkey merchant, had written in 1679, and Charles had cause to share his view. (*Verney*, II, 374.)

bours. " Then," recalled Lord Ailesbury, writing in a more costly age, " we had no generals to march themselves at the head of superfluous armies, nor had we one penny raised on land tax." Yet the very force and treasure which England poured out so lavishly in the wars of Marlborough, she drew from these quiet years when King Charles was leading her through green pastures. Everywhere men were laying up for themselves and their children treasure for the future. On every sea the adventurous ships of England sailed, coming home with treasure in their holds to enhance the wealth of a little island of squires, yeomen and homely merchants, and bringing silks and scents and delicate cloths for their ladies. In a quarter of a century, Evelyn's £250, invested in the stock of the East India Company, had multiplied itself threefold. Pennsylvania, whither Charles had dispatched the Quaker Penn in 1682, the Carolinas, New York and the shores of the Hudson; treaties with the Turks and the Moors to make Englishmen free of the Mediterranean; trading settlements at Bombay and Fort William, and dusky ambassadors bringing gifts from the great Mogul; companies to trade with Africa, Guinea and the coasts of Barbary; expeditions to find a new road to the golden East through the Arctic ice or discover the wonders of the South Seas: all these were milestones in England's commercial and imperial expansion, and all, in their greater or lesser degree, bore the impress of a Prince, who once told his sister : " The thing which is nearest the heart of this nation is trade and all that belongs to it."[13]

One colonial venture of the reign ended in failure— Tangier. The persistent refusal of Parliament to vote money for its support* made it impossible to hold it any longer, and in 1683, after nearly two millions of royal treasure and much

* " Hang Tangier," was the remark of the republican M.P., Sir Thomas Player, when asked why Parliament would not help to support the station. (C.S.P.D. 1680-1, 178.)

life had been expended in its defence, Charles dispatched Lord
Dartmouth with Samuel Pepys and a fleet to demolish the
Mole and fortifications and evacuate the garrison. "Tangier," wrote a courtier, summarizing the popular view, "is
utterly destroyed and blown up and all the people brought off
to England, and it had been better to have been done the
first hour it was taken in dower from the Portuguese." Of
England's first military station in the Mediterranean nothing
remained—save a mislaid copy of *Paradise Lost*.[14]

It was not only abroad that English trade prospered. The
King took an unfailing interest in the ways by which his
people lived, and never neglected an opportunity of increasing
his knowledge of them,* or of establishing a new industry.
When France revoked the rule of religious toleration which
his grandfather had given her, Charles offered every encouragement to the Huguenot silk-weavers to settle in England.
But his greatest effort was directed towards the sea.† In the
course of his reign the English Merchant Navy doubled its
size. "'Tis certain," testified one of his Ministers, "no
prince was ever more fitted by nature for his country's interest
than he was in all his maritime inclinations."[15]

In all this, Charles helped to create a newer and richer
England and instil into the minds of his subjects a love of a
more spacious and pleasant mode of life than they had known
before. The very luxury of his Court had served to bring
this about. Even the wild Buckingham took out a patent
for extracting glass and crystals from flint and founded a
factory at Lambeth. Evelyn saw it and praised the huge
vases of metal, clear and thick as crystal, and the looking-
glasses better than any from Venice. "He loved planting

---

* See his eager questioning of Sir John Reresby about that strange people,
the edged tool-makers of Hallamshire. (*Reresby*, 19 Sept., '81.)

† As a curious example of this, witness the anxiety he showed at the very
darkest moment of his reign, in 1680, on news that Louis was contemplating
building a ship canal between the Atlantic and the Mediterranean. (*Ailesbury*, 44.)

and building," recorded the same witness of his royal master,
" and brought in a polite way of living." The glories of
Windsor and Greenwich, the new faubourg of St. James, and
the London which arose from the ashes of the fire, posterity
owes primarily to him. Everywhere his subjects followed
his example, building those commodious and classical houses
which in the next age were to give a park and palace to every
village in England, encompassing gardens with walls to catch
the sunlight, making fountains and parterres and grottoes, and
planting walks of ash and sycamore.[16]

Being at peace, the King left things alone. His Ministers
were not perhaps quite as peaceful; an uneasy warfare waged
intermittently in the Cabinet between Halifax the trimmer,
and Rochester the High Tory. At the moment the latter
seemed to be in the ascendant, through the powerful patronage of York, who now, joyful in the defeat of his enemies,
was advancing from strength to strength. Behind him
marched the jackal, Sunderland, once more back in his old
secretaryship, and a host of place-seeking politicians, priests
and confessors, who saw in the coming accession of their
honest, stupid, fanatic master the approach of a golden age.
Since the King was now in one of his easy moods, the very
importunity of this party—the more irresistible for the real
industry and administrative capacity of its leader—gave it a
tremendous advantage; it seemed as though Charles " chose
rather to be eclipsed than troubled." Yet he never would
allow the balance in his Council to be altogether broken, or
relinquish his old habit of keeping an ear open to those of
other views—that humour, so irritating to those on the crest
of the wave, so comforting to others, of " hearing everybody
against everybody." For this reason, moderate men like
Halifax and Lord Keeper North, despite every attempt of the
reigning party to remove them, remained in his counsels.[17]

As the long cold winter of 1684 drew into a leafless

spring, there arose the old complication of foreign affairs. In the previous December the Spaniards, alarmed by Louis's encroachments, had declared war on France; now once more French armies beleaguered Luxemburg and threatened Flanders. Orange was on fire to arm all Europe against the lilies. But his uncle of England, appealed to, was coldly critical. Could Orange even carry his own Dutch countrymen with him? was any reliance to be placed on either the armies or promises of Spain?* why should England and its throne be placed in unknown dangers for the sake of obtaining a problematic future security? When Orange urged the time-honoured argument that, when the French had destroyed every rival on the Continent, they would fall on England, Charles replied that his realm was surrounded by water and guarded—despite all the refusal of his Parliaments to grant him money—by the finest fleet in the world. In the clearest possible manner he intimated that on no account would he endanger the settlement of his throne by a continental war. Abroad the result was the fall of Luxemburg and the conclusion of a twenty years' truce. But in England an uneasy sense remained that the French were far too powerful.[18]

The last spring of Charles's life dawned, as ever, at Newmarket. "The weather," wrote a country gentleman who was there, " was very unseasonable and dirty, so that walking the town with his Majesty he observed I had but thin shoes and advised me to get a stronger pair to prevent getting cold." Each year those present noticed that the King's Newmarket recreations grew more staid and regular; he walked daily till ten, attended horse-races after dinner, spent an evening hour

---

* Lord Preston, English ambassador at Paris, had justly summarized Charles's shrewd view of his would-be allies, in a letter of December 12th, 1682, to Secretary Jenkins : " The great aim of the allies is once to engage him in a war, and then to give him as little assistance as they can. For their great maxim is that England is rich, and that it ought to bleed in its turn as well as other estates; but as his Majesty hath long known their design, so he knows very well how to frustrate it." (H.M.C. Rep. 7, Graham of Netherby, 275.)

at the cock-pit or watched the country comedians at their play, supped with Louise and retired early to his own apartments to bed.   He was back at Whitehall for Easter, taking his communion with three of his tall sons kneeling by his side in the gilded chapel.   A day or two later, before his departure for Windsor, he was writing affectionately to his daughter, Lady Lichfield, about a house she was building at his expense and giving her a note to Mr. Wren to make it as high as he pleased, with a kindly caution not to prejudice the view of the corner house, which was intended for her sister, Lady Sussex.[19]

Charles was now master of as great a power as any King of England had wielded—the sweeter that it was founded, with little help of arms or money, on his people's love.   When he was to touch that spring for the evil, the press for tickets at the surgeon's door was so great that several persons were crushed to death.   Addresses of Abhorrence of the late conspiracy were still coming in—now from such remote dominions as Virginia, Connecticut and New Plymouth.   In the last passionate revival of loyalty to the ancient throne, it seemed as though English political liberty, fought for so long and fiercely, was to be thrown aside as a thing of no worth beside the greater blessing of a King at one with his people.   When Jeffreys took the Northern Assize that summer, charter after charter was laid at his feet, to be altered or amended as his master chose.   To immortalize the King's glory, the London merchants set up his statue in their Exchange, sculptured by Grinling Gibbons and arrayed in the habit of a Roman Cæsar.[20]

Never had the English people known such a King: the frailties of his life were now coloured by the kindly hand of time, the political bitterness of a few years back forgotten, his enemies discredited and in hiding.   There was nothing remote or inaccessible about this British Titus—receiving ambassadors amid the unchecked throng of his subjects, feeding his ducks while all the world watched, pulling off his hat to the meanest as he took his walk in the park or galleries. Beneath that lined face, so dark and stern—its shrewd, wrinkled eyes, the high, harsh nose and determined, delicately moulded chin—lurked a spirit, kindly and merciful and yet unaccountably puck-like, that was a contradiction to every known rule of physiognomy. When he chose to lay aside the King, among the friends and men of wit whom he loved to make his companions,* there were a thousand irresistible charms in his conversation; discoursing freely and without restraint on every subject under heaven and telling stories so well that, not out of flattery, but for mere joy of listening to them again, his Ministers would pretend they had not heard them. In such company he delighted to talk of humanity with Dryden or Wycherley, of architecture with Wren and music with Purcell, or lean familiarly—as one in after years recalled having seen him—over D'Urfey's shoulder to hum an air. Those who knew him best remembered his casual conversation as one of the great experiences of life—a window opened on to the world of men and affairs, and an unspeakable delight.† Yet, though he had words at will and knew the art of pleasing so well that he would send away a petitioner enchanted by the mere charm of his reception, he could, when he chose, by a mere change of countenance, put on a terrible majesty; once an inquisitive courtier, greatly daring, pushed his head between the velvet curtains of his Bed-chamber, only to draw it back a second later, crimson with shame. More often a witty word, spoken with a kindly smile,

---

* " A lover of mankind and a distinguisher of talent . . . whatever his favourites of State might be, yet those of his affection were men of wit." (Dryden, *Dedication to King Arthur*.)

† Lord Ailesbury spoke of his company as an " unspeakable delight " and attributed his knowledge of the world to his instructions, and Lord Keeper North told his brother that " he thought King Charles understood foreign affairs better than all his Councils and counsellors put together." (*Ailesbury*, 2; North, *Lives*, I, 329.)

WOODEN HEAD OF CHARLES II.

CARVED AFTER THE KING'S DEATH BY GRINLING GIBBONS.

" That lined face, so dark and stern—its shrewd wrinkled eyes, the high, harsh nose, and determined, delicately moulded chin."

sufficed to check the presumptuous; when the rich Quaker Penn kept his hat on in the royal presence, Charles politely removed his, explaining that it was the custom in that place for only one person at a time to remain covered.[21]

To the bustling York, now back in his old place in the Council, this inexplicable triumph of the monarchial principle over its once all-powerful enemies—for he never realized how much it was due to his brother's skill and patience—seemed an opportunity for reforming the Government on lines more amenable to his patriarchal intentions. His long, capable fingers were in every pie; while, ever whispering into his ear, his priests told him to be zealous and relentless in victory. It was his duty, so he and they conceived it, to maintain unceasing war on the King's defeated foes. It was beyond his comprehension that a victory could be pressed too far, or that old enemies might be wisely appeased. Since the discovery of the Rye House Plot, his mind moved in a constant orbit of assassinations; he suspected murderers behind every hedge, and refused to travel in the company of his brother, lest both should be killed at once. But when he expostulated with Charles for his habit of driving about the capital unguarded, he was assured that no one was likely to commit regicide to make him King. Charles, for his part, needed no slave at his shoulder to warn him of the transience of mortal triumphs. Walking one day in Hyde Park with Sir Richard Bulstrode— the English resident at Brussels—he opened his heart. After speaking of the people of Flanders as the most honest and true-hearted race he had ever met, he added that for his part he would never see them again. "I am weary," he added, " of travelling, and am resolved to go abroad no more. But when I am dead and gone, I know not what my brother will do: I am much afraid that when he comes to wear the crown he will be obliged to travel again. And yet I will take care to leave my kingdoms to him in peace, wishing he may long keep them so. But this hath all of my fears, little of my hopes and less of my reason." Time was to prove the truth of this shrewd, melancholy prophecy.[22]

The last summer of the King's life was such a one as no man in England could remember, a great drought and heat hanging over the land throughout the rose months. At the end of August Charles left Windsor for his annual visit to Winchester. Once more he saw his fleet riding at Spithead; once more rode hawking on the high downs and sat in the evenings watching the French players; once more could only be " drawn from his *divertissements* " with the utmost difficulty to return to London. He was full of his new house, and, for one so patient, unusually anxious to see it finished. Wren promised it him within the year, but he shook his head a little sadly, saying that a year was a great period at his time of life. To his daughter, Lady Lichfield, he wrote of the things nearest his heart—his love for her and his sailor son, the Duke of Grafton.

" Your excuse for not coming here is a very lawful one, though I am sorry I shall be long deprived of seeing my dear Charlotte. Your brother Harry is now here and will go in a few days to see Holland, and, by the time he returns, he will have worn out in some measure the redness of his face, so as not to fright the most part of our ladies here. . . . And so, my dear Charlotte, be assured that I am your kind father."

He was back in London at the end of September, reviewing his soldiers on Putney Heath. Thence he departed for a last fleeting visit to Newmarket, clouded by such terrible storms of wind and rain that for several days he was prevented from hawking. The sudden illness of Louise brought him hurrying back on October 23rd to a distracted Whitehall; till she was better all business was suspended. Then, as the winter set in, with early November snows and frost, the old routine began again.[23]

But the sands were running out. That November the Queen's birthday was kept with such bravery and richness of apparel as had not been seen since the Restoration; and while the young ladies and gallants of the Courts danced in the great Banqueting Hall, outside gaping subjects watched a tattoo of fireworks upon the Thames, with pageants of castles and battles upon the water, and the royal arms and mottoes inter-linked in letters of fire. Through it all the King passed as unconcernedly as ever—taking his two walks a day, working in his laboratory with his chemist, Dr. Williams, and showing his age a little by the regularity of his post-prandial slumbers. He was living very simply now, had given up the old plentiful suppers, and drank only for his thirst, but still, at levée and coucher, and twice daily in the Queen's withdrawing-room, diverted the company with his easy talk.[24]

Two things still haunted him. The old trouble of money had become pressing again of late : the discovery of serious frauds in his Treasury had led to a change of Ministers in the autumn, Rochester, first Lord of the Treasury, being suddenly promoted to the magnificent but powerless post of President of the Council—" kicked upstairs," as his delighted rival, Halifax, put it. An inquiry into the abuses was ordered, and some of the ablest brains in the city called in to examine them, Charles himself attending their meetings and showing an interest in financial details hitherto little known in him. With an infinite and almost pathetic patience he was paying off his debts and those of his father;* many curious little sums —for £100 lent him when he was Prince of Wales, for the wedding-clothes of his daughters, Sussex and Lichfield—figure in the Secret Service accounts of these last years. Those who were with him most knew that he was laying up in his

---

* In the autumn of 1684 he employed Samuel Morland to make a calculation of his total indebtedness. " I shall be able to pay the bankers' debts which I have so much at heart," he told Lord Bruce, " and if God gives me life I hope to pay at least some of the King, my father's debts." (*Ailesbury*, 21.)

Z

cabinet, month by month, every guinea he could spare, to make
a fund with which to discharge his obligations and provide for
his children. He would have, if his life was spared another
year, he said, a hundred thousand pounds.[25]

But there was no ledger-book to square the account of a
father with an ungrateful son, whom he could not help loving.
In the utmost secrecy, and with all that dissimulation of which
he was such a master, Charles conspired to bring back Monmouth to his life. For York's sake he would give him no
open countenance, and even protested publicly when Orange,
ever fishing in troubled waters, received him with royal
honours. But secretly he sent the exile money, and, as the
year 1684 drew to a close, mysterious rumours ran the round
of the town that Monmouth was in London, and a great
change impending.[26]

To such an alteration in his affairs many things were
driving the King. The manner in which York and his under-
strappers, Sunderland and Jeffreys, were conducting his affairs
was growing troublesome; they intruded themselves too much,
and their violence towards their enemies—who were after all
his own subjects—must, if persisted in, arouse the old spectres
of opposition which he had so hardly laid. He had small
liking for his brother's political philosophy—" *la sottise de
mon frère,*" as he called it. Some years before that shrewd
watcher, Barrillon, had noted that, while York wished to
increase the royal authority, Charles was averse to changing
the form of Government or to making himself any more
absolute than he was; his real aim was to preserve the prerogative and secure peace and an adequate revenue. Now that
he had obtained his ambition he was still the same.* " I would

* Even his enemies at the time admitted this. " If he had lived," wrote
Welwood, " it's probable we might in compliance with him have complimented
ourselves out of all the remains of liberty, if he had but a mind to be master of
them, which it's but charity to believe he had not, at least immediately before
his death." (*Welwood*, 131.)

have everyone live under his own vine and fig tree," he told Lord Bruce. " Give me my just prerogative and I will never ask more." A delicate sense of justice, which never deserted him, now caused Charles to revert to the one unchanging principle of his reign—to throw the weight of his authority into the lightest scale of his ever-warring Cabinet. York should be sent to govern Scotland again—it would be time enough for his brother to rule England when he was dead and gone—and Monmouth be forgiven and brought home.[27]

One other circumstance prompted the King—the old need of money. In the spring of 1684 Louis's subsidies under the agreement of three years before had ceased, and they were not renewed. Though they had never amounted to much—about £150,000 a year—in the fragile state of Charles's finances, even so small a loss of revenue could cause him grave inconvenience. There was only one way of making the deficiency good—to call a Parliament—and that, now faction was almost dead and the control of local government in loyal hands, seemed once more to be practicable. But so long as York, who still believed that a Parliament would strike at his right of succession, was near the throne, such a policy would be certain to meet with violent opposition.[28]

Charles acted with all his old secrecy and circumspection : nothing was to be hurried or done without deliberation. Above all there were to be no scenes or angry words; Louise would of course object, for she was fast tied to York's interest and to that of her liege King across the water, against whom a Parliament would certainly turn. But he would continue to show her favour and let her seem to share his confidence; still sup with her and treat her with the honours she so loved. And doubtless he would manage Louis somehow; and if the worst came to the worst, and that unforgetting monarch revealed, as he had once before threatened to do, the Secret Treaty of Dover, he would give his people their head, trust to

z*

his popularity to blazon it out, and unleash his gallant fleet:
then it would be seen whether England rode kitchen yacht
to any Grand Louis or no in the world.* So in cold, dark
December days it was settled: York should depart in peace
and honour to Scotland, where a Parliament was to be called
in the spring, the Council reformed, and Monmouth, who
returned secretly to Flanders to await the public recall, brought
again to his father's side. And old enmities between Englishmen and Englishmen should be laid for ever in the grave.[29]

Gazing that Christmas from his bedroom windows down
the river, the King could see the vanes of the city he
had helped to build—symbolizing, in its ordered red brick
houses and classical temples, a new age of wealth and far-
reaching responsibilities—and above it, rising higher every
week, the walls of its vast cathedral; on Saturdays he could
almost follow the upward passage of his little surveyor going
up in his basket to view the progress of his handiwork.
He had not done so badly, he reflected, by his people; he had
given them peace and prosperity after many years of unquiet;
he had stood by his friends; had kept his father's throne and
honour.† There were, of course, many things he regretted:
the scandal he had given by his too easy Court and life. But

---

* Halifax, in his *Trimmer*, written in 1684 to persuade Charles to call a
Parliament and declare war on France, observed: " . . . When England might
ride Admiral at the head of the Confederates, to look like a kitchen yacht to the
Grand Louis, is but a scurvy figure for us to make." To which Lord Mulgrave,
in his reply, *The Character of a Tory*, answered: " Whenever the Trimmer can
persuade the Parliament to give money enough for a fleet against France, the
Tory will engage to go a volunteer in it rather than command the kitchen yacht
to any Grand Louis of them all."

† " Let me end with this just and true remark: he wanted not money, he
was free from Parliaments that so greatly disturbed him, the succession was
settled in the due line, he had a good ministry, he was out of intrigues with
France—and to my knowledge, although a French lady and the ambassador of
that Crown were seemingly well (I was at Court: I may say seemingly)—and he
gave no countenance to loose and buffooning persons that flourished so in former
years. In fine his heart was set to live at ease, and that his subjects might
live under their own vine and fig tree; but the good God thought us not worthy
of these blessings." (*Ailesbury.* 24. See also *Ailesbury*, 97.)

he was sensible of his misspent time, and lamented it. He was not impatient to be reproached for these things; once he remarked to those about him that he was going to hear little Ken, whom, with his unfailing eye for true humility and saintliness, he made that Christmas a bishop, tell him of his faults.

Not that he set any great store by spiritual teachers and dogmas: he was apt to agree with his favourite, Mr. Dryden, that priests of all religions were the same. He loved to tell the story of that very honest blockhead, Dr. Woolley, to whom he had given a living in Suffolk, swarming with Nonconformists; how he had gone from house to house and brought them all to church, and how he had made him a bishop for his diligence, though what the good man could have said to the Nonconformists he could never imagine, except he believed that his nonsense suited their nonsense. But though Charles thought of all kinds of worship and Church government as but different fashions of the same cloak, he was no agnostic. He had large notions of God's mercy, and could never believe that He would damn one of His creatures for taking a little irregular pleasure by the way. Long ago he had told his sister that he was one of those bigots who regarded malice as a much greater sin than a poor frailty of nature. To design mischief, to be cruel and deny compassion, of these at least he had not been guilty; somehow, he trusted, he would climb up to Heaven's gate.[30]

CURTAIN

FEBRUARY LIGHT

CURTAIN

FEBRUARY LIGHT

" Death was denounced; that frightful sound
  Which even the best can hardly bear;
  He took the summons void of fear,
  And unconcernedly cast his eyes around,
  As if to find and dare the grisly challenger."
                                              —DRYDEN.

ON the evening of Sunday, February 1st, 1685, the pious
Evelyn visited Whitehall. " I can never forget," he wrote,
" the inexpressible luxury and profaneness, gaming and all
dissoluteness, and as it were total forgetfulness of God [it
being Sunday evening] which . . . I was witness of, the King
sitting and toying with his concubines, Portsmouth, Cleveland and Mazarin, a French boy singing love-songs in that
glorious gallery, whilst about twenty of the great courtiers
and other dissolute persons were at basset round a large table,
a bank of at least two thousand in gold before them." Of
the three ladies mentioned by the diarist, even the youngest
had attained what was then regarded as middle age, while
one had been the King's mistress, and another been proposed
to him for wife, just a quarter of a century before. If the
scene so graphically described was proof of iniquity in the
master of that Court, it was testimony also to his constancy.[1]
  The King had not been well for some days; whether it

was the excessive cold, gout, or a sore place in his heel, he had abandoned his wonted exercise for experiments in his laboratory and an occasional drive in the park.   But that evening he appeared to be quite his old self; made an excellent supper, and showed a more than usual affability.   Old Lord Ailesbury, who was making one of his rare visits to the Court, was transported with joy by the reception he received: "My Lord," said the King, "you make me blush whenever I see you, for whom I have done nothing in recompense for your constant adherence to me and mine; but "—motioning Lord Bruce—" your son is now near my person, and I will make it up to him, and he shall never quit me as long as I live." Afterwards in the Duchess of Portsmouth's apartments, where Charles went as usual to recreate himself with the company, he was in the most delightful and gracious of humours, so that those present could scarcely ever remember having seen him in so charming a mood.[2]

At the appointed hour, Bruce lit him to his Bedchamber. As he passed the candle to the page at the door, the flame went out, though there was no gust of wind in all that long, dark Gallery.

When he had put on his night-gown, the King went to ease himself, as was his custom, and remained laughing and talking to Bruce and Harry Killigrew for a long time in that strange but friendly place, where alone in all his vast palace he could be free from the press of company.   As he chatted, Bruce begged a colour in the Guards for a cousin of his: the King, smiling at such a trifling request, assured him that the Colonel would be only too glad to oblige him.   After that he spoke of the great house he was building at Winchester, telling Bruce, who had never liked to intrude himself there, that when modesty was not rewarded, it was the fault of the sovereign and not of the subject, and promising that next time he went there he would show him the place he so delighted in.   "I shall be so happy this week," he added, " as to have my house covered with lead."*

That night, Bruce and Killigrew, lying in the Royal Bedchamber, slept but little. A great fire of Scotch coal burnt all through the night, the King's dogs were never still, and several clocks, striking every quarter, kept up a continual chiming. Charles, to whom all this was habitual, slept through it, but his attendants noticed that he sometimes turned about in his sleep as though in unrest. In the morning when the servants, at the King's customary calling-out, came in to make the fire, Bruce, passing out through the Antechamber, where the surgeons were waiting to dress their master's heel, mentioned these uneasy movements to the Groom of the Bedchamber, who shook his head.[3]

When the surgeons entered, they found the King pale as ashes: he did not speak to them as was his wont, but addressed a few broken words in French to someone not present: he seemed to be speaking across time as though to a ghost. While Howard, who was buckling his garter, asked him how he was, he would not answer, but puffed a little, as he did when vexed, and, rising hastily from his chair, went out up the steps to his Closet: the world was swaying away from him, and he wished to be alone and to take some of his drops, if, in all that cold darkness, he could find them. There for some time he paced up and down, trying to be well and to bring himself back from the land of dreams: he knew vaguely that there was work before him that day, and that he was to meet the Commissioners of Accounts to examine the falsifications in the Hearth Money books—some great change was expected.[4]

Meanwhile, as minute passed minute, Bruce, in an agony of apprehension, sent Chiffinch—who alone had the right of

---

* " And God knows the Saturday following he was put into his coffin." (*Ailesbury*, 87.)

entry to the Closet—to beg his master to return to the Bed-chamber. But the King took no notice, and still paced up and down, and it was not till his old servant had returned a second time that he came out, pale and wan. At the foot of the stairs, where Lord Craven was waiting to receive the day's pass-word, he almost fell; he made no answer to the old man, but pointed to the book where the words were set down. Then, seeing the barber waiting by the window to shave him, he went over to the chair and sat down in silence, propping his knees against the glass as he always did.[5]

As the barber, tucking in his towel on one side, walked behind the chair to fix it on the other, Charles dropped back into Bruce's arms in a fit, his mouth foaming and screwing horribly upwards towards a white, pupil-less eye. Dr. King, who had remained in the room, hastily and with a shaking hand lanced a vein, while Bruce ran to fetch the Duke of York. When the latter arrived—a shoe on one foot and a slipper on the other—the physicians were trying to bring round their patient: bleeding him copiously, and applying blisters and pans of coal to every part of his body. About midday, after numberless emetics and purgatives had been forced down his throat, the King stirred and asked for his wife, who was kneeling at the end of the bed rubbing his feet. A few minutes later, when the faithful Bruce approached him, he was able to take his hand and whisper, " I see you love me dying as well as living."[6]

As the news of the King's seizure reached the outside world, a terrible hush fell. York—fearing an insurrection—ordered the ports to be stopped, lest any whisper of the crisis should reach Monmouth. But in the streets, beyond the barred gates of the Palace, a vast and silent crowd waited anxiously for news: it was hard, wrote an onlooker, to find anyone with dry eyes.[7]

Meanwhile, all that cold afternoon, in the darkened room

above the river, an ever-growing number of physicians cupped, blistered, purged and scarified the King's tortured body. Three things only they denied him—light, rest and privacy; nothing else was left untried. As evening came on, they prepared against the night a whole army of violent remedies; to meet the more ordinary needs of the human frame, they prescribed manna and cream of tartar in thin broth and barley-water, and a little light ale made without hops.[8]

Scarcely a quarter passed but the remedies were applied—purges forced down the mouth, sneezing powders to the nose, burning plasters for the feet, thighs and arms, shoulders and head. About two, when nature could respond no more to these attacks, Charles fell into a gentle sleep which continued till morning, when they woke him to tear off his plasters, rejoicing greatly to see that he felt the pain so keenly. Patiently he bore it all, and, when the pale light of day stole into his room, raised their hearts by the cheerful way in which he spoke of his sufferings.[*] To preserve his strength they forbade him to talk. Meekly he obeyed, observing that such a command would have killed Harry Killigrew.[9]

All day they followed each other: purgatives, juleps, cuppings, emulsions and that everlasting light broth. All day he lay with his eyes on the curtains of the great bed; all day the whispering throng crowded in and out of the room. His throat was sore and an aching pain racked his arm and shoulders. In the evening he was allowed to talk to the Secretary of State, and to send a message to his old friend Ormonde. Then night fell once more, and the watchers gathered in the firelight round the bed: the four doctors on duty, four Lords of the Council, three Lords of the Bed-chamber, the Bishop of Ely for ghostly consolation, and the

---

[*] " And about seven this morning he began to talk of the way he took his disease very cheerfully, to the unspeakable joy of all present." (Earl of Moray, H.M.C. Buccleuch, II, 3 Feb., '85.)

inferior servants moving about their business. Two of the doctors sat beside him with their eyes fixed on his, and the clocks continued to tick and chime. Sixteen times that night did those urgent remedies work.[10]

On Wednesday morning the tired King seemed better, and that afternoon the Privy Council issued a bulletin that he was out of danger. As the news passed out of the Palace gates, and the courtiers mounted their horses to awake sleeping towns, Charles, a little flushed and feverish, was talking cheerfully to the company about him. But as evening drew on and the candles began to gutter, he fell into a cold, clammy sweat. Then the physicians grew serious. Yet still those wonderful spirits did not play him false, and, after a restless night, he faced Thursday with the same cheerful courage.*[11]

But soon after midday a sudden and terrible change occurred. All that morning the physicians had been giving him the Jesuits' Bark: now a stronger dose put him into a sleep so deep that for a time it was feared he could never awake. Once more the gates of Whitehall were shut: once more men of all ranks and degrees walked about their business crying unashamedly.† Then those dark, suffering eyes opened, but this time there was no more hope. He lay there in intense pain, scarcely conscious—though he tried to hide it—of anything but that. The doctors announced that he could not live out the night.[12]

The watching Bishops gathered round the bed. Sancroft, with his low voice and timid, humble spirit, seemed unable to make the tortured man realize what he was saying, but Ken, whose voice was high and "like to a nightingale for the sweetness of it," implored him to receive the last rites of

---

* " He was very sensible of his condition all that Thursday, and spoke very freely and said many good things." (James Fraser, 7 Feb., '85, *Egmont*, II, 147.)

† " For near two hours the report was his Majesty could not recover out of it, which made all persons of all ranks and degrees melt into tears and fall a-crying." (James Fraser, 5 Feb., '85, *Egmont*, II, 146.)

that Protestant communion of which, for the few brief hours of life that still remained, he was the head. The King thanked him, and declared his sorrow for his sins, but begged him with great gentleness to desist from his entreaties. Somehow, he knew now, he must keep them away. Beyond the crowded darkness of the room, swaying and choking, his spirit was following a clearer trail, moving across the wet woods of Boscobel and the starlit meadows towards Moseley, where in a plain upper chamber two candles burnt before an ancient and secret altar. Strangely, it was his little sister who was leading him there.*[13]

But one whom he had loved, now weeping apart, had already divined the dying man's need. To the fat, astute Barrillon, Portsmouth in the deserted luxury of her room spoke urgently of the King's necessity; that she knew that at the bottom of his heart he was a Catholic, that he lay there, where she could not in decency go to him, surrounded by Protestant Bishops, with no one to tell him of his condition and speak to him of God, and that it would soon be too late. So prompted, Barrillon hastened back to the chamber of death, and, drawing York aside, bade him make some excuse to speak with him in the Queen's room. There he reminded him of his plain duty.[14]

York hurried back to the King, and, bidding the company stand back, knelt down and whispered in his ear. There, while the crowd stood watching at the door, he remained for nearly a quarter of an hour. Charles, whose senses were growing ever dimmer, seemed to have much difficulty in understanding him: then above the indistinct murmur he was heard saying clearly: " Yes, with all my heart! "[15]

York, despite his brother's entreaty to do nothing that might endanger himself, hurried back to the Queen's room,

* For this surmise there is no chapter and verse; but no other can adequately explain the strange incident that followed.

where he told Barrillon that the King had consented to see a priest. The immediate problem was to find one, for none of the Queen's Portuguese monks could speak a word of English, while to fetch one from one of the foreign embassies would entail the loss of many precious minutes, and the King was now sinking fast. But it so happened that in the little closet where the monks were huddled together, chattering and telling their beads, was Father Huddleston. The old man, who had been preserved at Whitehall by Charles during the Popish Terror, gladly agreed to risk his life once more for his master's sake. While the Holy Sacrament of the Altar was sent for from the chapel at Somerset House, he was smuggled, disguised in cassock and wig, to a side door of the Bedchamber.[16]

It was nearly eight before York turned to the crowded room and ordered all to retire save the Earls of Bath and Feversham, two Protestants upon whose loyalty and discretion complete reliance could be placed. As soon as the company had filed out, Chiffinch led in Huddleston, the Duke announcing him with the words: " Sire, here is a man who saved your life and is now come to save your soul." " He is very welcome," whispered the King.[17]

Kneeling beside the bed, Huddleston asked his sovereign whether he was prepared to be received into the arms of the Catholic Church and to receive her final rites. Charles answered that he desired to die in that communion, and to be absolved of the sins of his past life, for which he was truly sorry, and most of all for having so long delayed his conversion; he trusted none the less in the merits of Christ, was in charity with all the world, pardoned his enemies, and begged pardon of those whom he had offended. Then, at Huddleston's request, he made a full and sincere confession, afterwards lifting up his hands and repeating the last words, " Mercy, sweet Jesus, mercy," until the priest was ready to give him Extreme Unction. The Sacrament being now come,

Huddleston asked him if he desired to receive it: he replied that he did most earnestly, if he was thought to be worthy. While the final preparations were being made, the King struggled to raise himself, saying: " Let me meet my Heavenly Lord in a better posture than in my bed." But Huddleston bade him lie still. There, in his agony, Charles received with a gentle humility and gladness the final and greatest rites, entering, at the hour of his *viaticum*, the portals of the ancient communion in which all but two or three of the many Christian men and women from whom he was descended had lived and died.[18]

As Huddleston, still holding the cross before his eyes, withdrew, the door was flung open, and the crowd, after three-quarters of an hour of wondering suspense, pressed in. They saw the Protestant earls standing motionless, and the King's pale face gazing at them with faint recognition from the pillows. From that hour—it was close on ten—until the morning, Charles remained conscious, spoke clearly and with feeling, and seemed to be at peace. When they spoke to him of the pain through which he was passing, he did not any longer attempt to hide it, but answered without complaint or impatience: " Gentlemen, I have suffered very much, and more than any of you can imagine." Once he expressed a desire to be dissolved, and, asking the time, remarked: " My business will shortly be done." About midnight the Queen came to take farewell of him, and knelt with the others, weeping beside the bed. He spoke to her with great tenderness until she could bear the sight of his tortured body no longer, and was carried fainting to her room, whence she sent to beg his forgiveness. " Alas! poor woman! " he replied. " She ask my pardon? I beg hers with all my heart: take her back that answer." To York, whose grief was quite unrestrained, Charles showed every mark of affection, begging him to overlook all he had done towards

2A

him that seemed unkind, for he had been forced to it.   Then
he recommended to him the care of his wife and his sons, who
knelt in turn—all but Monmouth—beside the bed to receive
his blessing.   The Bishops asked him to bless his kingdom
and people; he raised himself, and, with all kneeling, prayed
for God's benediction to rest on his countrymen, and asked
that they would pardon him if in anything he had not been a
good king.   Throughout these scenes, the spasms of mortal
pain and the constant and degrading ministrations of the
doctors, he remained serene.*   For one moment a flicker of
the old wit returned: he was sorry, he said, to be so long
in dying.   Once more he called York to him and bade him
look to Louise and his poor children, and not let Nelly starve.
Then he gave him the keys of his cabinet and wished him
prosperity.[19]

About six in the morning he asked what time it was, and,
being told, murmured, "Open the curtains that I may once
more see day."   They drew them back, and the light of a
February dawn flooded in through the tall windows.   From
below came the voices of living men at their work on the river.
Once he spoke of one of his clocks: it must be wound that
day or it would stop.   As it grew brighter, his movements
stiffened, and he spoke no more.   To relieve the rigour of
his pain they blooded him, but he was past human help.   His
breathing came urgently and in spasms: they raised him
upright in the pillows.   By ten he seemed no longer to be
conscious.[20]

A little before noon—the river was then at high tide—
they began to press out, crying, from the Bedchamber into
the Gallery—first the divines, then the Gentlemen and Lords
of the Bedchamber, the Councillors of State, and, last of all,

---

* "He died as he lived, the admiration of all men for his piety, his contempt
of this world and his resolution against death." (Drummond to Queensberry,
6 Feb., '85, *H.M.C. Buccleuch*, II, 212.)

the new King with a great company of people attending him. Outside in the streets, anxious faces turned to a grief which none tried to hide: it was as though a family had lost a common parent.

Beside that motionless figure in the darkened chamber, the faithful Bruce watched all that day and night. " Thus ended," he wrote long after, " my happy days at a Court, and to this hour I bewail my loss and that of the three kingdoms. God's will be done on earth as it is in Heaven. . . . My good and gracious King and master, Charles the Second, and the best that ever reigned over us, died in peace and glory, and the Lord God have mercy on his soul."[21]

APPENDIX OF REFERENCES

For the sake of clarity, I have divided the list of references cited into four tables :

A. Contemporary Letters, Diaries and Accounts.
B. Memoirs, Histories, Tracts, Ballads, Newspapers, etc., by Contemporary Hands.
C. Parliamentary Debates, Journals, Statutes and State Trials.
D. Later Works not included in any of the above.

Of these the first are of far greater value as historical evidence than the second, for the writers of tracts and newspapers are inclined to distort facts to help their party, and memoir writers to justify their past conduct, while the latter (being generally retired statesmen occupying their leisure) suffer the additional disadvantage of failing memory. Burnet, Clarendon, Temple, North—the great memoir writers on whom English historians have mainly relied for their knowledge of the reign of Charles II—are only to be trusted implicitly when their statements are borne out by the evidence of letters and diaries, written not a generation later, but at the very time of the events which they describe.

Even the latter need to be used with caution, and with some knowledge of the opinions and characters of the writers. A letter-writer such as Sir Robert Southwell—shrewd, honest and disinterested—is of greater value to posterity, so far as the accuracy of his evidence is concerned, than a changeable careerist such as Ralph Montagu. Again, what the soldier said is not always evidence. When Pepys records gossip about his sovereign's nocturnal movements, obtained at third hand from the wife of the Court surgeon, he is not necessarily transmitting the truth to us; when, on the other hand, he describes a personal interview with the King, he is (as a man of proved honesty) entitled to every respect.

To avoid sprinkling the text page with digits, I have grouped the reference notes in paragraphs, re-numbering the notes in each chapter. This method has the obvious disadvantage of making it difficult to discover the source of any particular allusion or quotation without consulting all the references cited for the paragraph. But it has the corresponding advantage of causing the student to consider the authorities as a whole; much of the misunderstanding of the seventeenth century has been due to the habit of relying on the isolated statements of particular writers, who have thus acquired an influence out of proportion to their real importance. I have therefore tried to make each reference note a bibliography in miniature for the paragraph to which it refers.

In the case of well-known sources which are arranged in chronological order, notably the *Lords* and *Commons Journals*, *State Trials* and *Clarendon's History* and *Continuation*, I have omitted the page numbers in order to save space.

It will be noticed that in my references I have relied more on contemporary letters than on memoirs. The reason for this I have explained. The result has been to bring out the view of Charles generally held in his own day rather than that adopted for political reasons by the party writers of the next generation, and expanded by those constitutional historians of the nineteenth century who viewed the past mainly as a study in the advance of parliamentary sovereignty. Since the second Charles was one of the most successful statesmen who ever opposed this theory of government, his posthumous reputation has been somewhat roughly handled.

As over a hundred of the collections of contemporary letters cited in this Appendix are printed by the Historical Manuscripts Commission, I have tabled these separately.

LIST OF REFERENCES CITED

(Note.—Abbreviations used in Reference Notes printed in italics)

A. CONTEMPORARY LETTERS, DIARIES AND ACCOUNTS

1. PRINTED IN APPENDICES TO REPORTS OF HISTORICAL MANUSCRIPTS COMMISSION

(a) In Folio Volumes

Rep. 2. Earl *Spencer*; Lord *Lyttleton*; Duke of *Montrose;* Earl of *Mount Edgcumbe*.

Rep. 3. Duke of *Northumberland*; Marquis of *Bath;* W. *Dod*, Esq.; Sir P. de M. *Grey-Egerton*; Rev. F. *Hopkinson*; W. J. *Legh*, Esq.; Rev. W. *Sneyd*; Duke of *Montrose*; Marquis of *Ormonde*; John *Webster*, Esq.

Rep. 4. House of *Lords*; J. J. *Rogers*, Esq.; Countess of *Rothes*; Marquis of *Bath*.

Rep. 5. House of *Lords*; Duke of *Sutherland*; Sir Alexander *Malet*; Reginald *Cholmondley*, Esq.; J. R. *Pine-Coffin*, Esq.; Rev. H. T. *Ellacombe*; Mr. and Mrs. *Maxwell Witham*.

Rep. 6. House of *Lords*; Lord *Leconfield*; Sir Reginald *Graham*; Sir Henry *Ingilby*; P. B. Davies *Cooke*; Miss *ffarington*; T. Stamford *Raffles*, Esq.; Duke of *Argyle*; Sir Robert *Menzies*; Marquis of *Ormonde*.

Rep. 7. House of *Lords*; Sir Frederick *Graham of Netherby*; Sir Harry *Verney*; G. E. *Frere*, Esq.; G. Alan *Lowndes*, Esq.; Rev. Thomas *Webb*; Marquis of *Ormonde*.

Rep. 8. House of *Lords*; Duke of *Marlborough*; Earl of *Portsmouth*; Ralph *Bankes*, Esq.; Corporation *of Chester;* Corporation *of Leicester*; Royal *College of Physicians*; Trinity *House*; Duke of *Manchester*; Earl of *Ashburnham*; Marquis of *Ormonde*.

Rep. 9. Corporation *of Canterbury;* Corporation *of Carlisle*; House *of Lords*; Sir R. A. O. *Dalyell*; Marquis of *Drogheda*; Mr. Chandos *Pole-Gell*; Mr. *Alfred Morrison;* Mr. *Pyne* and Mr. Woodford; Mrs. *Stopford Sackville*.

NOTE.—The above are cited throughout with the number of the Report to which they are appended and prefixed by the initials *H.M.C.*

(b) In 8vo Volumes

Marquis of *Ailesbury*.

Earl of *Ancaster*, Vol. I.

Marquis of *Bath*, Vol. II.

Duke of *Beaufort*.

Lord *Braye*.

Corporation *of Bridgwater*.

Duke of *Buccleuch* and Queensberry (preserved at Drumlanrig Castle, Vols. I, II.

Duke of *Buccleuch* and Queensberry (preserved at Montagu *House*), Vols. I, III.
Bury St. Edmunds Corporation.
Miss *Buxton* (Rep. on MSS. in Various Collections, Vol. II).
Earl *Cowper* (Coke MSS.), Vol. II.
Earl of *Dartmouth*, Vols. I, III.
Marquis of *Downshire*, Vol. I, i.
Sir Archibald *Edmonstone* (Rep. on MSS. in Various Collections, Vol. V).
Earl of *Egmont*, Vols. I, II.
Corporation *of Eye*.
A. G. *Finch*, Esq., Vols. I, II.
Sir William *Fitzherbert*.
S. H. Le *Fleming*, Esq.
F. J. Savile *Foljambe*, Esq.
Family of *Gawdy*.
Glemham Hall MSS. (Rep. on MSS. in Various Collections, Vol. IV).
J. H. *Gurney*, Esq.
Duke of *Hamilton*.
Mrs. *Harford* (Rep. on MSS. in Various Collections, Vol. II).
R. Rawdon *Hastings*, Vol. II.
J. M. *Heathcote*, Esq.
J Eliot *Hodgkin*, Esq.
Lord *Hothfield*.
W. W. B. *Hulton*, Esq.
Lord *Kenyon*.
R. W. *Ketton*, Esq.
Laing MSS., Vol. I.
Duke of *Leeds*.
Le Strange Papers.
F. W. *Leyborne-Popham*.
Lincoln Corporation.
Earl of *Lindsey*.
S. Zachary *Lloyd*, Esq.
Earl of *Lonsdale*.
House of Lords (1678-88).
General *Lyttleton-Annesley*.
Marchmont MSS (in possession of Sir H. H. Campbell).
Sir J. *Stirling Maxwell*.
Earl of *Middleton*.
Major *Money-Kyrle* (Rep. on MSS in Various Collections, Vol. IV).
Lord *Montagu of Beaulieu*.
Charles S. H. *Drummond Moray*.
Marquis of *Ormonde*, o.s. Vols. I, II; n.s. Vols. III, IV, V, VI, VII.
Pepys MSS. (Magdalene College).
Duke of *Portland*, Vols. I, II, III, VIII.
Corporation *of Reading*.
James *Round*, Esq.
Mrs. F. *Russell-Astley*.
Duke of *Rutland*, Vol. II.
City of Salisbury (Rep. on MSS. in Various Collections, Vol. IV).
Duke of *Somerset*.
Corporation *of Southampton*.

Stewart of Alltyrodyn.
Stuart Papers, Vol. I.
Sir N. W. *Throckmorton.*
Marquis *Townshend.*
Earl of *Verulam.*
Wells Cathedral.
Earl of *Westmorland.*
County of Wilts. (Rep. on MSS. in Various Collections, Vol. I).
Sir George *Wombwell* (Rep. on MSS. in Various Collections, Vol. II).
The Hon. F. L. *Wood* (Rep. on MSS. in Various Collections, Vol. VIII).

N.B.—The above are prefixed throughout by the initials *H.M.C.* and arranged
alphabetically in each reference note.

2. CONTEMPORARY LETTERS, DIARIES, ACCOUNTS, ETC.—*cont.*
    (other than those printed in Hist. MSS. Com. Reports)

Aberdeen, George Earl of. *Letters.* (Spalding Club.)
*Add*itional MSS.* (in British Museum).
Ady, Mrs. Madame (for letters of Henrietta of Orleans). (1894.)
Archæologia, Vol. 68, Part I. (Ditchley letters of Charles II and Duke of York to
    Lady Lichfield.)
Arlington Letters. 2 vols. (1701.)
*Ashmole Papers (in the Bodleian). (For miscellaneous documents.)
Bailey. *Winchester Records.*
Baillie, Robert. Letters and Journals, Vol. III. (Bannantyne Club.)
**Ballard MSS.* (in Bodleian).
(*Blencowe* ed.) Diary and Correspondence of Henry Sidney. 2 vols.
Burnet Letters. (Camden Misc., XI.)
Burton, T. *Diary.* 4 vols.
Calendar of *Clarendon MSS.* (Ed. Macray.) 3 vols.
Calendars of State Papers, *Colonial* (*America and W. Indies*).
Calendars of State Papers, Domestic, 1625-49, 1649-60, 1660-81.
Calendars of State Papers *Venet*ian.
Calendars of Treasury Books, 1660-89. (Ed. W. A. Shaw.)
Camden Miscellany, I. (See *Lake.*)
Camden Miscellany, V. (For some letters of Charles II.)
Camden Miscellany, XI. (See *Burnet Letters.*)
**Carte MSS.* (in the Bodleian).
Carte. A Collection of Original Letters and Papers (Letters of Duke of Ormonde),
    1739. 2 vols.
Cartwright, Julia. (See *Ady.*)
Cary. *Memorials* of the Great Civil War. 2 vols.
Chesterfield, Philip Stanhope, Second Earl of. *Letters.* (Ed. 1837.)
Chevalier Journal. (Contained in *Hoskins*, Charles II in the Channel Islands.)
    2 vols. (See also *H.M.C. Rep.* 2, 158-64.)
Christie, Shaftesbury. Appendix.
**Clarendon MSS.* (in the Bodleian). (See also *Cal. Clar. MSS.* above.)
Clarendon State Papers, Vols. II, III and Appendix.
Clarendon, Second Earl of. (See *Singer.*)

Clarke Papers. (Camden Soc., ed. Firth.) III, IV.

Cosin Correspondence. (Surtees Soc.)

Council Notes of Charles II and Clarendon. (Roxburghe Club.) (Ed. Macray.)

Crawfurd, Raymond. Last Days of Charles II. (Contains translation of *Scarburgh MS*.)

Cromwell, Oliver. *Letters* and Speeches. (Ed. Carlyle.)

Dalrymple. Memoirs. (Ed. 1773.) Vol. II, Appendix.

Danby Letters, 1676-8. (Ed. 1710.)

D'Avaux. Négociations du Comte D'Avaux en Hollande. 6 vols.

Dugdale. Life, Diary and Correspondence.

Egerton MSS. (in British Museum).

Ellis. *Original Letters*. 1st Series, Vol. III; 2nd Series, Vols. III, IV.

Essex Correspondence. (Camden Soc.) 2 vols.

Evelyn. Memoirs. (Diary and Letters.) (Ed. Wheatley.) 4 vols.

Ferrero. Lettres de Henriette Marie à sa Sœur, Christine Duchesse de la Savoie.

Flanders Papers (in Public Record Office).

Foreign Entry Books (in Public Record Office).

Forneron. Louise de Kéroualle.

Fox. *James II*. Appendix.

Gentleman's Magazine, 1866. Parts I and II (for alleged letters of James de la Cloche).

Gordon, Patrick. *Diary*. (Spalding Club.)

Graham of Claverhouse, Letters of John. (Bannantyne Club.)

Hamilton MSS., The. (Ed. Lowry, 1867.)

Harleian MSS. (in British Museum).

Hatton Correspondence. (Camden Soc.) 2 vols.

Henrietta Maria, Letters of. (Everett Green.) (See also *Ferrero*.)

Holland Papers (in Public Record Office).

Instructions aux Ambassadeurs de France, Recueil de. (Angleterre.)

Jaffray. *Diary*.

Josselin. Diary. (Camden Soc.)

Jusserand. A French Ambassador at the Court of Charles II. (Letters of D'Estrades, Courtin, Cominges, etc.)

Lake, Dr. Diary. (Camden Misc., Vol. I.)

Lansdowne MSS. (in British Museum).

Lauderdale Papers. (Camden Soc.) 3 vols.

Lingard. History of England. (Ed. 1849.) Vol. IX. (For text of Secret Treaty of Dover.)

Lister. Clarendon. Vol. III. (For letters, etc., of Clarendon.)

Long of Draycot MS. (In Household Words, 9.)

Longleat MSS. (See *Foxcroft*, Halifax.)

Luttrell, Narcissus. Brief Historical Relation. (1857 ed.) Vol. I.

Lyme, House of. (Ed. Lady Newton.) (For Lyme Papers.)

Mackintosh MSS. (in British Museum).

Maids Moreton, Church Register.

Marvell. Works. (Ed. Margoliouth.) Vol. II for letters.

Mignet. Négociations relatives à la Succession d'Espagne. III, IV.

Miscellanea Aulica. (Ed. Brown, 1702.)

Momigliano, Eucardio. Cromwell. (For dispatches of Genoese and Venetian agents and envoys during Commonwealth.)

Moore, Diary of the Rev. Giles. (See *Ponsonby*.)

Newdegate. Cavalier and Puritan. (For Diary and News Letters of Sir Richard Newdegate.)
Nicholas Papers. (Camden Soc.) 4 vols.
Orrery, Earl of. State Letters. (1743.) 2 vols.
Parker. History of Wycombe. (For Wycombe Borough Records.)
Pepys. Diary. (Ed. Wheatley.)
Pepys. Life, Journal and Correspondence. (Ed. 1841.) (For *Narrative of Voyage to Tangier.*)
Pepys. Correspondence. (See *Tanner.*)
Pepys. Further Correspondence. (See *Tanner.*)
Ponsonby, A. English Diaries. (For diary of *Rev. Giles Moore.*)
Prideaux. Letters. (Camden Soc.)
Pythouse Papers.
Rawlinson MSS. (in Bodleian).
Rugge Diurnal. (*Add. MSS.* 10116, 10117.)
Russell, Lady Rachel, Letters of. (Ed. 1853.) Vol. I.
St. Evremond, Œuvres de. (Ed. 1865.) 3 vols.
Savile. Correspondence. (Camden Soc.)
Scarburgh MS. (See *Crawfurd,* Last Days of Charles II.)
Schwerin, Otto von. Briefe aus England 1674-8. (For Dispatches of Brandenburg Minister.) (Ed. Orlich.)
Secret Services of Charles II and James II. (Camden Soc.)
Sévigné, Lettres de. (1862.)
Seward. Anecdotes. (For a letter of Charles II to Jane Lane.)
Shakerley MSS. (at White House, East Claydon; formerly at Somerford Park, Cheshire).
Sidney, Algernon. Letters to Henry Savile. (Ed. 1740.)
Sidney, Henry. Diary. (See *Blencowe.*)
Singer (ed). Correspondence of Second Earl of Clarendon. Vol. I.
State Papers Domestic (in Public Record Office). (And see *Calendar of State Papers Dom.* above.)
State Papers, Colonial (America and W. Indies), see *Calendars* of.
State Papers Venetian, see *Calendars* of.
Tanner MSS. (in Bodleian).
(*Tanner* ed.) *Pepys Correspondence,* Vol. I.
(*Tanner* ed.) *Pepys Further Correspondence.*
Temple. Works. (1740.) (For letters of Sir Wm. Temple.) Vol. II.
Teonge, Rev. Hen. Diary. (Ed. Manaring.)
Thoresby, Ralph. *Diary.* Vol. I.
Thurloe State Papers. 7 vols.
Treasury Papers. See *Calenders of Treasury Books.*
Verney. Memoirs. (Ed. 1925.) 2 vols.
Warcup, Edmund, Journals of. (Ed. Feiling and Needham. Printed in *E.H.R.*, 40.)
Williamson Letters. (Camden Soc.) 2 vols.
Witt, de. Lady of Lathom. (For letters of Charlotte, Countess of Derby.)
Wynn Papers, Calendar of. (National Library of Wales.)
Wynne, W. Life of Sir Leoline *Jenkins.* 2 vols.

B. MEMOIRS, HISTORIES, TRACTS, BALLADS, NEWS-PAPERS, ETC., BY CONTEMPORARY HANDS

Absalom and Achitophel. (See Dryden.)
Account of Several Late Voyages and Discoveries, 1694.
Ailesbury, Thomas Bruce, Earl of. Memoirs. (Roxburghe Club.)
Alford, Captain. Narrative. (See *Fea, Flight of the King.*)
Aqua Triumphalis. (1662.)
" *Arraignment of the Devill for taking away Richard Bradshaw, The.*" (1659.)
Arthur, King. (See *Dryden.*)
Ashmole, E.   Order of the *Garter.* (1672.)
Aubrey. Lives. (Ed. Clark.) 2 vols.
Bagford Ballads. (Ed. Ebsworth.) Vol. II.
Baker Chronicle. (1684 ed.)
Balfour. Annals of Scotland. Vol. IV.
Bates, Dr. *Elenchus Motuum Nuperorum.* (See *Fea, Flight of the King.*)
Baxterianæ, Reliquæ. (1696.)
Blair. Life.
Blount, Thomas. *Boscobel.* (See *Fea, After Worcester Fight.*)
Bolingbroke. Works. (Ed. 1754.) Vol. II.
Bramston, Sir J., Autobiography of. (Camden Soc.)
Broadley, A. M. *The Royal Miracle.* (For contemporary tracts contained see App., Pt. I, Ch. I, n. i.)
Buckingham, Works of John Sheffield, Duke of. (2nd ed. 1729.) Vol. II.
Bulstrode, Sir Richard. Memoirs. (1721 ed.)
Burnet, Gilbert. History of My Own Time. (Ed. Airy, 1900). 2 vols.
Burnet, Gilbert. Lives of the Hamiltons.
Burnet, Gilbert. *Supplement.* (Ed. Foxcroft.)
Burney Collection (of news-sheets—in British Museum).
Butler, Samuel. *Hudibras.*
Calamy. Historical Account of My Own Life.
Cameron. Memoirs. (Abbotsford Club.)
Chamberlayne. Angliæ Notitia. (1671 ed.)
Child, J. *New Discourse of Trade.*
Choice Ayres. (1675.)
Cibber. Apology. (1740.)
Clarendon. History of the Great Rebellion. 6 vols. (Ed. Macray.)
Clarendon. (Life) *Continuation.* 2 vols. (1851 ed.)
Clarke. Life of *James II.* 2 vols.
Claustrum Regale Reseratum. (See *Fea, After Worcester Fight.*)
Coke, R. *Discourse of Trade.* (1670.)
Cook, Aurelian. Titus Britannicus.
Cosmo, Duke of Tuscany. *Travels.*
Courthop. Memoirs. (Camden Misc., XI.)
Crosby Records. A Cavalier's Notebook.
Defoe. " The *Review.*"
Delaune. Present State of London. (1681.)
Downes. (See *Roscius Anglicanus.*)

Dryden. Works. (Ed. Saintsbury.)

Dugdale. St. Paul's. (2nd ed., 1716.)

Earle, Bishop John. *Microcosmography.* (1897.)

Echard. History. (1720 ed.)

Eglesfield. Monarchy Revived. (1822 ed.)

" *England's Joy.*" (See *Stuart Tracts.*)

Evelyn. Sylva.

Examen. See *North.*

Fanshawe, Lady. Memoirs. (1907 ed.)

Fea, Allan. *After Worcester Fight.* (For contemporary tracts contained see App., Pt. I, Ch. I, n. i.)

Fea, Allan. *Flight of the King.* (For contemporary tracts contained see App., Pt. I, Ch. I, n. i.)

Ferguson. Robert Ferguson the Plotter. (For papers of.)

Fiennes, Celia. Travels. (Through England on a side-saddle.)

Fountainhall, Sir J. Lauder, Lord. *Chronological Notes.*

Fountainhall, Sir J. Lauder, Lord. *Historical Observes.* (Bannantyne Club.)

Fountainhall, Sir J. Lauder, Lord. *Journals.* (Scottish Hist. Soc.)

Fox, George. *Journal.* (1924 ed.)

Fox, Sir *Stephen, Memoirs* of the Life of. (1717 ed.)

Gallus Castratus. (1659.)

Gamaches, Père Cyprian de. Memoirs.

Gardiner. Papers illustrating the relations between *Charles II and Scotland in* 1650. (Scottish Hist. Soc.)

Gounter, Colonel. *Narrative.* (See *Fea, Flight of the King.*)

Grammont. Memoirs. (Ed. Goodwin, 1908.) 2 vols.

Growth of Knavery.

Growth of Popery. Marvell.

Guardian No. 67.

Halifax, Works of Geo. Savile, Marquis of. (Ed. Raleigh, 1912.)

Harleian Miscellany. Vol. IV.

Hearne. Collections. (O.H.S., 1901.)

Heath Chronicle (with Continuation.) (1676 ed.)

Higgons. Works. 2 vols. (1736.)

Hinton, Sir J. *Memoires.*

Hodgson. Original *Memoirs.* (1806.)

Huddleston. Short and Plain Way. A Brief Account of Particulars occurring at the Happy Death of King Charles II.

Impartial Case of the Earl of Danby. (1679.)

Kennet. Register.

King. Anecdotes of His Own Times.

King, Gregory. Natural and Political *Observations.*

King's Own Narrative of Flight from Worcester. (See *Fea, After Worcester Fight.*)

Kip. Britannia Illustrata.

Lansdowne. Works. (Ed. 1732.)

L'Estrange, Roger. *Brief History.* (See also *Observator.*)

Livingstone. Life.

London's Diurnal. (*Burney Collection,* 54.)

" *London Gazette.*"

Lord's Loud Call to England, The. (1660.)

Louis XIV, Œuvres de. 6 vols. (1805.)

"*Loyal Protestant* and True Domestic *Intelligence.*" (1681.) (*Burney*, 83.)
Loyal Songs, A Collection of. (1685.)
Lucy, Sir Francis, *Commonplace Book of.* (*English Review*, Oct., 1930.)
Ludlow. Memoirs. (Ed. Firth.) 2 vols.
Lying Wonders or the Wonderful Lyes, The. (1660.)
Macpherson. Original Papers. (1775.) Vol. I.
Marvell, Andrew. Poems and Letters. (Ed. Margoliouth.) Vol. I.
Maseres. Select Civil War Tracts.
"*Mercurius Publicus.*" (*Burney Collection*, 55.)
Mirabilis Annus. (1662.)
Miraculum Basilicon. (See *Broadley, Royal Miracle.*)
Montpensier, Mademoiselle. Memoirs.
Motteville, Madame de. *Memoires.*
Murray, Anne. (Lady Halkett) Autobiography. (Camden Soc.)
Nalson. Impartial Collection. Vol. II.
North, Roger. *Examen.* (1740.)
North, Roger. *Lives* of the Norths. (Ed. Jessopp, 1890.) 3 vols.
North. Memoires of Musick.
"*Observator.*" (*Burney Collection*, 88.)
Ogilby, J. *Account of the Coronation.* (1662.)
Oldmixon. History of Addresses. 2 vols.
Orleans, Dr. F. J. History of the Revolutions in England. (Ed. 1722.)
"*Parliamentary Intelligencer.*" (*Burney Collection*, 55.)
Phelipps, Robert. *Account.* (See *Broadley, Royal Miracle.*)
Plot, R. Natural History of *Oxfordshire.* (Ed. 1676.)
Plot, R. Natural History of *Staffordshire.* (1686.)
Price, John. Mystery and Method of His Majesty's Happy Restoration. (*Maseres* Select Tracts.)
"*Publick Intelligencer.*" (*Burney Collection*, 54, 55.)
Reresby, Sir John. Memoirs. (Ed. Andrew Browning and now in course of publication.)
Retz, de. Memoirs.
Richardsoniana.
Rochester, John Wilmot, Earl of. Poems.
Roscius Anglicanus. Downes.
Roxburghe Ballads. Vol. IV. (Ed. Ebsworth.)
Royal Oak, The. (See *Broadley, Royal Miracle.*)
Rushworth. Historical Collections. Vol. VIII.
Selden. Mare Clausum.
Shadwell. Humorists.
Somers Tracts. (Ed. 1809-15.) Vols. VI, VII, VIII.
Sophia, Duchess. *Memoirs.*
Spectator, No. 462.
Sprat, Bishop. History of the *Royal Society.*
Sprat, Bishop. *True Account* of the Horrid Conspiracy. (1685.)
State Poems. (Ed. 1697.)
Stuart Tracts. (Ed. Firth.)
Summary of Occurrences Relating to the Miraculous Preservation. (See *Fea, Flight of the King.*)
Temple. Works. (1740.) (For Memoirs of Sir Wm. Temple.) Vol. I.
Threnodia Augustalis. (See *Dryden.*)

Titus Britannicus. (See *Cook, Aurelian*.)
True Narrative of His Majesty's Miraculous Escape. (See *Fea, Flight of the King*.)
Turner, Sir J. *Memoirs*. (1829 ed.)
Walker. Historical Discourses.
Waller. Poems.
Welwood, James. *Memoirs*. (1718 ed.)
Whitelocke. Memorials.
Whitgreave, Mr. *Narrative*. (See *Fea, After Worcester Fight*.)
Wood. *Life and Times*. (Ed. Clark, 1891-1900.) Vols. I, II.
Wood, W. *Survey of Trade*.
Woodcock, Thomas. *Papers*. (Camden Misc., XI.)
Worcester, Great and Bloody Fight at. (See *Broadley, Royal Miracle*.)
" *Word to Purpose, A*." (1659.) (*Burney Collection*, 53.)
Wren. Parentalia.

C. PARLIAMENTARY DEBATES, JOURNALS, STATUTES AND STATE TRIALS

Chandler. Debates.
Commons *Journals*. Vols. VII, VIII, IX.
Grey, Anchitell. Debates of the House of Commons. (1667-94.) 10 vols.
Lords *Journals*. Vols. IX, X, XI, XII, XIII.
Old Parliamentary History. Vol. XXII.
Parliamentary History. (Ed. Cobbet.) Vol. IV.
State Trials. (Ed. Cobbet.) Vols. V, VI, VII, VIII, IX.
Statutes. Vol. I.

D. LATER WORKS NOT INCLUDED IN ANY OF THE ABOVE

Abbott, Prof. Wilbur. (See *English Historical Review*.)
Acton, Lord. *Historical Essays and Studies*.
Ady, Mrs. Sacharissa. (See also Section A.)
Barbour, Miss V. Arlington.
Beatson. *Political Index*.
Bell. The *Fire of London*.
Bell. The Great *Plague* in London.
Beresford, John. " Godfather of Downing Street."
Birch. History of the *Royal Society*.
Browning, Dr. Andrew. (See *History*.)
Bund, J. Willis, *Paper* by. (See *Broadley, Royal Miracle*.)
Burghclere, Lady. Ormonde. 2 vols.
Cambridge Modern History. Vol. V.
Carte. Life of Ormonde. 6 vols. (Ed. 1851.)
Cartwright, Julia. (See *Ady*.)
Corbett. *England in the Mediterranean*.
Courtenay, T. P. Sir William Temple. 2 vols.
Cunningham, P. Story of Nell Gwyn and Sayings of Charles II.
Cunningham, W. Growth of English *Industry and Commerce*, II, Pt. I.

Davidson.   Catherine of Braganza.
Dictionary of National *Biography*.
English *Historical Review*.
    Vol. 21.   Two articles by Prof. Wilbur C. *Abbott* on the Long Parliament of Charles II.
    Vol. 39.   Article by C. L. *Grose* on Anglo-Dutch Alliance of 1678.
    Vol. 40.   *Warcup* Journal.   (Ed. *Feiling*.)
    Vol. 45.   Article by Mrs. *George* on Elections of Exclusion Parliaments.
English Review, Oct., 1930.   (For *Commonplace Book of Sir Francis Lucy*.)
Feiling, Keith.   British *Foreign Policy*, 1660-72.
Feiling, Keith.   History of the *Tory Party*.   (See also *E.H.R.*)
Ferguson, J.   Ferguson the Plotter.
Firth.   *Last Years of the Protectorate*.   2 vols.
Fortescue, Sir J.   History of the *British Army*.   Vol. I.
Foxcroft, Miss H. C.   Geo. Savile, Marquis of Halifax.   2 vols.
Gardiner, S. R.   *Civil Wars*.   3 vols.
Gardiner, S. R.   *Commonwealth and Protectorate*.   3 vols.
Gardiner, S. R.   *History* of England.   10 vols.
George, Mrs.   (See English Historical *Review*.)
Grey.   *Hudibras*.   Vol. II.
Grose, C. L.   (See English Historical *Review*.)
Halliwell.   *Morland*.
Harris.   Lord *Sandwich*.   2 vols.
Hawkins.   *History of Music*.   Vol. IV.
History.   (n.s.) Vol. XIV for an article by Dr. A. *Browning* on the Suspension of the Exchequer and one by Prof. P. *Geyl* on De Ruyter.
Hoskins.   Charles II in the Channel Islands.   (See *Chevalier Journal*.)
Hume.   *History* of England.   (1848.)   Vol. VI.
Hunter.   History of *British India*.
Khan.   The East India Trade in the Seventeenth Century.
Klopp, Onno.   Der Fall des Hauses Stuart.
Lyon.   *Personal History of King Charles II*.
Marshall.   *Annals of Tennis*.
Mazure.   Histoire de la Revolution de 1688.   Vol. I.
Muddiman, J. G.   The King's Journalist.
Napier.   *Montrose*.
Pennant.   *London*.
Pollock.   *Popish Plot*.
Ranke.   History of England.   (Trans. 1875.)   6 vols.
Scott, Eva.   The *Travels of the King*.
Shaw, W. A.   *Beginnings of the National Debt*.   (See also Calendar Treasury Books.)
Sheppard.   Old Royal Palace of Whitehall.
Sitwell, Sir George.   The *First Whig*.
Steinman.   Barbara, Duchess of *Cleveland*.
Steinman.   *Althorp Memoirs*.
Strickland.   Lives of the *Queens of England*.   (Ed. 1871.)   Vol. IV.
Taylor.   Henrietta Maria.
Traill.   *Social England*.   Vol. IV.
Walpole.   *Royal and Noble Authors*.
Wodrow.   History of the Sufferings of the Church of Scotland.   4 vols.

PRELUDE

THE CHILD OF VANDYKE'S PICTURES

[1] *C.S.P.D.* 1629-31, 269; *Gardiner*, VII, 171; *H.M.C. Rutland*, II, 321.

[2] *C.S.P.D.* 1629-31, 269; *Eglesfield*, 5; *Gadbury, The Nativity of King Charles;* " *The Shining Star seen at Noon in London on May* 29*th*, 1630."

[3] *Chamberlayne*, 123; *C.S.P.D.* 1629-31, 282, 331; *Eglesfield*, 5-6; *Hacket*, II, 96; *H.M.C. Portland*, III, 27; *Laud*, Works, III, 103.

[4] *C.S.P.D.* 1629-31, 329, 334, 479; Letter formerly in the Imperial Library, St. Petersburg, cited *Strickland*, IV, 187.

[5] *C.S.P.D.* 1631-3, 12; 1660-1, 17; *H.M.C. Cowper (Coke)*, II, 11-12, 17-18, 26.

[6] *Burnet Supplement*, 48; *Clarendon, Hist.; C.S.P.D.* 1660-1, 162; *H.M.C. Hodgkin*, 297.

[7] *Chamberlayne*, 124; *Clarendon, Hist.*, VIII, 82; *C.S.P.D.* 1637-8, 357, 361, 510; *Eglesfield*, 8; *Ellis, Original Letters*, 1st S., III, 288-91.

[8] *Ellis, Original Letters*, 1st S., III, 286-7; *Harleian MSS.* 6988, f. 97-104; *H.M.C. Portland*, II, 134, 145, 152.

[9] *C.S.P.D.* 1639, 509; *Earle, The Child Microcosmography*, 1-2.

PART I

CHARLES LACKLAND

CHAPTER I

THE MIRACULOUS PROVIDENCE

[1] *Bibliographical Note.* For obvious reasons, there are no exact contemporary accounts of the events described in this chapter, the earliest recorded relation being made nine years later, and the most important of all, the King's own Narrative, after a lapse of thirty years. For this reason, it is impossible to be absolutely certain of the details of any particular incident in the Flight, and approximate truth can only be arrived at by a careful comparison of the various accounts. The references made are firstly to the ten tracts and narratives reprinted in Mr. Allan Fea's admirable books, *After Worcester Fight* and the *Flight of the King*. These are:

in *After Worcester Fight*

Tract I.   *The King's Own Narrative*, dictated to Samuel Pepys at Newmarket in 1681.

Tract II.   *Thomas Blount's Boscobel*, Pt. I (1660); Pt. II (1662).

Tract III.   *Mr. Whitgreave's Narrative* (first printed, from a MS. in the possession of the Whitgreave family in June, 1789).

Tract IV. *Clautrum Regale Reseratum; The King's Concealment at Trent,* by Anne Wyndham (1667).

Tract V. *Mr. Ellesdon's Letter to Lord Clarendon* (*Cl.S.P.,* II, 563-71).

in *The Flight of the King*

Tract I. *True Narrative of His Majesty's Miraculous Escape* (1660).

Tract II. *Summary of Occurrences relating to the Miraculous Preservation* (from personal testimony of Mr. Whitgreave and Father Huddleston, 1688).

Tract III. Extract from Dr. Bates's *Elenchus Motuum Nuperorum in Anglia* (1662).

Tract IV. *Captain Alford's Narrative* (*Tanner MSS.* 54).

Tract V. *Colonel Gounter's Narrative* (printed from the MS. from Racton, in Parry's *Coast of Sussex,* 1833).

Secondly, to certain other and rarer tracts contained in Mr. A. M. Broadley's invaluable work, *The Royal Miracle*—being: *Whiteladies* (1660); *The Royal Oak* (1660); *Broadside, History of His Sacred Majesty's Wonderful Preservation* (1660); *Miraculum Basilicon* (1664); *Robert Phelipps' Account* (MSS. *Eng. Hist., c.* 51).

Also and lastly to *Eglesfield's Monarchy Revived* (1822 ed.); *Plot's Staffordshire; Clarendon's History; Heath Chronicle* (1676); *Baker Chronicle* (1684); *Symonds' Pocket Book* (*Harleian MSS.* 991).

[2] *Blount, Boscobel; Broadley* (*Broadside,* 73-5; *Full and Perfect Relation of the Great and Bloody Fight at Worcester,* 300-1; *Miraculum Basilicon,* 12-17; *Paper by J. Willis Bund,* 233-6; *The Royal Oak,* 85; *Whiteladies,* 54-5, 60); *Cal. Clar. MSS.,* II, 563-4; *Cl.S.P.,* II, 560-2; *Eglesfield,* 121 *et seq.; Heath,* 296-8; *H.M.C.* (*Braye,* 175; *Edmonstone*); *Nash, Worcestershire; Turner, Memoirs,* 95.

[3] *Broadley* (*Miraculum Basilicon,* 117-18; *Whiteladies,* 55-6); *Eglesfield,* 131-3; *Fea, After Worcester Fight* (Tract I, 5-6; II, 71-3).

[4] *After Worcester Fight* (Tract II, 73); *Broadley* (*Miraculum Basilicon,* 118); *Eglesfield,* 133-4; *Heath,* 298.

[5] *After Worcester Fight* (Tract I, 74-6; II, 111); *Broadley* (*Miraculum Basilicon,* 118-19; *Whiteladies,* 56); *Eglesfield,* 134-6; *Flight of the King* (Tract I, 202-7; III, 240); *Heath,* 298-9; *Plot, Staffordshire.*

[6] For a study of Charles's life before 1651 the chief authorities are: *Baillie Corr.,* III; *Balfour, Annals,* IV; *Blair, Life; Burnet,* I; *Cal. Clar. MSS.,* I, II; *Cameron, Memoirs* (Abbotsford Club); *Carte MSS.* and *Clar. MSS.* (in the Bodleian); *Carte Papers,* I; *Cary, Memorials,* II; *Chevalier Journal,* contained in *Hoskins' Charles II in the Channel Islands; Clarendon, Hist. Reb.; Cl.S.P.,* II, III; *Edinburgh Review,* Jan., 1894; *Eglesfield, Monarchy Revived; Evelyn,* IV; *Fanshawe, Memoirs; Gardiner, Charles II and Scotland; Heath Chronicle; H.M.C.* (*Laing,* I; *Sutherland*); *Jaffray, Diary; Livingstone, Life; Lyon, Personal History of Charles II; Misc. Aulica; Montpensier, Memoirs; Motteville, Memoirs; Nicholas Papers,* I, III; *Eva Scott, The King in Exile; Duchess Sophia, Memoirs; Turner, Memoirs; Walker, Historical Discourses, Wigton Papers,* II. Occasional references will be found in *Acts of Parliament of Scotland; Aubrey, Lives; Burnet's Lives of the Hamiltons; Calendars State Papers Dom.; Clarke, James II,* I; *Ellis, Original Letters; Everett Green, Letters of Henrietta Maria; Ferrero,* Lettres de Henriette Marie à sa Sœur, Christine, Duchesse de la Savoie; *Gardiner, History; Hinton, Memoirs; H.M.C. Rep.* 9 (*Alfred Morrison*); *H.M.C.* (*Argyle; Beaufort; Braye; Buccleuch* (M.H.), III; *Buxton; Cowper,* II; *Dalyell; Dartmouth,* I, 40;

Egmont, I; ffarington; Hamilton; Hastings, II; Hodgkin; House of Lords; Jersey; Leyborne-Popham; Montagu of Beaulieu; Montrose; Pepys; Pole-Gell; Portland, I, II; Round; Traquair); Hodgson, Autobiography; Lake, Diary; Lister, III; Anne Murray, Memoirs; Napier, Montrose; Ranke, History; Rushworth; Somers Tracts, VI; Strickland, Queens of England; Taylor, Henrietta Maria; Verney, Memoirs; Whitelocke, Memorials.

7 After Worcester Fight (Tract I, 10-11; II, 83-4, 87-8); Broadley (Miraculum Basilicon, 119-21; Whiteladies, 57-8); Eglesfield, 138-9; Flight of the King (Tract I, 207-9; III, 240-1); Heath, 299.

8 After Worcester Fight (Tract I, 12-13; II, 89); Broadley (Miraculum Basilicon, 121-2; Whiteladies, 59); Clarendon, Hist.; Eglesfield, 139-40; Flight of the King (Tract I, 209-10; III, 241-2).

9 After Worcester Fight (Tract I, 14-15; II, 89-91); Broadley (Miraculum Basilicon, 122; Whiteladies, 59-60); Eglesfield, 140-1; Flight of the King (Tract I, 210).

10 After Worcester Fight (Tract I, 17; II, 91-3); Broadley (Miraculum Basilicon, 123-4; Whiteladies, 60-2); Eglesfield, 141-2; Flight of the King (Tract I, 211-12; II, 222-4); Heath, 299; Symonds.

11 After Worcester Fight (Tract II, 93-7); Broadley (Miraculum Basilicon, 124; Whiteladies, 62-6); C.J., VII, 15; Eglesfield, 142-3; Flight of the King (Tract I, 212-5).

12 After Worcester Fight (Tract I, 29; II, 84-6, 97-8; III, 158-62); Broadley (Whiteladies, 66); Eglesfield, 143-4; Flight of the King (Tract I, 215-16; II, 225-7; III, 244-5).

13 After Worcester Fight (Tract II, 98-102; III, 162-4); Broadley (Whiteladies, 67-8); Eglesfield, 144-5; Flight of the King (Tract I, 216-18; II, 227-30); Heath, 299.

14 After Worcester Fight (Tract II, 102-9; III, 162-8); Broadley (Whiteladies, 68-9); Eglesfield, 146-7; Flight of the King (Tract II, 230-6; III, 245-7).

15 After Worcester Fight (Tract I, 19-20; II, 124-5); Flight of the King (Tract III, 247).

16 After Worcester Fight (Tract I, 20-1; II, 125-6); Broadley (Miraculum Basilicon, 127-8); Flight of the King (Tract III, 248); Heath, 299.

17 After Worcester Fight (Tract I, 21-2; II, 126-7).

18 After Worcester Fight (Tract I, 22-3; II, 128-9); Broadley (The Royal Oak, 88); Clarendon, Hist.; Flight of the King (Tract III, 249-50).

19 After Worcester Fight (Tract I, 23-8; II, 130); Broadley (Miraculum Basilicon, 128; The Royal Oak); Flight of the King (Tract III, 250-2); Heath, 299-300.

20 After Worcester Fight (Tract I, 28-9); Broadley (Miraculum Basilicon, 130-1); Flight of the King (Tract III, 251-3).

21 After Worcester Fight (Tract I, 29-30; II, 131-3; IV, 183-92); Broadley (Miraculum Basilicon, 132); Flight of the King (Tract III, 253-5; IV, 271-3).

22 After Worcester Fight (Tract IV, 193-4; V, 226-9); Broadley (Miraculum Basilicon, 135-7); Flight of the King (Tract III, 255-6, 258-60; IV, 274); Heath, 300.

23 After Worcester Fight (Tract I, 32-4; IV, 197-8; V, 229-32); Broadley (Miraculum Basilicon, 134-5); Flight of the King (Tract III, 257-8; IV, 274-6).

24 After Worcester Fight (Tract II, 134; IV, 195-6, 197-200; V, 233); Broadley (Miraculum Basilicon, 135); Clarendon, Hist.; Flight of the King (Tract III, 256, 258).

25 After Worcester Fight (Tract I, 31; II, 135-8; IV, 189-206); Broadley (Phelipps' Narrative, 197-9).

26 After Worcester Fight (Tract I, 35-7; II, 138-41; IV, 209); Broadley (Miraculum Basilicon, 138; Phelipps' Narrative, 199-202); Echard; Heath, 300.

2B*

27 *After Worcester Fight* (Tract II, 139-40); *Broadley* (*Phelipps' Narrative*, 202); *Flight of the King* (Tract V, 281-92).
28 *Broadley* (*Phelipps' Narrative*, 202).
29 *After Worcester Fight* (Tract I, 37-8; II, 142-4); *Broadley* (*Phelipps' Narrative*, 202-3); *Clarendon, Hist.*; *Flight of the King* (Tract V, 292-6).
30 *After Worcester Fight* (Tract I, 38-41); *Broadley* (*Miraculum Basilicon*, 139-40); *Flight of the King* (Tract III, 265-6; V, 296-303); *Heath*, 300-1.
31 *After Worcester Fight* (Tract I, 41-4; II, 145-6); *Clarke, James II*, I, 52; *Eglesfield*, 149; *Flight of the King* (Tract III, 266; V, 303); *Heath*, 301-3.

CHAPTER II

EXILE

1 *Nicholas*, I, 276-8.
2 *Cal. Clar. MSS.*, I, Nos. 2361, 2488; II, Nos. 211, 270, 307, 390, 419, 471, 1818; *Cl.S.P.*, III, 22-4, 29; *Evelyn*, IV, 271; see *H.M.C. Bath*, II, 80-96, for Hyde's letters to his wife.
3 *Clarendon, Hist.*; *Cl.S.P.*, II, 307; *Grammont*, I, 95; *Nalson*, II, 746; *Nicholas*, I, 140-6; *Rushworth*, IV, 338; *Marvell*, I, 141.
4 *Cal. Clar. MSS.*, II, Nos. 679, 692; *Clarendon, Hist.*; *Cl.S.P.*, III, 35-6, 41-2, 46, 59, 63, 84, 88, 150, 162, 169, 171, 185, 250-1; *H.M.C. Harford*, 351.
5 *Cal. Clar. MSS.*, II, Nos. 721-2, 729, 769, 774, 776, 788, 793, 819, 844, 858-9, 872, 875-8, 1429, etc.; *Clarendon, Hist.*; *Cl.S.P.*, III, 46, 52, 57, 74, 81, 85, 89, 97, 124, 143, 157, 174, 215; *Evelyn*, IV, 262, 266; *H.M.C. Bath*, II, 99, 103; *Thurloe*, I, 248.
6 *Cal. Clar. MSS.*, II, Nos. 749-51, 761, 771, 789-94, 802, 804, 809-12, 826-7, 829, 831-2, 834, 846, 865-6, 870-1, 856-7, 948, 965, 1046, 1136, 1208, 2020-1; *Cl.S.P.*, III, 57, 75-6, 83, 91, 102, 105, 134, 165, 167, 171, 194; *Evelyn*, IV, 249, 260; *Gardiner, Commonwealth*, II, 297; *H.M.C. Rep. 6* (*ffarington*, 436-7; *Menzies*, 695); *Rep. 9* (*Alfred Morrison*, 442); *H.M.C.* (*Bath*, II, 107; *Harford*, 350; *Hodgkin*, 122-3; *Portland*, II, 139-40); *Holland Papers*, 159, f. 175; *Muddiman*, 30; *Nicholas*, II, 11; *Thurloe*, I, 241, 332, 640-1, 651; II, 25, 31.
7 *Cl.S.P.*, III, 71, 175, 198; *H.M.C. Rep. 6* (*ffarington*, 441); *H.M.C. Bath*, II, 104; *Nicholas*, I, 118, 276.
8 *Burnet Supplement*, 48; *Cal. Clar. MSS.*, II, Nos. 257, 742, 839, 1188, 1199, 1308-9, 1323, 1594-5, 1649, 1712; III, 316, 969; *Clarendon, Hist.*; *Cl.S.P.*, III, 46-50, 71, 108, 206-13; *Evelyn*, IV, 301; *Stephen Fox*, 13; *Lister*, II, 62-4; *Montpensier, Memoirs*; *Nicholas*, I, 135, 295; II (14 Jan., '54); III, 2, 4, 11, 15 *et seq.*; *Pepys* (11 Nov., '67); *Thurloe*, I, 232, 665, 672; III, 659.
9 *Barbour*, Ch. II, III; *Cal. Clar. MSS.*, II, Nos. 861, 2061; *Clarendon, Hist.*; *Cl.S.P.*, III, 109; *Evelyn*; *H.M.C. Rep. 6* (*Raffles*, 473); *H.M.C. Finch*, I, 65; *Lyon, Personal History of Charles II*; *Misc. Aulica*, 108-29; *Seward, Anecdotes*; *Thurloe*, I, 665, 674.
10 *Ady*, 127-8, 148-9; *Clarendon, Hist.*; *Evelyn* (18 Aug., '49); *Montpensier*; *Motteville*.

11 *Cal. Clar. MSS.*, II, Nos. 724, 1053, 1214, 1232, 1284; *Cl.S.P.*, III, 173; *Motteville*; *Thurloe*, I, 232.

12 *Cal. Clar. MSS.*, II, Nos. 374, 1046, 1188, 1270, 1430, 1802, 1919, 2033-4, 2042-3, 2055-8, 2062-9, 2096; Ill, 79; *Carte, Ormonde*, Bk. V, par. 250-62; *Clarendon, Hist.*; *Cl S.P.*, II, 414; III, 159, 180, 218, 222, 228, 233, 238, 242-4, 253, 257-9, 374; *Nicholas*, I, 147-50; *Thurloe*, II, 701.

13 *Baillie*, III, 86-90; *Cal. Clar. MSS.*, I, No. 2293; II, 1312, 1647; III, 291, 346, 549, 750; *Clarendon, Hist.*; *Cl.S.P.*, III, 186, 292, 299, 346, 567; *H.M.C. Rep. 9 (Dalyell*, 234); *H.M.C. (Beaufort*, 38-9; *Hamilton*, 137); *Nicholas*, III, 15; *Thurloe*, I, 622, 665, 681; II, 725; III, 76, 465; IV, 163, 580; V, 673.

14 *Cal. Clar. MSS.*, II, No. 1503; III, 282; *Ellis, Original Letters*, 2nd S., III, 376; *Misc. Aulica*, 115-20, 126-8; *Nicholas*, III, 61; *Thurloe*, I, 663, 665-7, 672-3, 681, 686; II, 242, 528, 591; III, 19.

15 *Cal. Clar. MSS.*, II, No. 1046; *C.S.P. Venet.* 1653-4, 164, 223; *Cl.S.P.*, II, 414; *Momigliano*, App., 295; *Thurloe*, III, 28, 42, 71, 75, 94, 98, 104, 122, 153, 160, 162-3, 197, 483; *Pepys* (4 June, '64).

16 *Clarendon, Hist.*; *Cl.S.P.*, III, 263, 265; *H.M.C. Rep. 6 (ffarington*, 438); *H.M.C. Ormonde (o.s.*), I, 14; *Ranke*, III, 139; *Thurloe*, III, 64-5, 77, 124.

17 *Cal. Clar. MSS.*, III, Nos. 28, 33-5, 47-8, 52-3, 55, 57, 67-8; *Clarendon, Hist.*; *Nicholas*, II, 173 *et seq.*

18 *Cal. Clar. MSS.*, III, Nos. 58-9, 65, 70, 72, 74, 78-9, 83; *Clarendon, Hist.*; *Nicholas*, II, 204.

19 *Clarendon, Hist.*; *Thurloe*, III, 205, 207, 209, 211, 216, 227.

20 *Cal. Clar. MSS.*, II, No. 86; *Clarendon MSS.* xlix, f. 402.

21 *Nicholas*, III, 2, 15, 19; *Thurloe*, I, 662; III, 427, 436, 445, 561, 659.

22 *C.S.P.D.* 1655, 405 *et seq.*; *C.S.P. Venet.*, 80, 100, 106, 110, 144, 191, 276; *H.M.C. Rep. 3 (Hopkinson*, 266); *Rep. 5 (Sutherland*, 176); *Rep. 6 (ffarington*, 438); *Rep. 7 (Webb*, 691); *Rep. 8 (Ormonde*, 514); *H.M.C. Rutland*, II, 5; *Ludlow (Firth*), I, 406; *Nicholas*, II, 253; III, 5, 8, 25, 37, 42-3, 59, 73, 85, 192-5, 218, 261; *Shakerley MSS.* (Lancashire and Cheshire Trials, 1656); *Thurloe*, I, 695; III, 219, 312, 445, 512, 523, 538, 676; IV, 117, 149, 179, 224, 274, 278, 315, 439, 522, 595, 622; *Verney*, II, 27, 35.

23 *Carte*, II, 50, 53-7; *Cl.S.P.*, III, 273, 275 *et seq.*; *C.S.P. Venet.* 1655-6, 2, 22, 24, 48, 62, 138, 140, 149, 188, 217, 190, 232; *Evelyn* (April, '55); *H.M.C. Rep. 6 (ffarington*, 439); *H.M.C. Portland*, I, 679; *Misc. Aulica*, 113, 123; *Nicholas*, III, 55, 70-3, 98, 102-3, 117, 125, 136, 143 *et seq.*, 188, 201, 207 *et seq.*; *Thurloe*, III, 16, 103; IV, 50, 65, 97, 103, 115, 131, 143, 170, 205, 301.

24 *Carte*, II, 65 *et seq.*; *Cl.S.P.*, III, 288; *Nicholas*, III, 232 *et seq.*; *Thurloe*, I, 663, 700-5; IV, 170.

25 *Cal. Clar. MSS.*, III, Nos. 301-3, 529; *Camden Misc.*, V, 10; *Cl.S.P.*, III, 288, 290 *et seq.*, 302; *Stephen Fox*, 18-19; *Misc. Aulica*, 127; *Nicholas*, III, 272 *et seq.*; *Thurloe*, I, 661; V, 4, 84, 141, 273.

26 *Cal. Clar. MSS.*, III, Nos. 429-30; *Cl.S.P.*, III, 300-1; *Evelyn*, IV, 320; *Thurloe*, V, 84, 108, 282.

27 *Carte*, II, 114; *Carte, Ormonde*, Bk. V, par. 270-2; *Clarke, James II*, I, 270-1; 277-81, 297; *Cl.S.P.*, III, 304-8, 318; *H.M.C. Laing*, I, 304; *Misc. Aulica*, 125-6; *Thurloe* V, 84, 198, 293, 315, 320, 325, 362, 383-4, 389, 431, 575, 645.

28 *Cal. Clar. MSS.*, III, Nos. 512, 518, 539, 549-50, 552, 578, 580, 583, 585, 595, 597, 604, 607, 610-15, 619-23, 626, 634-8, 647-8, 688-9, 1073; *Cl.S.P.*,

III, 311-14, 324 et seq., 341; H.M.C. Rep. 8 (Marlborough, 28); H.M.C. Hodgkin, 123; Thurloe, V, 320, 325, 389, 391, 447, 473, 503, 520, 575, 596, 608.
²⁹ Cal. Clar. MSS., III, Nos. 935, 1025; Cl.S.P., III, 315; H.M.C. (Bath, II, 117; Harford, 355, 357); Nicholas, IV, 6, 13; Thurloe, V, 578.
³⁰ Cal. Clar. MSS., III, Nos. 784, 787-8, 790-1; Carte, Ormonde, Bk. V, par. 274; Clarendon, Hist.; Flanders Papers, 31 (13, 18 April, '57); H.M.C. Harford, 355; Thurloe, VI, 151.
³¹ Cal. Clar. MSS., III, Nos. 713, 758, 788, 853, 883, 907, 910, 935, 937-9, 969, 971, 983, 990, 997, 1008, 1015, 1025, 1088; Cl.S.P., III, 346-7, 351-2, 354; Flanders Papers, 31 (16 June, '57); H.M.C. Rep. 5 (Sutherland, 162-3); Rep. 6 (ffarington, 441); Rep. 8 (Marlborough, 30); H.M.C. (Egmont, I, 582; Harford, 356-7); Nicholas, IV, 2, 4, 8, 10, 12-15; Thurloe, V, 645.
³² Cal. Clar. MSS., III, Nos. 22, 871, 994, 1024, 1029; Cl.S.P., III, 382, 387; Nicholas, III, 92; IV, 13.
³³ Cal. Clar. MSS., III, Nos. 1043, 1056, 1061-2, 1065, 1077, 1083, 1087, 1091, 1155; Carte, Ormonde, Bk. V, par. 275; Clarke, James II, I, 322-8; Cl.S.P., III, 347, 361; Thurloe, VI, 731.
³⁴ Cal. Clar. MSS., II, No. 770; III, 666, 874, 1171; Cl.S.P., III, 374; C.S.P.D. 1660-1, 366; Evelyn (25 Dec., '57; 7 March, 23 May, '58); H.M.C. Rep. 5 (Sutherland, 152); Rep. 6 (ffarington, 443); North, Lives, I, 185; Ranke, III, 60, 206; Tanner MSS. lii (21 Jan., '58); Thurloe, VI, 783.
³⁵ Cal. Clar. MSS., III, Nos. 1116, 1119, 1121, 1155, 1245-6, 1249, 1251-7; Carte, II, 118-24; Carte, Ormonde, Bk. V, 277-86; Clarendon, Hist.; Clarendon MSS. lvii, f. 37, 71, 134-5; lviii, f. 68-9; Clarke, James II, I, 330; Evelyn (31 May, '58); Firth, Last Years of the Protectorate, 61-80; H.M.C. Rep. 5 (Sutherland, 152, 166-7, 171, 180-1); Rep. 6 (ffarington, 443); Rep. 8 (Marlborough, 29); H.M.C. Bath, II, 122; Nicholas, IV, 33-4, 41, 46, 52-3, 55, 63; Ranke, III, 206; Thurloe, VI, 806; VII, 20-1, 27.
³⁶ Carte MSS. ccxiii (10 Sept., '58); Clarendon MSS. lviii, f. 166-7, 180, 189, 250-1; Cl.S.P., III, 387; Evelyn, IV, 323; H.M.C. (Bath, II, 123; Gurney, 164; Harford, 360); Thurloe, VII, 246, 307, 313, 360-2, 419. The story of Downing's visit to Charles rests on the doubtful authority of an insertion in Sir George Downing's MS. Journal. (See Beresford, 115.) Yet it is certain that Charles at this time visited Holland. For Downing's official reconciliation with the Crown in 1660 see Carte, II, 319-23. After the Restoration Charles made much use of this astute man, who not only made a vast fortune, but acquired immortality by leaving his name to the most famous street of modern times.
³⁷ Carte, II, 154-6; Carte, Ormonde, Bk. V, par. 291-2; Clarendon, Cont.; Clarendon MSS. lviii, f. 322-7, 412; lix, f. 56-7; Cl.S.P., III, 412; Thurloe, VII, 372, 390, 398.
³⁸ Evelyn (22 Oct., '58); H.M.C. Rep. 5 (Sutherland, 146, 172); Rep. 9 (Alfred Morrison, 444). For the growing unrest in England see H.M.C. Alfred Morrison, 445a; H.M.C. Westmorland, 46; Muddiman, 4; Sprat, Royal Society, 58; Wren, Parentalia.
³⁹ Cl.S.P., III, 413-14, 417-18; Maseres (Price, 707).
⁴⁰ Carte MSS. ccxiii (28 Jan., '59); Clarendon MSS. lix, 393-4, 417; Cl.S.P., III, 423 et seq.; C.S.P.D. 1658-9, 374, 583; H.M.C. Rep. 3 (Northumberland, 88); H.M.C. Bath, II, 132; Nicholas, IV, 75-6, 81-92, 98-106, 122-7, 130-1, 134-6, 138, 139-40, 146; North, Lives, III, 19-21; Verney, II, 145-6; Thurloe, VII, 615-16.

41 Carte, II, 173-4; Carte, Ormonde, Bk. V, par. 295; Clarendon MSS.
lx, lxi, passim; Cl.S.P., III, 409, 479, 481 et seq.; H.M.C. (Bath, II, 129,
133-5; Braye, 189-215; Leyborne-Popham, 118); Muddiman, 35; Nicholas, IV,
114-18, 126, 130, 141, 146-9, 156-69, 265; " A Word to Purpose " (Burney,
53).
42 Carte, Ormonde, Bk. V, par. 296; Clarendon MSS. lxi, f. 296-7, 383; Clarke,
James II, I, 370-1; Halliwell, Morland, 7; H.M.C. Heathcote, 13; Nicholas,
IV, 169-70.
43 Clarendon MSS. lxiii, f. 70, 123, 237-8, 240; Clarke, James II, I, 371-2; Cl.S.P.,
III, 535 et seq.; Flanders Papers, 32 (9, 16 Aug., '59); H.M.C. (Bath, II, 135
et seq.; Leyborne-Popham, 120); Egerton MSS. 2536, f. 447; Scott, Travels
of the King, 402-3.
44 Carte, II, 194-200; Clarendon MSS. lxiii, passim; Clarke Papers, IV, 28-48;
C.S.P.D. 1659-60, 87; H.M.C. Rep. 3 (Legh, 269); Rep. 7 (Verney, 483);
Nicholas, IV, 176-81; Scott, Travels of the King, 394.
45 Carte, II, 205-6, 217, 232, 242, 250-1, 257, 262-3; Carte MSS. ccxiii (1, 3 Nov.,
'59); Carte, Ormonde, Bk. V, par. 301-4; Clarendon MSS. lxiv, f. 26, 79-83,
187-8, 283; lxv, f. 39-40, 110-11, 130-1, 135-6, 173-7; lxvi, f. 3-6, 24, 30-1;
Cl.S.P., III, 596; Flanders Papers, 32 (3 Sept., 1, 5, 8 Nov., '59); H.M.C.
(Bath, II, 140; Heathcote, 15).
46 Ady, 52; Carte, II, 296-7; Carte, Ormonde, Bk. V., par. 305; Clarendon MSS.
lxvi, f. 95-6, 147-8; Clarke, James II, I, 395.
47 Clarendon, Hist.; Clarendon MSS. lxvii, f. 25-8; Cl.S.P., III, 636.
48 Carte, II, 219, 240; Clarendon, Hist.; Clarke, James II, I, 381; Cl.S.P., III, 636.

CHAPTER III

THE RESTORATION

1 " The Arraignment of the Divell for taking away Richard Bradshaw "; Burney
Collection, 53, 54 passim; H.M.C. Fleming, 24; Muddiman, 83-4, 92-4;
Rugge, f. 32-3, 36-7, 42.
2 Clarke Papers, IV, 153, 192 et seq., 212 et seq., 233-7; Echard, 748; Evelyn
(11 Oct., '59); " Faithful Intelligencer " (29 Nov., 3 Dec., '59); H.M.C.
Rep. 3 (Northumberland, 89); Rep. 6 (Argyle, 616); Rep. 7 (Verney, 461);
H.M.C. (Harford, 361; Leyborne-Popham, 198; Portland, I, 690; II, 99-100);
Maseres (Price, 730-44); Verney, II, 148, 150.
3 Clarke Papers, IV, 165 et seq., 186 et seq., 219 et seq.; Cl.S.P., III, 636, etc.;
H.M.C. Rep. 7 (Verney, 461); H.M.C. Rutland, II, 6; Nicholas, IV, 192;
Rugge, f. 50, 55; Verney, II, 149, 152; Muddiman, 78-81.
4 Clarke Papers, IV, 238; H.M.C. Rep. 6, 616; Maseres (Price, 744-50).
5 Clarke Papers, IV, 243 et seq.; H.M.C. Rep. 5 (Sutherland, 181, 193-4); H.M.C.
(Fitzherbert, 3; Leyborne-Popham, 144; Portland, I, 692; Rutland, II, 6);
Josselin, 132; Maseres (Price, 750-5); Pepys (30 Jan., 19 July, '60).
6 Clarendon, Hist.; Cl.S.P., III, 641; Cosin, I, 291-2; H.M.C. (Harford, 363;
Heathcote, 16); Clarendon MSS. lxviii, lxix passim.
7 Ady, 53-4; Cl.S.P., III, 646; H.M.C. Rep. 2 (Lyttleton, 37); Rep. 8 (Ashburnham,
6); H.M.C. Bath, II, 143; Clarendon MSS. lxix, f. 103.
8 Clarke Papers, IV, 247 et seq.; Cl.S.P., III, 645, 651, 664; H.M.C. Rep. 5

(*Sutherland*, 153); *Rep.* 7 (*Verney*, 462); *Rep.* 8 (*Corp. of Leicester*, 438); *H.M.C. Leyborne-Popham*, 142-5; *Maseres* (*Price*, 753-60); *Pepys* (Feb., '60); *Rugge*, f. 55; *London's Diurnal* (*Burney*, 54) (1-8 Feb., '60).

9 *Burnet*, I, 156; *C.J.*, vii, 837; *Cl.S.P.*, III, 674, 691-2; *H.M.C. Rep.* 7 (*Verney*, 462); *H.M.C.* (*Leyborne-Popham*, 142-3; *Townshend*, 23); *Maseres* (*Price*, 761-6); *Old Parl. Hist.*, xxii, 98; " *Publick Intelligencer* " (*Burney*, 54) (6-13 Feb., '60); *Pepys* (Feb., '60); *Rugge*, f. 58.

10 *Aubrey, Lives* (*Monk*); *Butler, Hudibras*; *Clarendon, Hist.*; *Cl.S.P.*, III, 681, 692-3; *Evelyn* (11 Feb., '59); *H.M.C. Rep.* 3 (*Legh*, 259); *Rep.* 7 (*Verney*, 461-2, 483); *H.M.C.* (*Bath*, II, 141-2, 145; *Leyborne-Popham*, 159-64; *Portland*, III, 218); *Maseres* (*Price*, 766-7); *Pepys* (Feb., '60); *Verney*, II, 153, 162-4; *Rugge*, f. 59.

11 *Clarendon MSS.* lxx, f. 120; *Cl.S.P.*, III, 689, 697, 722; *H.M.C. Rep.* 7 (*Verney*, 483-4); *H.M.C. Leyborne-Popham*, 171; *Nicholas*, IV, 196-203, 208; *Verney*, II, 162-4.

12 *Clarendon, Hist.*; *Cl.S.P.*, III, 725; *Echard*, 758-9; *H.M.C. Rep.* 7 (*Verney*, 463, 484); " *Publick Intelligencer* " (*Burney*, 55) (12-19 March, '60); *Pepys* (March, '60); *Rugge*, f. 67; *Thurloe*, VII, 855; *Verney*, II, 160. See also *Kennet*, 227, for the name and reward of this loyal painter, Michael Darby.

13 *Camden Misc.*, V (24 March, '60); *C.J.*; *Clarendon, Hist.*; *Echard*; *Maseres* (*Price*, 790-1); *Parl. Hist.*, IV, 15-23.

14 *Cl.S.P.*, III, 739; *Echard*, 759; *H.M.C. Rep.* 3 (*Northumberland*, 89); *Rep.* 7 (*Verney*, 484); *H.M.C.* (*Fleming*, 24; *Laing*, I, 310; *Leyborne-Popham*, 173); " *Parliamentary Intelligencer* " (*Burney*, 54); *Pepys* (April, '60; 8 March, '61).

15 *C.J.*, VIII; *Cl.S.P.*, III, 736 *et seq.*; *Evelyn* (May, '60); *H.M.C. Rep.* 3 (*Northumberland*, 89); *Rep.* 5 (*Sutherland*, 146, 149, 167, 199); *Pepys* (May, '60).

16 *C.S.P.D.* 1660-1, 69, 109, 314; *H.M.C. Rep.* 5 (*Sutherland*, 145); *Rep.* 8 (*Corp. of Leicester*, 438-9; *Manchester*, 65); *H.M.C. Portland*, III, 220-1; *Pepys* (May, '60).

17 *C.J.*, VIII, 18; *De Witt*, 241; *Echard*, 763; *H.M.C. Rep.* 5 (*Sutherland*, 167); *House of Lyme*, 210-11; *Josselin*, 134; " *Parliamentary Intelligencer* " (7-14 May, '60); *Parl Hist.*, IV, 33-4; *Rugge*, f. 91-3; *Verney*, II, 163.

18 *Ady*, 54-5; *Lansdowne*, Works, I, 481-2.

19 *Stephen Fox*, 25-59; *H.M C. Rep.* 3 (*Northumberland*, 89); *Rep.* 5 (*Sutherland*, 167, 181); *H.M.C. Fleming*, 24; *Rugge*, f. 97.

20 *Clarendon, Hist.*; *Clarendon MSS.* lxxii *passim*; *Echard*, 764-5; *Stephen Fox*; *H.M.C. Fleming*, 24.

21 *Clarendon MSS.* lxxii, f. 408; *Lister*, III, 106-7; *Pepys* (May, '60).

22 *Stephen Fox*, 69; *H.M.C. Rep* 5 (*Sutherland*, 205-6); *Pepys* (May, '60).

23 *Crosby Records*; " *England's Joy* " (*Stuart Tracts*, 427); *Stephen Fox*, 69; *Heath*, 450-2; *H.M.C. Rep.* 5 (*Sutherland*, 168, 181, 199, 206-7); *H.M.C. Fleming*, 24-5; *Gawdy*, 189); " *Parliamentary Intelligencer* " (21-28 May, '60); *Pepys* (25 May, '60); *Rugge*, f. 28.

24 *Ady*, 56-7; *Echard*, 766; " *England's Joy* " (*Stuart Tracts*, 427-8); *H.M.C.* (*City of Canterbury*, 165-6; *Fleming*, 25); *Pepys* (May, '60).

25 *Church Register, Maids Moreton*; *C.J.*, VIII, 49; *Clarendon, Hist.*; *Courthop, Memoirs*, 147; *Echard*, 766; " *England's Joy* " (*Stuart Tracts*, 429-30); *Evelyn* (29 May, '60); *Hearne, Collections*, 98-9; *Heath*, 452-4; *Hinton, Memoires*; *H.M.C. Rep.* 5 (*Sutherland*, 150, 167-8, 184); *H.M.C.* (*Egmont*, I, 612-14; *Fitzherbert*, 5; *Fleming*, 25-6); *Kennet*, 164-5; *L.J.*; *Parl. Hist.*, IV, 55-63; *Rugge*, f. 98-102.

INTERLUDE

ENGLAND OF THE RESTORATION

1 *Add. MSS.* 25124, f. 43; *Gallus Castratus, passim; H.M.C. Rep.* 2 (*Mount Edgcumbe,* 21); *Rep.* 7 (*Verney*, 465, 470; *Lowndes*, 575); *H.M.C.* (*Ailesbury*, 170; *Fitzherbert*, 25; *Fleming*, 62-3, 70; *Rutland*, II, 64); *Jusserand, passim; Pepys* (27 Nov., '60; 18 April, '61; 27 March, 26 July, '64; 3 March, '69); *Prideaux*, 11; *Reresby, passim.*

2 *Hatton*, I, 66, 119-21, 158; *H.M.C. Rep.* 2 (*Spencer*, 21-2); *Rep.* 4 (*Rogers*, 405-6); *Rep.* 5 (*Sutherland*, 159, 168, 177); *Rep.* 7 (*Verney*, 465, 469-70, 473, 478, 479-81, 484, 494); *Rep.* 8 (*H. of Lords*, 101, 122); *H.M.C.* (*Bath*, II, 160; *Dartmouth*, I, 75; *Fleming*, 62, 121; *Kenyon*, 116; *Montagu of Beaulieu*, 182; *Ormonde*, V, 281; VI, 117; *Portland*, III, 320; *Rutland*, II, 11, 17, 24, 27, 43-4, 62); *House of Lyme*, 245; *Newdegate*, 72-3, 78; *Nicholas*, IV, 263; *Pepys* (1 Feb., '64); *Reresby* (Sept., '60; 4 July, '61; 12 July, '63; July, '66; 19 March, '78); *Verney*, II, 314-15, 320-1; *Williamson*, I, 41-2, 86-7; II, 89-90.

3 *First Whig*, 95 *et seq.; Hatton*, I, 119, 157; *House of Lyme*, 259-60; *Jusserand*, 144, 148; *Williamson*, I, 85.

4 *Evelyn* (June, '70); *North, Lives*, III, 108; *Pepys* (31 Aug., '61; 21 Dec., '63).

5 *H.M.C. Rep.* 7 (*Verney*, 482); *H.M.C.* (*Hodgkin*, 17; *House of Lords*, 20; *Leyborne-Popham*, 151; *Ormonde*, IV, 18; VII, 278; *Rutland*, II, 52); *House of Lyme*, 271; *Jusserand*, 97; *Newdegate*, 76-7; *North, Lives*, I, 64-6; III, 108, 171; *Pepys* (27 Dec., '60; 5 June, 29 Sept., '61); *Prideaux*, 32-5; *Evelyn* (18 March, '69).

6 See *Aubrey's Lives* throughout. *North, Lives*, I, 294-5; III, 43, 91-3; *Pepys* (12 July, '64; 18 Aug., '67); *Shakerley MSS.* (2 Jan., '60; 6 Feb., '82); *Verney*, II, 272, 290-1.

7 *Pepys* (20 Oct., '60; 21 April, '61; 5 Sept., '67; 13 June, '68; 23 Jan., '69).

8 *Chamberlayne*, 203 *et seq.; C.S.P.D.* 1662-3, 86; *Hatton*, I, 231; *Newdegate*, 239; *Pepys* (2, 8 April, '68); *Thurloe*, II, 670.

9 *Pepys* (27 Nov., '60; 25 Sept., '61; 1 May, '63; 7, 12, 14 Nov., '66).

10 *Hatton*, I, 60-1; *North, Lives*, III, 105-6; *Pepys* (26 April, '63).

11 *Evelyn* (2 July, '61); *Pepys* (29 May, '62; 14 April, 1, 28 May, '67; 25 April, '69).

12 *Dryden, Sir Martin-Mar-All*, Act IV; *Gordon, Diary*, 85-6, 93; *H.M.C. Rutland*, II, 21; *North, Lives*, I, 66; II, 237; *Pepys* (29 May, '62; 23 July, '64; 13 March, 22 April, '68); *Shadwell, Humorists*, Act V.

13 *Celia Fiennes, Travels; Chamberlayne*, 6-11; *Evelyn* (31 Aug., '54); *Jusserand*, 168; *Pepys* (11 April, '61; 13 Oct., '62); *Shakerley MSS.* For a description of the countryside of Restoration England see *H.M.C. Portland*, II, 263-314.

14 *Diary of the Rev. Giles Moore*, Rector of Horsted Keynes; *H.M.C. Rep.* 6 (*Ingilby*, 375-6); *House of Lyme*, 266; *North, Lives*, I, 37-8, 175, 183; *Pepys* (23 Dec., '60; 14 July, '67); *Savile*, 135-6, 165, 179; *Shakerley MSS.* (16 May, '79).

15 *H.M.C. Heathcote*, 94; *Pepys* (22 Nov., '68; 23 April, 1 May, '69).

16 *H.M.C. Rep.* 6 (*Ingilby*, 373); *North, Lives*, I, 320; III, 67-88; *Pepys* (10 April, 8, 17 May, 26 Dec., '61; 15 Oct., '62; 27 Nov., '64; 22 Jan., 13 July, '65; 9 July, '66; 9 Oct., '67); *Reresby* (6 July, '66).

17 *Evelyn, passim; North, Lives,* II, 291; *Sprat, Royal Society,* 53-4; *Wren, Parentalia.*

18 *Birch, Royal Society,* I, 467; *Chamberlayne,* 327 *et seq.; Evelyn* (21 Oct., '69; 4 Aug., '65); *Pepys* (3 May, '68); *Sprat, Royal Society,* 93, 133, 158-82, 190-213, 215-40, 241-3, 246-51; *Williamson,* II, 7.

19 *Evelyn* (7 Sept., '60; 9 March, '61; 10 July, '67); *H.M.C.* (*Beaufort,* 49-50; *Hodgkin,* 175-6); *North, Lives,* I, 153-4, 320, 387-93, 434; II, 243-5; III, 63-6, and throughout; *Pepys* (4 March, '64; 14 March, '68); *Plot, Oxfordshire,* 227 *et seq.*

20 *Evelyn* (26 Aug., '76); *H.M.C. Rep.* 6 (*Ingilby,* 367); *North, Lives,* II, 8-36; *Pepys* (23 Sept., '60; 1 Feb., '64); *Sprat, Royal Society,* 152-3.

PART II

THE KING OF ENGLAND

CHAPTER I

THE FIRST FINE CARELESS RAPTURE

1 *Chamberlayne,* 155-90 *et seq.*; *H.M.C. Ormonde,* III, 2-5; IV, 642 *et seq.*; VII, 185; *Rochford, Travels; Sheppard, Whitehall, passim; State Papers Dom.* lxxvi, f. 67.

2 *H.M.C. Rep.* 6, 364; *Rep.* 7 (*H. of Lords,* 88-92); *Pepys* (27 Oct., '62; 13 April, '66; 6 Oct., '67; 5 Jan., '68); *Williamson,* I (8 Aug., '73).

3 *Ailesbury,* 93; *Essex,* I, II, *passim; Reresby* (Sept., '60); *Teonge,* 203.

4 *Ailesbury,* 15, 85; *C.S.P.D.* 1661-2, 350; *Essex,* I, 280; II, 33; *Evelyn* (14 May, 3 Oct., '61; 13 Sept., '66); *H.M.C. Rep.* 5 (*Sutherland,* 199); *H.M.C. Ormonde,* IV, 277; VII, 27-31; *Newdegate,* 23, 27.

5 *Carte, Ormonde,* Bk. VI, par. 89; *C.S.P.D.* 1660-1, 499; *Evelyn* (1, 23 Nov., 6 Dec., '60; 21 Oct., '61; 2 Sept., '80); *H.M.C. Rep.* 6 (*Ingilby,* 364); *Pepys* (3, 27 Oct., '60; 24 June, '64; 27 Aug., '67); *Secret Services,* 66.

6 *C.S.P.D.* 1661-2, 129; 1662-3, 58, 78, 152; *Evelyn* (10 Jan., '62; 2 Sept., '80); *H.M.C. Rutland,* II, 24; *Pepys* (18 June, 20 Oct., '62; 11 April, '69).

7 *Ailesbury,* 93; *Chamberlayne,* 207-9; *Evelyn* (23 April, 3 Aug., '67); *Halifax,* 203-4; *Lauderdale,* III, 28; *Pepys* (11, 25 July, '66; 8 Sept., '67; 4 April, '68); *Reresby* (29 Nov., '81). See also *H.M.C. Buccleuch,* II, 105.

8 *Ady* (28 Feb., '66); *Ailesbury,* 8; *C.S.P.D.* 1662-3, 139; *Cunningham,* 76; *H.M.C. Rep.* 5 (*Sutherland,* 204); *H.M.C. Fleming,* 29; *Kennet,* 175, 186, 208; *North, Lives,* III, 170; *Pepys* (17 June, 8, 29 July, 12 Aug., '64; 14 Oct., '60; 7 March, 6, 13 April, 18 May, '62; 8 Feb., 1 March, '63); *Woodcock Papers,* 56-7, 59.

9 *Ailesbury,* 75, 95-6; *Burnet,* I, 167; *C.S.P.D.* 1664-5, 225; *Evelyn* (20 Sept., '62); *H.M.C. Rep.* 6 (*Argyle,* 622); *Rep.* 7 (*Frere,* 531); *North, Lives,* I, 274; III, 171; *Pepys* (11 May, '63; 21 April, '66; 15 Jan., '69); *Prideaux,* 44; *Sprat, Royal Society,* 78; *Hatton,* I, 137; *Fountainhall, Chron. Notes,* 46.

10 *Cibber's Apology*, 26; *C.S.P.D.* 1661-2, 9; *Evelyn* (9 Feb., 29 March, '65); *Pepys* (16 Sept., 11 Oct., '60; 18 Aug., 4 Sept., '61; 16 March, '62; 26 April, '64; 17 Feb., '67); *Secret Services*, 82; *Marvell*, I, 167.

11 *C.S.P.D.* 1661-2, 25, 98; *Evelyn* (9 Feb., '65; 4 Feb., '85); *Hatton*, I, 65; *H.M.C. Rep.* 5 (*Sutherland*, 170); *Rep.* 6 (*Ingilby*, 365); *H.M.C.* (*Beaufort*, 66, 87; *Dartmouth*, I, 14; *Fleming*, 48); *Pepys* (19 April, 11 Aug., '64; 4 Sept., '67); *Secret Services*, 65; *Sprat, Royal Society*, 149; *State Poems*, I, 150.

12 *Ailesbury*, 84, 93; *Bramston* (1671); *Buckingham*, II, 78; *Burnet*, II, 456; *Aurelian Cook*; *Halifax*, 195, 202; *Pepys* (9 June, '60; 21 April, '66; 28 Oct., '67); *Reresby* (20 Nov., '81).

13 *Ailesbury*, 95; *Buckingham*, II, 79; *Burnet*, I, 167; *Evelyn* (14 May, 1, 2 Oct., 24 Nov., '61); *Halifax*, 198-201; *Pepys* (4 April, 2 Dec., '68).

14 *Ailesbury*, 96; *H.M.C. Rep.* 5 (*Sutherland*, 168); *Marshall, Annals of Tennis*; *Pepys* (2 April, '61; 15 May, 28 Dec., '63; 4 Jan., '64; 2 Sept., '67); *Rugge*; *Waller Poems*.

15 *C.S.P.D.* 1660-1, 22; 1661-2, 131, 179, 214, 613; 1662-3, 50, 191; 1666-7, 446; *Evelyn* (21 Dec., '62); *H.M.C. Rep.* 3 (*Hopkinson*, 266); *Rep.* 6, 779; *H.M.C.* (*Bath*, II, 165; *Rutland*, II, 22); *North, Memoires of Musick*; *Pepys* (8 June, '60; 3 Feb., '61; 14 Sept., '62; 22 Nov., '63; 12 Feb., 1 Oct., 16 Nov., '67; 28 Sept., '68); *Secret Services*; *Wood, Life and Times*, II, 69.

16 *Ady*, 137; *Evelyn* (1 March, '71); *Grammont*, I, 144-5; *H.M.C. Rep.* 6 (*Ingilby*, 368); *Rep.* 8 (*Portsmouth*, 91); *H.M.C.* (*Buccleuch* (M.H.), I, 427; *Fleming*, 191; *House of Lords*, 69); *Pepys* (20 Oct., '60; 9 Dec., '61; 19 June, '63); *Wren, Parentalia*.

17 *Evelyn* (18 Sept., '83); *Halifax*, 90-1; *H.M.C. Rep.* 2 (*Spencer*, 19); *Rep.* 6 (*Ingilby*, 372); *Rep.* 7 (*Verney*, 465); *H.M.C.* (*Beaufort*, 52; *Portland*, III, 292); *Jusserand*, 126; *Pepys* (30 Sept., '61); *Williamson*, II, 56-7.

18 *Ady* (5 March, '78); *H.M.C. Rep.* 6 (*Ingilby*, 367); *H.M.C.* (*Hamilton*, 149-50; *Wombwell*, 135); *North, Lives, passim*; *Pepys* (27 Nov., '62).

19 *C.S.P.D.* 1660-1, 4, 5, 49; *Evelyn* (4, 21, 30 June, 6 July, '60); *H.M.C. Rep.* 5 (*Sutherland*, 168, 194, 199, 206); *Rep.* 6 (*Ingilby*, 364, 367); *Kennet*, 206, 210; " *Mercurius Publicus* " (*Burney*, 55) (28 June – 5 July, '60); *Pepys* (23 June, 4, 22 July, '60; 31 Aug., '61; 30 Aug., '68); *Reresby* (27 Aug., '60).

N.B.—For the earliest signs of any restoration of the old orders at Court, see *Evelyn* (18 June, '60); *H.M.C. Sutherland*, 194; *Kennet*, 285.

20 *Evelyn* (3, 5 July, '60); *Grammont*, I, 142; *Hastings*, II, 140; *H.M.C. Rep.* 3 (*Northumberland*, 92, misdated); *Rep.* 5 (*Sutherland*, 145, 150, 168-9, 173-5, 184, 194, 204-7); *Kennet*, 176; *Pepys* (9, 19, 20, 28 June, 5 July, 15 Aug., '60); *Rugge*.

21 *Burnet*, I, 168-9; *Halifax*, 193; *H.M.C. Bath*, II, 160; *Pepys* (13 July, '60); *Reresby* (Oct., '60); *Steinman*.

22 *Cunningham, English Industry and Commerce*, II, Pt. I, 194-5; *De Witt*, 257; *H.M.C. Rep.* 5 (*Sutherland*, 174-5); " *Mercurius Publicus* " (*Burney*, 55) (2-9 Aug., 9-16 Aug., 16-23 Aug., '60); *Pepys* (4 Aug., '60).

CHAPTER II

THE AUGEAN STABLE

1 *Cl.S.P.*, II, 139; *Cunningham, Industry and Commerce*, II, Pt. I, 321; *Higgons*, I, 296-7; *H.M.C. Portland*, III, 222; *Nalson*, II, 750; *Ranke*, III, 312; *Reresby* (18 Jan., '82).

2 *C.J.*; *H.M.C. Rep.* 5 (*Sutherland*, 150-4, 168, 173-4, 184, 194-5, 199, 207-8); *H.M.C. Portland*, I, 2; III, 222-3; *Kennet*, 172, 183-4, 199, 203, 207, 212; *L.J.*; *Parl. Hist.*, IV, 67-80, 85-7 *et seq.*

3 *H.M.C. Rep.* 3 (*Northumberland*, 90); *Rep.* 5 (*Sutherland*, 155, 174, 177, 195, 199); *House of Lyme*, 213; *Kennet*, 212; *Parl. Hist.*, IV, 88-90.

4 *H.M.C. Rep.* 3 (*Northumberland*, 90); *Rep* 5 (*Sutherland*, 155-6); *Kennet*, 236, 239, 241, 256 *et seq.*; *Parl. Hist.*, IV, 91-114, 122-30.

5 *C.J.*, VIII; *C.T.B.*, I, Intr.; VII, Pt. I. Intr., ix-x, xxiv; *H.M.C. Rep.* 5 (*Sutherland*, 195); *H.M.C. Dartmouth*, III, 96-105; *Kennet*, 255.

6 *Baker Chronicle*, 730; *C.J.*, VIII, 172, 176-7, 189-91, 196-7; *C.T.B.*, I, Intr.; VII, Pt. I, Intr., x-xii; *De Witt*, 249-50; *Evelyn* (6 Oct., '60); *H.M.C. Rep.* 3 (*Dod*, 259); *Rep.* 5 (*Sutherland*, 157, 168); *H.M.C. Portland*, III, 226; *Kennet*, 240, 252, 256, 262; *Marvell*, II, 1-2; *Nicholas*, IV, 267; *Parl. Hist.*, IV, 123-4; *Statutes*, 12 Car. II, c. 2, 9, 10, 20, 26-8.

7 *C.S.P.D.* 1660-1, V, 1, 153, 159, 287, 292, 331, 620; and see throughout *C.S.P.D.* 1660-1 and 1661-2; *H.M.C. Rep.* 3 (*Northumberland*, 91); *Rep.* 5 (*Sutherland*, 175); *Rep.* 7 (*House of Lords*, 83 *et seq.*); *H.M.C.* (*Beaufort*, 49; *Hodgkin*, 300); *Verney*, II, 220.

8 *C.S.P.D.* 1660-1, 31, 53, 96, 159, 331; 1662-3, 96, 395; *Fea* (*After Worcester Fight*, xxiv-xxix; *Flight of the King*, 319-32); *H.M.C. Rep.* 3 (*Northumberland*, 91); *Rep.* 4 (*Rothes*, 505); *Rep.* 7 (*H. of Lords*, 82 *et seq.*, 138-9, etc.); *H.M.C. Kenyon*, 103; *Pepys* (29 June, 10 July, '60); *Secret Services*.

9 *C.S.P.D.* 1660-1, 295; *H.M.C. Rep.* 3 (*Northumberland*, 91); *Rep.* 5 (*Sutherland*, 194); *Nicholas*, IV; *Parl. Hist.*, IV, 80-2; *Pepys* (21 Oct., '61).

10 *Ailesbury*, 6-7; *Bramston, Autobiography*; *Burnet*, I, 176 (Dartmouth note), 287-9; *C.S.P.D.* 1660-1, viii-ix, 217; *H.M.C. Rep.* 5 (*Sutherland*, 205); *Kennet*, 232-3; *Parl. Hist.*, IV, 234-8; *Pepys* (7 March, '62); *Somers Tracts*, VII, 517-20.

11 *Ailesbury*, 21, 92; *C.J.*, VIII, 234, 238-44; *C.S.P.D.* 1662-3, 129, 149; *C.T.B.*, I, Intr.; VII, Pt. I, Intr., xii-xv.

12 *C.J.*, VIII; 498; *Clarendon, Cont.*; *C.T.B.*, I, Intr.; VII, Pt. I, Intr.; *H.M.C. Rep.* 5 (*Sutherland*, 156, 168, 195); *Kennet*, 241, 255; *Marvell*, II, 25; *Parl. Hist.*, IV, 114-15, 117-19, 143-52; *Ranke*, III, 320.

13 *C.J.*; *C.S.P.D.* 1660-1, 51, 324, 332; 1661-2, 77, 464; *Cunningham, Industry and Commerce*, II, Pt. I, 194-6; *H.M.C. Rep.* 5 (*Sutherland*, 157); *H.M.C. Portland*, III, 242; *Pepys* (31 July, '60); *Ranke*, III, 336-7.

14 *C.J.*, VIII, 498; *C.T.B.*, I, Intr.; VII, Pt. I, Intr., xv-xx; *Kennet*, 331, 336-9; *L.J.*; *Marvell*, II, 3-5, 12-13; *Parl. Hist.*, IV, 164-7; *Verney*, II, 171.

15 *H.M.C. Rep.* 5 (*Sutherland*, 168, 174-5, 204); *Kennet*, 273-86; *Pepys* (13, 15, 21 Oct., 6, 19 Nov., '60); *State Trials*, V.

16 *Burnet*, I, 281-2; *Cl.S.P.*, III, App. xlvi; *C.S.P.D.* 1660-1, 312, 500; *Evelyn* (30 Jan., '61); *H.M.C. Rep.* 5 (*Sutherland*, 158); *Kennet*, 281-3, 325-6, 367; *Marvell*, II, 7; *Parl. Hist.*, IV, 158-9; *Pepys* (4 Dec., '60; 28, 30 Jan., 5 Feb., '61).

17 *Baxterianæ*, 231 *et seq.*; *Burnet Supplement*, 68-9; *C.S.P.D.* 1660-1, 350; *H.M.C. Rep.* 5 (*Sutherland*, 178); *Kennet*, 175, 178, 182, 195, 197, 200, 205, 279 *et seq.*, 312 *et seq.*; *Parl. Hist.*, IV, 82-4; *Pepys* (17 June, 22 Oct., 60); *Ranke*, III, 320; *Wodrow*, 34.

18 *Burnet*, I, 329-30; *Cosin*, II, 10, 21; *C.S.P.D.* 1660-1, 308, 404; *Evelyn* (10 Nov., '61; March, '72); *H.M.C. Fleming*, 26; *Jusserand*, 120; *Kennet*, 210, 218, 231, 252, 272, 332; *Pepys* (8 July, 4 Oct., 4 Nov., '60; 20 March, '61); *Verney*, I, 486; II, 171.

19 *H.M.C. Rep.* 5 (*Sutherland*, 158, 196); *Kennet*, 248 *et seq.*, 279-83, 287, 301, 307, 311 *et seq.*; *Lister*, III, 110; *Marvell*, II, 6; *Parl. Hist.*, IV, 131-42, 152-4; *Reliquæ Baxterianæ*, 259 *et seq.*

20 *Clarke, James II*, I, 387; *C.S.P.D.* 1660-1, 271; *H.M.C. Rep.* 5 (*Sutherland*, 156-7, 168-9, 174); *Rep.* 9 (*Alfred Morrison*, 445); *H.M.C. Fleming*, 26-7; *Kennet*, 261; *Macpherson*, I, 17; *Pepys* (13, 16, 21 Sept., '60).

21 *Burnet*, I, 293-5; *Clarendon, Cont.*, 29 *et seq.*; *De Witt*, 254; *Grammont*, I, 160-5; *H.M.C. Rep.* 5 (*Sutherland*, 185, 195, 200); *Pepys* (7, 22, 24 Oct., 10 Dec., '60; 23 Feb., '61). But see also York's account in *Clarke, James II*, I, 387-8.

22 *C.S.P.D.* 1660-1, 324, 350; *De Witt*, 256-9; *Ferrero* (cit. *Taylor*); *H.M.C. Rep.* 5 (*Sutherland*, 175, 200); *Rep.* 6 (*Ingilby*, 363); *Kennet*, 250; *Pepys* (25 Sept., 6, 7, 27 Oct., 2 Nov., '60).

23 *Ady*, 75; *Cl.S.P.*, III, App. l; *De Witt*, 256, 260; *Gamaches*; *H.M.C. Rep.* 5 (*Sutherland*, 158, 199); *Rep.* 6 (*Ingilby*, 363); *Pepys* (22 Nov., '60).

24 *C.S.P.D.* 1660-1, 420, 424; *De Witt*, 257-60; *Pepys* (20-1, 24, 26 Dec., '60). See also *H.M.C. Rep.* 5 (*Sutherland*, 174).

CHAPTER III

SETTLING IN

1 *C.J.*, VIII, 485; *C.S.P.D.* 1660-1, 123, 127, 130, 270, 388, 447, 466; *De Witt*, 259; *H.M.C. Rep.* 3 (*Grey-Egerton*, 244-5); *Rep.* 5 (*Sutherland*, 201); *Rep.* 8 (*Bankes*, 211); *H.M.C. Buccleuch* (M.H.), I, 312; *Kennet*, 206, 286, 315, 326, 353, 356; *The Lord's Loud Call to England* (1660); *The Lying Wonders or The Wonderful Lyes* (1660); *Muddiman*, 131, 133; *Pepys* (New Year, '61); " *Parliamentary Intelligencer* " (10-17 Dec., 17-24 Dec., '60) (*Burney*, 55); *Ranke*, III, 320; *Wynn Papers*, 369.

2 *Baker Chronicle*, 734-5; *Burnet*, I, 278-9; *Burnet Supplement*, 76-7; *Clarke, James II*, I, 388-91; *C.S.P.D.* 1660-1, 470-3, 476; *De Witt*, 251; *Fortescue, History of British Army*, I, 290-2; *H.M.C. Rep.* 3 (*Dod*, 259); *Rep.* 5 (*Sutherland*, 201-2); *Rep.* 8 (*Corp. of Leicester*, 439); *Kennet*, 354, 357; *Muddiman*, 136; *Pepys* (7-14 Jan., '61); *Ranke*, III, 357-60; *Reresby* (6, 7 Jan., '61); *State Trials*, VI. For an earlier attempt to raise a royal army see *H.M.C. Rep.* 5 (*Sutherland*, 208).

³ *Fox, Journal*; *Josselin*, 112; *Kennet*, 288, 296, 356, 364; *Thurloe*, III, 693.

⁴ *Baxterianæ*, 298-9; *Kennet*, 359, 374, 383.

⁵ *Burnet*, I, 289-92; *Carte, Ormonde*, Bk. VI, par. 90; *Clarendon, Cont.*; *C.S.P.D.* 1660-1, 500; *De Witt*, 253, 261, 265; *Feiling, For. Policy*, 38 *et seq.*; *H.M.C. Rep.* 5 (*Sutherland*, 151, 158-9, 170, 202); *H.M.C.* (*Egmont*, I, 617; *Finch*, I, 85; *Heathcote*, 17); *Kennet*, 381-2, 394; *Pepys* (21, 29 Jan., 14, 28 Feb., '61); *Ranke*, III, 345 *et seq.*

⁶ *Cl.S.P.*, III, App.; *C.S.P.D.* 1660-1, 411; *H.M.C. Rep.* 5 (*Sutherland*, 159, 170, 202-3); *H.M.C. Dartmouth*, I, 6; *Jusserand*, 122; *Kennet*, 431; *Ranke*, III, 380.

⁷ *C.S.P.D.* 1660-1, 539; *De Witt*, 267; *H.M.C. Rep.* 3 (*Northumberland*, 90; *Dod*, 259); *Rep.* 5 (*Sutherland*, 146, 170, 175); *Josselin*, 138; *Kennet*, 382; *Pepys* (New Year, 21 Feb., 1 March, 13, 17 April, '61); *Ranke*, III, 363.

⁸ *Baker Chronicle*, 735-48; *C.S.P.D.* 1660-1, 536, 586; *De Witt*, 274-5; *H.M.C. Rep.* 5 (*Sutherland*, 151, 175, 205); *Rep.* 9 (*Alfred Morrison*, 445); *H.M.C. Portland*, III, 249; *Kennet*, 408-24; *Ogilby, Account of the Coronation*; *Pepys* (19-24 April, '61); *Ranke*, III, 364 *et seq.*

⁹ *E.H.R.*, 21 (*Abbott*, 22-4); *H.M.C. Rep.* 5 (*Sutherland*, 159-60, 181-2); *Rep.* 6 (*Ingilby*, 364); *H.M.C.* (*Fleming*, 27; *Portland*, III, 250); *Parl. Hist.*, IV, 178-81, 194-200; *Kennet*, 434-5.

¹⁰ *C.S.P.D.* 1660-1, 586; 1661-2, 29 *et seq.*; *H.M.C. Rep.* 5 (*Sutherland*, 151, 160); *H.M.C.* (*Finch*, I; *Fleming*, 28; *Heathcote*, 17-18; *Hodgkin*, 159; *Wood*, 65); *Kennet*, 471; *Lister*, III, 138; *Pepys* (10, 13 June, 17 Oct., '61).

¹¹ *C.S.P.D.* 1661-2, 16; *E.H.R.*, 21 (*Abbott*, 25); *H.M.C. Rep.* 5 (*Sutherland*, 208); *Josselin*, 138; *Kennet*, 436; *Lister*, III, 132; *Marvell*, II, 30-1; *Parl. Hist.*, IV, 209-15; *Ranke*, III, 363.

¹² *Ailesbury*, 9; *C.J.*, VIII; *C.S.P.D.* 1660-1, 77; 1662-3, 264; *C.T.B.*, I, Intr.; *History*, n.s. 14 (*Browning*, 333); *H.M.C. Rep.* 5 (*Sutherland*, 170, 203-4); *H.M.C.* (*Corp. of Bridgwater*, 316; *Gawdy*, 193); *Kennet*, 436; *Marvell*, II, 26; *Parl. Hist.*, IV, 291; *Pepys* (31 May, 14 Aug., '61); *Shaw, Beginnings of the National Debt.*

¹³ *Baxterianæ*; *Burnet*, I, 317 *et seq.*; *H.M.C. Fleming*, 28; *Kennet*, 407, 432, 450, 499-507, 629; *Ranke*, III, 368-70.

¹⁴ *C.S.P.D.* 1660-1, 536-9, 551, 561, 567; *H.M.C. Fleming*, 28; *Kennet*, 509; *Pepys* (23 March, '61); *Ranke*, III, 370.

¹⁵ *C.S.P.D.* 1660-1, 573; 1661-2, 7, 236; 1662-3; 157, 161; *Evelyn* (1 Oct., '61); *H.M.C. Finch*, I, 118; *Jusserand*, 140; *Pepys* (13, 15 Jan., 21 May, 13 June, 12 Sept., '61; 17 Aug., '65); *Rugge*.

¹⁶ *C.S.P.D.* 1660-1; 1661-2, *passim*; *De Witt*, 283; *Evelyn* (26 Nov., '61; 5 Feb., '64; 18 Oct., '66); *H.M.C. Rep.* 5 (*Sutherland*, 158); *Orrery*, I, 81; *Pepys* (7 Jan., 2, 23 July, 27 Aug., 7 Sept., 28 Oct., '61; 26 May, '62; 8 Jan., '63; 2 Aug., '64; 3 April, '65; 12 Feb., 25 Sept., 11 Dec., '67; 25 Feb., 28 Sept., '68; 19 Jan., '69); *Roscius Anglicanus*.

¹⁷ *Birch, Royal Society*; *Cl.S.P.*, III, App. xvi; *C.S.P.D.* 1661-2, 16; *Evelyn* (3, 11, 14 May, '61); *H.M.C. Rep.* 5 (*Sutherland*, 151, 159, 160, 170, 212); *H.M.C. Heathcote*, 17; *Parl. Hist.*, IV, 208; *Pepys* (11, 19 Aug., '61); *Sprat, Royal Society*, 53-4, 60, 133 *et seq.*

¹⁸ *C.J.*; *C.S.P.D.* 1661-2, 73, 85, 89, 107, 116, 129, 143, 160, 188; 1662-3, 160 *et seq.*; *Kennet*, 561 *et seq.*; *L.J.*; *Parl. Hist.*, IV, 224-8; *Pepys* (20 Nov., '61).

CHAPTER IV

BENEDICT—THE MARRIED MAN

1 *Echard*, 795; *Evelyn* (1, 3 Jan., 17 Feb., '62); *Heath*, 503; *H.M.C. (Somerset*, 93; *Wood*, 14 Feb., '62); *Kennet*, 627, 650; *Pepys* (3 Jan., 13, 18 Feb., '62).

2 *Ady* (16 Dec., '61).

3 *Ady*, 112; *Forneron*, 28; *Grammont*, I, 107; *H.M.C. Wood* (9 Feb., '62).

4 *Carte, Ormonde*, Bk. VI, par. 96; *C.J.*; *C.S.P.D.* 1661-2, 294, 307, 372; *De Witt*, 290; *H.M.C. (Ormonde*, III, 19; *Somerset*, 93-4; *Wood*, 14 Feb., '62); *Kennet*, 602-5, 626-34, 638-47, 657, 659, 661, 665, 670-2, 676, 680, 685; *L.J.*; *Parl. Hist.* IV, 230-3, 238-44; *Pepys* (10, 27 April, 7, 8, 15, 24 May, '62); *Ranke*, III, 370-5.

5 *Clarendon, Cont.*; *Pepys* (20 April, 23 July, 27 Aug., 7 Dec., '61; 22 Jan., 5 Feb., 10, 14, 21 May, '62); *Steinman, Cleveland*, 28.

6 *Cl.S.P.*, III, App. xxi; *Heath*, 508; *Kennet*, 689; *Macpherson*, I, 22; *Parl. Hist.*, IV, 244-8; *Pepys* (19 May, '62).

7 *Clarke, James II*, I, 394; *De Witt*, 257; *Heath*, 509; *Sousa, Historia Genealogica de Casa Real Portuguese*, VII (cit. *Davidson*); *Lister*, III, 195; *Aurelian Cook*, 481.

8 *Ady*, 120; *H.M.C. Heathcote*, 28.

9 *Clarendon, Cont.*; *De Witt*, 290; *Evelyn* (30 May, 2 June, '62); *Grammont*, I, 96-7; *H.M.C. Beaufort*, 53; *Jusserand*, 163; *Pepys* (25 May, '62).

10 *Evelyn* (9 June, '62); *Hist. Casa Real Portuguese* (cit. *Davidson*); *H.M.C. Stewart*, 111.

11 *Evelyn* (30 May, '62); *Ferrero* (cit. *Taylor*); *H.M.C. (Somerset*, 95; *Stewart*, 111); *House of Lyme*, 227; *Pepys* (23, 25, 31 May, 22 June, 7 Dec., '62); *Wynn Papers*, 370; *Reresby* (May, '62).

12 *Clarendon, Cont.*; *C.S.P.D.* 1661-2, 396; *De Witt*, 290; *Fanshawe*; *H.M.C. (Beaufort*, 52; *Fleming*, 28); *Pepys* (16 Aug., '61); *Verney*, II, 173.

13 *Clarendon, Cont.*; *H.M.C. Beaufort*, 53; *Pepys* (6, 16, 26 July, '62); *Register of St. Margaret's, Westminster*.

14 *Clarendon, Cont.*; *Pepys* (6, 26 July, '62).

15 *Clarendon, Cont.*; *H.M.C. Finch*, II, 147; *Lister*, III, 202; *Pepys* (19 June, '63). See also *Nicholas*, III, 98.

16 *Ady* (8 Sept., '62; 26 March, '69); *Evelyn* (28 July, '62); *Ferrero* (cit. *Taylor*, 542); *H.M.C. Finch*, I, 204; *Pepys* (19, 26, 28, 30 July, '62).

17 *Aqua Triumphalis*; *Carte MSS.* 31, f. 602; *Evelyn* (23 Aug., '62); *Ferrero* (cit. *Taylor*); *Gentleman's Magazine*, xciv, II, 516; *H.M.C. (Dartmouth*, I, 10; *Ormonde*, III, 23); *Pepys* (23 Aug., '62).

18 *Clarendon, Cont.*; *H.M.C. Heathcote*, 46; *Lister*, III, 222; *Pepys* (7 Sept., 9, 24, 27 Oct., 15, 23 Dec., '62).

19 *C.S.P.D.* 1661-2, 106, 385, 396-7, 404, 415, 431, 441, 452, 464, 466, 531, 541, 547, 614; 1662-3, 63, 72, *et passim*; *E.H.R.*, 21 (*Abbot*, 31); *Evelyn* (28 Oct., '62); *H.M.C. Portland*, III, 270; *Mirabilis Annus*; *Muddiman*; *Pepys* (31 June, 17 Aug., 3 Sept., '62); *Ranke*, III, 378; *Wood, Life and Times*, I, 465-6; *Wynn Papers*, 372.

20 C.S.P.D. 1661-2, 350, 366, 577; 1662-3, 57; C.T.B., I, Intr.; H.M.C. Hodgkin, 301; Pepys (27 March, 27 April, 21 July, 13 Aug., 30 Sept., '62; 2, 12 March, 13 April, 17 June, 2 Dec., '64; 19 March, 1 April, 12 May, '65); Evelyn (3 March, '68).

21 Burnet, I, 303; Clarendon, Cont.; Corbett, England in the Mediterranean, II, 12-21; C.S.P.D. 1661-2, 531; Feiling, For. Policy, 59; H.M.C. (Dartmouth, I, 10-11; Leyborne-Popham, 250; Portland, III, 270, see also 221-56); Lister, III, 491; Pepys (19 Oct., '62; 20 Feb., '65); Ranke, III, 386 et seq.

22 Carte, Ormonde, Bk. VI, par. 123-4; Clarendon, Cont., C.S.P.D. 1661-2, 525; Egerton MSS. 2538, f. 170; H.M.C. (Dartmouth, I, 11; Fleming, 29; Heath-cote, 54); Lister, III, 228; Pepys (16, 17 Oct., '62).

23 Cl.S.P., III, App. xlix; Evelyn (27 Nov., 29 Dec., '62); H.M.C. Heathcote, 55, 75; Pepys (27, 30 Nov., '62); Wynn Papers, 373.

24 Ady (4 Nov., '62); C.S.P.D. 1661-2, 583, 595-9; H.M.C. (Fleming, 29; Heath-cote, 48; Ormonde, III, 351); Lister, III, 198, 233; Misc. Aulica, 280; Pepys (26, 29 Oct., 6, 10 Nov., 1, 5, 7, 10 Dec., '62); Ranke, III, 394;

25 Cosin, II, 101-2; C.S.P.D. 1661-2, 603; 1662-3, 10, 50; Kennet, 848 et seq.; Pepys (6 Jan., '63); Ranke, III, 401-2.

26 Burnet, I, 345; Carte, Ormonde, Bk. VI, par. 94; Jusserand, 116, 206; Pepys (29 March, '69); Ranke, III, 397-401; Remarks on Ayre's Life of Pope, 12.

CHAPTER V

THE COURT OF CUCKOLDS

1 Pepys (31 Dec., '62).

2 Grammont, I, 156, 174-90; II, 2-3, 77; H.M.C. Rep. 7 (Verney, 463); H.M.C. (Fleming, 30; Heathcote, 55); Pepys (3 Nov., 15, 31 Dec., '62; 1, 19 Jan., 1, 8, 17, 23 Feb., 25 April, '63).

3 Ady (9, 16 Feb., '63); C.S.P.D. 1663-4, passim; Evelyn (7, 10 Jan., '63); Grammont, I, 92; Jusserand, 83-4, 91.

4 Ady (16 Feb., '63); C.J.; Clarendon, Cont.; E.H.R., 21 (Abbott, 32-3); H.M.C. Rep. 3 (Northumberland, 92); H.M.C. (Fleming, 30; Ormonde, III, 47); Lister, III, 243-4; Pepys (25-6, 28 Feb., 1, 3, 6 March, 1, 29 April, '63); Ranke, III, 402.

5 Barbour, passim; Burnet, I, 180; Feiling, For. Policy, 76-80; Grammont, I, 138; H.M.C. Heathcote, 50; Jusserand, 52, 77.

6 Ailesbury, 10; Burnet, I, 181-2; Burnet Supplement, 65; Clarendon, Cont., 195; Grammont, I, 93-4; Pepys (30 Aug., '68).

7 Ady (20 April, '63); Clarke, James II, I, 493; C.S.P.D. 1662-3, 552; Grammont, II, 132-4; H.M.C. Rep. 7 (Verney, 463); H.M.C. (Fleming, 29; Heathcote, 80); Pepys (24, 31 Dec., '62; 8 Feb., 4, 20, 23, 27 April, 4, 14, 15 May, '63).

8 Ady (11 May, '63); Grammont, I, 115-16; II, 139; H.M.C. (Heathcote, 46, 80; Portland, III, 265, 274); Jusserand, 89; Pepys (9 Oct., 15 Dec., '62; 4, 7 June, '63; 22 Feb., '64).

9 Ady (8 Sept., '62; 27 April, 24 June, '63); Grammont, I, 136; Jusserand, 90; Pepys (11, 15, 18 May, '63; 25 Nov., '66).

[10] *Feiling, For. Policy*, 64; *H.M.C.* (*Heathcote*, 45, 52, 63, 75, 104, 116, 118; *Portland*, III, 274; *Josselin*, 153; *Jusserand*, 63, 74, 125, 128; *Lauderdale*, I, 142; *Misc. Aulica*, 291-3; *Pepys* (29, 30 June, 4 July, '63); *Ranke*, III, 385.

[11] *C.J.*; *C.S.P.D.* 1663-4, 151; *H.M.C.* (*Fleming*, 31; *Heathcote*, 80, 83, 87; *Hodgkin*, 301-2; *Ormonde*, III, 53; *Portland*, III, 274); *Pepys* (18 Feb., 14 April, 31 May, 23, 30 June, '63); *Parl. Hist.*, IV, 265-9.

[12] *C.S.P.D.* 1663-4, 264; *Evelyn* (20 Aug., '63); *H.M.C. Rep. 3* (*Northumberland*, 92-3); *H.M.C.* (*Finch*, I, 297; *Ormonde*, III, 64, 78, 174, 177); *Josselin*, 143.

[13] *Carte, Ormonde*, Bk. VI, par. 105 *et seq.*; *Feiling, For. Policy*, 26; *H.M.C.* (*Finch*, II, 266; *Ormonde*, III, 113); *Lauderdale*, I, 136, 141, 142, 148, 150, 162; *Misc. Aulica*, 283-96; *Pepys* (2 March, '64).

[14] *C.S.P.D.* 1663-4, 175; *Lauderdale*, I, 148, 152; *Misc. Aulica*, 286, 290; *Pepys* (7 July, '63; 11 Jan., '64); *Reresby* (June, '63).

[15] *Burnet*, I, 350-2; *Burnet Supplement*, 74; *Clarendon, Cont.*; *Clarke, James II*, I, 427; *C.S.P.D.* 1663-4, 199, 254; *H.M.C. Rep. 3* (*Northumberland*, 92); *H.M.C.* (*Hastings*, II, 142; *Portland*, III, 274); *Jusserand*, 105-7, 214; *Lister*, III, 245, 441; *L.J.*; *Parl. Hist.*, IV, 270-83; *Pepys* (29 April, 4, 15, 31 May, 1, 3, 7, 10, 13 July, 10 Aug., '63); *Ranke*, III, 408; *State Trials*; *Wynn Papers*, 375.

[16] *Pepys* (13, 22 July, '63).

[17] *C.S.P.D.* 1663-4, 232; *Grammont*, II, 99-101; *H.M.C. Rep. 3* (*Northumberland*, 93); *H.M.C.* (*Heathcote*, 127; *Portland*, III, 276); *Jusserand*, 89; *Pepys* (27 July, 10 Aug., '63).

[18] *C.S.P.D.* 1663-4, 247, 264; *H.M.C.* (*Ailesbury*, 170-1; *Finch*, I, 274; *Hastings*, II, 142 *et seq.*; *Kenyon*, 71; *Ormonde*, III, 73, 81; *Reading Corp.*, 195); *Jusserand*, 90; *Lauderdale*, I, 177, 181, 185, 187, 189.

[19] *C.S.P.D.* 1663-4, 281; *Cl.S.P.*, III, App. xxxv; *Jusserand*, 92-3; *Pepys* (13 Oct., '63).

[20] *C.S.P.D.* 1663-4, 276, 290 *et seq.*, 322, 380, 405, 442, 512, 521; *H.M.C. Rep. 6* (*Graham*, 333); *Rep. 7* (*Verney*, 463); *H.M.C.* (*Fleming*, 30-1; *Lonsdale*, 93; *Portland*, II, 144); *Josselin*, 143-4; *Jusserand*, 115, 118; *Pepys* (13, 24 Oct., '63); *Reresby* (Aug., '63).

[21] *C.S.P.D.* 1663-4, 301; *Grammont*, I, 140-1; *H.M.C. Rep. 3* (*Northumberland*, 92); *Rep. 6* (*Graham*, 333); *Rep. 7* (*Verney*, 484); *Josselin*, 143; *Jusserand*, 88; *Misc. Aulica*, 306; *Pepys* (17, 19, 20, 22-4 Oct., '63); *Waller, Poems*.

[22] *Ady* (2, 20 Nov., '63); *H.M.C. Ormonde*, III, 98; *Pepys* (26-31 Oct, 1, 2, 4, 10, 22 Nov., '63).

[23] *Ady* (10 Dec., '63); *Jusserand*, 95; *Pepys* (22 Dec., '63).

[24] *C.S.P.D.* 1663-4, 400, 402, 414; *C.T.B.*, I, Intr.; *H.M.C.* (*Finch*, I, 197; *Hastings*, II, 144; *Ormonde*, III, 78).

[25] *Ady* (19 May, '64); *Choice Ayres*, 11; *Cunningham*, 84; *Grammont*, I, 140; II, 153-4; *Hatton*, I, 34; *H.M.C. Hastings*, II, 144; *Pepys* (6, 9 Nov., '63; 20 Jan., 8 Feb., 5 July, '64; 25 Feb., 26 April, '67); *Walpole, Royal and Noble Authors*, I, 154-5.

CHAPTER VI

SWORD, PESTILENCE AND FIRE

[1] *Ady* (23 Dec., '61); *Arlington*, II, 341; *Burnet*, II, 108; *Chamberlayne*, 164 *et seq.*; *H.M.C. Rep.* 2 (*Spencer*, 21); *H.M.C.* (*Fleming*, 118-19; *Hodgkin*, 170; *Leeds*, 3; *Portland*, II, 277); *Hoskins* (*Chevalier*); *Pepys* (12, 29 Nov., '61; 22 Feb., '64); *Selden, Mare Clausum.* See also *H.M.C. Lindsey*, 374.

[2] For the growth of the Anglo-Dutch rivalry see *Clarke, James II*, I, 399-403; *Feiling, For. Policy*, 83-138; *Khan, The East India Trade in the Seventeenth Century*; Downing's Letters to Clarendon in *Lister*, III; and *Ranke*, III, 417 *et seq.* For illustrations of English public opinion see *C.S.P.D.* 1663-4, 541, 561-2, 572; *H.M.C. Rep.* 5 (*Sutherland*, 160); *H.M.C.* (*Hastings*, 145; *Heathcote*, 146, 149); *Josselin*, 144-5; *Orrery*, II, 234; *Pepys* (28 Nov., '63; 15 Feb., 30 March, 1, 5, 20-1, 23, 26-7, 29 April, '64); *Temple*, I, 60-9.

[3] *C.J.*; *L.J.*; *Parl. Hist.*, IV, 292; *Pepys* (19, 20, 23 April, '64).

[4] *Ady* (2, 27 June, 14 July, '64); *C.J.*; *H.M.C.* (*Ailesbury*, 173; *Heathcote*, 152-5; *Montagu of Beaulieu*, 166); *Josselin*, 145; *Jusserand*, 87; *Pepys* (23 May, 30 June, 4, 5, 7, 8 July, '64); *Ranke*, III, 419, 420.

[5] *Ady* (23 Aug., 17, 24 Oct., '64); *C.S.P.D.* 1664-5, 235, 243; *Feiling, For. Policy*, 125; *H.M.C.* (*Buccleuch* (*M.H.*), I, 315; *Hastings*, II, 367; *Heathcote*, 165); *Josselin*, 146; *Pepys* (23 Aug., 8, 29 Sept., 1 Oct., '65); *Hatton*, I, 37.

[6] *Evelyn* (29 Oct., '64); *H.M.C. Rep.* 8 (*Trinity House*, 252); *Jusserand*, 135-7, 139; *Pepys* (5, 26 Oct., '64).

[7] *Ady* (19 Sept., '64; 27 Feb., '65); *C.J.*; *Clarke, James II*, I, 403; *C.S.P.D.* 1664-5 (9 Nov., '64; 9 March, '65); *Hatton*, I, 40-1; *Parl. Hist.*, IV, 296-308; *Pepys* (9, 21-5 Nov., 10, 15 Dec., '64).

[8] *Ady* (15 Dec., '64); *C.S.P.D.* 1664-5, 122; *H.M.C.* (*Heathcote*, 175; *Somerset*, 98); *Pepys* (21 Nov., 9 Dec., '64); *Carte MSS.* 33, f. 744; *Hatton*, I, 44.

[9] *Ady* (5, 12, 19, 22 Jan., '65); *H.M.C. Hastings*, II, 152; *Jusserand*, 140-4; *Parl. Hist.*, IV, 308-9; *Pepys* (Jan., Feb., March, '65, *passim*); *Wynn Papers*, 381.

[10] *Ady* (29 May, '65); *Clarke, James II*, I, 404-5; *H.M.C. Heathcote*, 191, 192; *Jusserand*, 150; *Pepys* (April, May, *passim*, 2 June, '65).

[11] *Ady* (8 June, '65); *Clarke, James II*, I, 407-20; *C.S.P.D.* 1664-5, 407-9, 420; *H.M.C.* (*Egmont*, II, 14; *Fleming*, 37; *Hothfield*, 85; *Portland*, III, 291-2); *Jusserand*, 145-8; *Pepys* (June, *passim*, '65); *Ranke*, III, 427.

[12] *C.S.P.D.* 1664-5 (29 June, '65); *C.T.B.* 1667-8, Intr.; *Evelyn* (26 May, 8, 20 June, '65); *H.M.C. Hodgkin*, 163-6; *Pepys* (6 Dec., '64; 1, 7, 12, 28 April, 21 June, 6 July, '65); *Verney*, II, 241.

[13] *Bell, Plague*; *Evelyn* (20 June, '65); *H.M.C. Rep.* 8 (*College of Physicians*, 230); *H.M.C. Hulton*, 177; *Josselin*, 147; *Jusserand*, 147, 159, 163, 166; *Pepys* (June, '65, *passim*); *Savile*, 5.

[14] *Ady* (13 July, '65); *C.S.P.D.* 1664-5, 460; *H.M.C.* (*City of Salisbury*, 244-5; *Fleming*, 37; *Hothfield*, 85); *Pepys* (29 June, 12, 23, 26, 27 July, '65).

[15] *Ady* (5 Aug., 9 Sept., '65); *C.S.P.D.* 1664-5, 526, 538, 550, 556, 568; *H.M.C. Rep.* 6 (*Graham*, 336); *H.M.C. Wombwell*, 120; *Jusserand*, 170, 171, 248; *Pepys* (12 Aug., 7 Sept., '65).

16 *Bell, Plague; Evelyn* (8 Aug., 7 Sept., '65); *H.M.C.* (*Heathcote*, 216-18; *Portland*, III, 292); *Josselin*, 148-9; *Pepys* (July, Aug., Sept., '65, *passim*); *Wynn Papers*, 383.

17 *Ady* (9 Sept., '65); *Bell, Plague; Cosin*, II, 195; *C.S.P.D.* 1664-5, 516, 520, 527, 538; *Evelyn* (28 Sept., '65); *H.M.C. Rep.* 6 (*Graham*, 339); *H.M.C.* (*Fleming*, 38; *Portland*, II, 102-4; III, 293); *Pepys* (5, 8, 19, 20, 28 Aug., 9, 10, 14, 18 Sept., '65); *Sprat, Royal Society*, 120.

18 *Burnet*, I, 390-1; *C.J.*; *E.H.R.* (*Abbott*, 37); *H.M.C. Rep.* 2 (*Spencer*, 19); *Jusserand*, 117, 174; *L.J.*; *Marvell*, II, 39-41; *Parl. Hist.*, IV, 317-32; *Pepys* (30 Sept., 1, 7, 15, 16, 27, 31 Oct., 27 Nov., 31 Dec., '65); *Ranke*, III, 433.

19 *Ady* (29 Jan., '66); *Evelyn* (29 Jan., 2 Feb., '66); *Hatton*, I, 48; *H.M.C. Rep.* 7 (*Verney*, 464); *H.M.C.* (*Ormonde*, III, 204-5; *Portland*, III, 293-4); *Pepys* (28, 31 Jan., '66; 1 May, '67).

20 *Ady* (9 Feb., '65; 29 Jan., 28 Feb., 2 May, '66; 2 Sept., '68); *Hatton*, I, 48; *H.M.C. Fleming*, 40; *Pepys* (25 Jan., '66); *Ranke*, III, 434.

21 *Clarke, James II*, I, 423-4; *C.S.P.D.* 1665-6, xix, 418, 430-4, 442, 449, 579; 1666-7, 22, 27, 28, 32; *Evelyn* (18 May, June, 17, 29 July, '66); *H.M.C. Rep.* 5 (*Malet*, 315; *Cholmondley*, 348); *Rep.* 6 (*Graham*, 338-9; *Ingilby*, 365); *H.M.C.* (*Dartmouth*, I, 14-15; *Fleming*, 40; *Heathcote*, 249-52; *Hodgkin*, 53-7; *Kenyon*, 77-8; *Lloyd*, 449-50; *Portland*, III, 297; *Wombwell*, 122-3); *Josselin*, 151-5; *Pepys* (31 May, June, July, *passim*, 15 Aug., '66); *Ranke*, III, 436-8; *Savile*, 9, 12-15; *Shakerley MSS.* (July, '66); *Temple*, I, 72; II, 128; *Hatton*, I, 49.

22 *Dugdale, St. Paul's*; *Evelyn* (25, 27 Aug., '66); *Wren, Parentalia*.

23 *C.S.P.D.* 1666-7, 94-5; *Evelyn* (3-5 Sept., '66); *H.M.C. Rep.* 7 (*Verney*, 485); *H.M.C.* (*Egmont*, II, 17; *Finch*, I, 435; *Fleming*, 41-2; *Hastings*, II, 369; *Hodgkin*, 306); *Lister*, III, 440; *Orrery*, II, 64; *Pepys* (2-5 Sept., '66); *Wynn Papers*, 385. For an admirable account see *Bell, The Great Fire of London*. See also *History*, n.s., 8, 40.

24 *C.S.P.D.* 1666-7, 99 *et seq.*, 104, 107, 214; *Evelyn* (5, 7, Sept., '66); *H.M.C.* (*Fleming*, 41-2; *Hastings*, II, 369; *Portland*, III, 298-9); *Pepys* (5 Sept., '66 *et seq.*).

25 *Bell, Fire of London*; *Burnet*, I, 469; *Chamberlayne*, 191 *et seq.*; *C.S.P.D.* 1666-7, 105, 111, 121; *Evelyn* (13 Sept., '66); *H.M.C.* (*Finch*, II, 2; *Fleming*, 42, 59, 97); *Marvell*, I, 166; *Pepys* (24 Feb., 23 Oct., 22 Nov., '67); *Reresby* (Sept., '66); *Sprat, Royal Society*, 149-50; *Verney*, II, 258; *Wren, Parentalia*.

26 *Burnet*, I, 211-16; *C.S.P.D.* 1666-7, 103, 108, 313; *Evelyn* (18, 30 Oct., '66); *H.M.C.* (*Beaufort*, 55; *Hastings*, II, 369; *Stewart*, 114-16; *Portland*, III, 301); *Pepys* (8, 15, 17 Oct., 22 Nov., '66); *Wynn Papers*, 385-6.

27 *Burnet*, I, 417 *et seq.*; *Cosin*, II, 158-9; *C.S.P.D.* 1666-7, xiii, 103, 108, 110 *et seq.*, 214, 313, etc.; *H.M.C. Rep.* 9 (*Dalyell*, 235; *Pyne*, 494); *H.M.C.* (*Fleming*, 43-4; *Hastings*, II, 374; *Portland*, III, 301-3); *Josselin*, 155-6; *Orrery*, II, 94-103; *Pepys* (Oct., Nov., Dec., '66, *passim*); *Ranke*, III, 507.

28 *Ady* (18 Oct., '66); *Feiling, For. Policy*, Ch. V.; *H.M.C. Kenyon*, 78; *Orrery*, II, 160, 169-70; *Ranke*, III, 440 *et seq.*; *Wynn Papers*, 388.

29 *Carte, Ormonde*, Bk. VI, par. 245; *C.J.*; *Clarendon, Cont.*; *C.S.P.D.* 1666-7, xxxi; 1667, xxiv-xxvii, 4-7, 77, 118; *C.T.B.* 1667-8, Intr.; *H.M.C.* (*Fleming*, 44; *Hodgkin*, 167-8; *Kenyon*, 78; *Portland*, II, 106); *Hoskins* (*Chevalier*); *L.J.*; *Marvell*, II, 42-54; *Parl. Hist.*, IV, 332-3; *Pepys* (13, 15, 24, 30 Oct., 5, 14, 25 Nov., 31 Dec., '66; 16, 25, 31 Jan., 13, 24 Feb., 6, 10, 13,

2C*

14 March, 1, 3-4, 10, 22, 26 April, 22 June, '67); *Ranke*, III, 441-3; *Tanner, Pepys Further Corr.*, 164.
³⁰ *C.S.P.D.* 1667, 62, 78, 89, 92, 103 *et seq.*, 108, 116, xii; *H.M.C. Fleming*, 49; *Pepys* (27 Feb., 6, 22, 23, 24 March, 3 May, '67); *Ranke*, III, 444; *Temple*, I, 71.
³¹ *Courthop, Memoirs*, 151-2; *C.S.P.D.* 1667, xxi *et seq.*, 156; *Evelyn* (June, '67); *Hatton*, I, 52-4; *History*, 14, n.s. (*Geyl*, 27-8); *H.M.C. Rep. 8 (Bankes*, 210); *H.M.C.* (*Egmont*, 17; *Fleming*, 49-50; *Hodgkin*, 57-60; *Kenyon*, 79); *Pepys* 3-12 June, '67).
³² *Burnet*, I, 448; *Carte, Ormonde*, Bk. VI, par. 246; *C.S.P.D.* 1667, xxiv, xxxii *et seq.*; *Evelyn* (17, 28 June, 29 July, '67); *H.M.C. Rep. 8 (Trinity House*, 253); *H.M.C.* (*Kenyon*, 79; *Lindsey*, 367; *Montagu of Beaulieu*, 168); *Josselin*, 157; *Marvell, I* (*Last Instructions to a Painter*); *Pepys* (13-30 June, July, *passim*, '67); *Savile*, 15-17. But see *H.M.C. Beaufort*, 53-4.

CHAPTER VII

THE KING'S ODYSSEY

The inspiration for the central idea of this chapter, as well as its title, I owe largely to Keith Feiling's brilliant study, *British Foreign Policy*, 1660-72.
¹ *Clarke, James II*, 1, 426; *C.S.P.D.* 1667, xxiv, xxxi, xxxiv, xxxix, 186 *et seq.*; *Feiling, For. Policy*, 223, 228-9; *H.M.C. Rep. 9 (Alfred Morrison*, 447); *Macpherson*, I, 38; *Pepys* (14 June, 19 Aug., '67); *Ranke*, III, 455.
² *Clarendon, Cont.; H.M.C.* (*Braye*, 180; *Egmont*, II, 17); *Pepys* (June, '67, *passim*); *Marvell*, II, 55-6.
³ *C.S.P.D.* 1667, lvi; *H.M.C. Rep. 3 (Northumberland*, 94); *H.M.C. Fitzherbert*, 5; *L.J.; Parl. Hist.*, IV, 363-4; *Pepys* (7, 25, 27, 29 July, '67); *Ranke*, III, 453.
⁴ *Burnet*, I, 169, 176 (Dartmouth note), 444-6; *Burnet Supplement*, 55; *Carte, Ormonde*, Bk. VI, par. 246-50; *Clarke, James II*, I, 427-9; *C.S.P.D.* 1667, lix; *Evelyn* (27 Aug., '67; 18 Sept., '83); *Feiling, Tory Party*, 113 *et seq.; H.M.C. Egmont*, II, 18; *Orrery*, II, 150, 299; *Marvell, I* (*Clarendon's House Warming*); *Pepys* (2, 17 March, '64; 15 Jan., '65; 26 April, 29 July, 2 Sept., 16 Dec., '67; 20 March, '69); *Reresby* (Feb., '82); *Verney*, II, 305. See also *Evelyn* (15 Aug., '62) for his description of Clarendon's coming to visit his house with his " purse and mace borne before him."
⁵ *Burnet*, I, 451; *Carte, Ormonde*, Bk. VI, par. 251 *et seq.; Clarendon, Cont.; H.M.C. Lindsey*, 369; *Lister*, III, 198, 468-9; *Macpherson*, I, 38; *Pepys* (25, 26, 27 Aug., '67); *Ranke*, III, 455 *et seq.; Savile*, 19.
⁶ *Clarendon, Cont.; Ellis, Original Letters*, 2nd S., IV, 39; *Lister*, III, 468-71; *Pepys* (30 Aug., '67).
⁷ *Burnet*, I, 456 *et seq.; C.J.; C.S.P.D.* 1667-8, 59; *Evelyn* (27 Aug., 26 Oct., 9 Nov., '67); *H.M.C. Rep. 3 (Northumberland*, 94-5); *H.M.C.* (*Kenyon*, 80-1; *Portland*, III, 305-6); *Lister*, III, 472-3, 476, 530; *L.J.; Marvell*, II, 58-9; *Parl. Hist.*, IV, 370-402; *Pepys* (29 Oct., 4, 11, 13, 21 Nov., 3, 12, 14, 17 Dec., '67); *Verney*, II, 305; *Wynn Papers*, 392-3.

[8] *C.S.P.D.* 1667, lv, 359; *H.M.C.* (*Fleming,* 53; *Lindsey,* 370); *Josselin,* 157; *L.J.; Marvell,* II, 56-7; *Orrery,* II, 314; *Parl. Hist.,* IV, 366-9; *Pepys* (10, 13, 14, 16, Oct., '67).

[9] *C.T.B.,* II, Intr.; *Pepys* (24 April, 1 May, '67); *Wynn Papers,* 389.

[10] *Ady* (30 Nov., '67); *C.J.; Feiling, For. Policy,* 252; *Lister,* III, 474; *L.J.; Orrery,* II, 324; *Pepys* (22 Oct., '67).

[11] *C.M.H.,* V, Ch. II; *Feiling, For. Policy,* 227; *Ranke,* III, 464 *et seq.; Temple.*

[12] *Ady* (23 Jan., '68); *Buckingham,* II, 78; *Carte MSS.* xlvi, f. 578; *Feiling, For. Policy,* 231, 371-2. And see *Foreign Entry Book,* 177 (16 Sept., '72).

[13] *Ady* (4, 10 Feb, 5 March, '68); *Arlington,* I, 190 *et seq.; Barbour; Courtenay's Temple,* I, 141 *et seq.; Feiling, For. Policy,* 231-66; *Pepys* (20 Jan., '68); *Ranke,* III, 464-78; *Temple,* II, 41-108, 137-55.

[14] *Burnet,* I, 465 *et seq.; H.M.C. Portland,* III, 306; *Macpherson,* I, 40; *Pepys* (21 Dec., '67; 21, 31 Jan., 23 Nov., '68); *Ranke,* III, 481.

[15] *Ady* (10 Feb., '68); *C.J.; Grey; H.M.C. Rep. 3* (*Northumberland,* 95); *H.M.C.* (*Hastings,* II, 376; *Kenyon,* 81-2; *Portland,* II, 106, 147-9); *L.J.; Marvell,* II, 64-75; *Orrery,* II, 350; *Parl. Hist.,* IV, 404, 408-26; *Pepys* (Feb., *passim,* 5, 10, 11, 17, 18, 30 March, 4, 7, 15, 22, 24, 28, 30 April, 1, 3, 9, 12, 15 May, '68); *Ranke,* III, 482-4; *Tanner, Pepys Corr.,* I, 7; *Arlington,* I, 211.

[16] *Burnet,* I, 474-5; *Commonplace Book of Sir Francis Lucy,* cit. *English Review,* Oct., 1930; *Cunningham,* 58-9; *Flecknoe, Euterpe Revived; Hawkins, Hist. of Music,* IV, 525; *Pepys* (8 Feb., '64; 7 March, 27 July, 5 Oct., '67; 14 Jan., 7, 19, 31 May, '68); *Roscius Anglicanus,* 23-4.

[17] *Ady* (26 Aug., '67; 23 Jan., 4 April, 7 May, '68); *Dalrymple,* II, 12; *Grammont,* II, 30, 154-60; *H.M.C. Rep. 7* (*Verney,* 485); *H.M.C. Fleming,* 46; *Pepys* (20 March, 1, 25, 26 April, '67; 8, 19, 31 May, '68).

[18] *C.T.B.,* II, 310, 316, 375; *Grammont,* II, 78; *Pepys* (14 Jan., 6 April, 8, 31 May, '68); *Steinman,* 112-15, 123-4, 157, 161, 163.

[19] *Ady* (4 April, 7, 14, 24 May, 14 June, 9 Aug., '68); *H.M.C. Buccleuch* (M.H.), I, 421 *et seq.*

[20] For confirmation of this view see *Ranke,* III, 413-500; *Feiling, For. Policy,* Ch. VII, particularly pp. 273-4, 292; the long series of letters—only a part of the whole—between Charles and Minette printed in *Ady's Madame; Dalrymple, E.H.R.,* 43, and the letters from Montagu to Arlington in *H.M.C. Buccleuch* (M.H.), I, 420 *et seq.* See also footnote on page 47.

[21] *Ady* (8 July, 3 Aug., 2 Sept., '68); *Dalrymple,* II, 6, 7, 12, 17 *et seq.; H.M.C. Hodgkin,* 140. For Charles's earlier attempt to procure a French alliance see *Ady* (26 Oct., '62; 16 Feb., 11 May, '63; 23 Aug., 17 Oct., 21 Nov., 15 Dec., '64; 5 Jan., '65).

[22] *Ady* (8 July, 3 Aug., 27 Dec., '68; 6, 24 June, '69); *Barbour,* 158; *Feiling, For. Policy,* 289 *et seq.; Forneron,* 25.

[23] *Ady* (2, 14 Sept., 3 Oct., '68; 20 Jan., '69).

[24] *Ady* (14 Dec., '68); *C.J.,* ix; *H.M.C. Fleming,* 58; *Lauderdale,* II, 170; *Pepys* (11 March, 11, 30 Aug., 17, 18 Sept., 5, 14 Dec., '68; 1 March, '69).

[25] *H.M.C. Fleming,* 63; *Pepys* (4, 25 Nov., 5, 23 Dec., '68; 24, 29, Jan., 14 Feb., 18, 21, April, '69); *Ranke,* III, 489-90.

[26] *Ady* (14, 27 Dec., '68; 20 Jan., 7, 12, 22 March, '69); *Clarke, James II,* I, 440-2; *Feiling, For. Policy,* 292-3; *Forneron,* 45; *H.M.C. Buccleuch* (M.H.), I, 422 *et seq.; Macpherson,* I, 50; *Mignet,* III, 73-4; *Ranke,* III, 496-7.

[27] *Dalrymple,* I, 44-52; *Feiling, For. Policy,* 295, 299; *H.M.C. Buccleuch* (M.H.), I, 421 *et seq.,* 430-5; *Pepys* (28 April, 69); *Ady* (20 Jan., '69).

[28] *Ady* (22 March, 25 April, 6 June, '69).

[29] *Ady* (7 March, 6 June, '69); *Camden Misc.*, V; *Carte, Ormonde*, Bk. VII, par. 13 *et seq.*; *Clarke, James II*, I, 443; *H.M.C. (Egmont*, II, 21; *Fleming*, 68; *Hastings*, II, 377; *Montagu of Beaulieu*, 169); *Lauderdale* II, 139, 140-1, 151, 166, 168, 171, 174; *Pepys* (17 Feb., 19 May, '69); *Ranke*, III, 507-9.

[30] *Ady* (6, 7 June, '69); *Arlington*; *Dalrymple*, I, 29, 34, 59-65; *Feiling, For. Policy*, 284-9, 303-4; *Forneron*, 51-3; *Khan*; *Ranke*, III, 492-3.

[31] *Barbour*, 163-4; *C.J.*; *C.T.B.* 1667-8, Intr.; *H.M.C. (Kenyon*, 83; *Portland*, III, 312); *Lauderdale*, II, 146; *Marvell*, II, 82-94; *Parl. Hist.*, IV, 428-31; *Pepys* (22 Oct., '67); *Ranke*, III, 506.

[32] *C.T.B.*, II, Intr., lxix-lxxxvi, 165, 259; *H.M.C. Rep. 8 (H. of Lords*, 128-33); *H.M.C. (Fleming*, 68; *Montagu of Beaulieu*, 177); *Marvell*, II, 94, 300; *Parl. Hist.*, IV, 441-7; *Wynn Papers*, 397.

[33] *Ady* (6 May, 7 June, '69); *Burnet*, I, 469-74, 492-3; *Clarke, James II*, I, 437-9; *H.M.C. Rep. 2 (Mount Edgcumbe*, 21); *Rep. 6 (Ingilby*, 365); *Rep. 7 (Frere*, 532); *H.M.C. (Buccleuch (M.H.)*, I, 425; *Fleming*, 64; *Kenyon*, 84; *Rutland*, II, 10, 14 *et seq.*; IV, 547; *Wombwell*, 128, 133-4); *House of Lyme*, 243; *Lauderdale*, II, 169-70; *Ludlow*, II, 503; *Macpherson*, I, 49; *Marvell*, II, 102, 301-3; *Parl. Hist.*, IV, 447-50; *Pepys* (27 July, '67; 9, 19 May, '68; 11, 19, 26 May, '69); *Ranke*, III, 509.

[34] *Ady*, 301-31; *Forneron*, 42; *H.M.C. (Buccleuch (M.H.)*, I, 451 *et seq.*; *Egmont*, II, 21; *Wombwell*, 135); *Lauderdale*, II, 145, 168-9.

[35] *Ady*, 331-55; *Barbour*, 166-70; *Clarke, James II*, I, 448-51; *Dalrymple*, II, 44-58; *Feiling, For. Policy*, 305-9; *H.M.C. (Egmont*, II, 22; *Fleming*, 70; *Hastings*, II, 319); *Lingard*, IX, 503-9; *Ranke*, III, 501-2; *Verney*, II, 297; *Arlington*, I, 438-47.

CHAPTER VIII

THE RETURN OF ODYSSEUS

[1] *Ady*, 359 *et seq.*; *Dalrymple*, II, 73; *Forneron*, 59; *H.M.C. Rep. 6 (Ingilby*, 367); *H.M.C. (Buccleuch (M.H.)*, I, 447; *Wombwell*, 150-1); *Ranke*, III, 502; *Savile*, 25.

[2] *Barbour*, 169-70, 173-4; *Dalrymple*, II, 69-72, 82-94, 98-9; *Feiling, For. Policy*; *H.M.C. Rep. 7 (Verney*, 488); *H.M.C. (Buccleuch (M.H.)*, I, 483 *et seq.*; *Fleming*, 71; *Laing*, I, 377); *Ranke*, III, 503, 511, 519.

[3] *Evelyn* (28 Aug., '70); *H.M.C. Rep. 5 (Maxwell Witham*, 652); *Rep. 6 (Ingilby*, 367); *H.M.C. (Hastings*, II, 321; *Rutland*, II, 19; *Wombwell*, 159); *Lauderdale*, II, 201-2.

[4] *Evelyn* (22 July, '70; 17 Dec., '84); *H.M.C. Rep. 6 (Graham*, 338); *Rep. 7 (Verney*, 488); *H.M.C. (Finch*, I, 266, 290; *Fleming*, 56; *Kenyon*, 84; *Leeds*,

9; *Portland*, II, 265; III, 314; *Russell-Astley*, 30; *Rutland*, II, 15); *Josselin*, 159; *Jusserand*, 162; *Pepys* (8 March, '69); *Savile*, 115; *Verney*, II, 316.

[5] *Barbour*, 170; *Dalrymple*, II, 78-82; *Evelyn* (28 Aug., '70); *H.M.C.* (*Fleming*, 72; *Hastings*, II, 328); *Marvell*, II, 107 *et seq.*, 304-5; *Parl. Hist.*, IV, 456-9; *Ranke*, III, 511-12.

[6] *Burnet Supplement*, 192; *Dalrymple*, II, 95-6; *Evelyn* (4 Nov., '70); *H.M.C.* (*Fleming*, 73-5; *Hastings*, II, 503-4); *Reresby* (Jan., '71); *Foreign Entry Book*, 176 (4 April, '69).

[7] *Evelyn* (4 Nov., '70); *Forneron*, 62-3; *Hatton*, I, 76-7; *H.M.C.* (*Buccleuch* (*M.H.*), I, 487; *Rutland*, II, 22).

[8] *Barbour*, 171; *C.J.*; *Dalrymple*, II, 92; *H.M.C.* (*Fleming*, 73; *Hastings*, II, 324; *Portland*, III, 318); *Parl. Hist.*, IV, 460; *Ranke*, III, 515.

[9] *Dalrymple*, II, 94, 100-1; *Feiling, For. Policy*, 268, 312; *Ranke*, III, 518.

[10] *Barbour*, 175-6, 178-9; *Feiling, For. Policy*, 314; *H.M.C. Egmont*, II, 25; *Josselin*, 162; *Marvell*, II, 117 *et seq.*; *Parl. Hist.*, IV, 473-6, 477-96; *Ranke*, III, 513-14; *Wynn Papers*, 401.

[11] *Evelyn* (1 March, '71); *H.M.C. Rep. 4* (*Rogers*, 405); *H.M.C.* (*Egmont*, II, 25; *Fleming*, 73-6; *Kenyon*, 87-8; *Portland*, III, 322); *Marvell*, I, 168-9; II, 122 *et seq.*, 307-8; *Parl. Hist.*, IV, 460-70.

[12] *Ailesbury*, 2; *C.S.P.D.* 1671, 335, 350; *Evelyn* (18 Aug., '73); *Dalrymple*, II, 97, 108; *North, Lives*, I, 114; *Ranke*, III, 515-22.

[13] *Burnet*, I, 547-8; *C.S.P.D.* 1671, 225, 384-5, 391-2, 395, 426, 433, 437, 487; *Echard*, 876-8; *Evelyn* (10 May, '71); *Feiling, For. Policy*, 316-18, 329; *Hatton*, I, 63, 66-8; *H.M.C. Rep. 2* (*Mount Edgcumbe*, 21-2); *Rep. 6* (*Ingilby*, 369-70); *Rep. 7* (*Verney*, 464); *Rep. 9* (*Alfred Morrison*, 447); *H.M.C. Fleming*, 78, 81-3; *Marvell*, II, 311; *Temple*, II, 248-9; *Wynn Papers*, 403.

[14] *Barbour*, 181-2; *C.S.P.D.* 1671, 488, 517; *Echard*, 876; *Evelyn* (Oct., '71); *Forneron*, 64-5, 68, 71; *Hatton*, I, 70; *H.M.C. Rep. 6* (*Ingilby*, 370); *Rep. 7* (*Verney*, 489); *H.M.C.* (*Fleming*, 84-5; *Kenyon*, 89).

[15] *C.S.P.D.* 1671-2, 127, 128, 348, 355, 364; *Dalrymple*, II, 105-7; *Feiling, For. Policy*, 325-9, 330; *Hatton*, I, 70, 72; *H.M.C.* (*Buccleuch* (*M.H.*), I, 501-4; *Hastings*, II, 379; *Portland*, III, 324); *Temple*, II, 250.

[16] *C.T.B.*, III, Pt. I., Intr.; *H.M.C. Rep. 6* (*Ingilby*, 368-9).

[17] For a careful study of the Stop of the Exchequer, or Suspension, as it more properly should be called, see *C.T.B.*, III, Pt. I, Intr., i-xiii, xxxi-xxxv, xlii-lxvii; *History*, n.s., 14, 33-7, for a brilliant article by Dr. Andrew Browning. See also *Arlington*, II, 349; *Clarke, James II*, I, 455; *Examen*, 37; *H.M.C.* (*Buccleuch* (*M.H.*), I, 512; *Fitzherbert*, 6; *Lyttleton-Annesley*, 270); *Hatton*, I, 74, 77. For the immediate responsibility in Council for the stop, see *Christie*, II, 56-71.

[18] *C.S.P.D.* 1671-2, 97, 191; *C.T.B.*, III, I, lxiii; *Feiling, For. Policy*, 330; *H.M.C. Rep. 7* (*Verney*, 490); *H.M.C. Fleming*, 87.

[19] *Arlington*, II, 335; *Clarke, James II*, I, 456-7; *C.S.P.D.* 1671-2, 194, 197-214, 218, 236, 243; *Evelyn* (March, '72); *Feiling, For. Policy*, 330, 339-44; *Hatton*, I, 78, 82, 84; *H.M.C. Rep. 8* (*Ashburnham*, 6-7); *H.M.C.* (*Fleming*, 87 *et seq.*; *Kenyon*, 88); *Ranke*, III, 524-5.

[20] *Baxterianæ*; *Clarke, James II*, I, 455; *Colbert's Memoir* (7 June, '71), printed in *Christie*, II, App., xii *et seq.*; *C.S.P.D.* 1671, 452, 562-3, 568; 1671-2, 136, 141, 183, 203, 235, 264, 302, 311, 315, 608, 609; *Evelyn* (4 April, '72); *H.M.C. Rep. 7* (*Verney*, 490); *H.M.C.* (*Fleming*, 90; *Somerset*, 103); *Josselin*, 162; *Ranke*, III, 522-3, 525-7; *Reresby* (March, '72).

21 Clarke, James II, I, 457-78, 480; Evelyn (May, '72); Hatton, I, 84-90; H.M.C. Rep. 2 (Mount Edgcumbe, 22); Rep. 6 (Leconfield, 318); Rep. 7 (Verney, 490); H.M.C. (Dartmouth, III, 6, 13-23; Fleming, 92-4; Hastings, II, 157, 159; Kenyon, 92; Ormonde, III, 450; Rutland, II, 24-5); Ranke, III, 528; Verney, II, 355. For King's activity see Foreign Entry Book, 176 (14 Jan., 4, 11, 13, 25 Feb., 3, 4, 14, 15, 31 March, 8, 9 April, 22 June, '72); 177 (5, 6, 8, 9, 11, 22, 23, 25 March, 1, 13, 18, 22, 28 April, 2, 3, 8, 9, 13, 15, 18, 19, 23, 29, 30—morning and afternoon—31 May et seq., '72).

22 Barbour, 188 et seq.; Feiling, For. Policy, 346-8; Hatton, I, 93-5; H.M.C. (Hastings, II, 379; Lindsey, 375; Portland, III, 326; Rutland, II, 25) Josselin, 163; Marvell, II, 311-12; Mignet, IV, 1-54; Ranke, III, 528-30.

23 Barbour, 188; Feiling, For. Policy, 349.

24 Barbour, 206-13; Christie, II, 137-41; C.J.; Dalrymple, II, 112-16; Essex, 161; Examen, 40; Feiling, Tory Party, 150; H.M.C. Rep. 7 (Verney, 490); Rep. 9 (H. of Lords, 25; Pole-Gell, 398); H.M.C. (Braye, 181; Fleming, 99; Hastings, II, 161; Portland, III, 334-6) House of Lyme, 252; L.J.; Parl. Hist., IV, 501-85; Ranke, III, 531-41.

25 Christie, II, 141 et seq.; Clarke, James II, I, 483-4; C.S.P.D. 1673, 380, 394; Dalrymple, II, 119; Hatton, I, 107-12; H.M.C. Rep. 4 (Rogers, 406); Rep 7 (Verney, 490); H.M.C (Fleming, 100-1; Hastings, II, 163; Portland, III, 336); Williamson, I, 2, 4, 6-7, 10, 14, 21, 24, 29, 34, 43-4, 47-51, 55-9, 62-4, 68.

26 Barbour, 211-13; Burnet, II, 5; C.S.P.D. 1673, 287, 293, 352, 353; Essex, I, 121; Evelyn (1 June, '73); Feiling, For. Policy, 353-4; History, n.s., 14, 30-1; H.M.C. Rep. 7 (Verney, 491); H.M.C. (Braye, 182; Dartmouth, I, 20-4; III, 9-13, 27-33; Fleming, 103; Hamilton, 144; Ormonde, III, 331; Stirling Maxwell, 80); House of Lyme, 255-8; Marvell, I, 197; Parl. Hist., IV, 593; Ranke, III, 545-7; Williamson, I, 24, 26-8, 36-44, 46-9, 52-4, 60-1, 65-85, 93-154, 158-95; II, 1-4, 9-20; Hatton, I, 104-7, 113-15.

27 C.S.P.D. 1673, 458-9; H.M.C. Rep. 2 (Spencer, 22); Rep. 7 (Verney, 491); H.M.C. (Dartmouth, III, 9; Fleming, 97, 102; Portland, III, 337); Williamson, I, 91-3, 106-7, 110, 118-20, 127, 130, 133, 137, 140, 143, 146, 148-9, 154, 156, 161, 177; II, 34-5.

28 Dalrymple, II, 102, 109; Examen, 40-1; Williamson, II, 21-2, 24, 29, 34-6, 39, 44-5.

29 Clarke, James II, I, 485; C.S.P.D. 1673, 372-3, 585, 589, 601; Essex, I, 130, 132; Feiling, For. Policy, 355; H.M.C. (Fleming, 103-6; Portland, III, 341); House of Lyme, 259-60; Josselin, 164; Macpherson, I, 70, 72; Parl. Hist., IV, 585; Ranke, III, 561-2; Williamson, I, 27, 36, 42, 49-53.

30 C.S.P.D. 1673, 99; Feiling, Tory Party, 152; Hatton, I, 118; H.M.C. Rep. 7 (Verney, 491); H.M.C. (Marchmont, 111; Portland, III, 341); Parl. Hist., IV, 586-608; Ranke, III, 546-8; Williamson, II, 56-60, 69-71.

31 Evelyn (25 July, 8 Aug., '73); Lauderdale, III, 9; Williamson, II, 40, 42, 46, 50.

CHAPTER IX

THE FAITHFUL COMMONS

[1] *Barbour*, 220; *Christie*, II, 155; *Hatton*, I, 119; *H.M.C. Portland*, III, 341 *et seq.*; *Lauderdale*, III, 2; *Parl. Hist.*, IV, 609-10; *Ranke*, III, 549-52; *Williamson*, II, 61, 67, 72, 78, 105.

[2] *Barbour*, 221; *Burnet*, II, 37; *Christie*, II, 185; *C.T.B.*, IV, xxxviii-xl, lxvi; *Essex*, I, 140, 153; *H.M.C. Portland*, III, 342; *Mignet*, IV, 239 *et seq.*; *Ranke*, III, 557; *Williamson*, II, 23-4, 82, 101, 104; *Wynn Papers*, 408.

[3] *Christie*, II, 149, note; *Essex*, I, 140; *Feiling, Tory Party*, 135-54; *H.M.C. Lindsey*, 377; *Williamson*, I, 61, 77, 92.

[4] *Essex*, I, 150; *H.M.C. Fleming*, 106; *Lauderdale*, III, 5 *et seq.*; *Williamson*, II, 73, 77, 85.

[5] *Barbour*, 225 *et seq.*; *Christie*, II, 187-9; *C.J.*; *Essex*, I, 153-4, 158, 161, 167; *H.M.C. (Hodgkin*, 136; *Portland*, III, 343-5); *L.J.*; *Parl. Hist.*, IV, 611-57; *Williamson*, II, 105-32; *Wynn Papers*, 408-9.

[6] *C.S.P.D.* 1673-5, 112, 116, 125, 139, 140, 144-5; *Dalrymple*, II, 132; *Feiling, For. Policy*, 362-5; *H.M.C. (Fleming*, 106-7; *Hodgkin*, 136; *Kenyon*, 98-9; *Ormonde*, III, 453; *Portland*, III, 343 *et seq.*); *Josselin*, 165; *Mignet*, IV, 264-73; *Parl. Hist.*, IV, 660, 665-6; *Temple*, I, 376-8; II, 288-95; *Williamson*, II, 133-7; *Instructions aux Ambassadeurs*, II, 134-8.

[7] *Christie*, II, 195; *C.J.*; *Clarke, James II*, I, 489-90; *Examen*, 61; *H.M.C. Fleming*, 106-7; *Lauderdale*, III, 22; *L.J.*; *Macpherson*, I, 77, 81; *Parl. Hist.*, IV, 666; *Williamson*, I, 138-58.

[8] *Bulstrode*, 424; *Burnet*, I, 449; *H.M.C. Ormonde*, III, 444; *Jusserand*, 98, 142; *North, Lives*, I, 81; III, 94, 100-1, 133; *Ranke*, IV, 23-4.

[9] *C.T.B.*, IV, xv-xvii *et seq.*; *Essex*, I, 181, 189, 199, 228.

[10] *C.T.B.*, IV, xiv, xviii-xix, xxxvi, xl, 540; *Essex*, I, 260; *Examen*, 37; *H.M.C. Rep. 6 (Ingilby)*, 374; *H.M.C. (Fleming*, 110, 125; *Hamilton*, 146).

[11] *Cunningham*, 125; *Essex*, I, 212, 265; *Forneron*, 108-10, 114, 178; *H.M.C. Rep. 3 (Hopkinson*, 266); *Rep. 6 (Raffles*, 473); *Rep. 7 (Verney*, 492); *Rep. 9 (Alfred Morrison*, 450, 456, 459); *H.M.C. (Hastings*, II, 165; *Leeds*, 9); *Hatton*, I, 80, 83; *Marvell*, II, 314; *Prideaux*, 21; *Secret Services*, 11; *Sévigné*, IV (11 Sept., '75); *Steinman*, 157, 161.

[12] *C.T.B.*, IV, xxxvi-xlvi, liii; *Evelyn* (10 Sept., '75; 4 Oct., '83); *H.M.C. Rep. 6 (Ingilby*, 367; *Raffles*, 473); *Rep. 7 (Verney*, 465-6); *H.M.C. (Portland*, II, 151; III, 353, 357; *Russell-Astley*, 50); *Marvell*, I, 181-9; II, 314-16; *Pepys* (26 April, '67); *Prideaux*, 55; *Williamson*, I, 109-10; II, 62. See also *H.M.C. Fitzherbert*, 7.

[13] *C.S.P.D.* 1673-5, 250, 265, 342; *Essex*, I, 258-60; *Evelyn* (21 Aug., '74); *H.M.C. (Fleming*, 112-13; *Hastings*, II, 165); *Mignet*, IV, 320; *Reresby* (11 May, '77).

[14] *Ailesbury*, 13; *Essex*, I, 195, 236-7, 248, 258, 263, 266-9, 280, 287; II, 74-5; *Lauderdale*, III, passim; *Macpherson*, I, 74; *Marvell*, II, 321; *North (Examen*, 78-9; *Lives*, I, 232).

15 *Add. MSS.* 25124, f. 25-9; *Burnet*, II, 79; *Christie*, II, 200-2; *Essex*, I, 294; *H.M.C. Rep.* 6 (*Ingilby*, 364); *Mignet*, IV, 330 *et seq.*; *Ranke*, IV, 7. See *E.H.R.*, 45, p. 58.

16 *C.S.P.D.* 1675-6, 19, 20, 28, 29, 34-5; *Essex*, I, 317-18; *Feiling, Tory Party*, 158; *H.M.C. Sneyd*, 288; *L.J.*; *Marvell*, II, 140; *Parl. Hist.*, IV, 672-8.

17 *Clarke, James II*, I, 499; *C.S.P.D.* 1673-5, 522; *Essex*, I, 302; II, 4, 6-8, 10; *Feiling, Tory Party*, 159-60; *Grey*, III, 261 *et seq.*; *H.M.C. Rep.* 7 (*Verney*, 465); *H.M.C.* (*Ailesbury*, 176; *Buccleuch* (M.H.), I, 321; *Fleming*, 114, 116; *Kenyon*, 100; *Laing*, I, 393; *Portland*, III, 348-50); *House of Lyme*, 272; *Parl. Hist.*, IV, 686-714; *Verney*, II, 305; *Marvell*, II, 142 *et seq.*, 319-20.

18 *Burnet*, I, 493; II, 81-5; *Christie*, II, 205-9; *C.J.*; *Essex*, II, 16, 23 *et seq.*; *Examen*, 61-4; *H.M.C. Rep.* 7 (*Verney*, 492); *Rep.* 9 (*H. of Lords*, 56-7); *H.M.C.* (*Beaufort*, 65; *Fleming*, 119-20; *Portland*, III, 352-3); *L.J.*; *Marvell*, II, 150-7, 319; *Parl. Hist.*, IV, 714-40; *Ranke*, IV, 9.

19 *C.S.P.D.* 1675-6, 184-90, 195-9; *Essex*, II, 33; *H.M.C. Laing*, I, 405.

20 *Burnet*, II, 101-2; *Christie*, II, 210; *C.S.P.D.* 1675-6, 203, 240, 272; *Essex*, II, 32; *H.M.C.* (*Fitzherbert*, 49 *et seq.*; *Lindsey*, 377; *Rutland*, II, 27; *Westmorland*, 37); *Mignet*, IV, 358-73; *Ranke*, IV, 13; *Savile*, 40; *State Poems* (*The Chequers Inn*).

21 *Burnet*, II, 86 *et seq.*; *Christie*, II, 209; *C.S.P.D.* 1675-6, 414; *Examen*, 70; *Feiling, Tory Party*, 161-2; *H.M.C.* (*Hastings*, II, 383; *Laing*, I, 408; *Kenyon*, 101); *L.J.*; *Marvell*, II, 159-71; *Parl. Hist.*, IV, 740-57, 764-803; *Ranke*, IV, 14, 18.

22 *C.S.P.D.* 1675-6, 473, 503, 505, 559-61, 562-3, 574, 576, 590; *H.M.C.* (*Fleming*, 124-5; *Laing*, I, 409; *Portland*, III, 353); *North, Lives*, I, 197-9; *Ranke*, IV, 25; *Marvell*, I, 191-6; *Wood, Life and Times*, II, 330.

23 *C.T.B.*, IV, vii-xv; V, Pt. I, ix, xxxvi, xxxix, xl-xli, 116; *Halifax*, 202; *H.M.C. Rep.* 7 (*Verney*, 493); *H.M.C.* (*Fleming*, 124; *Ormonde, o.s.*, I, 22); *Mignet*, IV, 375; *Newdegate*, 43; *Pepys* (3 April, '63); *Verney*, II, 373.

24 *Dalrymple*, II, 123, 128-31; *Forneron*, 122, 131, 132, 134, 136, 143; *H.M.C. Rutland*, II, 28-9; *Instructions aux Ambassadeurs*, II, 161-4, 197-200; *Mignet*, IV, 377-86; *Ranke*, IV, 21, 24-5.

25 *C.S.P.D.* 1675-6, 532; 1676-7, 25; *Essex*, II, 50-1, 60; *Forneron*, 21, 132, 147-9; 151; *Hatton*, I, 122-7; *H.M.C. Rutland*, II, 29; *Russell*, I, 24.

26 *C.S.P.D.* 1676-7, 57, 65, 70, 128, 131, 161, 165, 185, 200, 202, 219; *Essex*, II, 43, 50, 52-8, 63-5, 69-71, 83; *Hatton*, I, 132-3; *H.M.C. Rep.* 6 (*Ingilby*, 375); *Rep.* 7 (*Verney*, 467); *H.M.C.* (*Fleming*, 128; *Ormonde*, IV, 17-20; *Rutland*, II, 29); *North, Lives*, I, 191; *Singer*, I, 1-2.

27 *Dalrymple*, II, 128-31; *Hatton*, I, 129-30.

28 *Ailesbury*, 94; *H.M.C. Rep.* 7 (*Verney*, 467); *H.M.C. Rutland*, II, 31-2; *Josselin*, 166; *Spectator*, No. 462. See also *H.M.C. Ormonde*, III, 448; " *Loyal Protestant Intelligence* " (24 Nov., '81).

29 *C.S.P.D.* 1675-6, 4, 77, 166, 400; *Dalrymple*, II, 133; *Essex*, II, 80; *H.M.C. Rutland*, 31-2; *Mignet*, IV, 429 *et seq.*; *Prideaux*, 54; *Ranke*, IV, 20, 24-5; *Singer*, I, 2.

30 *C.S.P.D.* 1676-7, 459; *Essex*, II, 86, 92-4; *H.M.C.* (*Lindsey*, 379; *Rutland*, II, 33); *Mignet*, IV, 434.

31 *Reresby* (Feb., '77). For an illustration of the King's policy of leaving all to the laws, see *H.M.C. Fleming*, 140.

32 *Christie*, II, 226-7, 230-5; *Clarke, James II*, I, 404-7; *C.S.P.D.* 1676-7, 555, 565; *Echard*, 925-8; *Essex*, II, 100; *Examen*, 65-70; *Feiling, Tory Party*, 166;

H.M.C. Rep. 7 (Verney, 468); Rep. 9 (H. of Lords, 69-79); H.M.C. (Fleming, 132-3; Ormonde, IV, 20; Rutland, II, 33-40); L.J.; Marvell, II, 172-3; Parl. Hist., IV, 807-25; Ranke, IV, 27-9.

[33] *C.T.B., V, Pt. I, xlvii-li; Feiling, Tory Party, 166; Grey, IV, 118; H.M.C. Fleming, 134, 138; Marvell, II, 172 et seq.; Parl. Hist., IV, 825-42; Ranke, IV, 29-30; Reresby (10 Feb., 18 March, '77).*

[34] *C.J.; Dalrymple, II, 135; Essex, II, 110-11, 118, 141 et seq.; Feiling, Tory Party, 166-7; Forneron, 187; H.M.C. Rep. 7 (Verney, 469); H.M.C. (Egmont, II, 58; Fleming, 136; Lindsey, 381 et seq.; Portland, III, 354-5; Rutland, II, 40); Instructions aux Ambassadeurs, II, 213, 220; L.J.; Marvell, II, 190-8; Mignet, IV, 438 et seq.; Parl. Hist., IV, 859-91; Ranke, IV, 31-2; Reresby (29 March, 12, 19 April, 21, 28 May, '77).*

CHAPTER X

THE PATRIOT KING

[1] *Dalrymple, II, 135; Danby, 1-9; Mignet, IV, 477.*

[2] *Burnet, II, 129 (Dartmouth note); C.S.P.D. 1677-8, 691; Danby, 132 et seq.; H.M.C. Kenyon, 99; Marvell, II, 139; Ranke, IV, 32-8; Savile, 59.*

[3] *Dalrymple, II, 138-41; Danby, 13 et seq.; H.M.C. Rep. 9 (Alfred Morrison, 451-2); Mignet, IV, 477-501.*

[4] *C.S.P.D. 1677-8, 296-8, 303, 307, 311, 313-4, 316; H.M.C. Rep. 7 (Verney, 469, 494).*

[5] *Burnet, II, 128; Clarke, James II, I, 508-10; C.S.P.D. 1677-8, 378, 390, 401, 422, 427, 438, 452, 454; Hatton, I, 151-3; H.M.C. Rep. 6 (Ingilby, 383-4); Rep. 7 (Verney, 494); H.M.C. (Lindsey, 387; Money-Kyrle (30 Oct., '77); Ormonde, IV, 48, 53, 58, 376-81); Josselin, 172; Lake (21, 22, 23, 24 Oct., '77); Newdegate, 54-6; Temple, I, 454; II, 459; Verney, II, 324.*

[6] *C.S.P.D. 1677-8, 445; Hatton I, 154; H.M.C. Bath, II, 158-9; Lake (4, 5, 16, 19 Nov., '77); Ranke, IV, 38.*

[7] *Christie, II, 255; Dalrymple, II, 153-5; Danby, 160-3; H.M.C. Rep. 9 (Alfred Morrison, 453); H.M.C. (Lindsey, 389; Ormonde, IV, 71, 374, 385-90); Josselin, 172; Ranke, IV, 39-41.*

[8] *C.S.P.D. 1677-8, 526, 562, 565; Dalrymple, II, 155, 175; Danby, 38 et seq., 170 et seq.; Forneron, 197; H.M.C. Rep. 9 (Alfred Morrison, 453-4); H.M.C. (Bath, II, 160; Buccleuch (M.H.), I, 523-4; Egmont, II, 69; Hodgkin, 186-7, 189-92; Ormonde, IV, 79, 83, 87-90, 390-5; Rutland, II, 43); Mignet, IV, 519-30; Parl. Hist., IV, 896; Ranke, IV, 40.*

[9] *C.S.P.D. 1677-8, 412; H.M.C. Rep. 6 (Ingilby, 384-5); Rep. 9 (Alfred Morrison, 452); H.M.C. (Hamilton, 156-7; Ormonde, IV, 61-3, 69, 72-6, 386; Portland, II, 37, 39-40, 44-5; III, 354; Rutland, II, 43); Lauderdale, III, 88-103; Hatton, I, 158.*

[10] *Cunningham, 82; Hatton, I, 157; H.M.C. Rep. 7 (Verney, 469); H.M.C. (Buccleuch (M.H.), I, 323-4; Laing, I, 405; Lindsey, 387; Ormonde, IV, 105-6, 110, 376, 401).*

11 *Dugdale, St. Paul's; H.M.C.* (Fleming, 59, 141; *Ormonde,* IV, 83, 386-7, 390-1); *Hatton,* I, 156-7; *Lake* (30 Dec., '77); *Marvell,* II, 202; *North, Lives,* III, 122.

12 *C.S.P.D.* 1678, 121-3; *Dalrymple,* II, 157-8, 160, 167, 178-9; *Danby,* 53-4, 59-60; *E.H.R.,* 39, p. 358; *Feiling, Tory Party,* 170-1; *Forneron,* 207; *H.M.C.* (*Lindsey,* 389, 391; *Ormonde,* IV, 407-8); *Josselin,* 173; *Mignet,* IV, 533 *et seq.; Parl. Hist.,* IV, 896-9; *Ranke,* IV, 40, 44-57; *Reresby* (7 Jan., '78); *Singer,* I, 6-7.

13 *C.T.B.,* V, Pt. I, lii; *Dalrymple,* II, 179, 182, 189-90; *Feiling, Tory Party,* 168, 171; *H.M.C.* (*Ormonde,* I, *o.s.,* 23; IV, 131, 396-410, 412-14; *Portland,* III, 358; *Rutland,* II, 46-8); *Marvell,* II, 205 *et seq.; Parl. Hist.,* IV, 940-5; *Ranke,* IV, 42; *Reresby* (Feb., March, '78); *Singer,* I, 5.

14 *E.H.R.,* 39, p. 364; *Burnet Supplement,* 193; *C.S.P.D.* 1678, 2, 6, 10, 12, 78-9, 83, 118-19, 136, 516-17, 592; *Dalrymple,* II, 177, 180, 182, 189, 190; *Danby,* 189, 210, 217; *H.M.C. Rep. 4 (Bath,* 232); *Rep. 9 (Alfred Morrison,* 454-5); *H.M.C. Egmont,* II, 69; *Ormonde,* IV, 35, 125, 128, 136-7, 140, 407-10, 415, 422; *Ranke,* IV, 42; *Singer,* I, 12-13.

15 *C.S.P.D.* 1678, 98, 101; *C.T.B.,* V, Pt. I, lii-liii; *Dalrymple,* II, 165, 185; *H M.C.* (*Hodgkin,* 194: *Ormonde,* IV, 418-20); *Parl. Hist.,* IV, 951-61; *Reresby* (21 April, '78); *Add. MSS.* 25124, f. 139.

16 *Ailesbury,* 94; *C.S.P.D.* 1678, 61, 67, 91; *Danby,* 70 *et seq.; H.M.C.* (*Buccleuch* (M.H.), I, 524-5; *Hodgkin,* 194-5; *Ormonde,* IV, 139, 418; *Rutland,* II, 49); *Lauderdale,* III, 118 *et seq.; Mignet,* IV, 536 *et seq.; Ranke,* IV, 49; *Add. MSS.* 25124, f. 136.

17 *Burnet,* II, 150; *C.J.; C.S.P.D.* 1678, 2, 8, 26, 28, 53-4, 153-4, 158-9, 161, 168, 172-3; *Dalrymple,* II, 210; *Fountainhall, Chron. Notes,* 46-7; *Hatton,* I, 160; *H.M.C.* (*Bath,* II, 161, 164; *Fleming,* 145); *Lauderdale,* III (April, May, '78); *L.J.; Marvell,* II, 222-5; *Parl. Hist.,* IV, 961-77; *Reresby* (21 April, May, '78); *Singer,* I, 16-17.

18 *C.S.P.D.* 1678, 177-8, 182, 187; *Dalrymple,* II, 191-7, 204, 207, 209-12; *E.H.R.,* 39 (*Grose,* 532); *Lauderdale,* III (May, '78); *Mignet,* IV, 572-4, 578; *Ranke,* IV, 50.

19 *C.J.; C.S.P.D.* 1678, 187, 198, 204, 212-13, 224; *C.T.B.,* V, Pt. I, lxxix; *Dalrymple,* II, 214; *Feiling, Tory Party,* 173; *Grey,* V, 276 *et seq.; H.M.C.* (*Beaufort,* 69; *Ormonde,* IV, 144, 151, 425-38; *Portland,* III, 360; *Rutland,* II, 51); *Hatton,* I, 165; *L.J.; Marvell,* II, 225-35; *Mignet,* IV, 597 *et seq.; Parl. Hist.,* IV, 977-85, 994-1000; *Ranke,* IV, 50; *Reresby* (4 June, '78).

20 *Burnet,* II, 5; *C.S.P.D.* 1678, 237, 260; *C.T.B.,* V, Pt. I, lxi; *Dalrymple,* II, 221; *Evelyn* (21 Aug., '74); *Growth of Knavery; H.M.C. Rep. 2* (*Mount Edgcumbe,* 21); *Rep. 5* (*Sutherland,* 203); *Rep. 6* (*Ingilby,* 367); *H.M.C.* (*Bath,* II, 164, 166; *Egmont,* II, 71-2; *Fleming,* 45, 63, 98; *Hodgkin,* 138-9; *Montagu of Beaulieu,* 169; *Ormonde,* IV, 152, 155, 158-61, 423, 439 *et seq.; Portland,* III, 320; *Rutland,* II, 51); *Marvell, Growth of Popery; Newdegate,* 251-2; *Parl. Hist.,* IV, 1004; *Pepys* (4 July, '63); *Ranke,* IV, 50-1; *Verney,* II, 327-8; *Hatton,* I, 111, 128.

21 *C.J.; Courtenay,* II, 412-19; *C.S.P.D.* 1678, 244, 247, 253, 267, 271, 277, 302, 328; *C.T.B.,* V, Pt. I, lxii; *Dalrymple,* II, 222-35; *Danby,* 226 *et seq.; H.M.C. Rep. 7* (*Verney,* 471, 495); *H.M.C.* (*Beaufort,* 70; *Fitzherbert,* 9; *Ormonde,* IV, 167, 172-81, 193 *et seq.,* 444 *et seq.; Portland,* III, 360); *L.J.; Marvell,* II, 235; *Parl. Hist.,* IV, 1004-6; *Ranke,* IV, 51-5; *Savile,* 71; *Singer,* I, 21; *Temple,* II, 463 *et seq.*

CHAPTER XI

THE POPISH TERROR

[1] *Dalrymple*, II, 241; *Evelyn* (25 Aug., '78); *H.M.C.* (*Fitzherbert*, 9-10; *Fleming*, 147-8; *Hodgkin*, 66; *Lindsey*, 395; *Ormonde*, IV, 181, 197, 448; *Rutland*, II, 53); *Savile*, 69-70, 73. See also *Blencowe*, II, 30-1, 48.

[2] *C.S.P.D.* 1678, xi, 346, 353-6, 370, 416, 428; *H.M.C. Ormonde*, IV, 144, 147-8, 201, 206; *Essex*, II, 95; *Marvell*, II, 331.

[3] *Ailesbury*, 27; *Evelyn* (4 April, '72; 25 Aug., '78); *H.M.C.* (*Dartmouth*, III, 24-5; *Portland*, III, 343); *Shakerley MSS.*, 1660-78, *passim*.

[4] *Burnet*, II, 61; *Clarke, James II*, I, 513-20; *C.S.P.D.* 1678, 425-8, 431-3, 434; *Examen*, 157, 225; *First Whig*, 28-35; *Hatton*, I, 139; *H.M.C.* (*Fleming*, 147-8; *House of Lords*, 1 et seq., 97-9; *Kenyon*, 107; *Ormonde*, IV, 181-4, 207-8, 212, 214-17, 221-2, 454-7); *Impartial Case of the Earl of Danby*; *L.J.*; *Pollock, Popish Plot*, 12; *Ranke*, IV, 59-60; *State Trials*.

[5] *Burnet*, II, 161-5; *C.S.P.D.* 1678, 448, 451, 453, 462, 466, 472; *First Whig*, 35; *H.M.C. Rep.* 5 (*Pine-Coffin*, 371); *Rep.* 6 (*Ingilby*, 388); *Rep.* 7 (*Verney*, 471, 494); *H.M.C.* (*Fleming*, 148-50; *Hodgkin*, 315-16; *House of Lords*, 2-15, 46-8; *Ormonde*, IV, 219, 457-63; *Portland*, II, 154); *Luttrell* (*Oct.*, '78); *Muddiman*, 209; *North* (*Examen*, 177, 196-202; *Lives*, I, 69-70, 186); *Parl. Hist.*, IV, App. No. viii; *Reresby* (10 Oct., '78); *Singer*, I, 29. See also *H.M.C.* (*Fitzherbert*, 49-117; *Westmorland*, 35-44).

[6] *Ailesbury*, 29; *Bagford Ballads*, II, 670 et seq.; *Burnet*, II, 165; *C.S.P.D.* 1678, 475; *E.H.R.*, 40 (*Warcup*); *Examen*, 202-3; *First Whig*, 39; *H.M.C. Rep.* 7 (*Verney*, 471); *H.M.C.* (*Fleming*, 150; *Hodgkin*, 319-21; *Kenyon*, 105-9; *Ormonde*, IV, 461 et seq.; *Rutland*, II, 53); *Verney*, II, 329.

[7] *Clarke, James II*, I, 520; *First Whig*, 75-92; *H.M.C. Ormonde*, IV, 221-2, 380, 459; *North* (*Examen*, 176, 223, 226; *Lives*, I, 236). See *Blencowe*, I, 34.

[8] *H.M.C.* (*Lindsey*, 396; *Ormonde*, IV, 219, 465); *L.J.*; *Luttrell* (21 Oct., '78); *Parl. Hist.*, IV, 1016-17; *Ranke*, IV, 56-7; *Reresby* (25 Oct., '78). See *H.M.C.* (*Fitzherbert*, 49-117; *Westmorland*, 35-44).

[9] *Burnet*, II, 165; *C.J.*; *H.M.C.* (*House of Lords*, 1 et seq., 99; *Ormonde*, IV, 461-4); *L.J.*; *North* (*Examen*, 205; *Lives*, I, 216-17; II, 179-80); *State Trials*, IX, 490; X, 137, 1275, 1299; *Verney*, II, 329. See the endless grants to Oates (as to other informers) in *The Secret Services of Charles II, James II*. For his claim on his party see *H.M.C. Fitzherbert*, 25. After the Revolution of 1688, he was released from prison, in which, after a conviction for perjury, he had passed the reign of James II, and was pensioned by William of Orange.

[10] *C.S.P.D.* 1678, 494, 514, 580; *H.M.C.* (*Fleming*, 152; *Foljambe*, 124; *Kenyon*, 104-9; *Ormonde*, IV, 242-3, 465; *Portland*, III, 361; *Rutland*, II, 53); *Luttrell* (30 Oct., Nov., '78); *Parl. Hist.*, IV, 1021-4; *Reresby* (23 Oct., '78).

[11] *C.J.*; *Clarke, James II*, I, 523-6; *First Whig*, 63; *H.M.C.* (*Foljambe*, 123-4; *Ormonde*, IV, 227, 463-74); *L.J.*; *Luttrell* (9 Nov., '78); *Parl. Hist.*, IV, 1024-36, 1039-45; *Ranke*, IV, 62-7; *Reresby* (7, 13 Nov., '78).

[12] *Burnet*, II, 168-9, 178; *Christie*, II, 310; *C.J.*; *Clarke, James II*, I, 527-8; *C.S.P.D.* 1678, 503, 505-6, 517, 521, 533, 558, 562, 572, 576, 583; *Danby*, 263; *Examen*, 206; *H.M.C. Rep.* 6 (*Ormonde*, 778); *Rep.* 7 (*Verney*, 495); *Rep.* 8 (*College of Physicians*, 230; *Corp. of Chester*, 390); *H.M.C.* (*Beaufort*, 70-2; *Fleming*, 152, 168; *Foljambe*, 124; *House of Lords*, 16-22, 50 et seq., 99-100; *Kenyon*, 117-22; *Ormonde*, IV, 261-2, 265, 275, 311, 468 et seq., 475, 486; V, 41); *Luttrell* (Oct., Nov., '78;) *Macpherson*, I, 88; *Newdegate*, 89-91; *Parl. Hist.*, IV, 1036-8; *Reresby* (10, 21 Nov., '78).

[13] *Burnet*, II, 174; *Clarke, James II*, I, 528-9; *H.M.C. Rep.* 6 (*Ormonde*, 723); *Rep.* 7 (*Verney*, 471); *H.M.C.* (*Beaufort*, 73-4; *Foljambe*, 123, 125; *Ormonde*, IV, 244-5, 255, 257, 265, 473, 480 et seq.); *Macpherson*, I, 88-9; *Reresby* (26 Nov., '78); *Singer*, I, 52-6.

[14] *Burnet*, II, 180; *Examen*, 186.

[15] *Blencowe*, I, lxiv-lv; *Burnet*, II, 195-6; *E.H.R.*, 40 (*Warcup*, 260); *H.M.C.* (*Beaufort*, 71, 73, 76; *Dartmouth*, III, 129; *Fitzherbert*, 118 et seq.; *House of Lords*, 53-86, 100; *Ormonde*, IV, 242 et seq., 284 et seq.; V, 55); *L.J.*; *Parl. Hist.*, IV, 1050; *Prideaux*, 63.

[16] *H.M.C. Ormonde*, IV, 264-5, 485; *Parl. Hist.*, IV, 1052; *Ranke*, IV, 67.

[17] *Blencowe*, I, lxiii-lv; *C.J.*; *C.S.P.D.* 1678, 287, 579, 583; *Dalrymple* II, 171-2, 239-42, 250-1; *Danby*, 72-6, 94-122, 239; *Forneron*, 209; *H.M.C. Rep.* 6 (*Ingilby*, 389); *H.M.C.* (*Bath*, II, 166; *Beaufort*, 79-80; *Fitzherbert*, 14; *Fleming*, 151-2; *Foljambe*, 125-6; *Hodgkin*, 186-98; *Lindsey*, 397-9; *Ormonde*, IV, 256-7, 269, 276, 281, 284-6, 293, 443-4, 481, 486-94); *House of Lyme*, 288; *L.J.*; *Parl. Hist.*, IV, 1049-50, 1053-74; *Ranke*, IV, 68-71; *Reresby* (16 Dec., '78; 7 Jan., '79).

[18] *Ailesbury*, 96, 138-43; *C.S.P.D.* 1679-80, 15, 22; *H.M.C.* (*Beaufort*, 75; *Fleming*, 152-4; *Foljambe*, 127; *Ormonde*, IV, 276, 289, 325, 481 et seq.); *House of Lyme*, 289; *Josselin*, 174-5; *Luttrell* (7 Dec., '78); *North* (*Examen*, 229-30; *Lives*, I, 201, 203-4); *State Trials*. See *H.M.C. Ormonde*, IV, 495, for a long and very interesting letter from the Clerk of the Council to Ormonde, showing how the King fought in Council against Danby, Nottingham and Lauderdale, to save three condemned Jesuits' lives.

[19] *Bagford Ballads*, II, 586-9; *C.S.P.D.* 1679-80, 19-25; *Dalrymple*, II, 251, 280; *First Whig*, 75-92; *H.M.C.* (*Fleming*, 152-3; *Foljambe*, 127; *Ormonde*, IV, 293, 295, 297-8, 302, 494-6); *House of Lyme*, 290; *Josselin*, 175; *Luttrell* (7 Dec., '78); *Roxburghe Ballads*, IV, *passim*; *Verney*, II, 326.

[20] *Dalrymple*, II, 254-7; *H.M.C. Lindsey*, 403-4.

[21] *C.S.P.D.* 1679-80, 52; *H.M.C.* (*Foljambe*, 127; *Ormonde*, IV, 309); *Parl. Hist.*, IV, 1074-5; *Reresby* (24 Jan., '79).

[22] *Ailesbury*, 33; *C.S.P.D.* 1679-80, 78; *E.H.R.*, 45, pp. 553, 557; *Examen*, 320; *First Whig*, 54-6; *H.M.C. Rep.* 6 (*Ingilby*, 387-90); *H.M.C.* (*Fitzherbert*, 13; *Foljambe*, 128; *Montagu of Beaulieu*, 174-5; *Ormonde*, IV, 311-12, 314-17, 329; *Portland*, III, 362; *Russell-Astley*, 41-2); *Josselin*, 175-6; *Luttrell* (Feb., '79); *Muddiman*, 211; *Ranke*, IV, 72-3, 76; *State Trials*.

[23] *Burnet*, II, 179; *Clarke, James II*, I, 490, 537-42; *C.S.P.D.* 1679-80, 95; *Dalrymple*, II, 259-64, 323; *H.M.C. Rep.* 7 (*Verney*, 472); *H.M.C.* (*Dartmouth*, I, 30 (see also 36); *Fleming*, 156-7; *Foljambe*, 123, 128; *Ormonde*, IV, 335, 340-1, 345, 350, 470); *Luttrell* (3 March, '79); *Ranke*, IV, 73-5; *Reresby* (7 March, '79); *Sidney*, 52-3; *Verney*, II, 330; *Hatton*, I, 176-7.

[24] *C.J.*; *C.S.P.D.* 1679-80, 96, 98, 101, 106, 110, 123; *H.M.C.* (*Fleming*, 157-8; *House of Lords*, 86-7, 95-7, 110-12, 119; *Lindsey*, 399, 403-8; *Ormonde*, IV,

346-7, 356-61, 368-71, 498-501; V, 2 *et seq.*, 30-3, 38-9, 48-9; *Portland*, II, 154);
Parl. Hist., IV, 1079-1121; *Ranke*, IV, 77; *Reresby* (March, 17 April, '79);
Savile, 76, 80; *Sidney*, 20-2, 26, 29-31; *Hatton*, I, 178-86.

25 *Carte, Ormonde*, Bk. VIII, par. 26 *et seq.*; *H.M.C.* (*Foljambe*, 129 *et seq.*;
Hastings, II, 387; *Laing*, I, 416; *Ormonde*, IV, 29, 142, 251, 288-9, 306,
310, 322-4, 354, 361-6; V, 1, 4 *et seq.*, 13 *et seq.*, 80, 106, 370; *Lauderdale*,
III, 162; *Luttrell* (April, '79); *Sidney*, 25, 35.

26 *C.J.*; *C.S.P.D* 1678-9, 114; *H.M.C. Ormonde*, V, 7 *et seq.*, 66-70; *L.J.*; *Parl.
Hist.*, IV, 1125-7; *Reresby* (27 April, '79); *Savile*, 85; *Sidney*, 31-5.

27 *Ailesbury*, 35; *C.J.*; *Clarke, James II*, I, 548; *C.S.P.D.* 1679-80, 125; *First Whig*,
67; *Foxcroft*, 146; *H.M.C.* (*Dartmouth*, I, 32; *Foljambe*, 129 *et seq.*;
Ormonde, IV, 502-8; V, 55-9, 74); *L.J.*; *Luttrell* (April, '79); *North*
(*Examen*, 75, 320-1; *Lives*, I, 210, 215, 233-5); *Parl. Hist.*, IV, 1127-9;
Ranke, IV, 78-81; *Sidney*, 51-4; *Temple*, I, 333-4, 361-4.

28 *C.J.*; *C.S.P.D.* 1678-9, 158; *Dalrymple*, II, 264-71; *First Whig*, 68; *H.M.C.*
(*Dartmouth*, I, 33-4; *Foljambe*, 129-31; *House of Lords*, 30-7, 40-1; *Ormonde*,
IV, 508-20; V, 84-118; *Portland*, III, 363); *L.J.*; *Parl. Hist.*, IV, 1130-5, 1148;
Ranke, IV, 84-5; *Reresby* (11, 15, 21, 23, 29 May, '79); *Savile*, 89.

CHAPTER XII

THE FIGHT FOR THE SUCCESSION

1 *H.M.C. Rep.* 6 (*Ingilby*, 387); *Rep.* 7 (*Verney*, 472); *H.M.C. Ormonde*, IV, 364,
520; V, 119; *Prideaux*, 70; *Reresby* (29 May, '79).

2 *Blencowe*, I, 5-7, 20, 36-8; *C.S.P.D.* 1679-80, 169; *Dalrymple*, II, 283-5; *First
Whig*, 70-1; *H.M.C. Rep.* 7 (*Verney*, 472-3); *H.M.C.* (*Drummond Moray*,
131; *Egmont*, II, 83; *Foljambe*, 133-4; *Ormonde*, IV, 522-9; V, 123-36, 143-51,
155); *Newdegate*, 92-3; *North* (*Examen*, 79-87; *Lives*, I, 224, 230); *Reresby*
(22, 23 June, '79); *Savile*, 103; *Sidney*, 89-99, 104-10, 115-16, 122; *Temple*, I,
339-40.

3 *Blencowe*, I, 7-8, 14, 17, 86; *C.S.P.D.* 1679-80, 191; *Egerton MSS.* 1, 534, Letter
16 (trans. *Davidson*, 349-50); *Foljambe*, 134; *Ormonde*, V, 55, 121, 131,
157-8); *Luttrell* (20 June, '79); *Sidney*, 86, 100-3, 111, 123-5; *Verney*, II, 332.

4 *Blencowe*, I, 20-7; *C.S.P.D.* 1679-80, 195; *Evelyn* (24 July, '80; 16 June, '83);
H.M.C. Rep. 9 (*Alfred Morrison*, 450); *H.M.C.* (*Buccleuch* (M.H.), I, 332;
Ormonde, IV, 530-1; V, 157-8); *Luttrell* (12 July, '79); *Ranke*, IV, 84-5;
Savile, 54; *Sidney*, 131, 134-6; *Temple*, I, 340-1.

5 *Ailesbury*, 31; *Blencowe*, I, 34; *Evelyn* (18 July, '79); *Hatton*, I, 187, 207-10;
H.M.C. Rep. 7 (*Verney*, 474); *H.M.C.* (*Fitzherbert*, 18-20; *Fleming*, 160-1;
Ormonde, IV, 533, 535); *Josselin*, 177; *Luttrell* (1 Aug., '79); *North* (*Examen*,
182-5; *Lives*, I, 196); *Prideaux*, 70; *Ranke*, IV, 85-6; *State Trials*.

6 *Blencowe*, I, 58-9, 98, 114-20; *C.S.P.D.* 1679-80, 361; *Dalrymple*, II, 288-302;
First Whig, 74 *et seq.*, 88 *et seq.*; *H.M.C. Rep.* 7 (*Verney*, 474); *H.M.C.*
(*Fitzherbert*, 19-20; *Ormonde*, IV, 535-6; *Portland*, III, 364); *Josselin*, 177;
Longleat MSS. (31 July, '79) (cit. *Foxcroft*, I, 180); *Muddiman*, 225; *North*

(*Examen*, 540-1, 572-3; *Lives*, I, 111-12); *Ranke*, IV, 99; *Savile*, 44-8, 118; *Sidney*, 144. See, for a summary of this half military election, an article by Mrs. George in *E.H.R.*, 45, pp. 557-65.

[7] *C.S.P.D.* 1679-80, 210, 224-7; *Hatton*, I, 189-91; *H.M.C., Rep. 7 (Verney,* 495); *H.M.C. (Buccleuch (M.H.)*, I, 331; *Fitzherbert*, 20-1; *Ormonde*, V, 166, 176, 191, 193-4); *Newdegate*, 61-2; *Verney*, II, 317.

[8] *Ailesbury*, 40; *Blencowe*, I, 97, 121-2, 141; *Clarke, James II*, I, 564; *First Whig*, 72-3; *Foxcroft*, I, 187-8; *Hatton*, I, 189-92; *H.M.C. Foljambe*, 137; *Ranke*, IV, 92; *Savile*, 119-21; *Sidney*, 143; *Temple*, I, 342-3.

[9] *Blencowe*, I, 99-105, 114, 121-4, 146; *Clarke, James II*, I, 566; *C.S.P.D.* 1679-80, 227, 229, 231, 234; *Hatton*, I, 193; *H.M.C. Rep.* 3, 190; *Rep. 7 (Verney,* 475); *H.M.C. Fleming*, 161; *Ormonde*, V, 194, 196, 202); *Newdegate*, 62; *Ranke*, IV, 73; *Add. MSS.* 25124, f. 205.

[10] *Blencowe*, I, 145-7; *Clarke, James II*, I, 568; *C.S.P.D.* 1679-80, 234, 240, 246, 251-2; *Hatton*, I, 194-6; *H.M.C. (Fleming*, 162; *Foljambe*, 137-8; *Ormonde*, IV, 537-9; V, 204, 211, 213, 219, 223-4); *Luttrell* (15, 17, 24, 26 Sept., '79); *Newdegate*, 63-6; *North, Lives*, III, 214; *Verney*, II, 331.

[11] *Blencowe*, I, 161-3; *Clarke, James II*, I, 571-4; *C.S.P.D.* 1679-80, 260; *Hatton*, I, 197-9; *H.M.C. Rep. 7 (Verney*, 476); *H.M.C. (Dartmouth*, I, 37; *Foljambe*, 139; *Ormonde*, IV, 540-8; V, 223); *Luttrell* (12, 17 Oct., '79); *Reresby* (Oct., '79); *Verney*, II, 331.

[12] *Ailesbury*, 45; *Blencowe*, I, 176, 178-81; *C.S.P.D.* 1679-80, 39, 46, 69; *Dryden, Absalom and Achitophel*; *E.H.R. (Warcup*, 244-5); *Examen*, 88-9, 231-42, 256-68; *Hatton*, I, 199-202; *H.M.C. (Fitzherbert*, 21; *Kenyon*, 113; *Ormonde*, IV, 544, 552-8; V, 226, 233, 237-8; *Portland*, II, 155); *House of Lyme*, 296; *Luttrell* (31 Oct., 4, 25 Nov., '79); *Ranke*, IV, 94; *Sidney*, 152-4; *State Trials*; *Verney*, II, 329.

[13] *E.H.R.*, 40 (*Warcup*, 2, 3, 4 Nov., '79); *H.M.C. (Leeds*, 22-3; *Ormonde*, IV, 551); *Ranke*, IV, 95.

[14] *Bagford Ballads*, II, 659-62; *Blencowe*, I, 191, 207, 237; *C.S.P.D.* 1679-80, 295, 299; *Danby*, 121-2; *First Whig*, 96-8, 101-8; *Forneron*, 232; *Hatton*, I, 175, 203-9; *H.M.C. Rep. 7 (Verney*, 477-8, 495-6); *H.M.C. Dartmouth*, I, 38-9; *Fleming*, 163-4, 166; *Ormonde*, IV, 561-2, 564; V, 244-8; *Portland*, III, 364); *Muddiman*, 216-18; *Newdegate*, 69; *Parl. Hist.*, IV, App. No. ix; *Russell*, I, 53; *Verney*, II, 330-2.

[15] *Ailesbury*, 45; *Bagford Ballads*, II, 755-8, 773 *et seq.*; *Blencowe*, I, 183, 187-90; *C.S.P.D.* 1679-80, 296, 364, 425, 524, 566; *Examen*, 541-3; *First Whig*, 74-5; *H.M.C. Rep. 7 (Verney*, 496); *H.M.C. (Fitzherbert*, 21; *Ormonde*, IV, 560, 565 *et seq.*; V, 258); *Prideaux*, 75; *Ranke*, IV, 97; *Hatton*, I, 203.

[16] *Ailesbury*, 38; *Blencowe*, I, 230, 247-8, 252; *Burnet*, II, 266; *Hatton*, I, 211-13, 215-16, 218-20; *H.M.C. Rep. 7 (Verney*, 496); *H.M.C. (Fleming*, 165; *Hodgkin*, 316-17; *Ormonde*, IV, 566-9, 573-4; V, 266); *House of Lyme*, 298; *Luttrell* (11 Dec., '79; 13, 23 Jan., '80); *Newdegate*, 132-3; *Temple*, I, 346-7.

[17] *Ailesbury*, 37-40; *Blencowe*, I, 237, 252-3; *Hatton*, I, 214; *H.M.C. Rep. 7 (Verney*, 495); *Pepys* (28 Oct., '67); *Prideaux*, 75; *Savile*, 134; *Verney*, II, 332.

[18] *Ailesbury*, 40; *Blencowe*, I, 264-5, 272, 282; *Hatton*, I, 216, 221; *H.M.C. (Dartmouth*, I, 45; *House of Lords*, 172-93; *Ormonde*, IV, 578-80; V, 269-71, 274, 276, 278, 280); *Luttrell* (28, 31 Jan., '80); *Newdegate*, 70; *Prideaux*, 80; *Temple*, I, 347.

19 *Blencowe*, I, 293; II, 6; *Burnet Supplement*, 104; *H.M.C. Ormonde*, I, *o.s.*, 115; V, 272, 282-4; *North* (*Examen*, 77, 186; *Lives*, I, 302-3); *Ranke*, IV, 99; *Temple*, I, 345.

20 *Blencowe*, I, 247, 292, 301-2; II, 18, 39, 41; *Burnet Letters*, 16-18; *H.M.C.* (*Egmont*, 92; *Le Strange*, 104; *Ormonde*, V, 288; *Russell-Astley*, 44; *Portland*, III, 365); *Loyal Songs*; *Luttrell* (8, 23 March, 7 April, '80); *Reresby* (24 July, '80).

21 *Blencowe*, II, 22, 25; *Burghclere, Ormonde*, II, 325; *Burnet*, II, 292; *Burnet Letters*, 16 *et seq.*; *Carte, Ormonde*, Bk. VIII, par. 26 *et seq.*; *Clarke, James II*, I, 589; *H.M.C.* (*Ormonde*, V, 293, 295-324, 408-9, 438, 474 *et seq.*, 560; VI, 231, 348; *Portland*, III, 365); *Luttrell* (31 March, April, '80) *Reresby* (April, '80); *Add. MSS.* 25124, f. 229-31.

22 *Burnet Letters*, 19, 25, 28, 31; *C.S.P.D.* 1679-80, 447-52, 454-5, 460-1, 464, 481, 502, 509, 519; *H.M.C. Rep. 5* (*Malet*, 318); *H.M.C.* (*Fleming*, 167; *Ormonde*, V, 314-15, 320-1, 329); *Luttrell* (26 April, 8 June, '80); *Reresby* (8, 9 May, '80); *Hatton*, I, 225; *Somers Tracts*, VIII, 187 *et seq.* See *Blencowe*, I, 185, for further light on this box. See also *Clarke, James II*, I, 491, 589-90.

23 *Blencowe*, II, 57, 61, 64; *Burnet Letters*, 28, 30; *H.M.C. Rep. 9* (*Drogheda*, 329); *H.M.C. Ormonde*, IV, 568; V, 301, 305, 310, 316, 318-19, 322; *Reresby* (8 May, '80); *Savile*, 153 n.; *Verney*, II, 332.

24 *Blencowe*, II, 86-8; *Burnet Letters*, 38-40, 42; *C.S.P.D.* 1679-80, 554, 558, 569, 573; *E.H.R.*, 40 (*Warcup*, 252); *H.M.C. Rep. 7* (*Verney*, 479); *H.M.C.* (*Egmont*, II, 79; *Kenyon*, 116-17; *Ormonde*, V, 349-50, 356); *Luttrell* (11, 12 Feb., 11, 19 May, 23, 30 June, '80). See also *North* (*Examen*, 90-4; *Lives*, I, 157-62).

25 *Blencowe*, II, 30-1, 34 *et seq.*, 48-9, 54 *et seq.*, 73 *et seq.*; *Burnet Letters*, 25, 30-9; *Dalrymple*, II, 319-24, 349-53, 386-90; *Forneron*, 238-40, 245-6; *Hatton*, I, 232; *H.M.C. Rep. 7* (*Verney*, 496); *H.M.C.* (*Dartmouth*, I, 50 *et seq.*; *Hodgkin*, 177; *Ormonde*, V, 329-35, 342-7, 377-8, 403, 420); *Ranke*, IV, 100-5; *Savile*, 155, 160, 162.

26 *C.S.P.D.* 1679-80, 574-5, 597; *Dalrymple*, II, 373; *Hatton*, I, 237-8; *H.M.C.* (*Egmont*, II, 99; *Fleming*, 170-2; *Ormonde*, V, 339-40, 431, 437, 445, 449-50); *House of Lyme*, 305; *Luttrell* (29 Sept., Oct., '80); *Sacharissa*, 273; *Sidney*, 165.

27 *Blencowe*, II, 112-14; *Clarke, James II*, I, 594-60; *H.M.C. Portland*, III, 367; *L.J.*; *Macpherson*, I, 104-5; *North, Lives*, III, 159-61; *Parl. Hist.*, IV. 1160-1; *Verney*, II, 333.

28 *Ailesbury*, 46-7; *Blencowe*, II, 114-17; *C.J.*; *C.S.P.D.* 1680-1, 68, 72; *Dalrymple*, II, 334; *Foxcroft*, I, 235; *Grey*; *H.M.C. Rep. 7* (*Verney*, 496); *H.M.C.* (*Dartmouth*, I, 53; *Fitzherbert*, 23; *Fleming*, 168, 172-4, 176; *House of Lords*, 167 *et seq.*; *Ormonde*, V, 456-62, 467, 475, 561-2; *Somerset*, 107); *North* (*Examen*, 658; *Lives*, I, 163-4, 234, 239; II, 195-6); *Parl. Hist.*, IV, 1162-75; *Ranke*, IV, 108-9; *Reresby* (28 Oct., 7 Nov., '80); *Sidney*, 158-63, 166; *Thoresby* (17 Oct., '80).

29 *Ailesbury*, 49; *Blencowe*, II, 115, 121-8; *Christie*, II, 375-6; *C.J.*; *Clarke, James II*, I, 601-18; *C.S.P.D.* 1680-1, 86; *Dalrymple*, II, 356; *Dryden, Absalom and Achitophel*; *Examen*, 50-1; *Foxcroft*, I, 246-8; *Halifax*, 97; *H.M.C. Rep. 7* (*Verney*, 479); *H.M.C.* (*Fleming*, 173; *House of Lords*, 195-7; *Ormonde*, V, 476, 487, 490, 561-2); *L.J.*; *Macpherson*, I, 108; *Parl. Hist.*, IV, 1175-1215; *Ranke*, IV, 112-14.

30 *Ailesbury*, 49; *Blencowe*, II, 130, 134-6; *C.J.*; *Clarke, James II*, I, 619 *et seq.*;

2D

C.S.P.D. 1680-1, 90, 94; *Grey*, VIII; *H.M.C.* (*Fleming*, 175-6; *Ormonde*, V, 490, 496-508; *Portland*, VIII, 15-19); *Parl. Hist.*, IV, 1216-24; *Reresby* (22 Nov., '80); *Savile*, 170-7.

31 *Ailesbury*, 50-1; *Clarke, James II*, I, 635-7; *C.S.P.D.* 1679-80, 13; 1680-1, 94; *Evelyn* (30 Nov. *et seq.*, '80); *H.M.C.* (*Dartmouth*, I, 54; *Fleming*, 176-7; *House of Lords*, 42-5; *Kenyon*, 104-5; *Ormonde*, V, 511-22); *North* (*Examen*, 218-19; *Lives*, I, 204, 231); *Parl. Hist.*, IV, 1229-32, 1260-1; *Ranke*, IV, 117; *Higgons*, I, 38-9; *State Trials*.

32 *Ailesbury*, 52; *Blencowe*, II, 152-7; *C.J.*; *Evelyn* (12, 29 Dec., '80); *First Whig*, 141-3; *H.M.C.* (*Beaufort*, 98-116; *Dartmouth*, I, 42 (misdated letter of 25 Dec.), 55; *Fitzherbert*, 24; *Fleming*, 177-8; *House of Lords*, 220, 221 *et seq.*; *Kenyon*, 123-5; *Ormonde*, V., 530; *Portland*, III, 368); *Luttrell* (Dec., '80); *Macpherson*, I, 112; *Parl. Hist.*, IV, 1234-60; *Ranke*, IV, 118-19; *Reresby* (28 Oct., 24, 29 Dec., '80); *Singer*, I, 49-50; *Verney*, II, 334.

33 *Ailesbury*, 53; *Blencowe*, II, 158; *C.J.*; *Clarke, James II*, I, 654; *C.S.P.D.* 1680-1, 130; *Dalrymple*, II, 336, 338, 343; *E.H.R.*, 40 (*Warcup*, 8 Jan., '81); *H.M.C.* (*Fleming*, 178-9; *Ormonde*, V, 549, 563); *Muddiman*, 229-31; *Parl. Hist.*, IV, 1270-95; *Savile*, 176-8; *Verney*, II, 334.

34 *Examen*, 96-9; *H.M.C.* (*Kenyon*, 126; *Ormonde*, V, 555, 563-4, 566); *Luttrell* (19, 25, 31 Jan., 5 March, '81); *Newdegate*, 135; *Ranke*, IV, 127-8; *Sidney*, 8-9. See also *H.M.C.* (*Dartmouth*, I, 46 (letter of 23 Jan., misdated); *Ormonde*, VI, 1-2).

35 *Clarke, James II*, I, 662-5; *Dalrymple*, II, 335, 356, 362, 366; *H.M.C. Kenyon*, 124; *Ranke*, IV, 120.

36 *Clarke, James II*, I, 666; *Dalrymple*, II, 361-4, 369-70; *H.M.C. Hodgkin*, 139-40; *Ranke*, IV, 126-9.

37 *C.S.P.D.* 1680-1, 141, 186; *H.M.C. Rep. 6* (*Cooke of Owston*, 425); *H.M.C. Portland*, III, 380; *Luttrell* (Feb., '81).

38 *Ailesbury*, 53; *Bagford Ballads*, II, 998-1000; *Clarke, James II*, I, 668-9; *C.S.P.D.* 1680-1, 184, 173-5, 194-5, 675-8; *E.H.R.*, 45 (*George*, 566-8, 572-4); *E.H.R.*, 40 (*Warcup*, Feb., March, '81); *Examen*, 101-2; *First Whig*, 143-4; *H.M.C.* (*Beaufort*, 85-6; *Dartmouth*, I, 56-7; *Kenyon*, 125; *Ormonde*, V, 579 *et seq.*, 595, 599, 603-4, 609); *Luttrell* (1 March, '81); *Muddiman*, 235; *Prideaux*, 83; *Pythouse Papers*, 88-100; *Savile*, 183; *Sidney*, 10-11, 16-17; *State Poems*.

39 *E.H.R.*, 40 (*Warcup*, 3 Feb., '81 *et seq*); *Evelyn* (27 March, '81); *H.M.C.* (*Hastings*, II, 391; *Kenyon*, 126; *Ormonde*, V, 570, 575, 592, 599); *Savile*, 181-3.

40 *C.S.P.D.* 1680-1, 143-4; *H.M.C.* (*Fleming*, 180-1; *Montagu of Beaulieu*, 176; *Ormonde*, V, 616, 618; VI, 12-14); *Luttrell* (21 Feb., 2, 5, 12 March, '81); " *Loyal Protestant Intelligence* " (*Burney*, 83) (29 March, '81); *Reresby* (March, '81); *Wood, Life and Times*, II.

41 *Ailesbury*, 55; *Defoe, Review*, VIII, 614; *Examen*, 99-102, 107; *First Whig*, 144-6; *H.M.C. Portland*, 369; *L.J.*, xiii, 745; *Luttrell* (21 March, '81); *Muddiman*, 236; *Ranke*, IV, 129; *Reresby* (March, '81); " *Loyal Protestant Intelligence* " (17, 21 March, '81); *Wood, Life and Times*, II, 531.

42 *H.M.C.* (*Finch*, II, 106; *Ormonde*, VI, 8-9; *L.J.*; *Parl. Hist.*, IV, 1303-5; *Reresby* (23 March, '81).

43 *Blencowe*, II, 186; *Christie*, App., cxvi; *Examen*, 123-4; *H.M.C.* (*Beaufort*, 83-4; *Ormonde*, VI, 6-8); *Ranke*, IV, 130-1.

44 *Ailesbury*, 56; *Blencowe*, II, 177; *C.J.*; *Clarke, James II*, I, 671-2; *Grey, Debates*;

H.M.C. (Hodgkin, 321-2; Ormonde, VI, 5-6); Parl. Hist., IV, 1308-11; Ranke, IV, 130-2.

⁴⁵ *C.J.; C.S.P.D. 1680-1, 225; H.M.C. (Beaufort, 85; Lindsey, 428-31; Ormonde, VI, 9-12, 20-1; L.J.; Luttrell (March, '81); Parl. Hist., IV, 1314-38; Reresby (March, '81).*

⁴⁶ *Ailesbury, 56; Examen, 104-5.*

⁴⁷ *Ailesbury, 56-7; Blencowe, II, 185; Dalrymple, II, 368-70; App., Pt. I, 30; H.M.C. (Fleming, 181; Lindsey, 431; Ormonde, VI, 9, 21, 27-8); Higgons, I, 314; Hume, VI, 225; L.J.; North (Examen, 105; Lives, I, 187-8)); Parl. Hist., IV, 1339; Ranke, IV, 135-6; Savile, 191.*

CHAPTER XIII

THE FIGHT FOR THE BOROUGHS

¹ *Aberdeen Letters, 27, 44; Bagford Ballads, II, 715-19; Blencowe, II, 86; C.S.P.D. 1680-1, 265; Echard, 1009; E.H.R. (George, 570-7); H.M.C. Rep. 7 (Verney, 496); H.M.C. (Fitzherbert, 21; Kenyon, 125; Montagu of Beaulieu, 180; Ormonde, IV, 536; VI, 27, 35, 40); Luttrell (April, 31 Aug., '81); Muddiman, 234; North (Examen, 115-16; Lives I, 198-200); Savile, 107, 183.* See *Burney Collection*, 88, for " *Observator* " and 83 for " *Loyal Protestant Intelligence*."

² *Ailesbury, 58; C.S.P.D. 1680-1, 237, 258, 263, 270, 271, 277, 305-6, 352; Echard, 1007-8; Evelyn (2 June, '81); H.M.C. Rep. 7 (Frere, 533); H.M.C. (Kenyon, 127; Ormonde, VI, 46, 48, 50 et seq., 91; Reading Corp., 198); Loyal Songs; Luttrell (8, 17 April, May, June, July, '81); Muddiman, 238; North (Examen, 375; Lives, I, 235; II, 180); Oldmixon, History of Addresses; Parker, History of Wycombe; Singer, I, 60.*

³ *C.S.P.D. 1680-1, 270, 275-6, 278-80, 283-5; Feiling, Tory Party, 199; H.M.C. Ormonde, VI, 48, 62, 66-7; Luttrell (13, 14 May, '81); Muddiman, 239.*

⁴ *C.S.P.D. 1680-1, 194, 262-4, 270, 311-12, 340, 679; H.M.C. Ormonde, VI, 423; North (Examen, 117; Lives, I, 231, 315, 318; III, 175); Reresby (20 April, '81).*

⁵ *E.H.R., 40 (Warcup, 248-53); H.M.C. (Lindsey, 435; Ormonde, VI, 31, 48, 51-2, 59, 62, 68, 74, 80, 85); Luttrell (9, 16 June, 1 July, '81); Reresby (4 May, '81); Hatton, II, 2; State Trials.*

⁶ *E.H.R., 40 (Warcup, 23 June, '81); H.M.C. (Ketton, 181; Ormonde, VI, 36, 226, 272); North (Examen, 117-20; Lives, I, 236-7; III, 127-9).* See also *H.M.C. Rep. 7 (Graham of Netherby, 334).*

⁷ *C.S.P.D. 1680-1, 314-15, 346, 507, 656; E.H.R., 40 (Warcup, 252-7); Hatton, II, 1-2; H.M.C. Rep. 7 (Frere, 533); H.M.C. (Beaufort, 86; Dartmouth, I, 65; Lindsey, 435; Ormonde, VI, 82, 88-91); Luttrell (3, 16 June, '81); Muddiman, 241; Reresby (June, '81).* Those who prefer Burnet's account of these events will find it in *Burnet*, II, 293. It should be carefully compared with the contemporary accounts cited above.

⁸ *C.S.P.D. 1680-1, 320, 325, 330-1, 342, 352, 399, 404-6, 408; H.M.C. (Ormonde, VI, 87, 90, 95-6, 120; Throckmorton, 172); Luttrell (24 June, 8 July, '81); Hatton, II, 2-3; North (Examen, 585-7; Lives, III, 158-62); State Trials.*

2D*

9 *C.S.P.D.* 1680-1, 353, 359, 370, 374-5, 389, 391, 395, 408, 412; *E.H.R.*, 40 (*Warcup*, 17 July, '81); *H.M.C.* (*Fitzherbert*, 24; *Fleming*, 182-3; *Hodgkin*, 69; *Ormonde*, 98); *Luttrell* (14, 17 Aug., '81); *North* (*Examen*, 587-92; *Lives*, I, 188-9; III, 161-2); *Prideaux*, 88-9; *State Trials*.

10 *Blencowe*, II, 208-20; *Clarke, James II*, I, 690-3; *C.S.P.D.* 1680-1, 371; *Dalrymple*, II, App., Pt. I, 9-15; *Foxcroft*, I, 307; *H.M.C. Ormonde*, IV, 565; VI, 101-6, 111, 113-15, 117-21, 124; *Luttrell* (5 Aug., '81); *Macpherson*, I, 125-6, 131; *Ranke*, IV, 137-8; *Savile*, 199 *et seq.*; *Singer*, I, 59-60.

11 *Ailesbury*, 63; *C.S.P.D.* 1680-1, 404; *H.M.C.* (*Dartmouth*, I, 66; *Ormonde*, VI, 135); *Luttrell* (17 Aug., '81).

12 *Bulstrode*, 332; *Burnet*, II, 300; *C.S.P.D.* 1680-1, 421-2; *H.M.C. Rep.* 7 (*Verney*, 497); *H.M.C.* (*Fleming*, 183; *Ormonde*, VI, 111, 131-3, 137, 141-4, 154, 165-6, 182, 184, 187-8, 201, 204; *Throckmorton*, 172-3); *Luttrell* (27 Aug., Oct., '81); *Macpherson*, I, 130; *Muddiman*, 241; *Reresby* (Oct., '81).

13 *C.S.P.D.* 1680-1, 453, 456, 469; *H.M.C.* (*Finch*, II, 123; *Ormonde*, VI, 149, 160, 164); *Luttrell* (8, 14 Sept., 12 Oct., '81); *Prideaux*, 91, 101-2, 107; *Reresby* (22 Sept., '81).

14 " *Loyal Protestant Intelligence* " (20 Sept., '81); *Prideaux*, 91, 101-2, 106-7.

15 *C.S.P.D.* 1660-1, 582; 1663-4, 185; 1680-1, 680; *H.M.C. Ormonde*, VI, 144-5, 148, 193, 197-9, 208, 211; *House of Lyme*, 303; *Luttrell* (12 Oct., '81); *Prideaux*, 91, 96, 104, 109; *Reresby* (7, 19, 20 Oct., '81); *Savile*, 231-2.

16 *Aberdeen Letters*, 4; *Ailesbury*, 64; *C.S.P.D.* 1680-1, 544-5; *H.M.C. Rep.* 7 (*Verney*, 497); *H.M.C.* (*Ormonde*, I, *o.s.*, 33; VI, 142, 152, 155, 210, 212; *Throckmorton*, 173); *Luttrell* (29 Sept., 29 Oct., '81); *Reresby* (Oct., '81).

17 *Clarke, James II*, I, 713-14; *Examen*, 110-13, 572-8; *First Whig*, 118-20; *H.M.C.* (*Ormonde*, VI, 220, 229, 236-7; *Russell-Astley*, 47-8, 52; *Rutland*, II, 59-61; *Throckmorton*, 173-4); " *Loyal Protestant Intelligence* " (8, 19, 26, 29 Nov., '81); *Luttrell* (17, 24 Nov., '81); " *Observator* " (26 Nov., '81); *Reresby* (Nov., '81); *Shakerley MSS.* (20 Nov., '81); *State Trials*. See *Hatton*, II, 9-10; *H.M.C. Dartmouth*, I, 38 (misdated letter of 29 Nov.).

18 *Dryden, Absalom and Achitophel*; *Echard*, 1014; *Examen*, 112-13; *H.M.C.* (*Ormonde*, VI, 233, 239; *Throckmorton*, 174-5); *State Trials*, VIII, 782-7.

19 *Dalrymple*, II, App., Pt. I, 16-25, 30, 36-9, 98-103; *Foxcroft, Halifax*, I, 316-39; *H.M.C. Rep.* 7 (*Graham of Netherby*, 267-70, 276-7, 329, 333-4); *H.M.C.* (*Beaufort*, 87; *Dartmouth*, I, 70-1; *Lindsey*, 437; *Ormonde*, VI, 193, 208-9; 247-9, 257, 282-3, 287-8, 301, 307-8; *Rutland*, II, 58); *Luttrell* (Nov., '81); *Ranke*, IV, 143; *Savile*, 228 *et seq.*

20 *Ailesbury*, 95; *Clarke, James II*, I, 714; *Examen*, 597, 624-7, 629-31; *H.M.C.* (*Ormonde*, VI, 238, 244, 249, 273-4; *Throckmorton*, 173); *Luttrell* (Dec., '81); *Reresby* (16 Dec., '81); *Savile*, 262.

21 *Aberdeen Letters*, 11; *Dalrymple*, II, App., Pt. I, 54; *Evelyn* (14 Sept., '81; 11, 27 Jan., '82); *Stephen Fox*, 72-3; *Foxcroft*, I, 339-45; *H.M.C. Rep.* 5 (*Cholmondley*, 344); *H.M.C.* (*Bury St. Edmunds Corp.*, 149; *Hastings*, II, 392; *Hodgkin*, 137; *Kenyon*, 136, 139-41; *Ormonde*, VI, 350-3); *Luttrell* (20 Feb., March, 82); *Ranke*, IV, 152-3; *Reresby* (5, 11, 17 Jan., '82); *Savile*, 266.

22 *H.M.C.* (*Ormonde*, VI, 327, 334-5; *Sneyd*, 289); *Luttrell* (March, '82); *Reresby* (March, '82).

23 *Aberdeen Letters*, 9, 11-12; *Archæologia*, 68, Pt. I, 168; *Clarke, James II*, I, 720 *et seq.*; *Dalrymple*, II, App., Pt. I, 54; *Evelyn* (April, '82); *H.M.C. Rep.* 7 (*Graham of Netherby*, 351; *Verney*, 479); *H.M.C.* (*Dartmouth*, I, 67, 69 *et seq.*; *Ormonde*, I, *o.s.*, 34; VI, 271, 295-6, 327, 341-4, 347, 353, 357;

Rutland, II, 68-9; *Throckmorton*, 176); *Luttrell* (11, 22 March, '82); *Macpherson*, I, 132-5; *Ranke*, IV, 152-4, 156.

24 *Dalrymple*, II, App., Pt. I, 83-8; *Echard*, 1020; *Feiling*, *Tory Party*, 198; *H.M.C. Rep. 7 (Graham of Netherby*, 351-2); *H.M.C. (Ormonde*, VI, 362; *Rutland*, II, 72-4); *Luttrell* (27 May, '82); *Reresby* (May, '82); *Singer*, I, 67-73.

25 *Ailesbury*, 70; *H.M.C. Rep. 7 (Graham of Netherby*, 262, 352-3, 371); *H.M.C Buccleuch*, I, 168-9; II, 12-13; (*M.H.*) I, 327; *Ormonde*, VI, 376-7); *Reresby* (29 May, '82).

26 *Aberdeen Letters*, 20-36; *Ailesbury*, 64, 71; *Carte*, *Ormonde*, Bk. VIII, par. 120; *H.M.C. Rep. 7 (Graham of Netherby*, 352, 354); *H.M.C. (Buccleuch*, I, 174; II, 104; *Fleming*, 187-9; *Kenyon*, 144; *Ormonde*, VI, 423; *Russell-Astley*, 56-7); *Luttrell* (13, 24, 25, 26 June, 5, 12, 13, 14, 18 July, '82); *Muddiman*, 242-3; *North (Examen*, 595-624; *Lives*, I, 220-4; II, 181-3, 187); *Ranke*, IV, 160-1. See *Williamson*, I, 31, for a post Civil War case of this exercise of the Lord Mayor's right of nomination of one Sheriff.

27 *Aberdeen Letters*, 28, 51, 54, 58; *Archæologia*, 68, Pt. I, 170-5; *Bailey*, *Winchester Records*; *Hawkins*, *History of Music*, IV, 359; *H.M.C. Rep. 7 (Graham of Netherby*, 372); *H.M.C. (Buccleuch*, I, 238, 257; II, 15-16, 109; *Ormonde*, VI, 190, 213, 290, 429, 437, 442); *Luttrell* (30 June, 3 July, 30 Aug., 11, 12 Sept., '82); *Secret Services*, 41, 58-9.

28 *Aberdeen Letters*, 27, 44, 62, 65, 74-6; *Ailesbury*, 66, 71-2; *H.M.C. Rep. 3 (Northumberland*, 95-6; *Legh*, 269); *Rep. 7 (Graham of Netherby*, 338, 358, 372; *Frere*, 533); *Rep. 9 (Alfred Morrison*, 457); *H.M.C. (Buccleuch*, I, 175; II, 16-17, 111; *Kenyon*, 149; *Montagu of Beaulieu*, 181; *Ormonde*, VI, 438, 440-5, 451, 456); *House of Lyme*, 299-301; *Luttrell* (Sept., '82); *Prideaux*, 129; *Ranke*, IV, 162-4.

29 *Aberdeen Letters*, 81, 86; *Archæologia*, 58, Pt. I, 176; *Dalrymple*, II, App., Pt. I, 63; *H.M.C. Rep. 7 (Graham of Netherby*, 262, 358-60); *H.M.C. (Buccleuch*, II, 17; *Egmont*, II, 120-1; *Ormonde*, VI, 470, 486); *Luttrell* (4, 14, 22, 26 Oct., 6 Nov., '82); *Ranke*, IV, 165, 168.

30 *Aberdeen Letters*, 98; *Ailesbury*, 71; *Clarke*, *James II*, I, 740; *Examen*, 576, 579-80; *H.M.C. (Buccleuch*, I, 179, 184; *Fleming*, 190; *Kenyon*, 156; *Ormonde*, VI, 524); *Luttrell* (17 Nov., '82); *Prideaux*, 134; *Ranke*, IV, 166-8; *Ferguson*, 91-104.

31 *Aberdeen Letters*, 101, 103, 147; *Ailesbury*, 72-4; *Archæologia*, 58, Pt. I, 177; *Examen*, 376-7; *Ferguson*, App.; *H.M.C. Rep. 7 (Graham of Netherby*, 350, 363); *H.M.C. (Beaufort*, 87; *Downshire*, I, i, 16; *Ormonde*, VI, 546; VII, 52; *Rutland*, II, 55 (misdated)); *Luttrell* (3, 22, 26 March, '82); *Ranke*, IV, 172-4; *Savile*, 271 *et seq.*; *Sprat*, *True Account*, 51-7, 135.

32 *Aberdeen Letters*, 130-6, 147; *Ailesbury*, 74-6; *Carte*, *Ormonde*, Bk. VIII, par. 130-1; *Dalrymple*, II, App., Pt. I, 78-9; *Evelyn* (18, 28 June, '83); *Ferguson*, 128-68; *H.M.C. Rep. 3 (Northumberland*, 96); *Rep. 4 (Rogers*, 405); *Rep. 5 (Ellacombe*, 325); *Rep. 7 (Graham of Netherby*, 363-5); *Rep. 9 (Alfred Morrison*, 458-9); *H.M.C. (Buccleuch*, I, 192-3; II, 24, 121; *Dartmouth*, I, 82; *Fleming*, 191-2; *Montagu of Beaulieu*, 184; *Ormonde*, VII, 49-55, 60-5, 70-1, 82-3, 169; *Rutland*, II, 55, 79-80; *Somerset*, 110-11); *Luttrell* (22 March, 12, 23, 26, 29, 30 June, '83); *North (Examen*, 377-81; *Lives*, I, 205-6, 283); *Prideaux*, 139; *Ranke*, IV, 171-4; *Sprat*, *True Account*, *passim*; *State Trials*; *Hatton*, II, 22-7. See also, for the possibility of French complicity in the plot, *H.M.C. Rep. 7 (Graham of Netherby*, 341 *et seq.*).

33 *Aberdeen Letters*, 137, 143; *Ailesbury*, 78; *Carte*, *Ormonde*, Bk. VIII, par. 132,

Dalrymple, II, App., Pt. I, 72-4; *H.M.C. Rep. 3* (*Dod.* 259; *Legh*, 270); *Rep. 7* (*Graham of Netherby*, 288, 364-5); *H.M.C.* (*Buccleuch*, I, 194; *Fleming*, 192-3; *Kenyon*, 161-2, 166; *Ormonde*, VII, 65, 73-4; *Rutland*, II, 84); *House of Lyme*, 324; *Luttrell* (July, '83); *North* (*Examen*, 381-7; *Lives*, I, 205-6; II, 231; III, 127-9); *Ranke*, IV, 175-81; *State Trials; Evelyn* (13 July, '83); *Hatton*, II, 29.

34 *Aberdeen Letters*, 145-6, 148; *H.M.C. Rep. 7* (*Graham of Netherby*, 374); *Rep. 9* (*Stopford-Sackville*, 129); *H.M.C.* (*Buccleuch*, I, 194; *Glemham Hall*, 188-9; *Kenyon*, 162; *Ormonde*, VII, 74, 79, 88; *Rutland*, II, 80); *House of Lyme*, 325; *Luttrell* (July, '83); *Russell*, I, 96; *Hatton*, II, 31-2; *Wood, Life and Times*, II, 432. Compare with the contemporary accounts above *Burnet*, II, 376-84. See also *Bagford Ballads*, II, 1002-3.

CHAPTER XIV

AUTUMNAL FORTUNE

1 *Echard*, 1035-6; *H.M.C.* (*Kenyon*, 163-6; *Ormonde*, VII, 79-80); *Luttrell* (Aug., '83); *Ranke*, IV, 182. See also *North, Lives*, I, 316-17; II, 320-2; *Ashmole Papers*, 1818, f. 46.

2 *Aberdeen Letters*, 151, 153; *Ailesbury*, 87; *Archæologia*, 58, Pt. I, 179-81; *Echard*, 1036; *Evelyn* (23 Sept., '83); *H.M.C. Rep. 3* (*Sneyd*, 289); *H.M.C.* (*Buccleuch*, (*M.H.*), I, 339; II, 127, 131; *Dartmouth*, I, 89; *Ormonde*, VII, 22, 74, 83, 92; *Portland*, VI, 174; *Rutland*, II, 81); *House of Lyme*, 326; *Luttrell* (1 Aug., '83); *Savile*, 275; *Secret Services*, 58; *Wood, Life and Times*, III, 67.

3 *Evelyn* (9 Sept., '83); *H.M.C. Dartmouth*, I, 93; III, 122-4; *Savile*, 276.

4 *Aberdeen Letters*, 115, 124; *Archæologia*, 58, Pt. I, 181-2; *Echard*, 1036; *Evelyn* (18 June, '83); *Examen*, 624-46; *H.M.C. Rep. 3* (*Legh*, 270); *Rep. 7* (*Graham of Netherby*, 366; *Verney*, 498); *H.M.C.* (*Buccleuch*, II, 143; *Dartmouth*, I, 95-6 *Kenyon*, 167; *Ormonde*, VI, 423; VII, 49-50; *Rutland*, II, 55 (misdated)); *Luttrell* (28 Sept., Oct., '83); *Ranke*, IV, 169-71, 183-4; *Savile*, 277.

5 *Add. MSS.* 17677, FF, f. 566; *Archæologia*, 58, Pt. I, 183; *Forneron*, 268; *Halifax*, 193; *H.M.C. Rep. 7* (*Graham of Netherby*, 366-8); *H.M.C.* (*Dartmouth*, III, 127; *Ormonde*, VII, 146); *Luttrell* (8, 20, 29 Oct., '83); *Reresby* (30 Oct., '83): *Welwood*, 129.

6 *Burnet*, II, 405; *Carte, Ormonde*, Bk. VIII; *Dryden, Absalom and Achitophel*; *H.M.C.* (*Dartmouth*, I, 82; *Ormonde*, VI, 376, 428, 430; VII, 169; *Somerset*, 108); *Welwood*, 118, 142, 320.

7 *Ailesbury*, 81-2; *Burnet*, II, 405-6; *Foxcroft*, I, 399-403; *H.M.C.* (*Downshire*, I, i, 19; *Kenyon*, 169); *Roberts, Monmouth*, II, 340; *Welwood*, 142-3, App., 319-22.

8 *Ailesbury*, 82-4; *Bulstrode*, 152-3; *Carte, Ormonde*, Bk. VIII, 140-6; *Clarke, James II*, I, 742-3; *Dalrymple*, II, App., Pt. I, 64-5; *Foxcroft*, I, 408-10; *H.M.C. Rep. 7* (*Graham of Netherby*, 368, 375); *H.M.C.* (*Buccleuch*, I, 199; II, 168; *Dartmouth*, I, 100; III, 128, 131; *Ormonde*, VII, 169); *Macpherson*, I, 140; *Ranke*, IV, 185; *Sprat, True Account*, 136-41; *Welwood*, App., 322.

9 *Ailesbury*, 84; *Bulstrode*, 353-7; *Clarke, James II*, I, 742-4; *Dalrymple*, II, App., Pt. I, 66-7; *Echard*, 1039; *H.M.C. Rep. 7 (Graham of Netherby*, 295, 368, 375); *H.M.C. (Buccleuch*, I, 199-200; II, 28; *Dartmouth*, III, 129; *Ormonde*, VII, 164, 169-70; *Portland*, III, 377); *Ranke*, IV, 186-7; *Reresby* (Dec., '83).

10 *Bulstrode*, 357-9; *Burnet*, II, 404-5; *Echard*, 1037-8; *H.M.C. Rep. 7 (Graham of Netherby*, 375); *H.M.C. (Buccleuch*, I, 200; *Dartmouth*, III, 128-9; *Ormonde*, VII, 164-5, 169); *Newdegate*, 211-12; *Reresby* (7 Dec., '83); *State Trials*; *Verney*, II, 340.

11 *Ailesbury*, 85; *Echard*, 1040; *Evelyn* (23 Dec., '83; Jan., Feb., '84); *H.M.C. (Hodgkin*, 17; *Ormonde*, VII, 168, 181); *Luttrell* (Dec., '83; Jan., Feb., '84); *Newdegate*, 233-40; *Reresby* (Jan., '84); *Secret Services*, 81-2.

12 *Ailesbury*, 9-10; *Burnet*, II, 3; *Foxcroft*, I, 413; *North, Lives*, I, 316-17; *Reresby* (Jan., Feb., '84). But see *H.M.C. Ormonde*, VI, 388; VII, 3.

13 *Account of Several Late Voyages and Discoveries*, 1694; *Ady* (14 Sept., '68); *Ailesbury*, 97; *C.S.P. Colonial (America and W. Indies*, 1661-8), Preface; *C.S.P.D.* 1662-3, 184; *Cunningham, Industry and Commerce*, II, Pt. I, 198-202; *Echard*, 1041; *Evelyn* (18 Dec., '82; 2 Feb., '83); *H.M.C. (Dartmouth*, III, 5; *Downshire*, I, i, 5; *Fleming*, 72, 87, 102, 126, 128; *Middleton*, 195; *Rutland*, II, 62); *Hunter, British India*, II, 185; *Luttrell* (9 June, '81; 1 June, '82); *Reresby* (March, '83); *Secret Services*, 51; *Verney*, II, *passim*.

14 *Burnet Supplement*, 80; *C.S.P.D.* 1680-1, 29, 38, 94-178; *H.M.C. Rep. 7 (Verney*, 481); *H.M.C. (Buccleuch*, II, 167; *Dartmouth*, I, 77-119; III, 33-54, 127, 129-30; *Downshire*, I, i, 20-2, 25-7, 29; *Fitzherbert*, 23; *Ormonde*, VII, 146); *Pepys, Tangier Diary*. For some interesting details of this early adventure of English imperialism see *H.M.C. Heathcote*, 156 *et seq.*

15 *Ailesbury*, 44; *Buckingham*, II, 77-8; *Child, New Discourse of Trade*, 10; *C.S.P.D.* 1661-2, 277; 1680-1, 366, 526; *Cunningham, Industry and Commerce*, II, Pt. I, 213; *H.M.C. Fleming*, 57, 59, 72, 125; *Gregory King, Observations*; *Luttrell* (1 June, '82); *North, Lives*, I, 152, 176; *Reresby* (19 Sept., '81); *Savile*, 169, 189, 193, 198, 228, 229, 234, 236; *Traill, Social England*, IV, 615, 621; *W. Wood, Survey of Trade*.

16 *Evelyn* (1, 19 Oct., 6 Nov., '61; 19 Sept., '76; 4 Feb., '84); *Evelyn, Sylva*; *H.M.C. (Lonsdale*, 95; *Ormonde*, III, 446; *Portland*, II, 309); *House of Lyme*, 279-82; *Kip, Britannia Illustrata*; *North, Lives*, I, 171-2; *Pepys* (11 April, '62; 19 April, '64; 26 July, '65); *Aurelian Cook*, 502; *Reresby, passim* (particularly Spring, '66; March, '68; April, '71; Jan., '74); *Secret Services*, 82; *Shakerley MSS.* 1660-85, *passim*; *Sprat, Royal Society*, 149; *Verney*, I, 10.

17 *Burnet Supplement*, 49; *Dalrymple*, II, App., Pt. I, 90; *Halifax*, 196-7; *H.M.C. Rep. 7 (Graham of Netherby*, 362); *H.M.C. (Dartmouth*, I, 98; *Downshire*, I, i, 29-30; *Fleming*, 190; *Hastings*, II, 393; *Ormonde*, VI, 408, 532; VII, 3); *North, Lives*, I, 237, 319, 366; *Ranke*, IV, 190, 197, 200; *Reresby* (Feb., Oct., '83; Feb., '84); *Singer*, I, 83; *Welwood*, 131.

18 *Dalrymple*, II, App., Pt. I, 81-2; *Evelyn* (4 April, '84); *H.M.C. Rep. 7 (Graham of Netherby*, 275 *et seq.*); *H.M.C. (Ormonde*, VII, 195-6; *Russell-Astley*, 50); *North, Lives*, I, 329; *Œuvres de Louis XIV*, IV, 274 *et seq.*; *Ranke*, IV, 191-5; *Reresby* (May, '84).

19 *Archæologia*, 58, Pt. I, 184-5; *Evelyn* (30 March, '84); *H.M.C. Rep. 7 (Graham of Netherby*, 369, 376); *H.M.C. Ormonde*, VII, 198, 205, 212; *Luttrell* (March, '84); *Ranke*, IV, 196; *Reresby* (March, '84).

²⁰ *Bulstrode*, 388; *Echard*, 1044; *Evelyn* (28 March, '84); *H.M.C. Rep. 8 (Corp. of Leicester*, 440); *Rep. 9 (Corp. of Carlisle*, 200); *H.M.C. (Bury St. Edmunds Corp.*, 150; *Lincoln Corp.*, 109-10; *Russell-Astley*, 50); *Luttrell* (March, '84); *Higgons*, I, 318; *North, Lives*, I, 278, 307-8.

²¹ *Ailesbury*, 2, 85, 93-6, 109; *Buckingham*, II, 79-83; *Burnet Supplement*, 48; *Cibber, Apology*, 26; *Aurelian Cook*, 477-508; *Dryden, Introduction to King Arthur, Threnodia Augustalis; Evelyn* (11 Jan., '82); *Grey, Hudibras*, I, 376; *Guardian*, No. 67; *Halifax*, 198-205; *H.M.C. (Beaufort*, 87; *Dartmouth*, I, 100, *Downshire*, I, i, 30; *Leyborne-Popham*, 263); *North (Examen*, 657; *Lives*, I, 315, 321-2); *Lansdowne*, I, 435; *Welwood*, 128-31. There are several contemporary accounts of Charles in his late years; though drawn by very different hands, they all agree in their main essentials. The most intimate and moving is that of Lord Ailesbury, recalling the happy, far-off years when as Lord Bruce he had served the best and most gracious of masters; yet in its way almost as lovable is that of Dr. Welwood, a Whig partisan. Other excellent characters of the King are those of Lord Halifax— the sketch, it should be remembered, of a brilliant, shrewd but vain man, who had not always seen eye to eye with his master—of Lord Mulgrave (Duke of Buckingham), of Roger North, both in his *Examen* and the *Life of Lord Guilford*, of Cook (in *Titus Britannicus*), and of his foe Burnet in his original and contemporary MS. sketch in the British Museum, printed in *Foxcroft's Supplement*. For a delightful vignette of the King, recalled by an anonymous subject in after years, see *Spectator*, No. 462. See also the lines in Dryden's *Threnodia Augustalis*, too beautiful to be mere Court flattery.

²² *Bulstrode*, 424-5; *Burnet Supplement*, 51; *Foxcroft*, I, 415-16; *King, Anecdotes of His Own Times*, 61.

²³ *Archæologia*, 58, Pt. I, 185-7; *Bulstrode*, 338; *Evelyn* (2 July, 10, 24 Aug., 26 Sept., 2 Nov., '84); *Forneron*, 276; *H.M.C. (Buccleuch*, II, 31-2; *Hodgkin*, 178; *Ormonde*, VII, 274, 277-8); *Luttrell* (July, 26 Aug., 25 Sept., 4 Oct., '84); *Newdegate*, 251-2; *North, Lives*, I, 330; II, 207; *Secret Services*, 97.

²⁴ *Ailesbury*, 85, 93, 96; *Evelyn* (15 Nov., '84); *Halifax*, 195; *H.M.C. Portland*, III, 383; *Luttrell* (15 Nov., '84).

²⁵ *Ailesbury*, 21, 92; *Bulstrode*, 385-6, 389-90; *Burnet*, II, 461; *Dalrymple*, II, App., Pt. I, 103-10; *Evelyn* (26 Sept., '84); *Foxcroft, Halifax*, I, 421-2, 433-4; *H.M.C. Rep. 5 (Sutherland*, 186); *Rep. 7 (Graham of Netherby*, 310, 376); *H.M.C. (Buccleuch*, I, 206; *Ormonde*, IV, 596; VII, 267; *Luttrell* (24 Jan., 1 Feb., '85); *North, Lives*, I, 329-30; II, 192, 202-7; *Reresby* (23 Oct., '81; 27 Aug., '84); *Secret Services*, 91; *Singer*, I, 94.

²⁶ *Add. MSS.* 17677, GG 170; *Ailesbury*, 112; *Bulstrode*, 390-2, 425-7; *Burnet*, II, 454; *Clarke, James II*, II, 26; *Dalrymple*, II, App., Pt. I, 90; *D'Avaux, Négociations*, IV, 85-7, 183-8, 217; *Egerton MSS.* 1527, f. 73; *H.M.C. Rep. 7 (Graham of Netherby*, 378); *H.M.C. (Buccleuch*, I, 212; *Laing*, I, 440; *Ormonde*, VII, 298); *Macpherson*, I, 142, 144; *Reresby* (20 Sept., '84); *Welwood*, 144-7.

²⁷ *Ailesbury*, 22, 24, 95, 97; *Bolingbroke, Works*, II, 97; *Buckingham*, II, 79; *Burnet*, II, 454-5; *Dalrymple*, II, 174; *Echard*, 1046; *Foxcroft*, I, 420-34; *H.M.C. Rep. 7 (Graham of Netherby*, 310, 342); *H.M.C. Buccleuch*, II, 38, 203; *North, Lives*, I, 278-9, 318-20; *Reresby* (10 Feb., 11 May, '77; *Welwood*, 131, 146.

28 *Dalrymple*, II, App., Pt. I, 90; *Halifax*, 61; *Mazure*, I, 365.

29 *Ailesbury*, 24, 86, 97; *Buckingham*, II, 61, 78; *Egerton MSS*. 1527, f. 17, 74; *Dalrymple*, II, App., Pt. I, 98-102; *Fox, James II*, App. vii; *Halifax*, 195-6; *H.M.C. Rep. 7* (*Graham of Netherby*, 313, 323, 378); *H.M.C. Buccleuch*, II, 212; *North, Lives*, I, 427; *Welwood*, 144-5, 322-3.

30 *Ady* (22 July, '64); *Ailesbury*, 7, 22, 24, 93-4, 97; *Burnet*, I, 464-5; II, 28, 180, 461; *Burnet Supplement*, 50; *Carte, Ormonde*, Bk. VI, par. 94; *Halifax*, 206; *H.M.C.* (*Buccleuch*, II, 212; *Fleming*, 114; *Wells Cathedral*, 264); *House of Lyme*, 287-8; *North* (*Examen*, 657; *Lives*, I, 329-30; II, 238); *Ranke*, IV, 79; *Reresby* (30 Jan., '81).

CURTAIN

FEBRUARY LIGHT

1 *Evelyn* (4 Feb., '85).

2 *Ailesbury*, 23-4, 85-6; *Burnet*, II, 455-6; *Long of Draycot MSS*. (cit. *Household Words*, 9, 278).

3 *Ailesbury*, 23-4, 86-8.

4 *Add. MSS*. 17677, GG 186; *Ailesbury*, 87-9; *Burnet*, II, 455; *Chesterfield*, 45; *Hatton*, II, 51; *Long of Draycot MSS*. (cit. *Household Words*, 9, 278); *Longleat MSS*. (cit. *Foxcroft*, I, 434); *Ranke*, IV, 201; *Welwood*, 323.

5 *Ailesbury*, 87-9; *H.M.C. Ormonde*, VII, 316; *Long of Draycot MSS*. (*Household Words*, 9, 278).

6 *Ailesbury*, 88-9; *Chesterfield*, 45; *Ellis, Original Letters*, 1st S., III, 335; *European Magazine*, Vol. 27, p. 22; *Hatton*, II, 51; *H.M.C. Rep. 3* (*Northumberland*, 96); *Rep. 5* (*Sutherland*, 186); *H.M.C.* (*Buccleuch*, II, 41; *Egmont*, II, 149; *Kenyon*, 176; *Ormonde*, VII, 316); *Long of Draycot MSS*. (*Household Words*, 9, 278); *North* (*Examen*, 648; *Lives*, I, 331); *Scarburgh MS*. (cit. *Crawfurd, Last Days of Charles II*, 69-70); *Mackintosh MSS*. 34501, f. 18-19.

7 *Dugdale Corr*., 448; *Hatton*, II, 52; *H.M.C.* (*Downshire*, I, i, 36; *Egmont*, II, 149); *North* (*Examen*, 647; *Lives*, I, 332; II, 207; III, 177); *Ranke*, IV, 201; *Van Citters* (cit. *Crawfurd*).

8 *Ailesbury*, 89; *H.M.C.* (*Buccleuch*, II, 41; *Ormonde*, VII, 316); *Long of Draycot MSS*. (*Household Words*, 9, 278); *Scarburgh MS*. (*Crawfurd*, 70-3); *Dugdale Corr*., 449.

9 *H.M.C.* (*Egmont*, II, 149; *Ormonde*, VII, 316); *Long of Draycot MSS*. (*Household Words*, 9, 278); *Scarburgh MS*. (*Crawfurd*, 73).

10 *Chesterfield*, 45; *H.M.C.* (*Egmont*, II, 145; *Ormonde*, VII, 317); *Long of Draycot MSS*. (*Household Words*, 279); *Scarburgh MS*. (*Crawfurd*, 74-6).

11 *Ailesbury*, 89; *Evelyn* (Feb., '85); *Examen*, 649; *H.M.C. Rep. 8* (*Corp. of Leicester*, 440); *H.M.C.* (*Buccleuch*, II, 212; *Egmont*, II, 145-7; *Rutland*, II, 85); *London Gazette* (5-9 Feb., '85); *Reresby* (6 Feb., '85); *Scarburgh MS*. (*Crawfurd*, 75-6); *Van Citters* (*Crawfurd*, 32-4).

¹² *Dalrymple*, II, App., Pt. I, 116; *Egmont*, II, 145-7; *Portland*, III, 383); *North (Examen*, 649-50; *Lives*, I, 331); *Scarburgh MS.* (*Crawfurd*, 75-6).

¹³ *Ailesbury*, 89-90; *Chesterfield*, 46; *Clarke, James II*, I, 746-7; *H.M.C. Stuart*, I, 4; *Mackintosh MSS.* 34501, f. 19.

¹⁴ *Dalrymple*, II, App., Pt. I, 117; *Ranke*, IV, 201.

¹⁵ *Clarke, James II*, I, 747; *Dalrymple*, II, App., Pt. I, 117; *Mackintosh MSS.* 34501, f. 19.

¹⁶ *Clarke, James II*, I, 147-8; *Dalrymple*, II, App., Pt. I, 118-19; *H.M.C. Stuart*, I, 4; *Huddleston, Short and Plain Way*, 84-5; *Mackintosh MSS.* 34501, f. 19, 20.

¹⁷ *Ailesbury*, 90; *Clarke, James II*, I, 748; *Dalrymple*, II, App., Pt. I, 118-19; *H.M.C. Stuart*, I, 4; *Mackintosh MSS.* 34501, f. 20.

¹⁸ *Ailesbury*, 90; *Clarke, James II*, I, 748-9; *Dalrymple*, II, App., Pt. I, 119; *H.M.C. Stuart*, I, 4; *Huddleston, Short and Plain Way*, 84-91.

¹⁹ *Burnet*, II, 459; *Chesterfield*, 46; *Clarke, James II*, I, 749; *Dalrymple*, II, App., Pt. I, 119; *Dryden, Threnodia Augustalis*; *Ellis, Original Letters*, 1st S., III, 335-7; *Evelyn* (Feb., '85); *Fountainhall* (*Chron. Notes*, 46; *Hist. Observes*, 147); *Halifax*, 190; *H.M.C.* (*Buccleuch*, II, 212; *Egmont*, II, 147; *Stuart*, I, 4); *Huddleston, Short and Plain Way*; *Long of Draycot MSS.* (*Household Words*, 279); *Mackintosh MSS.* 34501, f. 15.

²⁰ *Ailesbury*, 90; *Dalrymple*, II, App., Pt. I, 120; *H.M.C. Egmont*, II, 147; *Mackintosh MSS.* 34501, f. 15, 21; *Scarburgh MS.* (*Crawfurd*, 80).

²¹ *Ailesbury*, 90, 97; *Calamy*; *Crawfurd*, 47; *Dalrymple*, II, App., Pt. I, 120; *Ellis, Original Letters*, 1st S., III, 334-5, 336-8; *Evelyn* (Feb., '85); *Higgons*, I, 319; *H.M.C. Rep. 5* (*Sutherland*, 186); *H.M.C.* (*Buccleuch*, II, 42, 212; *Egmont*, II, 147; *Kenyon*, 177; *Portland*, III, 383); *Long of Draycot MSS.* (*Household Words*, 280); *North* (*Examen*, 647; *Lives*, I, 332; II, 207; III, 177).

INDEX